Reconceptualizing the Literacies in Adolescents' Lives

Second Edition

Reconceptualizing the Literacies in Adolescents' Lives

Second Edition

Edited by

Donna E. Alvermann
University of Georgia

Kathleen A. Hinchman
Syracuse University

David W. Moore
Arizona State University

Stephen F. Phelps
Buffalo State College

Diane R. Waff
WestEd, Oakland, CA

 LAWRENCE ERLBAUM ASSOCIATES, PUBLISHERS
2006   Mahwah, New Jersey   London

Lawrence Erlbaum Associates, Inc., Publishers
10 Industrial Avenue
Mahwah, New Jersey 07430
www.erlbaum.com

Cover design by Tomai Maridou

Library of Congress Cataloging-in-Publication Data

Reconceptualizing the literacies in adolescent's lives / edited by Donna E. Alvermann ... [et al.]. — 2nd ed.
    p. cm.
Includes bibliographical references and index.
ISBN 0-8058-5385-5 (cloth : alk. paper) — ISBN 0-8058-5386-3 (pbk. : alk. paper)
1. Language arts (Secondary)—Social aspects—United States. 2. Literacy—Social aspects—United States. 3. Critical pedagogy—United States. I. Alvermann, Donna E.
LB1631.R296 2006
428'.0071'2—dc22

2005054715

CIP

Books published by Lawrence Erlbaum Associates are printed on acid-free paper, and their bindings are chosen for strength and durability.

Printed in the United States of America
10 9 8 7 6 5 4 3 2 1

Contents

Foreword   vii
Richard T. Vacca

Preface   ix

Contributors   xi

Introduction   xxi
Donna E. Alvermann, Sarah Jonas, Ariel Steele, and Eric Washington

PART I: SITUATING ADOLESCENTS' LITERACIES

Introduction to Part I   3
Stephen F. Phelps

1   Playing for Real: Texts and the Performance of Identity   5
Lorri Neilsen

2   "Struggling" Adolescents' Engagement in Multimediating: 29
Countering the Institutional Construction of Incompetence
David O'Brien

3   Re/constructing Identities: A Tale of Two Adolescents   47
Josephine Peyton Marsh and Elizabeth Petroelje Stolle

4   Adolescents' Multiple Identities and Teacher Professional   65
Development
Alfred W. Tatum

PART II: POSITIONING YOUTH AS READERS AND WRITERS

Introduction to Part II   83
David W. Moore

5   Adolescent Identities as Demanded by Science Classroom Discourse   85
Communities
Elizabeth Birr Moje and Deborah R. Dillon

6   Utilizing Student's Cultural Capital in the Teaching and Learning Process: 107
"As If" Learning Communities and African American Students'
Literate Currency
Jennifer E. Obidah and Tyson E. J. Marsh

7   Adolescent Agency and Literacy   129
David W. Moore and James W. Cunningham

8   Fallen Angels: Finding Adolescents and Adolescent Literacy   147
in a Renewed Project of Democratic Citizenship
Helen J. Harper and Thomas W. Bean

PART III: MEDIATING PRACTICES IN YOUNG PEOPLE'S LITERACIES

Introduction to Part III   163
Kathleen A. Hinchman

9   Self-Fashioning and Shape-Shifting: Language, Identity, and Social Class   165
James Paul Gee

10   Exploring Race, Language, and Culture in Critical Literacy Classrooms   187
Bob Fecho, Bette Davis, and Renee Moore

11   New Literacies, Enduring Challenges? The Influence of Capital   205
on Adolescent Readers' Internet Practices
Phillip Wilder and Mark Dressman

12   Literacies Through Youth's Eyes: Lessons in Representation   231
and Hybridity
Kathleen A. Hinchman and Kelly Chandler-Olcott

PART IV: CHANGING TEACHERS, TEACHING CHANGES

Introduction to Part IV   255
Diane R. Waff

13   The Literacies of Teaching Urban Adolescents *in These Times*   257
Susan L. Lytle

14   Learning from Learners: Student Voices and Action Research   279
Jody Cohen, Cambria Allen, Heather Davis, Bruce Bowers, Elena Darling-Hammond,
and Li Huan Lai

15   Reconceptualizing Adolescent Literacy Policy's Role: 297
Productive Ambiguity
Lisa Patel Stevens

Author Index   311

Subject Index   317

Foreword

The second edition of *Reconceptualizing the Literacies in Adolescents' Lives* is more powerful—and will probably have a greater impact on what happens in middle and high schools under the guise of literacy instruction—than the first edition, which was published nearly a decade ago. The first edition was timely and remarkable in its own right, making a strong case to view adolescent literacy within a broader context that encompassed a "multiple literacies" perspective. But when the first edition was published in 1998, other than a diehard circle of adolescent literacy educators, who was listening or joining in on the conversation?

Just 8 years ago, most adolescent literacy educators were deeply perplexed over the lack of attention paid to the academic and nonacademic literacies of adolescents. The emphasis placed on the development of "reading and writing skills" by political leaders, state and local school boards of education, and policymakers focused almost exclusively on literacy learning and teaching in the early grades and in elementary school. It was about then that the International Reading Association established the Commission on Adolescent Literacy. Through its position statements, outreach, and advocacy efforts, the Commission positioned itself to create a national consciousness—an identity, if you will—for adolescent literacy. The Commission, along with groundbreaking books such as the first edition of *Reconceptualizing the Literacies in Adolescents' Lives*, argued that educators and policymakers must advocate for curricula, instructional programs, and educational policies that take into consideration the academic and nonacademic literacies that function in the lives of adolescents.

What a difference 8 years make! Today the surge of support for adolescent literacy is felt everywhere. As the editors of this edition note in their preface, interest in adolescent literacy has "skyrocketed," due in no small part to single-minded efforts at the national level to hold schools accountable for meeting standards of excellence for all students, especially for older readers who struggle with a wide range of texts in various content areas. However, it is my belief that "accountability" alone will not create permanent or profound differences in the literate lives of adolescents. Knowledgeable educators, curriculum planners, and policymakers will.

And this is why the second edition of *Reconceptualizing the Literacies in Adolescents' Lives* is in a powerful position to impact adolescent literacy instruction for the next decade or two. The chapter authors tackle head-on the important issues of adolescents' personal identities, their social experiences, and their cultural capital in relation to literacy learning and literacy use. They provide critical insights into why adolescents do what they do as readers and writers and how teachers can best support their literacy learning in and out of school.

For example, personal identities—the self-understandings and perceptions we have of ourselves as readers and writers in various contexts—are inextricably tied to literacy learning and the varied ways we engage in literate activity. Allow me to illustrate this point from my own life experience. Thirty-something years ago at the age of 23, I began full-time doctoral studies at Syracuse University. I had just completed my third year as a high school English teacher. Throughout my brief tenure as a public school teacher, I was continually perplexed as to why my students, many of whom were at risk of school failure, were "helpless" in the face of school-related reading assignments. Many of these students, the yong men in particular, could read *Popular Mechanics* without batting an eyelash. But just try assigning them a Hemingway novel!

My concern for these students led me to doctoral studies in the field of reading, focusing mainly on adolescent learners. My initial motivation for studying reading was to better understand why older students who struggled with text found it difficult to view themselves as readers and to use reading to learn. Soon into the doctoral program, however, I found myself struggling with learning—and doubting myself—in ways that my students did. Although I could read a best-selling novel with ease in 5 or 6 hours, I found myself taking similar amounts of time to read chapter assignments from my statistics and research methods textbooks—only to come up short in understanding what I had read. I soon eschewed reading these "incomprehensible" texts altogether in favor of taking copious notes and participating in study groups.

During my first year of doctoral study, I often wondered why I had ever left the classroom. Six years earlier, I was Richie Vacca, point guard on my high school basketball team. In college, I was Richie, the "frat boy" and future teacher. At age 23, my identity was wrapped in that of "teacher"—not scholar, not researcher. I was a doctoral student in name only. My mom and dad were impressed. But I was depressed. Was I out of my league? Not as smart or as wise as my fellow doctoral students, who in many cases were a decade or two older than I? On more than one occasion, I thought about quitting and returning to classroom teaching where I had been successful.

What I know now that I didn't know then is that personal identity, what one chooses to read, how one reads, and why, are inextricably tied to one another. That first year as a doctoral student, I had experienced an "identity crisis" and lacked the self-perceptions and confidence to read difficult technical material that for all intents and purposes may as well have been written in a foreign language. Over time, however, I began to identify myself, not as a former point guard who was out of his league, but as a teacher/scholar/researcher, and that made all the difference in the way I approached and read technical texts and research reports.

The second edition of *Reconceptualizing the Literacies in Adolescents' Lives* is a book that you will read and reread several times. It's not Hemingway. But the ideas and issues encountered are powerful ones that will help educators and policy makers to understand what it takes to make lasting differences in the literate lives of adolescents.

—Richard T. Vacca,
Professor Emeritus
Kent State University

Preface

In the nearly 8 years since *Reconceptualizing the Literacies in Adolescents' Lives* first appeared, interest in improving young people's reading achievement has skyrocketed. This interest, which shows no signs of abating, is being fueled by coordinated efforts at the national level to hold schools accountable for meeting standards of excellence for all students, and especially for older readers and writers who struggle to comprehend a wide range of materials their teachers assign in the various disciplinary areas (e.g., the English language arts, social studies, mathematics, and the natural sciences). Advocacy groups representing a broad spectrum of public and private interests are getting behind what some leaders in the field are calling the "adolescent literacy movement" to bring about change through increased funding for research and professional development. Not surprisingly, policymakers are finding it increasingly difficult to ignore these groups' concerted call for improved literacy teaching and learning in the upper grades. Finally, not to be outdone and in an effort to claim their own ground in the push to spotlight adolescent literacy, professional organizations (e.g., the International Reading Association, the National Reading Conference, and the National Council of Teachers of English, to name but a few) are commissioning and adopting position statements that spell out what their memberships believe should be the objectives of effective literacy instruction at the middle and high school levels.

As editors of the second edition of *Reconceptualizing the Literacies in Adolescents' Lives*, we appreciate the attention being showered on youth and their multiple literacies, for it is the case in this age of information communication technologies and increasing global awareness that young people's learning from and with texts can no longer be confined to print alone. Many of our colleagues both in North America and elsewhere would say that it's about time literacy professionals and policymakers acknowledge that reading and writing instruction doesn't end with elementary school. At the same time, we question the degree to which this newfound advocacy takes into consideration issues concerning young people's personal, social, and cultural experiences in relation to literacy learning.

We submit in this second edition that unless such issues are acknowledged in terms of their impact on youth's identity-making practices, much of what will pass in the name of adolescent literacy reform may miss its mark, or worse yet, harm the very individuals for whom it holds the greatest potential. To prevent this from happening and to increase the chances that literacy reform efforts will take hold in ways that respect youth's multiple literacies, we invited chapter authors to explore the impact of young people's identity-making practices in mediating their perceptions of themselves as readers and writers. Specifically, we asked the authors to draw examples from their own research that illustrate the importance of valuing adolescents' perspectives in an era of externally mandated reforms and accountability measures that have the potential to change young people's literate identities.

The book is divided into four parts. The chapters in Part I: Situating Adolescents' Literacies address how young people use favorite texts to perform their identities, how they counter school-based constructions of incompetence, and how they re/construct their literate identities in relation to certain kinds of gendered expectations, pedagogies, and cultural resources. Part II: Positioning Youth as Readers and Writers features chapters that stress the importance of classroom discourse, cultural capital, agency, and democratic citizenship in mediating adolescents' literate identities. The chapters in Part III: Mediating Practices in Young People's Literacies speak to issues of language, social class, race, and culture in shaping how adolescents represent themselves and are represented by others. Part IV: Changing Teachers, Teaching Changes captures the productive ambiguities associated with teaching urban adolescents to read and write in changing times, encouraging students to conduct action research on topics that are personally relevant, and using "enabling constraints" as a concept to formulate policies on adolescent literacy instruction.

Substantial changes have been made in the second edition of *Reconceptualizing the Literacies in Adolescents' Lives*. For example, 9 of the 15 chapters in Parts I through IV are new. Beginning with the Introduction and carrying through in each of the other chapters, students' voices and perspectives are featured front and center. Finally, chapters that appeared in the first edition have been updated to reflect the second edition's claim that, in times of large-scale reform aimed at improving adolescents' literacy achievement, it is vitally important to stay grounded in the day-to-day lived experiences of those whose literate identities are being affected the most.

Contributors

Cambria Allen grew up in West Hartford, Connecticut, surrounded by remarkable men and women (including her mother) who have dedicated their lives to the noble occupation of teaching. She feels truly honored and humbled to be a part of this project with school professionals, her peers, and her education professor, whom she credits with reinvigorating her interest in urban pedagogy. Cambria recently earned a BA in political science from Bryn Mawr College, and is currently living in her hometown, working for state government, and silently brooding over the meaning of Life.

Donna E. Alvermann is Distinguished Research Professor of Language and Literacy Education at the University of Georgia. Formerly a classroom teacher in Texas and New York, her research focuses on youth's multiple literacies in and out of school. From 1992 to1997 she codirected the National Reading Research Center, funded by the U.S. Department of Education. With over 100 articles and chapters in print, her books include *Content Reading and Literacy: Succeeding in Today's Diverse Classrooms* (4th ed.), *Popular Culture in the Classroom: Teaching and Researching Critical Media Literacy*, *Bridging the Literacy Achievement Gap, Grades 4–12*, and *Adolescents and Literacies in a Digital World*. A past president of the National Reading Conference (NRC), cochair of the International Reading Association's Commission on Adolescent Literacy (1997–2000), and member of the 2009 NAEP Reading Framework, she currently edits *Reading Research Quarterly* and serves on the Adolescent Literacy Advisory Group of the Alliance for Excellent Education. She was elected to the Reading Hall of Fame in 1999, and is the recipient of NRC's Oscar Causey Award for Outstanding Contributions to Reading Research, the Kingston Award for Distinguished Service, College Reading Association's Laureate Award, and the Herr Award for Contributions to Research in Reading Education.

Thomas W. Bean is a professor in literacy/reading and coordinator of doctoral studies in the Department of Curriculum and Instruction, College of Education, at the University of Nevada, Las Vegas, USA. Tom is considered a leading scholar in content area literacy. He is the co-author of over 18 books, 25 book chapters, and 95 journal articles. He was recently honored with the College of Education Distinguished Faculty Research Award for his studies of students' discussion of multicultural young adult literature in content-area classrooms. Tom is co-author of recent books, including: *Content Area Literacy: An Integrated Approach* (8th ed., 2004, Kendall/Hunt Publishers) and *Targeted Reading: Improving Achievement in Middle and Secondary Grades* (2004, Kendall/Hunt), devoted to addressing strategies for meeting No Child Left Behind requirements and test preparation. He is also a co-author of the International Reading Association position paper, *Adolescent Literacy: A Position Statement*, designed to guide policy decisions aimed at increasing literacy development efforts for adolescents.

Bruce Bowers is currently a humanities teacher at Mastery Charter High School in Philadelphia, Pennsylvania, where he has been teaching for the last 4 years. He had previously taught for 15 years at Strawberry Mansion Middle and High School for the School District of Philadelphia, where he also served as the school coordinator for the Coalition of Essential Schools. His teaching career began in special education and he has taught classes in this area in both Pennsylvania and Minnesota. His interest in the connections between social justice and literacy have been supported and nurtured by his active work in teacher research, funded in part by the Spencer Foundation and the Arthur Vining Davis Foundation. He has been a facilitator for Seeking Educational Equity and Diversity (S.E.E.D.) since 1992, and a teacher consultant (T.C.) for the Philadelphia Writing Project since 1993. The affiliations to these dynamic teacher networks have nurtured and sustained his practice.

Kelly Chandler-Olcott is an associate professor in Syracuse University's Reading and Language Arts Center, where she directs the English Education program and teaches undergraduate and graduate literacy courses. She was awarded a Meredith Recognition Award for excellence in university teaching in 2000. A former secondary English and social studies teacher, she holds undergraduate and master's degrees from Harvard University and a doctorate from the University of Maine. Her research on classroom-based inquiry and adolescents' technology-mediated literacy practices has been published by such journals as *English Education*, *Journal of Teacher Education*, *Journal of Adolescent & Adult Literacy*, and *Reading Research Quarterly*. She has also co-authored or co-edited four books, the most recent being *Tutoring Adolescent Literacy Learners: A Guide for Volunteers* (Guilford, 2005) with Kathleen Hinchman. With funding from the National Science Foundation, she and three colleagues are currently investigating the literacy demands that reform-based mathematics curricula present for students in urban secondary classrooms.

Jody Cohen has been a faculty member in the education program at Bryn Mawr and Haverford Colleges since 1998. She teaches undergraduates courses, including Schools in American Cities, Literacies, and Multicultural Education, in which she coaches her students as they take on teaching roles, usually in urban schools. She also teaches writing in the Bryn Mawr College Seminar Program and directs the Writing for College Summer Program for high school young women. Jody's research has focused on working with urban students, teachers, and parents as part of school reform initiatives. From 1993 to 1998, Jody was a director at Research for Action, where she was principal investigator on a number of qualitative research projects, including research commissioned by the American Association of University Women into girls in middle school (documented in *Girls in the Middle*), and an action research project called Sisters Together in Action Research (STAR), funded by the Ms. Foundation Collaborative for Healthy Girls/Healthy Women. More recently, she conducted research with college students on issues including urban education and diversity in education. Jody also serves as a mentor with the Posse Program, which sends groups of urban youth leaders to top colleges and universities, including Bryn Mawr.

James W. Cunningham is Professor Emeritus of Literacy Education at the University of North Carolina-Chapel Hill. He has over 100 publications, including books, book chapters, research articles, professional articles, and scholarly reviews. He was on the editorial boards of *Reading Research Quarterly, Journal of Literacy Research, National Reading Conference Yearbook, Literacy Teaching and Learning: An International Journal of Early Reading and Writing,* and *Reading Psychology* prior to his retirement. He was elected Fellow by the National Conference on Research in Language and Literacy, and was an elected member of the Board of Directors of the National Reading Conference. He has presented many papers at national and international conferences, and served as a consultant to public schools, school systems, and other education agencies in 24 states.

Elena Darling-Hammond is a recent graduate of Haverford College, where she majored in education and sociology through Swarthmore College. Her interests are in creating schools that work for all types of learners and that promote critical learning and thinking. She plans on working in preschool settings and creating programs to promote literacy for young children.

Bette Davis is an assistant professor of English at William Carey College in Hattiesburg, Mississippi. Before assuming this position 9 years ago, she taught in Mississippi public high schools and at a community college, where, involving students as co-researchers, she began documenting students' agency in their own linguistic development. A grant from the Spencer Foundation facilitated the extension of this inquiry at William Carey College. She also served as codirector for the South Mississippi Writing Project, a National Writing Project affiliate, based at the University of Southern Mississippi. Davis' (formerly Bette Ford's) work as a high school teacher is featured in Mike Rose's *Possible Lives* (Houghton Mifflin, 1995). In addition, she has published articles in the English Journal and American Quarterly, as well as a chapter in *The Nearness of You: Students and Teachers Writing On-line* (Teachers and Writers Collaborative, 1996).

Heather Hopkins Davis is an undergraduate at Bryn Mawr College, pursuing an independent major in educational policies and practices. She has worked in many different educational contexts, serving as a City Year corps member in an elementary school in Texas for a year before coming to Pennsylvania, where she has worked in roles ranging from tutor to coresearcher to assistant and student teacher. She plans to continue studying and learning through experience, and aspires to improve the quality and equality of the North American educational system.

Deborah R. Dillon is a professor of literacy at the University of Minnesota. Her research focuses on the literacy practices of teachers and learners in K–12 schools, particularly adolescents, and the role of motivation in literacy learning. Dillon also researches the preparation of preservice literacy teachers. She has published four books, including *Kids InSight: Reconsidering How to Meet the Literacy Needs of All Students,* and numerous articles in journals such as the American Educational Research Journal, Reading Research Quarterly, National Reading Conference Yearbook, International Journal of Qualitative Studies in Education, Journal of Educational Research, Journal of Research in the Teaching of Science, and the Reading Teacher. Dillon's research has been funded by the National Science Foundation, the Spencer Foundation, the Bush Foundation, and the U.S. Department of Education. Dillon is past president of the National Reading Conference, former Vice Chair of the English Language Arts Early and Middle Childhood Standards Committee of the National

Board for Professional Teaching Standards, and former Associate Editor of The Reading Teacher and the Journal of Research in Science Teaching. Dillon has won two teaching awards and was recently awarded the 2004 University of Georgia, College of Education Alumni Lifetime Achievement Award.

Mark Dressman is Associate Professor of Curriculum and Instruction at the University of Illinois at Urbana-Champaign, where he teaches courses in English and secondary literacy education. He is a former middle and secondary teacher who taught for more than a decade as a Peace Corps volunteer and at schools on the Navajo Reservation and in the midwestern United States. He is the author of *Literacy in the Library: Negotiating the Spaces Between Order and Desire* and co-editor of *Kaleidoscope: A Multicultural Booklist*, as well as articles in Reading Research Quarterly, Research in the Teaching of English, Curriculum Inquiry, and Language Arts, and numerous chapters in edited volumes. He is currently Reviews Editor for Journal of Curriculum Studies and serves on the editorial board of several major journals. His research has examined cultural assumptions and practices of literacy instruction and policy in school libraries, across multiple discourses of "best practice," and most recently in programs for adolescents with a history of struggle in school. In addition to his interest in technology, his current research focuses on the uses of theory in literacy research articles and the teaching of poetry in the United States over the last century.

Bob Fecho is an associate professor in the reading program of the Language and Literacy Department at the University of Georgia (Athens, Georgia, US). To date, his work has focused on issues of language, identity, sociocultural perspectives, practitioner research, and critical inquiry pedagogy as they relate to adolescent literacy, particularly among marginalized populations. He has published articles in Harvard Educational Review, Journal of Literacy Research, Research in the Teaching of English, and English Education, and articles he has written have garnered both the Richard A. Meade and Alan C. Purves awards. A book, *"Is This English?" Race, Language, and Culture in the Classroom* (Teachers College Press), tells of his experiences teaching across culture in an urban school and was awarded the James Britton Award for Teacher Research from the National Council of Teachers of English, along with receiving Honorable Mention for the 2004 Myers Outstanding Book Awards by the Gustavus Myers Center for the Study of Bigotry and Human Rights. Most recently, he, along with co-authors, completed a book, *No Deposit, No Return; Community, Responsibility, and Risk Taking in Critical Inquiry Classrooms*, to be published in late 2005 by the International Reading Association.

James Paul Gee received his PhD in linguistics from Stanford University in 1975. His work over the last two decades has centered on the development of an integrated theory of language, literacy, and schooling, a theory that draws on work in socially situated cognition, sociocultural approaches to language and literacy, language development, discourse studies, critical theory, and applied linguistics. Professor Gee has extended this work to deal with the so-called "new capitalism" and its cognitive, social, and political implications for literacy and schooling. More recently he has worked on digital literacies and has published two books on the theories of learning embedded in video and computer games. He has published widely in journals in linguistics, psychology, the social sciences, and education. His books include *Sociolinguistics and Literacies* (1990, Second Edition 1996); *The Social Mind* (1992); *Introduction to Human Language* (1993); *The New Work Order: Behind the Language of the New Capitalism* (1996, with Glynda Hull and Colin Lankshear); *An Introduction to Discourse Analysis: Theory and Method* (1999; Second Edition 2004); *What Video Games Have to Teach Us About Learning and Literacy* (2003); and *Why Video Games Are Good for Your Soul* (2005).

Helen Harper is an associate professor in the College of Education at the University of Nevada, Las Vegas. She formerly taught at the University of Western Ontario. Her teaching and research intersect cultural studies and English/literacy studies in education, focusing on issues and theories of identity, representation, and social difference in pedagogical contexts. Her publications include *Wild Words/Dangerous Desires: High Schools Girls and Feminist Avant-Garde Writing* (Peter Lang, 2000) and, with Meredith Cherland, *Advocacy Research in Literacy Education* (Lawrence Erlbaum Associates, in press).

Kathleen A. Hinchman is Professor and Chair of the Reading and Language Arts Center at Syracuse University. Once a middle school teacher, she now teaches undergraduate and graduate classes in childhood and adolescent literacy education. With a wide array of book chapters and articles, she has published in such journals as The Reading Teacher, Language Arts, Reading Research Quarterly, Journal of Literacy Research, and Reading Research and Instruction, and serves on the editorial boards of several journals. She has coauthored *Principled Practices for a Literate America: A Framework for Literacy and Learning in the Upper Grades*, *Teaching Adolescents Who Struggle With Reading and Writing: Practical Strategies*, and *Tutoring Adolescent Literacy Learners: A Guide for Volunteers*. She also coedited *Struggling Adolescent Readers: A Collection of Teaching Strategies* and the *National Reading Conference Yearbook*. Her research is concerned social perspectives of adolescent literacy and literacy teacher education, with a focus on theorizing teachers' and students' views of what it means to be literate. Her most recent work explores teachers' and students' views in urban middle-level English and mathematics classrooms.

Sarah Jonas is the Director of Education Services for the Children's Aid Society in New York City. She has conducted staff development for youth workers through The After School Corporation, the Partnership for After School Education, The Harlem Educational Activities Fund, and The Literacy Assistance Center. She is a certified teacher and taught for 7 years in public elementary schools in Los Angeles (as a charter member of Teach for America) and New York City. She holds an EdM in Administration, Planning and Social Policy from the Harvard Graduate School of Education and a BA in English Literature from Yale University.

Li Huan Lai was born in Huizhou, China. She moved to Boston, Massachusetts at age 8 and attended urban public elementary and middle school. Later she attended a private high school in Boston called Commonwealth High School. Currently, she is a senior at Bryn Mawr College studying East Asian Studies and Anthropology. She is also a recipient of the Posse Scholarship, the Alumnae Regional Scholarship, and the Freeman-Asia Scholarship.

Susan L. Lytle began her career in education as an English teacher in public secondary schools in Massachusetts, California, and, as a Peace Corps volunteer, in Manila, Philippines. At the University of Pennsylvania since the early 1970s, she began as a supervisor of secondary English interns and later, as a faculty member, was coholder of the Joseph L. Calihan Term Chair in Education, awarded for her collaborative research on teacher inquiry. She is currently chair of the Language in Education Division and director of the Program in Reading/ Writing/ Literacy. Dr. Lytle is also the founding director of the Philadelphia Writing Project (PhilWP), a teacher collaborative project with the School District of Philadelphia. PhilWP has been the primary site of her research, for which she has received a number of major grants, including one from the Spencer Foundation on teacher inquiry and the epistemology of teaching. Dr. Lytle has published widely on literacy and urban teacher education. Her co-authored book, *Inside/Outside: Teacher Research and Knowledge* (Teachers College Press, 1993), received the AACTE Outstanding Professional Writing Award in 1995. Dr. Lytle is a past president of the National Conference on Research in Language and Literacy as well as the NCTE Assembly on Research.

Josephine Peyton Marsh is an associate professor of language and literacy at Arizona State University where she teaches courses in adolescent literacy. Her past experiences as a high school reading teacher influence her research interests in adolescent literacy and her commitment to working with teachers in schools to find ways to engage adolescents in literacy and learning.

Tyson E. J. Marsh received his Masters Degree in Higher Education and Organizational Change at the University of California, Los Angeles where he is currently a doctoral student in Urban Schooling. Specializing in African American student literacy acquisition, he studies the African American oral tradition and the use of spoken word poetry and Hip Hop as critical teaching tools. His research is informed by his passion for rap music and his work as a poet and spoken word poetry teacher in a Los Angeles area high school.

Elizabeth Birr Moje is an Arthur F. Thurnau Professor of Literacy, Language, and Culture in Educational Studies at the University of Michigan, Ann Arbor. Moje teaches undergraduate and graduate courses in secondary and adolescent literacy and in cultural theory and qualitative research methods in the Literacy, Language, and Culture unit and the Joint Program in English and Education. Moje also serves as a Faculty Associate in the University's Institute for Social Research. Her research interests revolve around the intersection between the literacies and texts youth are asked to learn in the disciplines (particularly in science) and the literacies and texts they engage outside of school. In addition, she studies how youth make culture and enact identities from their home and community literacies, and from ethnic cultures, popular cultures, and school cultures. Moje has published two books and numerous articles in journals such as the *Reading Research Quarterly, Teachers College Record, Journal of Literacy Research, English Education, Journal of Adolescent & Adult Literacy, Urban Review, Journal of Research in Science Teaching, Science Education, International Journal of Learning, Journal of Educational Research,* and the *International Journal of Qualitative Studies in Education*.

David W. Moore is a professor of education at Arizona State University, where he teaches secondary-school teacher-education courses in classroom instruction and management, specializing in adolescent literacy. His vita shows a 25-year publication record that balances research reports, professional articles, book chapters, and books. Noteworthy co-authored items include an International Reading Association position statement on adolescent literacy and a *Handbook of Reading Research* chapter on secondary school reading. Recent co-authored books include *Developing Readers and Writers in the Content Areas: K–12* (4th ed.) and *Starting Out: A Guide to Teaching Adolescents Who Struggle with Reading*. He cochaired the International Reading Association's Commission on Adolescent Literacy from 2000 to 2004.

Renee Moore holds a full-time position as English instructor at Mississippi Delta Community College. Once a journalist, she also taught high school English and journalism in Mississippi. She completed her BS in English Education at Delta State University (1990) and earned a Master of Arts from the prestigious Bread Loaf School of English at Middlebury College in Vermont (1997). Actively involved in teacher research, Renee is also a Writing Project Fellow (Delta Writing Project) and has received numerous awards and grants, including $30,000 from the Spencer Foundation. She is a National Board Certified Teacher in Adolescent English Language Arts and serves on the Board of Trustees of the Carnegie Foundation for the Advancement of Teaching (California). She also currently serves on the State Commission on Teacher and Administrator Education, Certification, and Licensure. Ms. Moore is the first educator in Mississippi to win both the State Teacher of the Year award and the $25,000 Milken Educator Award in the same year (2001). Her writings have been published as chapters in several books and professional journals. She is currently pursuing her doctoral degree in education through Oral Roberts University.

Lorri Neilsen is the author and editor of several books on literacy, research methods, and arts-based inquiry. *Knowing her Place* (Caddo Gap, 1998) was the 1999 recipient of NCTE's Richard A. Meade Award. Her most recent poetry collection, *All the Perfect Disguises* (Broken Jaw Press), was the 2003 recipient of the Poet's Corner Award in Canada. She was appointed Poet Laureate of Halifax for 2005–2009. Currently, she is writing a book on lyric inquiry (and scholartistry), completing a collection of essays on grief and loss, and researching the role of place in women's poetry.

Jennifer E. Obidah is an associate professor of Urban Schooling in the Graduate School of Education and Information Studies at UCLA. Her area of research is the socio-cultural contexts of schools and students' lives. She focuses specifically on the socio-cultural contexts of (a) teacher–student interactions in urban classrooms; (b) violence in communities and schools; and, (c) urban school reform. Dr. Obidah is the first author of the book *Because of the Kids: Facing Racial and Cultural Differences in Schools*, published by Teachers College Press. She has published research papers in distinguished journals such as the Harvard Educational Review Journal, Teachers College Record, and The Journal of Negro Education. Her paper published in the Harvard Educational Review Journal was selected, as part of an edited volume, for a Critics Choice Award by the American Educational Studies Association in November, 2000. *Because of the Kids: Facing Racial and Cultural Differences in Schools* received the 2001 Gustavus Myers Outstanding Book Award, which "recognizes works that increase understanding of intolerance and bigotry, and most importantly, that inspire and inform strategies and actions that can lead to greater equity in our society." Dr. Obidah is currently the Principal Investigator of a 5-year study of urban school reform aimed at increasing college access for economically disenfranchised African American and Latino students.

David G. O'Brien is professor of Literacy Education at the University of Minnesota, Twin Cities, where he conducts research and teaches courses in content literacy, foundations of instructional leadership in K–12 reading, and interpretive research methods. His scholarship and teaching focus on the literacy practices of adolescents. He has studied how adolescents use literacy to learn content across the disciplines and how their teachers learn to support their students' learning by integrating both traditional literacies and "new" literacies practices into various disciplines. In current projects, O'Brien is collaborating with colleagues at an urban high school in Minneapolis on academic literacy support for struggling adolescents and with colleagues at a suburban middle school in a project focusing on how low-achieving students bridge traditional print-based practices with more progressive digital literacies practices. O'Brien has authored and edited books, including *Constructions of Literacy: Studies of Teaching in and Out of Secondary Schools* with Elizabeth Moje, and published numerous chapters and articles in the areas of content literacy, engaging at-risk or struggling learners, and using digital media literacy with struggling learners. He has also been a junior high reading teacher, a Title I project director, and reading curriculum coordinator.

Stephen F. Phelps is a professor of Elementary Education and Reading at Buffalo State College. He teaches courses in the graduate reading specialist program, as well as undergraduate reading methods courses for preservice secondary teachers. He is co-author of *Content Reading and Literacy: Succeeding in Today's Diverse Classrooms.* Steve is particularly interested in helping teachers to understand the cultural, social, and linguistic factors that influence adolescents' literacy.

Lisa Patel Stevens is an assistant professor in the Lynch School of Education at Boston College. Prior to working in academe, Lisa was a policymaker, a literacy consultant, a reading strategist, and a middle school teacher. Her primary research interests include the use of literacy practices by young people to mediate their sense of self and the world, and the cultural construction of adolescence.

Elizabeth Petroelje Stolle currently is pursuing her doctoral degree in Language and Literacy at Arizona State University, where she also teaches both undergraduate and graduate literacy courses. As a former classroom teacher, she directly connects her research to student learning with an emphasis on critical literacy and the new literacies research.

Alfred W. Tatum is an assistant professor in the Department of Literacy at Northern Illinois University. Before joining NIU's faculty, he served as a senior program associate in the Center for Literacy of the North Central Regional Educational Laboratory (NCREL). His research foci are adolescent literacy, teacher professional development in urban middle schools and high schools, and the literacy development of African American adolescent males. Alfred has provided professional development support in schools across the nation. Most recently, he was a reading consultant for a high school in Washington, DC. Alfred has published in several journals, including *The Reading Teacher*, the *Journal of Adolescent & Adult Literacy*, *Reading Research Quarterly*, the *Illinois Reading Council Journal*, the *Journal of College*

Reading and Learning, and *Principal Leadership.* He also serves on the National Advisory Reading Committee of the National Assessment of Educational Progress. Alfred began his career as an eighth-grade teacher in Chicago.

Diane R. Waff is a Senior Program Associate at WestEd in Oakland, California, and a doctoral candidate at the University of Pennsylvania. She is a member of the National Writing Project Task Force and served as the codirector of the Philadelphia Writing Project from 1996–2003. She is currently a member of the Philadelphia Writing Project's advisory board. She facilitates Seeking Educational Equity and Diversity Seminars for the National SEED Project in Philadelphia and New Jersey and Reading Apprenticeship Seminars for the Strategic Literacy Initiative at WestEd. She is an advisory board member for the Practitioner Initiated Inquiry Series for Teachers College Press, a member of the Bread Loaf Teacher Network, serves on the NCTE Executive Committee, and was recently elected Secondary Section cochair. Diane was a recipient of a 2-year Carnegie Foundation Fellowship (1999–2001) awarded to school and university-based scholars to conduct classroom-based research. She is also a recipient of the National Writing Project's Fred Hechinger Award in 2002 for connecting research and practice in a body of work that includes articles and book chapters focused on language and literacy.

Phillip Wilder is currently a doctoral student in curriculum and instruction at the University of Illinois at Urbana-Champaign with an emphasis in language and literacy. A former English and social studies teacher, he is presently the school-wide literacy coordinator at a high school in Illinois, where he teaches freshmen reading courses and collaborates with teachers from a variety of content areas regarding effective literacy instruction. His current research interests include the new literacies of struggling adolescent readers, teacher conceptions of best practice instruction regarding new literacies, and models of effective secondary literacy programs.

Introduction

Donna E. Alvermann
University of Georgia

Sarah Jonas
The Children's Aid Society

Ariel Steele
Eric Washington
Dunlevy Milbank Center of The Children's Aid Society

People tell others who they are, but even more important, they tell themselves and then try to act as though they are who they say they are.

—Holland, Lachicotte, Skinner, & Cain, 1998, p. 3

It is these ways of telling and acting that produce self-understandings, which Holland and her colleagues refer to as *identities*, especially when those self-understandings are associated with strong emotional resonance for the tellers. Importantly, these identities are conceived of "as always forming" (Holland et al., 1998, p. 8), which is a way of incorporating the social weighing of expression and the history-in-person constructs theorized, respectively, by Bakhtin (1981) and Vygotsky (1971). These are constructs that make possible the notion of subjectivities (or always-forming identities). We find Holland et al.'s conception of identity a useful one in framing this introduction and laying the groundwork for the chapters that follow.

In this, the second edition of *Reconceptualizing the Literacies in Adolescents' Lives*, the focus is on exploring the impact of young people's identity-making practices in mediating their perceptions of themselves as readers and writers in an era of externally mandated reforms aimed at improving all students' literacy achievement. For example, are their perceptions inextricably tied to their teachers' perceptions of achieving readers? Or, is such interdependency more theory bound than practice driven? Do adolescents value reading against the grain—sometimes described as reading the subtexts or "hidden" messages of texts that authors may have con-sciously or unconsciously concealed? More to the point, have they been taught to read in this manner, and if so, do they recognize that texts of all kinds (print, visual, aural, digital) position them in ways that produce certain meanings and literate identities from the cultural resources available within specific social situations? Fi-nally, and perhaps most importantly, might the small but growing trend to do re-search *with*, rather than exclusively *on*, youth (Lee, 1999; Reeves, 2004) signal the field's openness to valuing adolescents' perceptions of themselves as readers and the literate self-understandings that mediate those perceptions?

The extent to which these questions can be answered depends in no small measure on the research that has been conducted since the first edition of *Reconceptualizing the Literacies in Adolescents' Lives* appeared 8 years ago. For although it was the first edi-tion that gave rise to these very questions—they were stated originally in the form of "imagined possibilities" (see chapter 16, Alvermann, 1998)—it is the second edition that addresses them more fully, and it does so in at least two important ways. First, a substantially greater number of students' voices are included in the second edition, primarily to make visible their identity-making practices, that is, the things they tell others and themselves about who they are as literate beings and the actions such tellings induce. Second, greater attention is given to the policies that are driving fed-eral and state efforts to improve adolescents' reading achievement, and especially to the implications these policies have for the questions just posed.

We have divided the introduction into three main sections. We begin with a brief overview of the No Child Left Behind Act (2001) and the influence this controversial piece of legislation is having on groups advocating for increased student reading achievement at the middle and high school levels. Although it is only one piece of the larger accountability-driven education reform movement that uses high-stakes testing as a policy tool (Hamilton, 2003), NCLB is garnering considerable attention because of its emphasis on raising reading achievement levels for students from ev-ery type of family background. Next, we describe why calls for improved literacy achievement must take into account, at a minimum, the following factors: the situatedness of adolescents' literate identities; the ways in which young people are positioned as readers and writers in school; the sociocultural and linguistic prac-tices that mediate identity formations in youth; and the impact of teachers and school-wide reform on students' literate identities. We conclude with a conversa-tion that highlights the literate identities of two adolescents whose voices, like those in the chapters that follow, speak to the importance of listening deeply to what youth have to tell us.

NCLB'S IMPACT ON YOUTH ADVOCACY GROUPS

Unlike primary schools, which have experienced the force of No Child Left Behind legislation for over 2 years through federally funded programs such as Reading First that mandate certain prescribed ways of teaching "scientific" reading princi-ples, secondary schools have remained relatively outside of NCLB's immediate gaze. However, this is changing rapidly due to increased media and public atten-tion focused on high-stakes testing and its implications for determining annual yearly progress (or lack thereof) in high schools across the United States. For exam-ple, according to Educational Testing Service's fifth annual nationwide survey ti-tled *Ready for the World: Americans Speak on High School Reform*:

One-third of the American public believes that America's public education system is most responsible for the country's success in the world—even more important than the democratic system of government or military strength—but two-thirds believe that America's ability to compete will be threatened if American high schools do not improve in the next twenty-five years. http://www.all4ed.org/publications/StraightAs/Volume5No13.html# Grad)

Advocacy groups such as the Alliance for Excellent Education (http://www.all4ed. org), the National Adolescent Literacy Coalition (Williamson, 2004), and the Carnegie Corporation's recently formed Advisory Council on Advancing Adolescent Literacy (Henríquez, 2005) have been instrumental in keeping educators and policymakers focused on the need to bridge the literacy achievement gap, especially among readers who struggle (or strive) to meet the increasingly higher standards set for high school graduation. Although such support is greatly welcomed and adds immeasurably to these heady times in school reform, the second edition of *Reconceptualizing the Literacies in Adolescents' Lives* is an excellent reminder of a basic premise that can easily get overlooked in the rush to close the achievement gap.

That premise is this: Advocating for higher literacy achievement for all students, although a worthwhile goal in its own right, has the potential for even greater impact when adolescents' identity-making practices are taken into consideration and their voices are invited to the table for discussion. To explore the feasibility of such actions, the chapter authors in this book have provided documented evidence based on their research that underscores the importance of understanding key factors that mediate young people's views of themselves as readers and writers, and in turn, how those same factors may influence both positively and negatively the very policies that are put in place to improve literacy achievement among adolescents.

FACTORS TO CONSIDER IN CALLS FOR IMPROVING LITERACY ACHIEVEMENT

The second edition of *Reconceptualizing the Literacies in Adolescents' Lives* is divided into four parts. To situate the content of these parts in the larger literature, chapter authors have drawn from fields as diverse as cultural and media studies, education, psychology, communication, sociolinguistics, political science, and anthropology. They have also called on equally diverse perspectives, including but not limited to theories derived from postpostivistic, critical, sociohistorical, and poststructural frameworks.

Situating Adolescents' Literacies

In Part I of the second edition, chapter authors provide grounded examples from their research that show how adolescents' literate practices in specific contexts are linked to broader social processes. A common starting point for this work can be found in what is commonly referred to as the New Literacy Studies (Gee, 1996; Street, 1995). Another commonality shared by the chapters in this section is the implicit acknowledgment of how "one's history-in-person is the sediment from past experiences upon which one improvises, using [or resisting] the cultural resources available, in response to the subject positions afforded one in the present" (Holland et al., 1998, p. 18).

For example, in chapter 1, Lorri Neilsen's account of how two "touchstone texts" that David and Eleanor read as adolescents contributed to their identities then and continue to assist them in resisting certain resources available to them in the cultural and economic mainstream, we see the workings of both the history-in-person construct and the notion that all literacies are situated within larger, structuring social processes. Similarly, in David O'Brien's updated chapter 2, we see how adolescents who struggle with school reading tasks can change their perceptions of themselves as literate beings when reading competency is redefined in the context of some highly sophisticated literacies, such as those required in the mediasphere.

Chapter 3 is new and chronicles Josephine Peyton Marsh's and Elizabeth Petroelje Stolle's examination of how critical literacy practices opened up spaces for what the authors call identity "re/construction"—in this instance, a restructuring of stereotypical images of gender and ethnicity as two adolescent girls produced self-understandings of what these identity markers had to do (or not do) with their lives. Chapter 4, another new chapter in the second edition, features Alfred W. Tatum's detailed account of how teachers, by improvising pedagogically with the cultural resources available, can accommodate young people's socially situated literacy practices and improve their own literacy instruction at the same time.

Positioning Youth as Readers and Writers

Young people develop more or less conscious conceptions of themselves as readers and writers in socially and culturally constructed spaces both in and out of school, and these sensed identities (to the extent that they are conscious and objectified) permit youth, through the kinds of semiotic mediation described by Vygotsky (1986), at least a little agency or control over their own identity-making activities. Holland et al. (1998) refer to such socially produced and culturally constructed activities as "figured worlds" (p. 41) in which participants' positions matter. As they further note, "Some figured worlds we may never enter because of our social position or rank; some we may deny to others; some we may simply miss by contingency; some we may learn fully" (p. 41). Applied to the figured world of adolescent literacy, this would mean as Moore (this volume) points out in his introduction to Part II, that adolescents' identity-making practices jointly produce storylines that position themselves and others in particular ways.

Three of the four chapters in Part II show how such positioning occurs while adolescents engage with various literacy practices in academic subject areas (science, persuasive writing, and poetry) and while coenacting these practices with their teachers and classmates. For example, in chapter 5, Elizabeth Birr Moje and Deborah R. Dillon revisit their chapter from the first edition of *Reconceptualizing the Literacies in Adolescents' Lives*, and offer new interpretations of their supporting data that demonstrate how the figured worlds of two particular high school science classrooms produced storylines that at times alternately invited or barred a particular student's participation in science-related literacy practices.

In chapter 6, which is new to the second edition, Jennifer E. Obidah and Tyson Marsh write about African American youth participating in a learning community that intentionally positions each learner as if he or she were someone important—a figured world in which possibilities exist for learning more fully how positioning works and why it should matter to those of us interested in advancing adolescents' literacy achievement. In an updated and streamlined Chapter 7, David W. Moore and James W. Cunningham account for the role of agency in adolescents' literate identities by attending to individuals' internal dialogues in the midst of complex, semiotically mediated contexts.

The fourth chapter in Part II, which is new and co-authored by Helen J. Harper and Thomas W. Bean, takes into account the politics of advocating for improved adolescent literacy and argues for a renewed project of democratic citizenship. Claiming that the capabilities and sensibilities found in adolescents' multiliteracies have the potential to refigure a stronger and more pluralistic democracy, the authors call for a practical form of pedagogy to support students' 21st-century literacy practices and the new positionings that such practices might well afford.

Mediating Practices in Young People's Literacies

The chapter authors in Part III focus largely on how young people's literate identities both mediate, and are mediated by, the social worlds in which they live. This kind of reciprocity, like Holland et al.'s (1998) notion of semiotic mediation as a means of agency, allows for the possibility that "one modifies one's environment with the aim, but not the certainty, of affecting one's own behavior—and it requires a sustained effort" (p. 38). This, coupled with the fact that "except for rather small-scale changes [the process] is clearly beyond the ability of any individual to accomplish alone" (p. 38), suggests that adolescents' literate identities are always forming (never static) in relation to the social world around them.

It is a concept certainly at play in chapter 9. There, James Paul Gee illustrates through discourse analysis how adolescents' shape-shifting identities and self-fashioning tactics mediate, and are mediated by, language and social class differences. Similarly, in chapter 10, Bob Fecho, Bette Davis, and Renee Moore explore how race, language, and culture mediate, and are mediated by, young people's literacy practices in three different classrooms that espouse critical inquiry into young people's language use. In chapter 11, which is new to the second edition of *Reconceptualizing the Literacies in Adolescents' Lives*, co-authors Phillip Wilder and Mark Dressman explore the extent to which a group of adolescents' academic and social practices in school, over time, may have so thoroughly structured their cognition and identity as social actors as to curtail their ability to capitalize on the benefits afforded by literacy instruction using digital computer technology. In contrast, chapter 12, by Kathleen Hinchman and Kelly Chandler-Olcott, suggests that tapping into young people's insights about factors that mediate, and are mediated by, their literate lives might very well produce a different picture of who they are and the pedagogical practices necessary for meeting their needs.

Changing Teachers, Teaching Changes

Part IV of the second edition of *Reconceptualizing the Literacies in Adolescents' Lives* is comprised of all new chapters dealing with conceptual change about literacy teaching and learning in a time of policy-driven federal and state efforts to improve adolescents' reading achievement. And aptly so, for as Waff (this volume) explains in her introduction, these three chapters challenge readers "to rethink the logic of one-size-fits-all school reform efforts while benefiting from the wisdom of inclusive local inquiry communities to transform teacher practice, advance student learning and bring about lasting school improvement." Imagining alternative worlds out of seemingly ordinary forms of communal life at the local level is a concept that Holland et al. (1998) explore in their work on identity and agency in cultural worlds. Although not situated in schools per se, their work offers glimpses into how different constructions of being a teacher and learner might evolve from politically mediated literacy practices that foster the development of agency and a sense of self-understanding among adolescents and their teachers.

For example, in chapter 13, Susan L. Lytle describes a collaborative practitioner inquiry community comprised of teacher leaders and college/university-based researchers who explore from their different vantage points how diverse experiences of race, class, gender, student advocacy, and social justice can effect change in local and national policies to improve adolescent literacy. With an eye toward engaging adolescents in collaborative action research projects and the political process, Jody Cohen, Cambria Allen, Heather Davis, Bruce Bowers, Elena Darling-Hammond, and Li Huan Lai wrote chapter 14 to document the ways in which a group of high school students investigated their school's dress code, while a group of middle school students explored the implications of the No Child Left Behind Act for urban schools. What Cohen and her colleagues learned from this study was the value of doing research *with* (rather than simply *on*) adolescents about their perceptions of themselves as stakeholders in meaningful intellectual work.

Finally, in chapter 15, Lisa Patel Stevens pulls together several diverse threads of stakeholder interest in adolescent literacy reform by proposing that policymakers develop a set of what she calls "enabling constraints." These constraints, she argues, would require that school districts draw on local knowledge and expertise to imagine an alternative world of policy-driven reform, one in which young people and their teachers would have opportunities to share their views of how they use a range of textual practices to mediate their sense of selves and the world, and what they need educationally.

A CONVERSATION WITH SARAH JONAS, ARIEL STEELE, AND ERIC WASHINGTON

The following commentary, interspersed with directly quoted excerpts from an audiorecorded conversation between Sarah Jonas, Director of Education Services for The Children's Aid Society in New York, and two adolescents who participate in programs sponsored by the group, is a preview of what can be learned from carefully listening to youth talk about how they identify with particular reading and writing practices both in and out of school. As such, it is but a brief sampling of the more in-depth analyses of what counts as literacy in young people's eyes in the chapters that follow. And not to be overlooked, this conversation hints in important ways at Holland et al.'s (1998) understanding of identity and the self-understandings that develop when young people tell others and themselves who they are as literate beings.

Who They Are

Both Ariel and Eric participate regularly in out-of-school time programs at the Dunlevy Milbank Center of The Children's Aid Society, near where they live in Central Harlem. Ariel, a 10th grader, is involved in the Center's evening teen program, helps in supervising younger children in the Saturday "Study Now, Play Later" program, and is currently a counselor at the Center's summer camp. Eric, a sixth grader, attends the summer camp, and during the school year, he also attends the after-school MASPAS program (a tutoring and project-based learning program for middle school youth). Although both young people expressed confidence in their own abilities to learn through reading and writing, they were also cognizant, as their comments suggest, that literacy is highly valued in today's society and that their teachers worked hard to help them achieve in school. At the same time, they seemed well aware that the other half of the learning equation involves them, as students, and that not all their friends are as motivated as they are to engage with literacy.

Self-Identified Readers and Writers

Sarah noted how pleased she was to learn, first and foremost, that both Ariel and Eric love reading and writing and that both of them choose to engage in these activities on their own time, outside of school. In fact, both Ariel and Eric described themselves, with pride, as avid readers and writers. Ariel specifically cited her uncle, who worked in a library, as influencing her love of reading:

> When I was a little girl I used to read to my uncle all the time. He worked in a library, so he always bring me books, so that's what got me into reading. So you know as a little child I was always curious about books. I wasn't worried about playing and stuff.

Eric said that reading was his favorite subject in school. He specifically mentioned what he felt reading does for him:

> It relaxes me when I come off from playin' and it cools me down. Like action books, like suspension, that leaves you thinkin' all night about it, so you want to go back to school and read the rest.

He also made specific mention of enjoying the way his reading teacher made reading fun by holding class discussions in which students could offer their own insights and opinions about what they'd read.

Types of Reading Matter

Ariel and Eric said the number one thing that makes them love reading is the kind of books they read. They both listed action/adventure books, such as the Harry Potter series, as being among their favorites. Second to that were books that have to do with "real life" issues that young people have to work through. For example, Ariel, who said she often reads on the subway, prefers to read books about people who grew up in Harlem as well as books about young people like herself. She said she uses ideas gained from reading books to writes stories of her own, including screenplays about teens and the issues they are facing. Asked if she had shown these to her friends, Ariel said yes, and added that she had shared them with one of her teachers, who had encouraged her to submit them for publication (but she hasn't done that yet).

Both Eric and Ariel said they enjoy reading on their own time about the music business, particularly about the daily lives of the music stars they admire. They were less interested in the "glitzy" star image of these musicians, and much more interested to read the details of their lives that make them seem more like regular people. They pointed out that they preferred to read how the stars "rose up" from humble beginnings to become hugely successful because this makes it seem like it could happen even to you. Eric mentioned he likes to read sports magazines for the same reasons.

Eric also noted that he loves comic books and has written some of his own. When asked why comic books appeal to him, Eric said that besides the action, he loves how the characters talk. He mentioned how a character may have two bubbles above his or her head, one for what is being said aloud and another—a "thought bubble"—that shows what the character is really thinking. He pointed out that often these two bubbles are at odds. He said he likes this because he gets insight into what the character is actually thinking:

> Once I read it [a comic book], I was like, he's insulting him. But how does he know that because he's just smilin', and then I learned that that's the bubble of what he's thinkin'.

Eric also mentioned repeatedly how much he likes to write in his free time. For example, he said:

> Like when there's nothin' to do, I'll probably grab a book and start writing…about my life and stuff, and how I feel. Like I write about myself if I have powers or anything, and if I was in the Olympics, if I was racing at 180 miles per hour.

Like Ariel, Eric made specific mention of the fact that while he is grateful for the opportunity to do creative writing in school, he still treasures the "aloneness" of writing on his own time, outside of school, without any structured writing activity to guide him or rein in his imagination.

Both young people shared a dislike of reading in science class and described their science texts as "boring." For example, Eric said that his science textbook had nothing in it that kids can relate to, nothing to do with the "street," as he put it:

> Like in science, it [his textbook] talks about the body and stuff, and when it gives you like stuff you won't use a lot when you walkin' around on the street, you just walkin'. You might not even remember it, you might not think about it.

However, Eric did point out an exception to his general dislike of reading his science text. He specifically mentioned a time when writing was fun in science class. It was when the class did a project that involved making a volcano, and then writing a short paragraph about it.

Ariel said kids don't want to read about things that happened, like "a thousand years ago," but are, instead, looking for topics that have immediate relevance:

> The books are so old, I mean they published them in 1950 something. I try my best—I get pretty good grades when I write reports [in science class], but it's hard to remember something that is so boring. It [the textbook] didn't seem too helpful to me so I have to use the Internet or something to fill in. It's hard to write when it's dry and dull.

On Testing and the Push to Become Better Readers and Writers

Both Ariel and Eric felt personally confident about being tested in reading and writing, but they had plenty of friends for whom this causes great stress.

Ariel described what she viewed as the reason for taking so many tests in school:

> Actually they have us doin' a lot of tests, and they always test on what we read the day before. Um, the books they give us, they're challenging, and they want us to build our literature up, vocabulary, and stuff.

Eric felt teachers should emphasize that reading and writing are important to succeeding in life, but he was adamant about how that message should be communicated to students:

> Like they [teachers] shouldn't say that you *have* to do this to pass the test. Just tell them that it's really important, that you want them to pass, that it's important to their mother and father that you pass.

Things Ariel and Eric Wished Their Teachers Knew About Them as Readers and Writers

Ariel wished that her teachers wouldn't make everyone in the class wait while others finished reading something in class:

> Actually, I just wish, you know, that if a group of people finish a book in class, we shouldn't be penalized to wait for the rest of the group to finish. They [teachers] should allow us to do a report on the book for extra credit or something, or maybe just let us start a new book on our own.

She also said she wished that teachers knew how much kids like to choose their own topics when they write:

> Like if you have a report, they usually give us one topic the report should be on. I think they should give us numerous topics to choose from, but all based around that main topic so we wouldn't be forced, like, to write something that we weren't comfortable with … like maybe pick something we'd be motivated to write about.

From Eric's point of view, he said that he thought his teachers did not know that he likes to write stories outside of school and that he writes about himself. When asked if he'd like them to know this information, Eric hesitated and then replied:

> Not really. It's something I like to have to myself because I can create something that only I know about.

Both young people spoke of teachers who creatively and enthusiastically found ways to engage students in literacy activities. Eric, in particular, emphasized the importance of having what he called "free reading" time in school, where he is at liberty to choose what he likes to read and to be left alone to read. He mentioned that he appreciates having his teachers show an interest in what he and the other kids are reading on their own time.

Things Eric and Ariel Wished Their Families Knew About Them as Readers

Neither Ariel nor Eric were certain that their families understood just how important reading was in their lives. For example, when asked what he wished his family knew about him as a reader, Eric responded this way:

> I would tell 'em that I really like to read. I might not show it sometimes when I'm playing video games a lot. But I really do read, like for 30 minutes, about an hour sometimes.

Ariel's response that she needed more time by herself to enjoy reading at home suggests that privacy is often difficult to come by as a young person, whether in school or after school:

> In my house when there's nothing to do—I have a little brother so I kinda go in a room by myself—sit on my bed and read. Like my grandmother, she's like, "You always reading in the dark!"

Text Messaging and Instant Messaging (IM)

Ariel said she and her friends text message and IM all the time, even sometimes during school when it is technically not allowed. Eric text messages sometimes and enjoys using the computer in the after-school program because he does not have a computer with Internet access at home. When asked what young people their age like so much about text messaging/IM, both Ariel and Eric stressed that it's easier, often, than talking. They said that sometimes they just don't feel like talking and that they can express themselves better by texting/IM.

Both Ariel and Eric said they know plenty of young people who strongly dislike writing in school, and never write (pencil to paper) outside of school, but who will think nothing of writing entire paragraphs in text messaging. In fact, Ariel described a friend who creates alternate (screen) identities for herself when IMing in chat rooms, which Ariel described as being akin to writing a story. In elaborating on an incident in which her friend shared a "story" written under one of her various screen names, Ariel explained the situation this way:

> You know, you're not manipulating somebody, but you know, you're kinda tricking them, and you get a thrill out of it. And she' [her friend] would always send us the conversation that she would have with the person, whoever she met [in the chat room], and it was funny, it was so funny, 'cuz I'm like that's not her, that's not the real person!

Yet this friend, Ariel explained, would never think of herself as a writer and does not enjoy writing stories in or out of school. Eric mentioned a boy he knows who hates writing but has a cell phone with an elaborate keyboard that he uses to text message whole paragraphs to his friends all day long.

Both spoke as well of the new language young people are creating with the new technologies. Ariel called them "shortcuts," which allow the writer to write much more quickly, such as using only first letters to represent words (e.g., "BRB to stand for "be right back" and using letters that sound like whole words in place of the words, such as "U" for you). However, Ariel was quick to point out that she knows when and where it is inappropriate to use these shortcuts:

> I wrote an essay one day in school and instead of writing "too" (meaning "also"), I wrote the number 2. It was a good thing I had someone over-read it for me.

When asked if any teachers in their schools made use of text messaging or some of the other new technologies as a way of engaging young people in reading and writing, the answer was a resounding "no." The only example Ariel and Eric could think of was using computers to do Internet searches prior to writing a research report. When pressed further as to whether they would be interested in class activities that made use of the new technologies (Sarah gave the example of an activity where students would have to write a persuasive argument to a friend entirely through text messaging), the answer was a resounding "yes."

Eric said that he would be especially interested if his school could supply the phones for text messaging. He explained that he did have a cell phone but that it didn't allow him to do text messaging easily. He said that he likes text messaging because it allows people to express themselves better, especially when they just don't feel like talking:

> Disabled people who can't really talk a lot, they can explain in words. Like if you're in the summer and you do a lot of text messaging, it's kinda like writing in school. It's easier to express yourself in words instead of your mouth …. My cousin [name omitted to protect the privacy of his cousin] he has this phone that you flip it, and there's a whole bunch of buttons, and I don't think he likes to write [but he does a lot of writing on his cell phone].

When asked if he reads from a computer at home, or uses one to write reports or to instant message, Eric explained:

> I don't have a computer at home, well I do, but it's not linked up for the Internet. But um, in MASPAS [the middle school tutoring and enrichment program at the Dunlevy Milbank Center] I wrote a short biography of myself, and drew my self-portrait so that was kinda a way that was fun for me.

Sarah noted that it was through projects such as this one, which included posting Eric's autobiography on a special Web site for others to read, that the Center hoped to not only engage youth in after-school literacy activities, but also to democratize the situation a bit for those who are left behind on the technology superhighway because they don't have the right gear.

STAYING GROUNDED IN YOUTH'S PERCEPTIONS OF THEIR LITERATE IDENTITIES

We predict that just as this brief conversation with Ariel and Eric has revealed how rich the inner lives of adolescents are—how thoughtful and insightful they can be—so, too, will the detailed and deeply nuanced accounts of other young people's literate identities that are chronicled in this book. As David Moore noted after reading an initial draft of the introduction (and reflecting on the chapters to come):

Young people's voices offer great authenticity and intensity. Reading them—rather than what is said about them—encourages me to slow down, reflect on what they are saying, connect with other conversations I've had with flesh-and-blood kids, and be more empathetic to their situation.

In closing, we (Donna, Sarah, Ariel, and Eric) would like nothing better than to hear David Moore's words echoed by all who read this, the second edition of *Reconceptualizing the Literacies in Adolescents' Lives*. For as he has reminded us, in an age of externally mandated, life-changing accountability, educators and policymakers alike need to remain grounded in the day-to-day lived experiences of those whose literate identities are being affected the most.

REFERENCES

Alvermann, D. E. (1998). Imagining the possibilities. In D. E. Alvermann, K. A. Hinchman, D. W. Moore, S. F. Phelps, & D. R. Waff (Eds.), *Reconceptualizing the literacies in adolescents' lives* (pp. 353–372). Mahwah, NJ: Lawrence Erlbaum Associates.

Bakhtin, M. M. (1981). *The dialogic imagination: Four essays by M. M. Bakhtin* (M. Holquist, Ed., C. Emerson & M. Holquist, Trans.). Austin: University of Texas Press.

Gee, J. P. (1996). *Social linguistics and literacies: Ideology in Discourses* (2nd ed.). London: Falmer.

Hamilton, L. (2003). Assessment as a policy tool. *Review of Research in Education, 27,* 25–68.

Henríquez, A. (2005). The evolution of an adolescent literacy program: A foundation's journey. *Reading Research Quarterly, 40,* 376–380.

Holland, D., Lachicotte, W., Jr., Skinner, D., & Cain, C. (1998). *Identity and agency in cultural worlds.* Cambridge, MA: Harvard University Press.

Lee, P. W. (1999). In their own voices: An ethnographic study of low-achieving students within the context of school reform. *Urban Education, 34,* 214–244.

No Child Left Behind Act (2001). PL 107-110, 115 Stat.1425, 20 U.S.C. 6301 *et. seq.* Retrieved May 31, 2005 from http://www.ed.gov/nclb/landing.jhtml?src=pb

Reeves, A. R.(2004). *Adolescents talk about reading: Exploring resistance and engagement with text.* Newark, DE: International Reading Association.

Street, B. V. (1995). *Social literacies: Critical approaches to literacy in development, ethnography and education.* New York: Longman.

Vygotsky, L. S. (1971). *The psychology of art.* Cambridge, MA: MIT Press.

Vygotsky, L. S. (1986). *Thought and language* (rev. ed.). Cambridge, MA: MIT Press.

Williamson, K. (2004). Progress on the issues: Adolescent literacy policy update and what's ahead in 2005. Retrieved July 21, 2005 from http://www.ncte.org/about/gov/cgrams/news/118641.htm

I

Situating Adolescents' Literacies

CHAPTER 1

Playing for Real: Texts and the Performance of Identity   5
Lorri Neilsen

CHAPTER 2

"Struggling" Adolescents' Engagement in Multimediating: 29
Countering the Institutional Construction of Incompetence
David O'Brien

CHAPTER 3

Re/constructing Identities: A Tale of Two Adolescents   47
Josephine Peyton Marsh and Elizabeth Petroelje Stolle

CHAPTER 4

Adolescents' Multiple Identities and Teacher Professional   65
Development
Alfred W. Tatum

Introduction to Part I: Situating Adolescents' Literacies

Stephen F. Phelps
Buffalo State College

In our first edition of *Reconceptualizing the Literacies in Adolescents' Lives*, Donna Alvermann urged us to question simplistic notions of adolescence and literacy. Policymakers, researchers, teacher educators, and teachers need to understand and value adolescents' perspectives as well as the ways in which their identities and subjectivities mediate their literate endeavors both in and out of school. This takes on increasing urgency as federal policymakers turn their attention to adolescent literacy. Consequently, we begin this new edition with four chapters that look specifically at how adolescent identity and literacy are intertwined.

In Chapter 1, Lorri Neilsen updates her original *Reconceptualizing* chapter by reacquainting us with David and Eleanor, first as adolescents talking about how certain "touchstone texts" were involved in their identity formation, and 8 years later, how they see themselves both in retrospect and now, as politically astute, literate young adults who resist the cultural and economic mainstream and who are still very much in the process of identity formation. David O'Brien in chapter 2 looks at adolescent readers who are struggling with the traditional text-based literacies most often equated with school, yet who will persevere and create complex and sophisticated literate products when they set their own personally meaningful tasks and choose the media through which they express themselves. He demonstrates the link between self-perception and competency, and argues that if we redefine competency in light of the highly sophisticated literacies of the "mediasphere," we can change how students perceive themselves. In chapter 3, Josephine Marsh and Elizabeth Stolle look at school experiences of two adolescent girls that demonstrate how critical literacy practices can open up space for what Marsh and Stolle call identity "re/construction," that is, how adolescents can simultaneously reconstruct stereotypical images of gender and ethnicity as they are constructing their own gender or cultural identity. Finally, Alfred Tatum in chapter 4 gives a detailed account of what can happen when teachers move toward purposefully accommodating adolescent cultural and community identity in literacy instruction.

These opening chapters build a foundation for our continued reconceptualization of adolescent literacies. Five themes are established that will be revisited and elaborated in later chapters:

1. Literacy has an important function in the development of adolescents' individual, cultural, and social identities.

2. The full range of adolescent literacies is much more complex, dynamic, and sophisticated than the narrow confines of school-based literacy.

3. As adolescents have multiple literacies, they also have multiple texts. An expanded concept of "text" must transcend print-based texts to also include various electronic media and adolescents' own cultural and social understandings.

4. Understanding the full range of adolescent literacies and texts requires a reconceptualization of literate competency.

5. Adolescents need spaces in school to explore multiple literacies and multiple texts, to experiment, to critique, and to receive feedback, encouragement, and guidance from peers and adults.

1

Playing for Real: Texts and the Performance of Identity

Lorri Neilsen
Mount Saint Vincent University

… Old paint on canvas as it ages sometimes becomes transparent. When that happens it is possible, in some pictures, to see the original lines: a tree will show through a woman's dress, a child makes way for a dog, a large boat is no longer on an open sea … This is called pentimento … the old conception, replaced by a later choice, is a way of seeing and then seeing again.

—Lillian Hellman (1973), *Pentimento*

This chapter is in two sections: Adolescence and Early Adulthood. The first section, Adolescence, is an abbreviation of an earlier chapter written for the first edition of this handbook (Neilsen, 1998b). The earlier chapter, written 8 years ago, focuses on identity creation, and on what I call *"touchstone" texts* informing the lives of two adolescents in high school. These touchstone texts shape the lives of David and El in ways that suggest that reading in adolescence is an activity of interpolation—whether the texts are film, cultural practices, or literary works, they inhabit the reader and the reader, in turn, writes the texts into his or her life. This earlier chapter, "Adolescence," suggests that, as educators, we must learn which texts resonate for adolescents and why. Both the substance of "Adolescence" and the theoretical inferences have remained as they were 8 years ago in order to preserve the original data, analyses and theoretical perspectives of both the participants and the researcher in context at that time. The reader is encouraged to read this section as though he or she might be reading it 8 years ago.

The second section of this chapter is an update; here, in "Adulthood," we meet again the two friends, David and El, 8 years after high school and after their first conversation with the researcher. What are their textual preoccupations now? What role do they believe their readings have played in shaping their lives? And what insights, given their experience, might they offer to educators today? This section, like the earlier chapter, invites an aesthetic as much as an efferent reading. Because much of our reading in school and the academy is efferent (and much writing is thus propositional, theoretical, and closed), this chapter offers the possibility of understanding research and scholartistry (Neilsen, 2002), which is, like texts, students, and data themselves, open to multiple interpretations.

ADOLESCENCE

Prologue

"Who am I?" is a question of central importance in adolescence. No longer children unself-consciously acting out story in the school yard or playing dress-up in the basement, adolescents try on roles in their lives at school, at home, and in the community. Unlike the play of young children, however, adolescent play often is marked by the awareness of its purpose: to explore identities in order to find a place in the world. Although play at all ages is serious, adolescent performance-as-identity has a particular urgency and intensity. Eva Hoffman (1989) describes this intensity about life as being marked by "fire, flair, a holy spark of inspiration" (p. 154). Who will I be today, tomorrow, next year?

This study explored the role of text in the lives of two adolescents in a Nova Scotia rural community. Here the term *text* refers to sets of signifying practices and discourses available to us in local and larger discourse communities: a novel in English class, the conversation about that novel, teen 'zines, mall cultures, music videos, advertising, and television sitcoms, for example. The premise of this study is that our engagements with everyday texts help all readers and writers to shape and reshape our identities, but that adolescents, in particular, engage in more fluid, intentional and often more passionate identity-play in their encounters with such symbolic resources. These resources not only help the adolescent make sense of her or his experience, but also offer opportunities for trying on or taking up often multiple and conflicting roles or identities. In this way, a text is both role and reality. Adolescents, who typically demonstrate as much zeal in taking up roles as they do in resisting them, become at once the performer, the audience, and the theatre. By performing the texts of their lives, they are reading and writing themselves.

As researcher, mother, and community member, I have observed the participants, Eleanor and David, in a number of social, personal, and school settings since their first grade in school. The in-depth interviews about the role of key texts in their lives, however, were taken over two months late in their Grade 11 (junior) year in high school. Emerging from transcripts of 6 hours of individual and paired interviews is a recurring theme: the fluidity of text in performance and role-playing as Eleanor and David make and shape meaning in their lives through literacy. Their understanding and "scripting" of principal—or what I refer to as "touchstone"—texts in their lives is woven into their school and social behavior in a process of ongoing revision. Here the texts are the novel, *The Catcher in the Rye*, and the film, *Pulp Fiction*. Their motifs and influences shift, recede, and emerge, seeming at times like the phenomena of pentimento in painting (Hellman, 1978) or the layered scripts of a palimpsest. The text or texts, as the adolescents themselves, resist stasis and defy definition.

The Players

Eleanor.   Eleanor and her older sister moved with their mother (a single parent) to this rural Nova Scotia community before Eleanor started school. She lives with her mother, the owner of a craft store, and her stepfather, a fifth-generation Nova Scotian, in a recently converted boathouse on St. Margaret's Bay.

Interviews with El took place just before she turned 17. El is independent, has traveled alone to Ireland to visit relatives, travels every other weekend to see her birth father, and works part-time at a local restaurant/coffee house and occasionally as a sign painter. She goes into Halifax regularly to see films, hang out in coffee houses, or to visit her current boyfriend, an art student.

El's dress is distinctive, what some might call "nonconformist." She wears several earrings, including a nose ring; her dark hair has sported many hairstyles. She is short, quiet, but not shy, and often questions her parents' and her teachers' decisions. Art, drama, English, and history are her favorite school subjects. She has attended school in the same school system since grade primary.

David. David, 17, moved to the community from western Canada 13 years ago with his parents, both of whom are educators. He has a 9-year-old brother. David and Eleanor have been close friends since Grade 1, but never romantically paired. David, like El, has been independent from childhood, and has traveled frequently out of Nova Scotia. He attended school in the same classes as Eleanor. Highly verbal, he performs in school settings (as class clown), has studied drama with the local theatre school, and served as a youth judge at the local film festival. David is on two baseball teams, has been an avid skater and snowboarder, and when not with his girlfriend, Cheryl, hangs out with El and other friends from school. Ross, David, Simon, and El have made several home videos based on material they have written or improvised.

David dresses in a style he calls unique ("I am not preppie, not jock, and not punk"), but is in the contemporary style of skateboarders (large shirts, long skirt-like shorts). Like El, David's heritage is European, largely Caucasian; his great-grandmother was Cree. His brown hair, once worn in a ponytail, is now short and dyed dark blond. David is tall and solidly built. El's and David's strong sense of justice is demonstrated in their ongoing challenge of what they see as sexist or racist practices of their teachers or the community. Both frequently "diss" the rural community for what they see as its provincial attitudes.

Researcher/Narrator. As a 13-year resident of the rural community, I have researched and written about the literate behavior of adults in the area (Neilsen, 1989). As David's mother and a volunteer in their schools, I have seen both David and El in a variety of literacy and schooling contexts over the 11-year period in which they have known one another. Having moved intellectually from an atomistic, functional notion of literacy and literacy research in the 1970s, I am now engaged in ongoing research into gender and literacy that might be characterized as phenomenological.

The Texts

The Catcher in the Rye. J.D. Salinger's 1951 story of a prep-school runaway is perhaps one of North America's most controversial and enduring novels. Typically described as the only novel to successfully "convey contemporary youth's dissatisfaction with adult society" (Benet's, 1987), it deals with the two days following Holden Caulfield's departure from school. Holden Caulfield is considered by many adolescent and adult readers to represent the voice of disaffected youth. Indeed, although readers in the 1950s were avid readers of the novel (the language was frank and racy enough for the times to ensure a wide readership), the work continues to attract succeeding generations of young readers.

Pulp Fiction.   The controversial movie (Tarantino 1994) about low-rent hit men won the 1994 Cannes Film Festival's highest prize, the Palme d'Or, and a 1994 Academy Award for Best Original screenplay for the writer/director, Quentin Tarantino. Celebrated as the work of one of cinema's "enfants terrible," the movie also marked actor John Travolta's long-awaited return to the screen.

Like Salinger, Tarantino has been praised for his authentic, engaging dialogue and his originality. In Tarantino's case, the film is flagrantly derivative of other films and of pop culture narratives and, ironically, it is this derivative "bricolage" quality, in part, that wowed the critics. The term *pulp fiction* refers to the 5-cent novels popular a generation ago, and the movie is replete with pop culture images and references and allusions to well-known movies. The film disrupts the conventional narrative and linear plot line; viewers must piece together "what happened" through a series of flashbacks (and jumps forward). Martin and Porter (1996) describe it as a "trash masterpiece" in which the writer/director "spares the viewer little in this tale of the underbelly of Los Angeles where philosophizing hit men and techno-crazed druggies live on the thrill-packed edge" (p. 103) Vincent Vega (Travolta) and Jules (Samuel Jackson) are the hapless gangsters whom we follow on the trail of a suitcase, the contents of which remains a mystery.

The movie, like its director/writer, is not without its critics. Some have called the film "blaxploitation," claiming that actor Samuel Jackson's Afro and exaggerated sideburns (part of the movie's 1970s motif) make him just another Black stereotype, and that Travolta's "White negro" attitude, as well as the script's frequent use of the word "nigger," makes the movie both dangerous and racist. Feminists, in particular, have attacked the film for its graphic violence: heroin addiction, execution-style murder, male rape, and bondage.

Theoretical Backdrop

This study assumes that becoming literate is a lifelong process, and that literacy learning and literate behaviors are semiotic activities (Neilsen, 1989) in which we learn to read and write within value-laden code systems. Becoming literate is a process not only of acquiring functional skills of decoding and encoding printed material, but also of developing critical awareness and agency in one's own life.

Adolescents in particular draw from popular culture to "actively create and define their own social identities ... 'reading' and 'writing' popular culture are thus inherently social processes" (Buckingham & Sefton-Green, 1994, p. 108). As young people learn to see themselves in social and political terms, they have the opportunity to actively choose or to resist the discourses and roles available to them. Although it is true that choice itself is framed and shaped by myriad personal and social influences, it is also true that the more diverse and discrepant the choices provided for young adults, the greater the chance their choices will move them beyond the insular and the local. Buckingham and Sefton-Green (1994) offer this observation:

> Becoming critical could be seen simply as a matter ... in Bourdieu's terms, of acquiring a kind of cultural capital ... on the other hand, (it) could be seen from a Vygotskyan per-

spective … (emphasizing) the way in which critical understanding offers the individual a degree of power and control over his or her thought processes. (p. 182)

Adolescents supported in multiple opportunities to work with a range of texts, both school-sanctioned and popular, would seem, then, to be well positioned for growth in their critical literacy development.

Cherland (1993) and others have shown how young girls take up gender identities through reading as a social practice. Rogers' (1993) study of preadolescent girls makes apparent that entry into adolescence creates for young girls a "crisis of courage" (p. 290) in which they struggle to maintain their outspokenness and strength in the face of pressures to assume societal roles and expectations for feminine behavior. Finders' (1996a, 1996b) work on the "underlife" of junior high school girls' literacy practices illustrates how social roles are shaped and maintained through girls' reading and writing outside of school-sanctioned literacy practices. Humans, regardless of age, tend to resist an official view of who they must be and what they must do (Finders, 1996a).

Boys, as much as girls, can be constrained by limited constructions of their gender identities in school and society. Most work in gender over the last decade has affirmed that cultural values about males and females are inscribed in literacy practices and can reinforce strongly the stereotypical male/female polarities of activity/passivity, dominance/submission, and public/private. Finders (1996a) calls for opportunities that examine:

the social, historical and cultural motivations of particular roles available—in texts, classrooms, and the larger culture—(that) will lead students to more critical awareness and thus, it is hoped, to the ability to revise those roles … Students, both male and female … need opportunities to practice dealing with intellectual uncertainties and political tension. (p. 126)

The texts of students' lives, regardless of the context, often undergo a process that Jenkins (1992) calls "becoming real," whether the text is in the private or the public domain. First the text—particularly if it is interesting to the reader/viewer—is incorporated into lived experience; then it is reread and rewritten so that it is more productive and more able to sustain its original appeal; and finally, it is shared within social practices as assumed and tacit knowledge, particularly among friends.

As this study shows, the touchstone texts that inform Eleanor's and David's lives—*The Catcher in the Rye* and *Pulp Fiction*, respectively—undergo such a process of becoming real, culminating, finally, in the insertion of these texts into their social world. In this way, whether it is a Saturday Night Live sketch seen alone at home and then reenacted in the school hallway as a piece of shared text (and then subsequently used as a "shorthand" reference for a social phenomenon), or whether it is a touchstone novel or film that plays an important role in their lives, these young people live the private in concert with the public. Each script, or text, has the potential for reenactment in public in some form, whether the enactment is explicit (in speech or writing) or tacit (changed behavior, for example).

To learn about the texts in their lives, I asked two questions of El and David: "Tell me about your reading and writing in school" (I asked this question of them individually, and together); and "Tell me about your favorite "text" (book, movie)" (I explained my perspective on "text," and that my meaning included other media). Each talked with only my occasional prompting for further explanation. Because we know each other so well, the conversations were, at first, awkward, as though we each recognized the performative nature of such talk. For David, especially, knowing me as "Mom," interested in his learning and his academic progress, he seemed at times caught between what he wanted to say and what he thought I might want to hear, both as a parent and a researcher. As a researcher, however, I did not consider this wrinkle problematic: Issues of stance and disclosure, identity and performance adhere in most research interviewing, regardless of the relationship between the people involved. El and David seemed remarkably candid and willingly offered their thoughts. Later, they read transcriptions of our recorded conversations, made changes, then read and revised a draft copy of what became the chapter.

Presenting the data in this format is an attempt, like breaking down the fourth wall in theatre, to collapse the distinctions between text and audience (or text and reader)—to make this a reading event, not an object—and to move away from viewing our own interactions with text as an activity separate from who we are (Rosenblatt, 1978).

Eleanor

> Then I'd throw my automatic down the elevator shaft—after I'd wiped off all the finger prints and all. Then I'd crawl back to my room and call up Jane and have her come over and bandage up my guts. I pictured her holding a cigarette for me to smoke while I was bleeding and all.

> The goddam movies. They can ruin you. I'm not kidding …. Holden Caulfield, *The Catcher in the Rye* (Salinger, 1951, p. 104)

Why El Likes Catcher in the Rye

I think it's just the way he goes on these spiels … there's this one chapter—I actually did bits of it for a monologue once in drama—and Holden's in this crap hotel, and he's in the lobby, in this, as he calls it, "vomity- looking chair," and all of a sudden he starts thinking about Jane, the girl he's still in love with, and it just goes off for the whole chapter about Jane—just the way he goes all over the place and he goes so deep into the way he's thinking, and you just relate to that, I mean that's how it happens in life …. chapter eleven … here it is [she reads]:

> "All of a sudden, on my way out to the lobby, I got old Jane Gallagher on the brain again. I got her on, and I couldn't get her off. I sat down in this vomity-looking chair in the lobby and thought about her and Stradlater sitting in that goddam Ed Banky's car, and though I was pretty damn sure old Stradlater hadn't given her the time—I know old Jane like a book—I still couldn't get her off my brain." (Salinger, 1951, p. 76)

and then he just goes on and on and on …
And this is probably my favorite part in the whole book … when they're out on the screened-in porch and it was the first time they had even got close to necking, and they didn't really, and it was raining, "raining like a bastard out" and

> " all of a sudden this booze hound her mother was married to came out on the porch and asked Jane if there were any cigarettes in the house … Anyway, Jane wouldn't answer him … she didn't even look up from the game" (Salinger, 1951, p. 78).

Jane just started crying. And he (Holden) talks about how this teardrop fell on a red square on the checkerboard, and how she just rubbed it in. And you can just see it so well, the way he describes it. So well. It makes me really feel the respect that he had for Jane, how he cared for her, I dunno. You almost think he doesn't have any respect for anything else but her ... well, except Phoebe (El pronounces this "foe-bee"), his sister. I love to hear him talking about his kid sister, and how she dances, and the little things about her that make him happy.

Another scene that really gets to me is when he was in his sister's school, when he went to get Phoebe to tell her he was leaving, and he saw "fuck off" written on the wall, and he was so angry, he wanted to go and smash the guy who did it, that it was so horrible that little kids would see this ...

On seeing Catcher in the Rye as a film

Never. No way. Because I have got it so clearly in my head if it was on film it would ruin it, unless I made the film ... I mean the only thing anyone ever says about him is Sally, and she talks about his crew cut, so I don't know what he looks like. He's probably not big, cause he was worrying about old Stradlater stretching his jacket, and he's tall, I think, and he has a little bit of grey hair, it says that somewhere. I see him, like now, how he would dress now, because I don't know what the fashion was then. It does relate now, it's timeless, really.

I can't even think who I would have play him as an actor ... I wouldn't. I couldn't. Because then it just turns all Hollywood. I don't want to see it like that. Yuk! Tom Cruise as Holden Caulfield? If it was going to be a movie it would have to be someone young, not big, who had never played anything before. Everyone else has a reputation and that takes over their character in a lot of movies. I could see people I know playing Holden Caulfield, but not anybody well known .... I know he's tall, skinny, with short hair, not a crew cut, short at the back, kind of long at the front. With casual pants, button-up shirts. I can hear his voice in my head, but I could never describe it exactly. Kinda low, but not real deep.

Reading and rereading

When I first read the book, I was in 7th grade, and I was, like, so sad. Just because I want this person to be alive, to really exist, so that I could know them .... when I finished the book, I thought, what do I do now? Because I just felt like I knew this person .... I wanted him to be around to talk to. I think I was a little in love with him.

But the more I read it—like the last time I read it through was a while back—and I was more distanced from it, I think. I just felt he was too pissed off at everything, and that bothered me. Nothing pleased him .... I've heard people say it's a really depressing sort of book, I don't find it that way, but I think the more I read it, the more I get out of it. Maybe the first time I read it I didn't really understand what he was going through. It was just a story, he was just a cool guy who did whatever he felt like doing ....

He couldn't relate to society because he thought it was all bullshit ... A lot of people would like to have the guts that Holden did, just to say screw it and leave school, and get away, but they don't. I dunno, he just sounds like an adolescent sounds, even now. He says 'goddam' all the time. I just love that. He just says what he wants. And all these people he knows; they all represent different people in the teenage social structure. I know people like Stradlater. I'm friends with people like Holden. And I know people like Ackley—the guy with the mossy teeth—people who have disgusting fingernails and stuff. I know these people.

Sometimes I see all the negative stuff in Holden, and I just want to tell him to smarten up … other times it seems as though it's the complete truth. I think I reread it because it sounds realistic, and I would reread it just for the section on Jane and the tear on the checkerboard. That really struck me. It was just so obvious that he cared about her so passionately. That really gives him another dimension. And I reread that and wondered about the stepfather and Jane, whether we were supposed to take from that that there was some kind of abuse going on. It's subtle, but it's there. And Holden's feelings of protectiveness toward Jane. If you didn't reread and see those things then he wouldn't be a good character, he'd just be a joke. So many people are like that. They'd never tell their little sister what they're thinking, like how much they really care about her. I remember the time at the end when he was so exhausted, and sick, I think, and he was watching Phoebe going around and around the carousel, he was so full of happiness he wanted to cry. He loved her but didn't say. He didn't talk to Jane the whole time even though he had the opportunity … he's deeper than you'd expect … But last time I read it, I wondered actually if Holden was homophobic. Remember at the end when he leaves his drunk teacher's house so quickly? Who knows if the guy was making a pass at him, but I think Holden thought so …. And something else I noticed the last reading. Remember how he went to see his teacher, Spencer, and old Spencer showed him his terrible essay on the Egyptians? Well, at the end of the book, he's in the museum, and he starts telling these little kids all about the Egyptians, like he actually knows something about them. It's as though he finally found a use for all that information in real life. He becomes the teacher. You know what I mean? It's like he's in between being a child and an adult.

On Playing

Every single person Holden meets is interesting. Like his professor, the woman on the train. I just laughed at him telling her all those lies about her son …. Me and Nic have this routine that we do sometimes. It's sort of like Holden's. We act like I'm from Ireland and he's from Germany and we're just traveling around Nova Scotia, and we put on accents and have this great big story we tell people downtown. Remember when Holden was dancing with that girl and he told her she just missed seeing a movie star? That was so funny. I'd love to do that.

On Connecting With Male and Female Characters

I spend a lot of time with guys. I have friends who are girls, too, but I connect with guys more I think …. For music I choose mostly women artists. Sinead O'Connor. But I like older music, mostly male artists. Like Donovan, The Doors, Cream, The Beatles, Neil Young, America. It was my sister, though, who suggested I read *Catcher*. And my science teacher just freaked out when she saw I was reading it—she didn't read it until she was in university. I think she was shocked because most people my age were reading the *Babysitter's Club* and *Sweet Valley High* books. I read those in Grade 5: they were, like, chewing-gum reading. I wish there was stuff for girls to read that wasn't so empty. Things that would also make you think a little bit, maybe learn something. Instead of living in Sweet Valley and wishing for a convertible. I like novels, and poetry, and stories where there is more interpretation and where your own experience comes into it.

On Pulp Fiction

I liked the way the story was told—the storyline all jumbled. I liked the cinematography and the dialogue. It was both vulgar and smart. I liked the way the dialogue got into detail about little things. Like Vincent and Jules get into this big thing about Mia and foot massage outside the door of where they're supposed to pick up the briefcase. It had nothing to do with what they were there for, they just went on a rant. Like the kind of rant that Holden would go on.

I went not because of Travolta, but because everyone was raving about it. It scared me, actually, because of my reaction to the violence. Some of the violent scenes just were nothing, which made me wonder if I was overexposed to violence, they were brutal, but what got to me—when I really freaked out—was when Vincent was putting the needle into Mia's heart. You know, the adrenalin to revive her. I mean he was saving her life, not killing her like all the rest of the violence in the movie, but saving her, and that's the part that really affected me.

David

Buddy: Hi I'm Buddy, what can I get 'cha?

Vincent: I'll have the Douglas Sirk steak.

Buddy: How do you want it, burnt to a crisp, or bloody as hell?

Vincent: Bloody as hell. And to drink, a vanilla coke.

Buddy: How about you, Peggy Sue?

Mia: I'll have the Durwood Kirby burger—bloody—and a five-dollar shake.

Buddy: How d'ya want that shake, Martin and Lewis or Amos and Andy?

Mia: Martin and Lewis

Vincent takes a look around the place. The Yuppies are dancing, the diners are biting into big, juicy hamburgers, and the icons are playing their parts. Marilyn is squealing, the Midget is paging Philip Morris, Donna Reed is making her customers drink their milk, and Dean and Jerry are acting like fools.

Mia: Whaddya think?

Vincent: It's like a wax museum with a pulse rate. (*Pulp Fiction*, Tarantino, 1994)

Why David Likes Pulp Fiction:

I thought it was hilarious. And I really liked the way Tarantino messed with linear structure and chopped up the film … that was just not done in any movie I have ever seen. Plus I fell in love with John Travolta—he was just wicked; it was his comeback film. Plus the writing was really good. You know, dialogue about nothing.

Often in movies, every word that someone says is critically important, you know, very, very significant. This was just casual conversation between guys … what they said was important, because it added to their characters or added to the scene, but it didn't have life or death consequences. Like Travolta describing his trip to Amsterdam, saying to his partner:

> You'd really like it cause you can get a glass of beer at McDonald's. And you know what they call a quarter pounder with cheese at McDonald's? You mean they don't call it a quarter pounder with cheese? No man, they got the metric system. They wouldn't know what the fuck a quarter pounder is. What do they call it? Royale with cheese. Royale with cheese? Yeah, Royale with cheese.

Later on, they go:

> You want some bacon? No man, I don't eat pork. What, you Jewish or something? No man, I just don't dig on swine. Yeah, but bacon tastes good, pork chops taste good. Yeah, it might taste like pumpkin pie, but I'd never know 'cause I wouldn't eat the filthy motherfucker. Pigs eat and root and shit; pigs are filthy animals.

And they go on like that. This is right after Jules has found redemption because of some divine intervention where this guy hauled off and fired six shots from a hand cannon and missed them. But he's not talking about how he's found God, or how he's going to leave and find his true path, or nothing like that, he's talking about bacon … you know what I mean? It's really well done. It's really laid back. It's hilarious.

On Having Point

There's *Forrest Gump*. Where every word brought you closer to feeling compassion for Forrest Gump. Where you're really manipulated. But then there's TV, like *Seinfeld,* and all these new Generation X TV shows like *Friends* or the *Single Guy, Caroline in the City,* talking about nothing. Larry David and Jerry Seinfeld came up with the idea of a show about nothing, and it's made millions. And that's what it is. Just casual encounters and funny situations. It doesn't have to follow a direct plot line. It doesn't have to be boy meets girl, stuff like that. It's just everyday life. That's what it showed in *Pulp Fiction.* Just the everyday, underground life of two second-rate gangsters. They might be a little more philosophical than most, but …

I'm not part of Generation X, but I think these guys [Generation Xers] are sick of always having a plot line, or sick of things always having an inner meaning. I think every show has a point. But I don't think that it has to be a big one. I think life is like that. It doesn't always have a big point. Just lots of little ones.

On the Writer/Director

People just write what they know … I dunno, if you lived in Iceland you wouldn't write about the desert. Obviously Tarantino had a vast knowledge about certain kinds of movies. That's why he hasn't done a romance film, cause he really liked gangster films. He's like a geek. It's not the same old, same old, let's cast Arnold Schwarzennegger where we can make a million dollars cause it's a film where we blow up everything. And it's not a Disney cartoon borrowed from a book. He's coming up with original stuff. *Pulp Fiction* was never a book.

Pulp Fiction … ten cents. Book format … cheap entertainment, you know? Maybe the movie has some similarities with those old novels. The entertainment value. They're second-rate gangsters.

On Fiction and Reality

I think it's a portrayal of that kind of life, but it's not real life, 'cause real life isn't like that. People want to see real life, but they want to see it done more cleverly and more exciting. They don't want to see it done over the top—at least I don't—I want to see it as close to reality, but still far away. That's a paradox, isn't it. It's an impossible reality, I guess.

On Cultural Texts

I mean, I understood all those things in the restaurant scene. Mamie Van Doren, cherry cokes, all that. I mean, I didn't live in the 50s, so I don't really know it, but I think the media has taught me to know what all that is, even though I didn't live it. So I could place it right away.

On Viewing and Re-Viewing: The Text Becomes Real

It certainly boosted my interest in movie-making and being in films. About that time I was in a lull, I didn't know if I was going to continue in theatre or study film, and then seeing that movie … it was like, ohmygod, this is something entirely new. I liked it more when I got to see it more, talk about it more, share it more with my friends. I probably wouldn't have liked the movie as much if I was the only person I knew who saw it. My close friends and I got the sound track which was a kick-ass soundtrack which also added to my love for the film because there were excerpts from the movie on the soundtrack, which I memorized. Gave me a greater appreciation for music at that time. One of Jules' lines, for example, is "That's all right … that's Kool n' the Gang."

We even went so far as to do our own *Pulp Fiction* movie, Simon and I. We took the video camera from Simon's house, went downtown to an apartment building and did the scene about the foot massage. We found a place on Queen that looked kind of 70s, carpeted and all that, went up to one of the floors and asked Simon's sister to film us. We walked around, we were dressed up, and then we went downstairs and did the scene about Royale with cheese.

Then we did the play at school, which I directed. It intrigued me. I loved that script. The dialogue made the characters and the characters were wicked. I found the script on the Internet, printed off sections I wanted. I would have printed off other sections but because it was for the school, it couldn't contain "motherfucker" and all that. I had to be selective. It was too bad, because I had to leave out some of the best scenes, like the foot massage one because it was talking about, like, oral sex.

Ross and I still want to put *Pulp Fiction* in its linear order and see what kind of movie it turns out to be. It could totally suck.

On Identities and the Future

There's always fantasy, like it would be cool to be Vincent Vega, to be like those guys. There's nothing more I want right now than to live in the big city. I want to live in a city, to know the goings-on, to be able to walk out my front door, and be there. But do it outside Canada. There's times when I would like to be Quentin Tarantino. To have made it.

I hate Canadian movies. I know they are deeper, have more meaning, win all these awards, but that's not the attraction for me ... I mean if I were in Canadian music, I would stay here. Canadian music rules. Canadian music—that's where it's at nowadays. But not our movie industry. It's too boring. I'm attracted to the fame, I guess, and you won't get that in Canada. I'm not just talking about *Pulp Fiction* now. I'm talking about my life. I want my life to be exciting. To mean something.

On Performing

Quentin Tarantino seems like us. Hanging around making films, hanging out with friends. Our conversations are like that kind of dialogue. Or like Seinfeld. I mean, maybe we're mocking them, but ... we joke around with each other. A lot of our dialogue we borrow from *Pulp Fiction,* from shows, and stuff—that's the way we live our interactive life with each other. I mean I might live differently with my parents, or with Cheryl, but when I'm with all my friends together I'm being myself but I'm also performing, and everyone is. We borrow from the film, argue about nothing and are funny. Like Ross will go, hey, I like your shoes, let's just say. And I go, yeah, man, they ARE the shoes. And Ross will say, Oh, they ARE the shoes. And then we just go off talking about shoes. Just think of a situation and we'd try to one up each other, playing, not like competition, but to try to come up with better lines. One up each other.

Adults have lived a lot of their life, and they've had time to mature, develop into a person, and I know they keep learning, but teenagers are so impressionable. And we're borrowing from everything we see that we think is cool. I mean, like maybe this will fit on me. This will look cool on me; this kind of conversation, this kind of attitude. According to what we think is cool at that time. Your favorite song might be from the 60s, but mine is still changing. Right now, I'm still picking my favorites. I'm trying out new personalities from different sources, and if I think it's cool, maybe I'll try it out. Maybe it will be me. Then again, maybe it won't be me, but it will stay with me, and so that adds to my personality, and so I also have that little facet of me, because I use it as knowledge. So by doing this my whole life I kinda gain a way of being.

I think certain attributes of mine are going to remain the same. I think I'm a funny person, and I know I'm not very good at listening. I've always talked a lot and I don't think that will change. I think you just change according to your surroundings, your age, your experiences, but that core personality that you start out with is still there.

I don't think you ever lose anything as a person. It all helps to make up who you are. Maybe, like with Travolta, you gain his coolness, but then by gaining the coolness you've added his arrogance, which means you've lost your kindness. But maybe it's not lost, maybe it's buried underneath there, underneath this John Travolta mask you're wearing.

For a lot of time I even had my hair like Travolta. I don't think that 20 years from now I could look back on Vincent Vega, and say, how could I ever have liked him? I think he's super cool. If you can look back and it still intrigues you, still draws you in, still makes it happen for you then it's part of you. I couldn't think this way if it had been Tom Hanks.

On Catcher in the Rye

When I read that I walked around for a week annoyed at people because all they were doing was bullshitting. Everyone seemed to be so phony. Holden was a character I really liked but he didn't touch me personally, not like Vincent. Holden gave me an insight into how some teenagers live and think, but that's about it. I'm not a book kinda guy anyway. I don't like to read. I like movies and films. And music.

El and David on Teachers and Teaching: Selected Dialogue

David: I learned a lot last year in history—about Roman times and that—but this year is so much more useful knowing how political and social things got to be the way they are because of events 50 years ago …

El: Like I never knew what a Fascist pig was …

David: I knew the name Mussolini, but until we had Mr. M, I used to think he was like this Italian mobster, from Sicily who killed guys …

El: Amazing the conclusions you come up with yourself.

David: I find out he was the first Fascist leader. And here I thought he was Jimmy Hoffa, or the Godfather …. Mr. M gives us amazing detail …

El: Yeah, he's still so passionate about it. He's been teaching the same course for 16 years …. and he still LOVES it ….

—

David: A teacher shouldn't be the kind of person who has the book with all the answers at the back. You know what I mean? The teachers' edition. You got to have Mr. M. who knows everything there is to know about modern history … and you need Ms. M who is an actual artist—

El: —who went to art school

David: And you need an English teacher like Ms. A. or Mr. H. and who have experienced life …. Mr. H. has been in Vietnam … he's been a hippie … he's seen world change … he was there when the Berlin wall came down, for example—

El: —Interesting experiences at least … a teachers' life shouldn't affect how we learn, but it does. When you know somebody has a flair for life, they obviously have a flair for other things.

Epilogue

Texts are symbolic resources for these two; they are imaginative possibilities, sometimes a costume, and sometimes a mask. Texts house dreams, too, and El and David have dreamed through *Catcher* and *Pulp Fiction*. If we "read" them one way, we can read El's dreams as including the romance story; her reaction to the teardrop scene—through which Holden reveals his love for Jane—seems to indicate her wish to be loved the same way. (Nic, El's boyfriend, is known for his antiestablishment beliefs). The admiration she has for Holden's love for his sister, Phoebe, also seems to show the centrality in her life of human values such as caring, preservation of the innocent, and the male's role as protector. Watching *Pulp Fiction*, El is struck most, for example, by the moment where Vincent's violent act (a needle plunged in the heart) revives Mia, the female playing a supporting role in the movie.

If we read El's dreams another way, we can imagine her wish to have the freedom and flexibility that Holden has—and perhaps which many males share—to live his life the way he wishes, if only for a couple of days. El's stated wish to live an exciting life is consistent with her enjoyment of a character who has created his own excitement. Yet we are left to wonder whether she sees herself playing the lead role in her life, as Holden seems to do, or to play a supporting role on stage with a man. Furthermore, is El forced, because of lack of options in school, to see life through the curtain of male protagonists and male leads?

El dislikes anything that has "gone Hollywood," a phrase she seems to associate with inauthenticity, phoniness. Her love for reading and writing propel her to use literacy to pursue what she believes to be authentic, particularly through journal writing and the reading of poetry and novels. But, left without adult support in this goal, she typically finds male-centred texts to fuel her interest; what would happen if she found similarly strong and vivid female characters? The English curriculum for her senior year does not look, at this point, to represent perspectives other than male Eurocentric perspectives, and so I will, as a result of these conversations, offer to pass along books or to assist her in any of her assignments.

David's dreams are made explicit: For this year, at least, he wants to be famous. He is unabashedly frank in his admiration of Travolta, Tarantino, and the character Vincent Vega, seeing them perhaps as role models to emulate, as symbolic resources to try on identities. Consistent with the social construction of masculinities, David dreams of having the power and control that his role models enjoy. David's observations seem to write the story of the hero, the master of his fate.

Although David espouses antisexist and antiracist practices in school and society, his rereading of the film does not include a condemnation of what others see as its racist or sexist elements. When David and I have a follow-up conversation, he claims that teachers, because of their role as sources of knowledge for students, must guard against racist and sexist practices. Film-makers, however, are merely "showing real life, and real life is sexist and racist."

ADULTHOOD: 8 YEARS ON

Looking is what saves us … Simone Weil, *Waiting for God*, p. 125

More than 8 years have elapsed since I interviewed El and David about the texts that informed their lives. Although the two have undergone considerable change in their circumstances, they have remained in touch over the years. Both play on the same softball team that meets weekends on the Halifax Common; they get together socially now and then, and run into each other at local cultural events.

El, now 25, moved into Halifax after high school to complete a Bachelor's Degree in Art at the Nova Scotia College of Art and Design. She hosts a radio program on the local university network (spin handle: Miss Darla Kitty). She lives with Stephen, the technical director at the station, refuses plastic at the grocery store, and finds as many ways as she can as a citizen and artist to jam culture (interrupt the given cultural texts or undercut them; see www.adbusters.com for more information on culture jamming). El is now an artist, and has had several shows, one of which included a compilation video focusing on the gender stereotypes in a month of television advertising. For income, El works in a number of art galleries as a curator and administrator. Being in the field seemed a natural step: *"My art teacher in High School helped me pull a portfolio together, my boyfriend was at the art college, and I was always hanging around with people in the arts community."* Her program at the Nova Scotia College of Art and Design allowed her to do off-campus study and develop some of her own curriculum, one part of which was a "road trip" down from Canada around the perimeter of the United States:

> *That journey was instrumental in shaping the way I think about things, and the way I make art. Now that I've graduated, it's a struggle to keep going—to balance the art, the business of the art (getting grants and support), making enough for bread and butter. To find time to create. To develop my own work when part of my job is to curate others' work. I don't have kids, I don't have a mortgage; this is the time I can keep pushing the poverty line and try to keep my art at the forefront. You can't have it both ways, unless you're making something really commercially viable. Sometimes I get sucked into that whole cycle of wanting to be affluent, of wanting money. But then finally, I think, I don't care about money. I've been really fortunate to have a job in the arts community and do my art, instead of having to sling beer. Although I'm feeling the pressure, I'm resistant to having children—a lot of my friends are. My art is my baby ... How do you balance those things in life?*

David, now 26, is finishing a cultural studies degree at Mount Saint Vincent University, works as a chef at My Other Brother Darryl's, and as a DJ at *"whatever places will have me."* He wants to travel to Ireland with his girlfriend after graduation, then return to finish a graduate degree. *"You can't do anything with a B.A., and besides, I'm really interested in the ideas."* After enrolling in university after high school—*"basically, I went because my girlfriend at the time was going"*—he left before completing a year because *"I suddenly asked myself, what am I doing? This wasn't me. I broke up with my girlfriend and left the province."* He moved to Alberta, where he worked in a series of McJobs in a tourist town in the Rockies, tried *"every experience available to me there ... what's that saying? The paths of excess lead to the path of wisdom? Those years are blurry."* He returned to Nova Scotia ready to resume his education on his own terms.

> *I was interested in visual communications of some sort. I tried theatre during high school and in my first year, and that was fine. But I read about this cultural studies program (the only one East of Toronto) and saw it was about visual and media literacy, and film and art. I was never a big reader, but now I read more than ever. Not fiction, though. Articles on culture, the semiotics of things. I watch a lot of film. Males generally are more visual, I think, when it comes to learning. It's funny. I'm still in the media, but no longer as the actor or player or director. Now, I'm in the role of critic, looking at the media and its influence. In a theoretical context—thinking more than doing."*

Review: The Players Look Back at Themselves

David: I feel like I've learned a hell of a lot, but it feels like no time at all. Don't feel old yet. That person 8 years ago was a product of his generation. I took in what was there, reworked it as my own. We all latch on to something we think is our own at that age. *Pulp Fiction* appealed to me because it was different from the mainstream. Tarantino challenged the status quo. El and I have always been critical thinkers, when I think about it now. We got into trouble in high school not for fights in the hall, but because we were always questioning authority.

That photocopying scam—remember that? Matt's in grad school now—obviously turned him into a criminal (laughs). When I used to do the announcements at Sir John A (high school), I remember saying "Here at SJA, we put the 'fun' in funeral," and thinking that was hilarious. I regret that. I was an asshole. And I remember getting into trouble with the secretary because I announced over the intercom that "on this day"—however many years ago, I can't remember—"John Lennon announced that the Beatles were bigger than God." Oh, she was so upset and I just couldn't understand it.

El: It's weird to see yourself like that. That was me, though. For yourself, you don't see the change. I have friends who are turning thirty—I can't believe it. But I can see how who I am now was always there. But back then we were so optimistic! Now we're jaded and depressed. (both laugh).

Re-visioning: Texts in Lives

David: I was so interested in the glamour of *Pulp Fiction* at that time. I was so impressionable. Now, I can't trust anything anyone tells me. Ever. There are some sources of authority, perhaps, but definitely not the media. In those days, I believed in Tarantino and his fresh way of storytelling—his fresh perspective. I think I wasn't caught up so much in the content of the movie as its presentation. Tarantino's passion, his energy. You just feel it. The teacher we talked about—Mr. McNair—same thing. We loved him because he was enthusiastic. I'm still drawn to that kind of enthusiasm.

El: *Catcher in the Rye* is still the most important book for me. And it still changes, every time I read it. Never has been any other text I return to like that, except my art work. When I took a road trip on my own around the United States, I read all of Salinger's other work ... he draws on the same contexts and people, which I find interesting. I was in New York recently and found myself in Central Park, thinking "Where is the carousel?" I wanted to do a Holden Caulfield tour.

David: Holden Caulfield's New York.

El: Exactly. When I was doing an independent study in art school, I went to Montreal and shot video of all the places Leonard Cohen hung out. When my friend Andrea went to school there, her class went to all the places mentioned in (Mordecai Richler's) *Duddy Kravitz*. That's what we need to do more of in schools. Nowadays, I don't read a lot of fiction. When I did my tour of the States I read and reread *A Picture of Dorian Gray*. That was significant for me. It's about morality, though, more than anything: The painting changes (his face) as he does things he shouldn't. It's still relevant. Usually, I read *The Guardian Weekly*. I want to do more reading about theory, like David is now. I didn't pay a lot of attention to theory while I was in art school, and should have.

David: When I was working in Canmore, something really hit me. It's about a larger text, I guess. It's a tourist town and I realized that people buy anything if you feed it to them properly. Eighty dollars for a t-shirt with a logo—insane. Now I make t-shirts on my own that send up corporate America, but I give them away as gifts. I know there is potential there for making money. But I can't do that to myself. John Berger's work really got me to understand how and why we look at each other, how we frame things, our gaze .... men act, women appear, that sort of thing. When I put on those cultural studies glasses, well, I realized what we're immersed in. It wasn't a fish who discovered water. Even rereading the chapter you wrote about us, seeing Bourdieu's name, and now understanding, reading our pop culture articles, Adbusters, all that good material that keeps me interested, thinking.

El: It's about being aware. Everything around us influences us. It wasn't until I traveled on my own—outside of Halifax without any support system—that I felt like I could really invent myself.

I went to art school in part because Nic was going. Then when I broke up with Keith I didn't know what I'd buy at the fucking grocery store! I had not lived outside my parents' house long enough before I started dating him and having him influence my taste; that's a lot of the reason why we broke up. I can't live my life not knowing what I would do on my own, completely, by myself. That's why I think travel is important—like you did, David, going to Canmore for a couple of years. It allows us to invent ourselves outside of any context.

Rethinking Schools

El: We're never really taught that saying yes to yourself is good. We're supposed to follow rules, what our parents want, what the school wants. We need to learn to find out what's best for us. Our associations restrict us, and we don't have a chance to figure out who we are. I'm my sister's sister, my parents' daughter, Stephen's girlfriend, and I play into those roles. I stay that way because people expect it of me. We need to encourage students to get outside school. They herd us into university right after school, and we have no time for reflection on what we might want to do with our lives. What we might study, if we might go at all? No one pushes trades or practical skills and we need people who know those things. Those are important jobs. We have a highly educated generation of people who went to university and can't get a fucking job: a B.F.A. means B.F.A.

David: There is a big gap between what we learn in school and what we need in life. So much in life is trial and error. We could learn about credit, business, finances. Schools could teach more media literacy. I'd love to see a course in high school—"let's jam this billboard," that sort of thing. Creative ways of looking at the world. I don't think teenagers know, for example, that their music is completely constructed. The power that Disney has.

El: Even in art school. When you're a practicing artist, a whole lot of it is about writing grant applications, getting a show ready, knowing how to be a business person for your own work. In art courses for our degree, we have great touchy-feely critiques, but we're not dealing with the nuts and bolts of getting your work out there. Skills like that are necessary. In high school, we teach skills but we don't allow kids to learn their applications. Math is useless for everyday. When Keith and I were in Mexico renting a car, he got out his calculator and did a parabola to figure out the best value. But he was a finance major.

David: Shouldn't the everyday person know how to do that? Schools are teaching basically in the same way they did a hundred years ago. Nothing's really changed. And we're still teaching to produce doctors and lawyers, and to take one path and stay with it. My biggest concern in life is job security. People change jobs four, five different times or more in a life nowadays. Used to be a ladder, promotions, some kind of stability, having a pension. It's not like that now. I always feel I'm in a position where I have to sell out in order to survive.

Replay: Media as Text:

El: Horrific things are happening all the time everywhere. No one gives a shit about people dying of AIDS in Africa. It's not what's hip in the media nowadays. The media drives everything.

David: When you think about the way we learn, though, no wonder we are all the same. We all read the same books, go to school, exposed to the same media events. We are only slightly different from one another. The media gets kids' attention more than parents do. Kids get more instruction from media than from teachers. Eight years ago, it was the same—I think I'm just more aware.

El: I didn't watch as much TV when I was younger. It was always on in the house. I went into my room to draw or paint. Aside from *Kids in the Hall*, or *Saturday Night Live*, I never watched. Now I watch the news a lot because I'm much more interested in world events. I get angry at how political debate is covered, how they do "balanced" reporting but always show their political leanings. I'm almost addicted to watching it because I want to see what people are being told. It's important to be aware, so that I can formulate an opinion. I seek out other texts in my life that help me do that—newspapers, for example. So many people don't question what they watch. In fact, the media, as David said, is making the choice for us. Everything is presented in sound bytes, and black and white arguments. In terms of disasters, we're oversaturated with information, images, numbers—the death toll for the tsunami is rising, we see how horrific it is but we have no real sense or consequence of that, we're still here, whining …

David: … in our own little worlds—Oh, I wish it didn't snow last night, or …

El: Interviewing people from the comfort of their suburban couch makes me angry…people have no idea what reality is like. Or they're in their own safe reality.

David: The media fascinates me. I know I could make money advertising, but I have an ethical problem with that. I could be Mr. Jingle Man, if I wanted, working for some radio station, making a hundred grand because I can alliterate—but I can't see myself pimping for the man. I'm angry about the way we are duped—who gets the voice, who gets left out, who gets represented and who doesn't. Whenever I'm watching TV I'm always studying, I'm not relaxing any more. I watch less than I ever have. I want to be in the industry, but I want to change it. When I was in high school, I watched everything. Unlike El, who just chose what she watched in high school, I was a passive watcher, into things like *Little House on the Prairie*, for God's sake, and *Saved by the Bell*. Now, who's speaking to me here? Half Pint? What does her life on the prairies have to do with me? I was just filling time. Escape, suspending reality. Out in Hubbards it was hard to have a social life like in the city, so a lot of times I just parked in front of the TV, and didn't think. A lot of bad things can happen when you don't think. At this point, I guess I can look at it as research—I pull out quotes now and then I can use—(laughs).

El: The ads always do me in. I rent movies, or box sets of shows so I don't have to watch ads. The ads make me furious. I did an art piece about that in August—it was a video in which I had logged television ads for 3 months. Looking at the gender constructions in advertising—the women's products are always about a better face or better hair or cleaning the house, and men's are shaving and beer and they're always attached to virile sexuality. I'm shaving and then there's a hot chick right on me, or I'm having a beer and there's tits over there and tits over here. Women's beauty ads are all about I'm not sexy enough—so I have a hard time watching. They're absurd. The products and the wasteful attitudes we have. There's an ad about a disposable dish wipe. The soap is already in the dish wipe, you use it, and then you throw it away! And then she says "and there's plenty more where that came from." We are living in an unsustainable world. We're not making the association between our excess consumer habit—problem, addiction—with climate change and our environment failing.

David: I'm free—I have a right to my SUV.

El: Freedom becomes the right to choose from dozens of options. To me, freedom is having air to breathe, to be able to walk somewhere. We should be forced to use hybrid cars; someone should be forced to make them.

David: People should be paying more at the pumps for starters.

El: Go to Europe and try to buy gas. We like deals. We go to Wal-Mart so we can buy more stuff. The dollar store. Where did that come from? Whose back is that on? Nobody cares.

David: We're appalled by the fact that Nike gets people in Asia to make their shoes. The person who just recently told me he was appalled by that is working at a call center. What are these call centers for? for big U.S. business in the U.S.. They come in to the economically poorer places in the continent, lure people in with jobs—we live these contradictions. I do. I shop at Wal-Mart. I'm a student—I can't afford anything else.

El: You can drive 500 miles every day and stay in the same hotels, eat the same meals, listen to the same station.

David: A deejay I know came up to Reflections; he's a house legend from Chicago. Tommy, the owner of the bar, has $200.00 in his pocket, ready to take this guy out for a big seafood dinner, the downtown bars. No, no need to stop, this guys says, just take me to a Best Western and pick up a Big Mac meal on the way. Hey, no problem! $6.99. But think about it—in this culture we all stay in the same place and eat the same food. Cultural imperialism. It's safety.

El: People are resistant to change right about now … we don't think we have to change, we won't give up our luxuries to save anybody else.

David: The rest of the world doesn't expect to be happy, but we in Western society expect to be. A right to be happy. A tremendous amount of emphasis on the individual, rights, and free will.

Reality Bites

El: It's hard to be able to live and keep your principles. I try to go to the grocery store and buy groceries without any plastic. Just try that. Fruits, vegetables. I remember in high school wanting to be an individual. Now I'm more interested in social issues, turning toward concern for one another.

David: I wonder if what we had as youth was enthusiasm or ignorance? I'm taking a course in humor this year—let me tell you, nothing's funny anymore once you've analyzed it! Most of my sarcasm or general discontent or critical abilities come from the culture—take Michael Moore, his films are agenda-based, but he is also opening new perspectives on things. Or think of Noam Chomsky—in a democratic society we can't control what people do but we can control what they think. Manufacturing consent through images, texts, representations—the general effect is compliance. The older we get, the more we're aware. I still love learning, but things are more serious for me now.

El: In art school, I was overwhelmed with what was possible, learning new skills; it was exciting to see what my peers and teachers were doing, what was happening internationally. Now, working at the gallery, very few students can get my attention with their work. I can't figure out where the change happened. Was it because I was so invested in the individuals behind the work when I was seeing it before? Knowing the creators? Was it that the quality was higher than it is now, or is it just that I am a lot more critical and not as involved with the student body? As I archive stuff, I find I can't remember what the work was. You also get so saturated with the imagery and with all the works and the magazines and whatever that you now only really get jazzed by something that's really exceptional. I'm more art literate now, I guess.

David: Reminds me of that comment that knowledge kills curiosity....the earlier stuff, you were invested in, you were interested, and perhaps that suspends some kind of critical thought.

El: People say that art school will teach the art right out of you because learning the history and contexts and technical information takes the enjoyment out. There's a split that happens in school: those who want to get into the critical side—contemporary thought, history; and then a whole other faction who just want to paint because they like it. And those are the people who get into a craft to support their art; keeps them doing the work without getting into the critical side of things. Art comes from a strictly personal place but it needs to transcend the personal. When you're in high school, you don't realize that. You think art is just about the expression and the creativity, not about the wider conversation. Now that's what's most important to me. The art I want to do is based in the populist—radio, video. I want to be able to talk to people in the medium that's most available to them. I want to have an expanded audience, not to be esoteric.

David: Let's do this in another 10 years. Turn this into a reality program? (everyone laughs).

House Lights

This is a hermeneutic process—reading El and David, writing them, having El and David re-read themselves 8 years later, talk about who they are now and what texts they engage with that shape or reconfirm their identity as young adults. Then—here, now—writing their words (condensed for this chapter, the essences remaining intact), and in so doing, reading what seems to be significant. Then, in a further act of interpretation, describing what I, as researcher and parent, see happening. What resonates for me, obviously, depends on what ideas and preoccupations are shaping my own reading of the world 8 years later. Herakleitos was right—we can't step in the same river twice. Everything moves. There are no fixed meanings, and no answers. But there are points of illumination we cannot ignore. Rather than summarize what the conversations with El and David now and then "mean" (everything doesn't have to have a point, after all; it's only our Western desire for rationalist explanation that causes us to believe this), let me offer three among many connections I made as a researcher and educator. The reader of this chapter will, of course, have his or her own places of resonance.

- Desire is a form of seeking home—who we are in heart and mind. Reading and literacy are forms of desire. David and El's wish to be at home in the world (Neilsen, 1989) propelled them toward certain texts, texts that fed ontological desire: Who am I? Is this my identity? Is this how I write myself? That both of them first entered university influenced by peer group, familiar territory, and current love interest is not insignificant. These social factors and cultural offerings are texts as powerfully influential as any work of fiction. What do schools offer that incites desire in youth? What ways can schools be places where seeking home is encouraged?

- Literacy and reading are forms of inscribing ourselves into a landscape. As we move from beginner to apprentice to fully functioning reader (student, working adult), we develop a greater sense of agency: Yes, I can move this world. For El and David, participation in the art world and in cultural studies, respectively, years of induction into the landscape have made each of them more aware, more active, and more critically attuned to the field. El, in fact, sees the world from a feminist perspective. Each is critically aware—as Simone Weil says, "Looking is what saves us"—not only of their respective fields as texts, but of the world as larger text. The price for this awareness may be the very idealism we, as educators, admire in the young. When does being aware and critical destroy the desire to move the world? When does critical awareness begin to destroy imagination?

- Schools have much work to do in Western culture, a culture that influences youth daily with films, television, video games, branding, and inscriptions into most everything we eat, drink, ride, read, or speak. We need to develop media literate readers and writers; but we need to accept the fact that schools are largely anachronistic and unwilling to accept the cultural texts that students engage with. We need to answer questions about relevance, engagement, social justice, and ways of knowing; we need to reduce our dependence on fundamentalism, intellectual safety, homogeneity, and control in reading—indeed, in all curricula. The terrible truth is that there is no single preferred reading of any text, no script that works for all, just as are no basics and no magic formulae. There is only life, its complexities and insistent forces, and the love for learning and participating in the world we hope to continue to foster in youth.

Both El and David have become political activists in their own local, but significant ways—refusing plastic at the grocery store, resisting (and rewriting) labels on clothing, for example. Both feel trapped—wanting to pursue work they love, but knowing that to do so will compromise their principles. Each wants to resist being co-opted by corporate values, by American economic and political imperialism, by the thousand of little ethical compromises each of us makes when we do what we must do to live in the world as it is. Both these adults are playing for real now, trying to find place and balance: Cultural texts are juggernauts, and David and El invent their roles as they go, resisting, adapting, coming to a greater understanding both of their possibilities and their limitations (Neilsen, 1998a). It's bittersweet, this play, and as educators, we know it has had—and will continue to have—a long run. We live it ourselves.

REFERENCES

Benet's Reader's Encyclopedia (3rd ed.). (1987). New York: Harper & Row.

Buckingham, D., & Sefton-Green, J. (1994). *Cultural studies goes to school.* London: Taylor & Francis.

Cherland, M. R., with Edelsky, C. (1993). Girls and reading: The desire for agency and the horror of helplessness in fictional encounters. In L. Christian-Smith, (Ed.), *Texts of desire: Essays on fiction, femininity and schooling* (pp. 28–44). London: Falmer Press.

Finders, M. (1996a). "Just girls": Literacy and allegiance in junior high school. *Written Communication, (13),* 93–129.

Finders, M. (1996b). Queens and teen zines: Early adolescent females reading their way toward adulthood. *Anthropology and Education Quarterly, 2,* 71–89.

Hellman, L. (1973). *Pentimento*. New York: Signet.
Hoffman, E. (1989). *Lost in translation*. New York: Penguin.
Jenkins, H. (1992). *Textual poachers*. New York: Routledge.
Martin, M., & Porter, M. (1996). *Video movie guide 1996*. New York: Ballantine Books.
Neilsen, L. (2002). Learning from the liminal: Fiction as Knowledge. *Alberta Journal of Educational Research, 48*, pp. 206–214.
Neilsen, L. (1989). *Literacy and living*. Portsmouth, NH: Heinemann Educational Books.
Neilsen, L. (1998a). Exploring reading: Mapping the personal text. In *Knowing her place: Research literacies and feminist occasions* (pp. 63–85). San Francisco: Caddo Gap Press.
Neilsen, L. (1998b). Playing for real: Performative texts and adolescent identities. In D. Alvermann, K. Hinchman, D. Moore, S. Phelps, & D. Waff (Eds.), *Reconceputalizing the literacies in adolescents' lives*, (1st ed., pp. 3–26). Mahwah, NJ: Lawrence Erlbaum Associates.
Rogers, A. G. (1993). Voice, play and a practice of ordinary courage in girls' and women's lives. *Harvard Educational Review, 63*(3), 265–295.
Rosenblatt, L. (1978). *The reader, the text, the poem: A transactional theory of the reading process*. Carbondale, IL: University of Illinois Press.
Salinger, J. D. (1951). *The catcher in the rye*. New York: Bantam.
Tarantino, Q. (1994). *Pulp fiction*. Miramax Films.
Weil, S. (2001). *Waiting for God*. New York: Harper Perennial.

2

"Struggling" Adolescents' Engagement in Multimediating: Countering the Institutional Construction of Incompetence

David O'Brien
University of Minnesota

Prior to writing this chapter, I explored digital literacies as a set of New Literacies practices for so-called "at-risk" adolescents. (O'Brien, 1998, 2003; O'Brien, Springs, & Stith, 2001). The work focused on how those practices expand our conceptions of literate competence while helping the students, many of whom have been disengaged from school for years, redefine their own competence. In this chapter, I extend this work by looking more closely at how current conceptualizations of literacy practices involved in using and creating digital media change adolescents' perceptions of their own literate competence by using examples from two projects.

In order to set the stage for looking more closely at literate practices involved in using digital media, I provide a brief background of my previous work and discuss and contrast traditional or "print-centric" and newer "digital media-centric" notions of literacy competence. I then define the newer competence through a framework called *multimediating* (Doneman, 1997; Lankshear & Knobel, 2003), using vignettes from the two projects. Finally, I discuss the future implications of the work in schools.

BACKGROUND

From 1992 to 1997, I worked with school-based colleagues to set up a program for "at-risk" high school students—the Lafayette Jefferson High Literacy Lab (O'Brien, Springs, & Stith, 2001). In the years between the end of the project and now, we continued to analyze data, working to make sense of how the program engaged the students enrolled in it and studying how that engagement contributed to both their sense of agency and actual improvement in achievement (O'Brien, 2001, 2003). Our initial goal was to better assess the students so that we could provide them with strategies that would improve their comprehension. After the first year of this work, it was apparent that fostering effective strategies was a necessary but insufficient way to address the problem.

What unfolded was a complex syndrome: Low achievement led to low perception about abilities, which resulted in increasing disengagement from reading, which, in turn, resulted in lack of practice, low fluency, lagging decoding skills, and the absence of strategies. These Literacy Lab students lost ground each year in relation to peers, and believed that the plight they faced was beyond their control, leading to "learned helplessness" (Seligman, 1992). When students discover, early in their academic careers, that they are not doing well in reading (it could be any school discipline), and they *attribute* success to stable factors outside of their control (e.g., the texts are too hard, effort doesn't yield results, the teacher is hard, they just don't have the ability), success is perceived as unattainable, universal, and permanent. Helplessness is learned as a response to something you can't explain—something that you don't have control over. When you see that you are not improving, even though your peers are, you assume that you lack ability (perceived as a stable, unchangeable factor). Yet, you might rationalize the failure to external factors like the teacher, or luck—for example, the teacher did not like me or it was just an unlucky day. As time goes on, though, the rationalizations don't help, and you continue to fall behind, you are less motivated to read, you avoid reading, and the more you avoid it, the less practice you have, and you fall further behind. When I met the Literacy Lab students, most of them read little; most considered themselves poor readers and viewed print as all but inaccessible. About half of them had a profound dislike of school. No wonder.

Toward the end of the first year of the project, we started to study and implement ways to motivate the Literacy Lab students so that they would engage with literacy practices in ways that boosted their perceptions of their abilities. We decided to engage them with digital media because, on the surface level, we thought it would, in and of itself, "motivate" them. We soon discovered that this was an oversimplification and quickly corrected. We set out to design tasks that, when completed, the students could attribute success to actions within their control; this sense of agency was unlikely during years of failure with print-based tasks. The approach was later rooted in a considerable body of research in achievement motivation, a lot of which had not been written at the inception of the project (e.g., Alderman, 1999; Wigfield, 1997; Wigfield & Guthrie, 1995, 1997) but at the time was mostly informed by the then-emerging engagement theme of the National Reading Research Center at the Universities of Georgia and Maryland (Alvermann & Guthrie, 1993).

In a nutshell, we "discovered" in the Literacy Lab setting what had already been substantiated in controlled interventions: When students perceived that they were successful, and they could set personally relevant goals and see that they were improving, they would read and write more, build fluency, and decide to persevere, even on tasks that they perceived as being difficult (Anderman et al., 2001; Pintrich and Schunk, 1996). Coupled with the motivation of choosing topics and tasks and using popular media (Alvermann, 2004; Alvermann, Moon, & Hagood, 1999; Kellner, 1995, 2002; Sefton-Green, 1998; Semali & Pailliotet, 1999) this proved a powerful way to both reengage the disengaged, and to change their perceptions of themselves as not only literate, but highly so given an expanded notion of what it means to be literate.

Specifically, we set up an inquiry-based approach in which students selected topics of their choosing (with broad topical guidelines) and used a variety of tools, including media-authoring hardware and software, to construct projects associated with tangible goals. For example in a major project, which we termed the *Violence Project*, students selected from among film and TV media to show how the violence in each medium impacted adolescents. They were required to use a variety of media, including print, to make their case, and the goal was to present the final project for parents on open house night.

In a current project, we are studying seventh-grade students' literacy practices in a 2-year, media-rich, language arts class offered at Hawthorne, a suburban middle school. The students engage in a range of literacy practices including reading, writing (print and media authoring), Web browsing, and playing video games, to attain personally relevant goals through the use of tools they control and connect to outcomes. Students engage in media-rich inquiry projects resulting in presentations about topics of their choosing and play video games in both "free form" game play as well as with participation structures we set up. For example, students learn the digital and conceptual tools related to urban planning and living similar to the SIMs video games and engage in an activity of designing a community.

In the current study (O'Brien, Beach, & Scharber, 2005), we are looking at how media-rich activities help learners connect their various lived worlds, some of them virtual rather than actual. Among other things, we are studying how these activities transform the students' senses of competence and agency, particularly as it has been defined in relation to print-based activities. In all of the work, we are continuing to address two key questions: First, why do adolescents who "struggle" with reading print text—a complex processing act, but not as complex as reading and writing a range of media—competently engage in these media-rich practices and choose to engage in them? Second, what is the nature of that competency and how is it connected to engagement?

At the core of the issue is how competencies are defined within the traditional "print-centric" world in comparison to how they are defined in the newer digital "media-centric" world. The caveat here is that these worlds are not distinct. Youth and adolescents navigate in and out of them seamlessly, but the literacy that officially counts is the print-centric one—the one that is formally assessed, the one they get feedback on from day to day in school, and the one that, in their minds, is the sole measure of their literate competence. In the next section, I present vignettes from the two projects to accentuate how students lacking in print-centric competence according to formal tests, succeed with media tasks. As a follow-up, I compare and contrast print-centric and media-centric literacies. Finally, I elaborate on media-centric competence by looking closely at some more activities in the two projects with a focus on the process of using and creating media rather than on the media themselves—a process that has been termed *multimediating*.

FRAMEWORKS FOR THINKING ABOUT COMPETENCE AND ENGAGEMENT

In these vignettes, adolescents classified as "at risk" or "struggling," labels they usually acquire early in their academic careers, competently engage in media-centric tasks, most of which involve using media as well as engaging in traditional literacy practices. As you read the two vignettes, note the literate practices the struggling adolescents engage in and think about why they might consider themselves competent using the practices in these tasks.

The Literacy Lab: Eddie and Ron

In the Jefferson High Literacy Lab, students identified as most at risk in reading were scheduled into an English elective that was actually a special reading class. The focus of the class was on using media to engage the struggling readers (at that point, they were referred to as "at-risk" learners) and to improve their reading achievement.

Eddie and Ron, both freshmen, were self-selected project partners in the Literacy Lab. Each, when assessed with standardized tests and content reading inventories, read at about third-grade level. Both of them devoted limited attention to reading and writing activities in school and neither expressed much interest in reading and writing related to school tasks. Both boys expressed a range of interests when given the choice of picking project topics. Football was one of those topics.

When given the opportunity to work on a media project, they delighted in their shared interest in Jim Harbaugh, the star quarterback of the Indianapolis Colts at the time. They decided to create a Web site honoring their football hero, planned it, storyboarded it, and divided up tasks. Eddie found images of Harbaugh in the *Indianapolis Monthly* magazine, which was running a feature story on Harbaugh. Ron located video clips of some of Harbaugh's best plays from television sports highlights he had taped, saved these into files, and wrote captions for them. Eddie rounded up some biographical information and news stories about Harbaugh from the *Indianapolis Monthly*, *Sports Illustrated*, and other sources and synthesized the material.

As Eddie and Ron worked together, they continued to sort out the text and images and modify their plan for Web pages. They collaborated using SuperCard©, an authoring package they were both learning at the time that allowed them to mock-up the Web pages with displays of text, pictures, and video clips. Eddie looked up information in the SuperCard documentation to help Ron as Ron used menus to explore button options, select background colors, and put hyperlinks on pages. Eddie served as the format editor, double-checking Ron's layouts of the objects on each page. The final product was a SuperCard stack that logically and aesthetically displayed text and pictures about Harbaugh's personal life, the evolution of his career, and key plays that played as video clips in windows on separate pages with captions and descriptions.

The Reading and Writing Intervention 7 Class:
Darnell, Arthur, and Jonathan

This seventh-grade class, team-taught by an English teacher and a reading specialist, is designed for the struggling readers and writers in Hawthorne middle school. The class of about 15 adolescents meets once per day and is organized around both traditional and media-centric activities designed to improve the students' reading and writing skills. This scenario comes from an after-school video game club for students in the reading class.

Darnell, Arthur, and Jonathan, who show varying interests in reading and writing, but struggle with traditional school reading and writing tasks, joined the after-school video game club set up by Brock and Cassie, our doctoral students. The boys started out by playing "Harry Potter—Chamber of Secrets," but after 10 minutes they became disinterested in it because it is a single player game (you get to be Harry Potter). It was clear that they viewed the game club as a social group. Darnell told me that he liked to play the Harry Potter game on his own. When I queried him about the relations between the game and the films, he said that you could do better in the game if you understood the "storyline" from watching the Harry Potter films.

While I talked with Darnell, Arthur and Jonathan had already migrated over to the other side of the room where Brock was setting up a Game Cube© and the game Symphonia, a multiplayer option Role Playing Game (RPG) in which two worlds, unaware of each other, share Mana, the same life force. Darnell left the Harry Potter game and joined them. Darnell and Arthur said they had played Symphonia before. They swapped the controllers, and whoever did not have a controller was willing to help the person with the controller to strategize. The discourse during gameplay was a mixture of fun, razzing, and offering strategy advice as the game progressed.

As they played, I asked them about reading the narrative text on the screen—when the story is presented in text or when the text is presented with oral narration. They said that they read the narrative text when it contains something crucial to playing the games, but don't read it when it does not. When the storyline text came up, if they viewed it as important they paused to read and listen. If they already knew it, they were frustrated with the screen time taken up by it. I asked them if they read any of the printed documentation for the games they play and they said that they didn't—but they noted that they used such references as a last resort. I also asked about the "strategy" magazines for games and Jonathan said that he has them but seldom uses them for strategies. He said that he uses them as a last resort if he gets stuck, but admitted that he reads the reviews of new games or revised games to see what the best new games will be.

RECONCEPTUALIZING COMPETENCE

Eddie and Ron are the classic struggling readers who seldom engage in reading and writing in school. Yet, when given an opportunity to choose both a topic (Jim Harbaugh) and task (designing a Web site) based on interest, they planned a composition (the storyboard of the site), read sources (both visual and print-based), synthesized texts—not just print but all media—and put all of the media together. In the process they used a range of tools, including reading, writing, and a media-authoring tool on a computer, while overcoming a series of challenges. The media project they produced included print texts they could write and read, even though those print texts exceed the level at which they are supposed to competently read and write based on traditional reading assessments like the Stanford Diagnostic Reading Tests. Also, students like Ron and Eddie, who spent a lot of engaged time on projects, improved in reading as assessed on the state standardized tests.

Darnell, Arthur, and Jonathan, although more capable readers than their counterparts in the Literacy Lab project, did not do well on reading and writing in comparison to their same-age peers. The video game vignette shows that they are more than happy to read narratives that they believe will help them use tools (game controls, strategies) they need. They understand story lines in games and how those story lines connect to strategies. The game organizes a discourse community in which the boys are adept at using a range of social and strategic practices. They talk about the game, about their relative prowess with different genres of games (e.g., RPGs, shooter games, strategy games, simulations). They are also quick to offer advice about strategies to peers with the controllers while the game is being played. When playing another game, *WarioWorld*, they laughed, almost in synchronicity, at the same points in the game when a particularly interesting or surprising thing happened. The discourse was about familiarity with the game—the game, as a media text genre, is a given. As in all of the games, the boys automatically swapped controllers, and less knowledgeable peers, who haven't played a particular game, easily slid into controlling it with help from their more adept companions. Contrary to gender and discourse studies that indicate how males have conversational goals that place ultimate value on maintaining status (whereas girls and women use discourse to achieve connection and intimacy), for example in knowing things and knowing how to do things (e.g., Kendall & Tannen, 2003; Tannen, 1990), the boys in the video game club seemed willing to take advice from peers and to assume the position of being less knowledgeable than peers.

As the two vignettes show, literate competence is not a static, universal phenomenon. Rather, it is socially constructed, and relative to the use of certain tools, to complete certain goals. In terms of the reconceptualizing theme of this book, this is a New Literacies perspective (Gee, 1990; Lankshear & Knobel, 2003; Street, 1993). That is, it deviates from the traditional psychological notion that targets the processes and processor rather than practices, it situates the practices in the context of particular events in which they are used to complete a goal, and it relies on new tools like digital technologies that redefine texts and literacies. The vignettes show "reading" and "writing" as multidimensional and situated (Barton, Hamilton, & Ivanic, 2000; Street, 1993).

A Print-Centric View of Competence

The predominant processing definition of "struggling" adolescent learners is that they lack the skills and strategies that competent readers possess. They are struggling to be like their more competent peers. Just as the term *struggling* was starting to catch on, policymakers decided that "struggling" is too negative: Struggling readers are helplessly, hopelessly floundering; when we hear the term struggling, we see the "remedial" readers we have taught looking into hallways from "special" classrooms where they stay forever and never catch up with their peers. These kids are now called *striving* readers by the Bush administration (Long, 2005) because striving connotes moving forward rather than floundering. The formerly struggling readers are now seemingly reaching for lofty goals; they are optimistic, making progress, and self-assured that they will not be left behind. "Progress" in terminology aside, I use the term *struggling* readers because it was still the predominant term when this chapter was written, and messing with shades of meaning changes little about how labels affect the students.

Adolescents who struggle started out as primary-age readers who likely had trouble with decoding and fluent word recognition, including recognizing sight words; they were also kids unable to connect ideas in running text and make inferences (e.g., Pressley, 2002). They have been characterized as having "core linguistic deficits," something attributable to all struggling readers, particularly with weaknesses in phonological processing and word recognition (Moats, 2001). The affective correlate of this deficit view is that struggling adolescent readers, because they have been unsuccessful early in their academic careers, have not "practiced" reading because once they realized they were not good at it (because of deficits and poor instruction) they avoided it.

One instructional complement to this deficit view is that these older struggling readers would likely have ended up on a more positive academic trajectory if they had more effective instruction when they were in primary grades (Lyon, Fletcher, Torgesen, Shaywitz, & Chhabra, 2004). Hence, the solution to their deficit is that they need more and better instruction on the things that they didn't learn in the first place so that they can catch up to "grade level" where their more competent peers reside. If they catch up, they will learn to like to read, they will do it more often, and through this practice, get better and better at it. The evidence indicates that these kids are not likely to ever catch up to their more competent peers (Allington & Walmsley, 1995; Juel, 1988). From about fourth grade on, in addition to fluent decoding and word recognition, competence also means being able to comprehend increasingly complex texts that are inaccessible to even some competent readers. Competence means that readers need to self-regulate, automatically drawing on a repertoire of skills and strategies and monitoring their understanding of written discourse that is increasingly disconnected as texts become compendia for more and more information (Jetton & Alexander, 2004). High school students and teachers I work with now on literacy coaching and academic literacy support say that many of the texts they try to use are so difficult that even the most competent readers are unlikely to tackle them.

In school, by the time you leave the primary grades, you believe that you have ability or you don't, and this self-appraisal is usually related not only to specific disciplines but to specific tasks within those disciplines (Anderman et al., 2001; Pintrich & Schunk, 2002). Even second-graders will render honest appraisals of their academic prowess by saying, "I am a good reader but I am not good at math" or "Marlene is better at reading than me." From the print-centric view, your perception of your competence in reading is based on what Street (1984, 1993, 2005) termed the *autonomous* view of literacy. Autonomous literacy, as defined in national and international campaigns, is a sort of decontextualized, "homogenized," absolute set of skills one is supposed to attain; the skills are assessed statistically and linked to technical and economic consequences. Literacy, in and of itself, autonomously, will exert predictable effects on social and cognitive practices. High stakes testing, meeting standards, reading texts in approved core curricula, completing assignments in which you recall questions about sections of textbooks, are all articulations of autonomous literacy. This relatively narrow, print-centric literacy has been most recently termed the "deep grammar of schooling" (Lankshear & Knobel, 2003, p. 30).

Within the secondary school as institution, perception about ability is also tied to labels and "special" programs to which one is assigned, and the institution, in labeling students as "at-risk" (substitute "struggling" or "remedial"), usually unwittingly abdicates ultimate responsibility for helping them (O'Brien, Springs, & Stith, 2001). This is not to say that we set up programs so we don't have to help them; rather, the special programs provide a way of helping them that lets us off the hook in terms of providing experiences and opportunities that are afforded other students, particularly academic track students.

In the next section, I discuss a media-centric view of competence. Although the second definition of competence is supported by the work in multimediating presented in the two vignettes, that work, based on our research and that of others, has the potential to positively change learners' sense of competence from the frameworks supported by both definitions—with both print and media.

A Digital Media-Centric View of Competence

Even though literate competence is defined almost exclusively by national, state, and local standards related to facility in processing print, adolescents are developing new competencies as they increasingly use and create a range of electronic print and media texts. A national survey conducted by the Kaiser Family Foundation (Rideout, Roberts, & Foehr, 2005) unsurprisingly found that both children and teens are spending more and more time engaged with a variety of "new media" including computers, the Internet, and video games, and that during a quarter of their media use time (26%) they use more than one medium at a time. Even 4 years ago, 71% of teens said that they used the Internet as their primary source of information for completing school assignments (Lenhart, Simon, & Graziano, 2001). Clearly, the Internet is *the* new academic text, and being able to read it will be crucial to academic success in the years ahead.

Adolescents, along with the larger population, are developing new literacies in order to negotiate their media worlds. I like the term, *multimediating* (Doneman, 1997; also discussed in Lankshear & Knobel, 2003) as a way to define this new competence with digital media. It captures the complexity of simultaneous use of multiple media. Rather than *multimedia*, which focuses on the noun, the *production* of media, Doneman opts for the verb to capture the active processes of engaging in a variety of media environments. Multimediators move seamlessly in and out of the real world and virtual worlds, rapidly and automatically using various technologies that they embrace as extensions of themselves. As I discuss shortly, some of the processes used in multimediating are New Literacies.

Adolescent multimediators can work on a paper using a word processor with multiple IM windows open, some windows for conversations with peers also working on the assignment, some windows for social conversations, while listening to MP3 music files, intermittently looking aside from the computer screen to check a cell phone for text messages. In fact, researchers in the Kaiser Family Foundation study already cited (Rideout, Roberts, & Foehr, 2005) found that youths, who spend on average of 6½ hours per day using media, do not displace older media with new media—they simply spend more time with all media and use multiple media simultaneously; in short, they engage in multimediating.

Multimediating involves not only a simultaneous allocation of attention to different tasks, it also involves multimodal channel switching and/or simultaneous channel use plus rapid attention shifts, some self-initiated, some as automatic responses to a media field (e.g., pop-ups and banners on Web pages, audible signals of information coming into e-mail and text messaging). We have typically explained this shifting—which the new Kaiser Family Foundation report, I think erroneously, termed *multitasking*—to the resource allocation flexibility of the cognitive processor. I say more about this misconception later. The New Literacies, in this paradigm, would be part of this efficient cognitive processor that has simply adapted to multimediating. There is another, perhaps more compelling and certainly more futuristic, explanation for how multimediators develop new competencies: cyborg theory.

Cognitive scientists, philosophers of mind, and neurologists are exploring the likelihood that the cyborg human brain is adapting to the expanding mediasphere, not by fine-tuning resources allocation but by rewriting its neural networks. Clark (2003), one of the breed of "new humanists," who is a philosopher and cognitive scientist, states that we should never underestimate the plasticity of the human brain, which, he contends, is always adaptable and modifiable to environmental "props and scaffolds" so as to be ready to grow into extended "cognitive and computational architectures" (p. 67). The cognitive and linguistic adaptations the brain may be making to permit multimediating could mean that reconceptualizing literacies is not only academic, it is neurobiological.

This cyborg theory rings of science fiction creepiness; the Borg on *Star Trek* chant in unison as they "assimilate" entire races, "Resistance is futile!" Yet, it is a perfectly good *partial* explanation for why adolescents who have grown up with computers and related technologies have developed and enhanced new ways of interfacing their brains and language systems with digital media. The multiliteracies and multimediating are the result of a brain "upgrade." Restak (2003), a neurologist and neuropsychiatrist, has actually coined the term the *New Brain*, which helps to partly explain what new media literacies are. Like the philosophers of mind, except in taking the route of neuroimaging rather than intellectual argument, he contends that media and technologies can permanently alter, although sometimes in harmful ways, the human brain. Like Clark, he supports the notion of brain plasticity, the ability of the neurobiology of the organ to adapt, and in a major split with traditional neuroscience, contends that brain plasticity does not stop at adolescence. Rather, Restak contends, plasticity continues throughout one's life. Although we know relatively little about the neurobiology of these new digital media literacies, it is incumbent upon us to find out more.

MULTIMEDIATING AND THE MEDIASPHERE

As I noted, traditional learning theorists might want to classify multimediating as a form of multitasking. The synthesis of media use in the Kaiser Family Foundation study cited previously (Rideout, et al., 2005) characterized it just that way. In my view, that parallel is inaccurate. Multimediating is not the purposeful juggling of multiple tasks. Multimediating is constructing and reconstructing the community we live in—a community that, itself, melds the real with the virtual in the datasphere or mediasphere (Rushkoff, 1996). It involves using media, producing media, and engaging in literate practices as a way of fitting in the world (Lankshear & Knobel, 2003). The new competencies subsume the old ones of processing print text but are more complex.

The *millennials*, students we teach who were born between 1980 and 2000, have also been referred to in the last 10 years by a variety of techno terms like the *Internet Generation* and the *Digital Generation* and, most recently, *Generation M* (M for mediacentric) because of their increasing facility with digital media and ICTs as a routine way of life. They are constantly immersed in the mediasphere and they negotiate it seamlessly.

The competencies adolescents are developing with these new media texts, if tapped and applauded, should drastically change our conceptions of what literacy means. More importantly, it will change adolescents' perceptions of their literacy abilities. And perceptions of abilities, particularly for adolescents who have been disengaged and have viewed themselves as incompetent with print texts since about second or third grade, may be as important, or even more important, to their future engagement, perseverance, goal setting, than either strategies or skills instruction alone (Anderman et al., 2001; Guthrie and Wigfield, 2000; Wigfield, 2004). The significance of the multiple "new" literacies in this reengagement of disengaged youth is just starting to unfold (Lankshear & Knobel, 2003).

In the remainder of the chapter, I explore multimediating more directly using additional vignettes from both the high school and middle school literacy projects. I also use some specific multimediating literacy frameworks to better explicate how the latest reconceptualizations of adolescent literacy, in the realm of multimediating, are redefining struggling adolescents' literate competence.

ANOTHER VIEW FROM THE FIELD: A CLOSER LOOK AT COMPETENCE IN MULTIMEDIATING

Some of these vignettes are selected and adapted from some previous work with a new analysis based on the multimediating frameworks. Others are so new that they are still evolving, but I render an analysis of them as I understand them now. As before, read each with an eye for what these adolescents who struggle with print in typical schooled literacy tasks do when they are multimediating.

Katie: The Virtual Life of the Grateful Dead

Unlike Eddie and Ron and most other students in the Literacy Lab, Katie was a relatively high achiever but lacked "motivation," although she was about two grade equivalents behind her peers in reading. The slight lag could be attributable to her disengagement. We found out that she was interested in the Grateful Dead, a band she discovered via her parents' music collection. She was particularly interested in the band following the death of band leader Jerry Garcia. My colleague, Dave Stith, talked with her about the music. Being a musician himself, Dave facilitated her interest in the topic and she decided to do a media project on the Dead. For several weeks, Katie read everything she could find about the band in *Rolling Stone* and other music publications. Via her reading, she became fascinated with images of the band, both pictures and the various symbols the band used. She scanned in pictures of Garcia working with the band and relaxing at home. She integrated symbols into her print text, appropriately selecting San Francisco font to write text for her documentary. One day when we were videotaping various projects, she presented some of her work, talking very passionately about the band and their music and enthusiastically explaining how she used various hardware and software to create the project.

Denise and Lynn: CSI on CD

When I met her, Denise had been in the Literacy Lab 2 years. She was mostly positive about her academic accomplishments, but thought that she struggled in reading because she didn't concentrate enough and viewed reading as erratic. "Some days I just can't read—I like, can't get it." Lynn was more typical of the Literacy Lab students with a lower achievement profile across subject areas. But Lynn was always upbeat and ready to work to improve herself. Denise, on the other hand, noted that she was fulfilling her promise to her parents to get Cs so she could continue to play basketball. Both Lynn and Denise were slow starting, but Lynn had more difficulty finding topics that interested her. Both girls reported that they thought they were reading better because of the Literacy Lab. The two girls were friends and liked to work together. The project that I became interested in studying was not a media project they worked on but something they did when they finished their main project tasks for the day—playing a CD-based mystery game, "Who Killed Elspeth Haskard: The Magic Death" written by Shannon Gilligan, an acclaimed author and producer of the "Who Killed ..." interactive multimedia series. In the game, the players, Denise and Lynn, assumed the role of police detectives. They went to a virtual crime scene and gathered evidence (this was well before the popular CSI TV series), they accessed lab reports to check blood evidence and combed through telephone logs, they went through videos of interviews with suspects whose records they also pored over. As they became overwhelmed with evidence, they took copious notes and classified information in several ways to cross-check it. At one point, they even discovered that the CD contained conflicting information—for example, listing two different blood types for the same person in different places. When they solved the game, they decided to author one themselves, and over a period of about 4 weeks constructed a murder mystery with them, their friends Lynn and Raylene, and teachers (Dave, Rebecca, and me) as characters.

Tania: Multimediating a Minnesota Tradition

One of several activities we studied at the Hawthorne middle school focused on why and how the seventh graders put together media productions—why they picked the topics they did, what they were thinking as they constructed them, who the audience was. The vignettes were constructed from interviews we conducted using a retrospective thinkaloud format in which we elicited responses as the students showed us their productions. Tania's was atypical (although maybe not so unusual in Minnesota) in that she chose a male-oriented game about a male-oriented sport—deer hunting. She created a PowerPoint presentation on *Deerhunter*, a PlayStation® format game about hunting—getting gear, setting up a deerstand, picking the weather (a truly amazing virtual option), lining up a shot, and bagging "a big buck deer." She selected it because, like her dad, she was "addicted" to playing it. It was the way she could hunt with her dad before she was old enough for the real thing. And for the last year, as she played it, she said she was preparing to join the affinity group (Gee, 2003) of hunters—she noted excitedly that next year will be her first season in the real deer blind.

To show me a mockup of the actual virtual experiences, she assembled a set of slides showing how the deer looked in the rain, fog, snow, sun—she showed me what the deer looked like from a view in the game through binoculars and then through the scope of the rifle just before you bag him. Tania put the PowerPoint slides together by capturing screens from the game and from the game Web site. She didn't know where to look so she went to Google™ and typed in "images deer hunter" and, of the 50 pages that came up, some were from Deerhunter. She downloaded the images and placed them so that they would appeal to her intended audience—deer hunters, potential hunters, and her dad—whom she was trying to impress. She wrote the text for the images "mainly from memory" but pulled some text from the Web. Tania classified media writing as easier than regular report writing because you have pictures; however, she noted that the visual composition that precedes the writing can be difficult because you have to think carefully and plan what features you want to show—and do it one slide at a time.

Mapping the Space of Multimediating

One of the focus group interview activities we did with the Hawthorne students involved drawing maps about the different worlds they live in and talking about the maps. These places that the kids inhabit represented geographical space, social/cultural spaces, and the so-called *third space* (Leander & Sheehy, 2004; Lefebvre, 1991; Soja, 1989) in which they engage in different discourses and enact various identities over space and time. In the focus group session, the kids also talked about pictures they took of various places, describing them, talking about why they took them. Some of the stories were linked to history or neighborhood stories about the places, like building features or natural features like important trees. Some were of family places. Some were of school, mostly social spaces (seeing friends between classes) and extracurricular activities like sports.

In a related activity, they drew maps of ideal communities, collaborating with peers to include all of the things they thought they needed or would like in such a community. The maps included neighborhoods for "richies" by the lake, houses with convenient shopping spaces, health clubs, and restaurants. One team constructed an elaborate school campus in one corner of their town where all of the schools from kindergarten through a 4-year college were located. They said they did this so you can "get all of the education you need and never have to leave home." Another group I interviewed about their map planned an ideal community, with all of the amenities in other maps, except it included no schools. When I asked them about it, they simply said, "In an ideal world, there is no school."

As you can see in the vignettes, multimediating involved a variety of literacy practices and a range of purposes. But the common feature across vignettes is that it is part of what the adolescents did naturally in completing projects to help explain themselves, their interests, their pleasures, and the worlds they inhabit or would like to inhabit. In the next section, I delve further into what sorts of New Literacies practices were enacted in the multimediating vignettes and what they mean.

LITERACY FRAMEWORKS FOR CRITIQUING
NEW LITERACIES COMPETENCIES

In this section, I use a few of the many New Literacies frameworks to critique the vignettes of struggling readers engaged in or talking about multimediating, with a focus on redefining literate competence. These frameworks or conceptualizations, which are rapidly evolving, sometime overlap but also offer differing angles or important nuances on what multimediating is, what processes it involves and, by implication, what competencies it entails.

Multimodality

Kress's (2003; Kress & Van Leeuwen, 2001) framework of multimodality explores how representation of ideas using different semiotic modes (e.g., modes of representing knowledge and modes of practice) distributes meaning in new ways beyond representation with print or even traditionally linguistic means. According to Kress, we have moved from the page to the screen. The shift is not merely modal; rather, it is spatially more compelling. In two dimensions, I might use a print text description of a lesson I planned. In three dimensions I might use a video clip showing what I did during the lesson so viewers might read my plan and see how it actually played out. Based on careful planning or *design*, I can show a video accompanied by a narrative text and present a video and allow viewer/composers to extend text by writing what they see in the video. I can use techniques such as *framing* (or lack thereof) to set off elements in different semiotic modes or to try to seamlessly merge them. Semiotic modes are subject to respective *grammars* or ways of saying things in different modes and knowing what can be said in each. The *production*, the articulation of the semiotic event, and *distribution*, the selection of the media, are interlinked and dictate how different media work together.

Katie designed her Grateful Dead documentary to maximize the use of different semiotic modes. She not only used print text and pictures but selected a font with regional significance to the band. What is more, she appropriated the band's own semiotic system by incorporating their symbols into her production. She exploited the spatial and modal dimensions of both print text and visual texts by juxtaposing them to create a more powerful message than the respective modes could carry alone in their original, linear form. Hence, Katie exhibited competence with framing the elements (e.g., a picture of Jerry Garcia relaxing, next to a picture of the band performing, accented by narrative about both photos with San Francisco font and embedded band symbols).

Denise and Lynn moved from the screen (the Magic Death CD) to the page and back to the screen as they used the media on the CD to construct notes and used notes to check the information on the CD. They negotiated various semiotic modes (videos of the crime scene, printed information telephone logs, and lab reports) and audio texts (interviews of the suspects) to synthesize what they learned into notes.

Tania composed her project on Deerhunter by carefully selecting images that highlighted what she believed to be the most compelling aspects of the game, and she both transposed text from Web sites and wrote text to accompany the images. Like adolescents in the other vignettes, she explored the respective grammars of the modalities she used and used them to fit her goal of producing something to convince others to play the game.

Focus group interviews that probed the various worlds these adolescents represented in their media productions and on their multimediating experiences, showed that they transition easily from the page to screen, from geographical space to virtual space and easily appropriate the literacies needed to succeed in virtual space. As consumers, they are adept at using the semiotic systems of each space they inhabit.

Textured Literacy

Yancey (2004) defines textured literacy as the ability to comfortably use and combine print, spoken, visual, and *digital* processes in a multilayered composition of a piece of writing. Essentially, this perspective can be used to characterize multimediating as a form of composition. The composition involves decisions about which media and artifacts to select to represent what one *knows* and wants others to know or feel. Ultimately, it also means using interactions with peers in constructing new, negotiated texts in which the media artifacts are expanded and critiqued.

Denise and Lynn tried to recreate the text of the CD-ROM *Magic Death* games in their own CD. Their composition is a good example of textualizing and intertextuality (Bloome & Egan-Robertson, 1993) as a cross between schooled and nonacademic literacy. The texture of their new media included the medical, technical, and law enforcement discourses Denise and Lynn experienced in the *Magic Death* game, photos they took of friends and teachers who became characters in the game, and storyline scenarios from Denise and Lynn's immediate social and school worlds. Both Tania's and Katie's productions were also sophisticated, textured compositions that involved decisions about which media to use, how much of each to use, and how to organize the print and visual media to impact an intended audience.

Technoliteracy and Literacies of Technology

Unlike the previous two frameworks, I use this one to focus on what we as teachers do to *provide educationally sound opportunities* for students to engage in multimediating rather than on what students do when multimediating. Both technoliteracy and the literacies of technology frameworks seem to address the thoughtful use of technologies in education.

Selfe & Hawisher (2004), in discussing the literacies of technology, have found it necessary to move beyond the oversimplified practice of literacy tied to particular tools like computers (hence, "computer literacy") to the notion of literacies of technology that more broadly connects social practices, people, technology, values, and literate activity within a larger "cultural ecology." Lankshear and Snyder's (2000) technoliteracy project explores the integration of technologies and literacy in useful ways while also presenting some caveats: First, there is pressure to technologize education in ways that may be detrimental; second, using technologies effectively requires a concerted effort to think deeply about literacy, learning, and technology together in critical, cultural, ways.

Technoliteracy and *Literacies of Technology* refer to an understanding of how literacies and technologies as implicitly integrative and mutually transformative practices come together when knowledgeable teachers use them in the arena of schooling. Unlike the other constructs used to critique New Literacies practices of students, this one allows a critique of the way teachers construct multimediating experiences for kids.

Katie's Grateful Dead project was one of many in a series of inquiry projects in which students in the Literacy Lab were to select both topics and tasks, using media authoring tools (hardware, software, collaborations with tech-savvy peers) to produce something they constructed to meet a personally relevant goal. The requirement was that the students include a range of media, not that they complete certain tasks with the media. Tania's Deerhunter project was similar, except her tools were a little more limited—using PowerPoint to display the inquiry and picking a topic within the realm of video games. Both of these projects were designed to allow the students to transform their understanding of literacy practices like reading and writing, rather than to focus on a tool like the computer to make something.

Denise and Lynn's video game playing was something that emerged out of the open structure we provided in the Literacy Lab where students had free access to the technologies. Playing games was transformed by them into a focused intermedial project—they wanted to make something like the *Magic Death* game. The intensity of the work on the project surprised both them and us, but they pursued it not because they were trying to use certain tech tools or to create something for an assignment; rather, they worked and watched what evolved out of their interest and perseverance.

Finally, the mapping spaces activity shows that kids intuitively understand technoliteracies as they understand other literate practices. For example, they are aware of the projective identities they have in video games (Gee, 2003) and how these identities need to be separated from their real-world identities; they matter-of-factly talk about IMing and text messaging as ways of being in the world—they do not stop to reflect on the technoliteracies that enable them to do these things. This is the very essence of the transformative nature of these technoliteracies. The pedagogical lesson from these literacies enacted outside of school is to look at how kids' engagement in these practices, and their feelings of competence, can be designed into school to bring out the best of what they can do, not with traditional print-centric literacies alone but with multimediating.

THE FUTURE OF MULTIMEDIATING IN SCHOOLS

The New Literacies practices morph so rapidly that it is impossible to step back and say, "So this is what literacy is now;" rather, we must constantly retool, redefine, and figure out what to attend to during the evolution (Leu, 2000, 2002; Leu, Kinzer, Coiro, & Cammack, 2004). Multimediating is reshaping our traditional notions of literate competence at the same time it critiques the print-based notions of literacy tied to schooled practices. These practices have recently been referred to as the deep grammar of schooling (Lankshear & Knobel, 2003) and characterized as institutional practices and artifacts of the Institution of Old Learning, IOL for short (O'Brien & Bauer, 2005). The IOL protects and nurtures print-centric notions of literacy; it supports both assessment and instructional practices that keep schooled practices significantly behind what adolescents are engaging in outside of school. As in that cited article, I want to emphasize that the IOL is the *institution*, with its deeply held, historically grounded, organizational routines and practices, not the *teachers* within the institution. Many teachers are engaging in exciting New Literacies practices, but, overall, nationally, teachers can only progress as far as the IOL and national policy allow them.

The current "schooled literacy" response to New Literacies is to teach, model, coach, and provide practice in print strategies that struggling readers have never learned—more of the same in spite of the fact that the approaches, for a host of reasons, did not work earlier in these adolescents' academic careers. While this often ineffective institutionalized practice is occurring in school, these same adolescents spend more and more time outside of school engaged in multimediating. As they do so, they build fluencies with the texts and technologies, develop positive perceptions about their abilities to engage in these New Literacies practices to meet personally relevant goals, and attribute much of their success to factors they control, based on their interests and connections to popular culture.

These multimediating adolescents are developing a very clear self-regulation of complex linguistic, cognitive, technical, and social skills and strategies. Few of the literate practices they master in multimediating are ever officially sanctioned in school as literate competencies. For example, the digitally rich inquiry projects, Internet use, IMing, and playing video games, all of which involve complex literacies, are typically viewed as either unimportant in school or as detractors from print-centric schooled literacies.

Research on how and why these new literate competencies develop is in its infancy. We need to design multidisciplinary studies that wed frameworks like socio-cognitive theories of motivation and engagement (which informs most of the engagement work in reading) and offer suggestions for how multimediating, which now occurs mostly outside of school settings, can be used in school to not only support adolescents' literate practices with print, but to address the largely neglected "affective" dimensions of years of failure.

REFERENCES

Alderman, M. K. (1999). *Motivation for achievement.* Mahwah, NJ: Lawrence Erlbaum Associates.

Allington, R. L., & Walmsley, S. R. (1995). *No quick fix: Rethinking literacy programs in America's elementary schools.* New York: Teachers College Press.

Alvermann, D. E. (2004). Media, information communication technologies, and youth literacies: A cultural studies perspective. *American Behavioral Scientist, 48*(1), 78–83.

Alvermann, D. E., & Guthrie, J. T. (1993). *Themes and directions of the National Reading Research Center* (Perspectives in Reading Research, No. 1). Athens, GA: National Reading Research Center, Universities of Georgia and Maryland.

Alvermann, D. E., Moon, J. S., & Hagood, M. C. (1999). *Popular culture in the classroom: Teaching and researching critical media literacy.* Newark, DE: International Reading Association.

Anderman, E. M., Eccles, J. S., Yoon, K. S., Roeser, R., Wigfield, A., & Blumenfeld, P. (2001). Learning to value mathematics and reading: Relations to mastery and performance-oriented instructional practices. *Contemporary Educational Psychology, 26,* 76–95.

Barton, D., Hamilton, M., & Ivanic, R. (Eds.). (2000). *Situated literacies: Reading and writing in context.* London: Routledge.

Bloome, D., & Egan-Robertson, A. (1993). The social construction of intertextuality in classroom reading and writing lessons. *Reading Research Quarterly, 28,* 305–333.

Clark, A. (2003). Natural born cyborgs? In J. Brockman (Ed.), *The new humanists* (pp. 70–77). New York: Barnes & Noble.

Doneman, M. (1997). Multimediating. In C. Lankshear, C. Bigum, & C. Durant (Eds.), *Digital rhetorics: Literacies and technologies in education—current practices and future directions* (Vol. 3, pp. 131–148). Brisbane, AU: QUT/DEETYA.

Gee, J. P. (1990). *Social linguistics and literacies: Ideology in discourses.* Hampshire, UK: Falmer.

Gee, J. P. (2003). *What video games have to teach us about learning and literacy.* New York: Palgrave Macmillan.

Guthrie, J. T., & Wigfield, A. (2000). Engagement and motivation in reading. In M. L. Kamil, P. Mosenthal, P. D. Pearson, & R. Barr (Eds.), *Handbook of reading research* (Vol. III, pp. 403–422). Mahwah, NJ: Lawrence Erlbaum Associates.

Jetton, T. L., & Alexander, P. A. (2004). Domains, teaching, and literacy. In T. L. Jetton & J. A. Dole (Eds.), *Adolescent literacy research and practice* (pp. 15–39). New York: Guilford.

Juel, C. (1988). Learning to read and write: A longitudinal study with 54 children from first through fourth grades. *Journal of Educational Psychology, 80,* 437–447.

Kellner, D. (1995). *Media culture.* London: Routledge.

Kellner, D. (2002). New media and new literacies: Reconstructing education for the new millennium. In L. Lievrouw & S. Livingstone (Eds.), *The handbook of new media* (pp. 90–104). London: Sage.

Kendall, S., & Tannen, D. (2003). Discourse and gender. In D. Schiffrin, D. Tannen, & H. E. Hamilton (Eds.), *Handbook of discourse analysis* (pp. 548–567). Malden, MA: Blackwell.

Kress, G. (2003). *Literacy in the new media age.* London: Routledge.

Kress, G., & Van Leeuwen, T. (2001). *Multimodal discourse: The modes and media of contemporary communication.* London: Edward Arnold.

Lankshear, C., & Knobel, M. (2003). *New literacies: Changing knowledge and classroom learning.* Buckingham, UK: Open University Press.

Lankshear, C., & Snyder, I. (2000). *Teachers and techno-literacy: Managing literacy, technology and learning in schools.* St Leonards NSW, Australia: Allen & Unwin.

Leander, K. M., & Sheehy, M. (Eds.). (2004). *Spatializing literacy research and practice.* New York: Peter Lang.

Lefebvre, H. (1991). *The production of space.* Cambridge, MA: Blackwell.

Lenhart, A., Simon, M., & Graziano, M. (2001). *The Internet and education: Findings of the Pew Internet and American Life Project.* Available: http://www.pewinternet.org

Leu, D. J. (2000). Deictic consequences for literacy education in an information age. In M. L. Kamil, P. Mosenthal, P. D. Pearson, & R. Barr (Eds.), *Handbook of reading research* (Vol. III, pp. 743–770). Mahwah, NJ: Lawrence Erlbaum Associates.

Leu, D. J. (2002). The new literacies: Research on reading instruction with the Internet. In A. E. Farstrup & S. J. Samuels (Eds.), *What research has to say about reading instruction* (pp. 310–336). Newark, DE: International Reading Association.

Leu, D. J., Kinzer, C. K., Coiro, J. L., & Cammack, D. W. (2004). Toward a theory of new literacies emerging from the Internet and other information and communication technologies. In R. B. Ruddell & N. Unrau (Eds.), *Theoretical models and processes of reading* (5th ed., pp. 1570–1613). Newark, DE: International Reading Association.

Long, R. (2005). New year, full agenda. *Reading Today, 22*(4), 28.

Lyon, G. R., Fletcher, J. M., Torgesen, J. K., Shaywitz, S. E., & Chhabra, V. (2004). Preventing and remediating failure: A response to Allington. *Educational Leadership, 61*(6), 86–88.

Moats, L. (2001). When older students can't read. *Educational Leadership, 58*(6), 36–39.

O'Brien, D. G. (1998). Multiple literacies in a high school program for "at-risk" adolescents. In D. E. Alvermann, K. A. Hinchman, D. W. Moore, S. F. Phelps, & D. R. Waff (Eds.), *Reconceptualizing the literacies in adolescents' lives* (pp. 27–49). Mahwah, NJ: Lawrence Erlbaum Associates.

O'Brien, D. G. (2001). "At-risk" adolescents: Redefining competence through the multiliteracies of intermediality, visual arts, and representation. *Reading Online, 4*(11). Available: http://www.readingonline.org/newliteracies/lit_index.asp?HREF=/newliteracies/obrien/index.html

O'Brien, D. G. (2003). Juxtaposing traditional and intermedial literacies to redefine the competence of struggling adolescents. *Reading Online, 6*(7). Available: http://www.readingonline.org/newliteracies/lit_index.asp?HREF=obrien2/

O'Brien, D., Beach, R., & Scharber, C. (2005, December). *Struggling middle school students' multimediating: Countering institutionally defined notions of incompetence.* Paper presented at the Annual Meeting, National Reading Conference, Miami, FL.

O'Brien, D. G., Springs, R., & Stith, D. (2001). Engaging at-risk students: Literacy learning in a high school literacy lab. In E. B. Moje & D. G. O'Brien (Eds.), *Constructions of literacy: Studies of teaching and learning in and out of secondary schools* (pp. 105–123). Mahwah, NJ: Lawrence Erlbaum Associates.

O'Brien, D. G., & Bauer, E. (2005). Essay book review. New Literacies and the institution of old learning. *Reading Research Quarterly, 40,* 120–131.

Pintrich, P. R., & Schunk, D. H. (1996). *Motivation in education.* Englewood Cliffs, NJ: Merrill.

Pintrich, P. R., & Schunk, D. H. (2002). *Motivation in education: Theory, research, and applications* (2nd ed.). Englewood Cliffs, NJ: Merrill.

Pressley, M. (2002). *Reading instruction that works: The case for balanced teaching* (2nd ed.). New York: Guilford.

Restak, R. (2003). *The new brain: How the modern age is rewiring your mind.* New York: Rodale.

Rideout, V. J., Roberts, D. F., & Foehr, U. G. (2005). *Generation M: Media in the lives of 8-18 year-olds.* Menlo Park, CA: Kaiser Family Foundation.

Rushkoff, D. (1996). *Media virus.* New York: Ballantine.

Sefton-Green, J. (Ed.). (1998). *Digital diversions.* London: UCL Press.

Selfe, C. L., & Hawisher, G. E. (2004). *Literate lives in the information age: Narratives of literacy from the United States.* Mahwah, NJ: Lawrence Erlbaum Associates.

Seligman, M. (1992). *Helplessness.* New York: Freeman.

Semali, L., & Pailliotet, A. W. (Eds.). (1999). *Intermediality: The teachers' handbook of critical media literacy.* Boulder, CO: Westview.

Soja, E. W. (1989). *Postmodern geographies.* New York: Verso.

Street, B. V. (1984). *Literacy in theory and practice.* Cambridge, UK: Cambridge University Press.

Street, B. V. (Ed.). (1993). *Cross-cultural approaches to literacy.* Cambridge, UK: Cambridge University Press.

Street, B. V (2005). Recent applications of New Literacy studies in educational contexts. *Research in the Teaching of English, 39*(4), 417–423.

Tannen, D. (1990). *You just don't understand: Women and men in conversation.* New York: Ballantine.

Wigfield, A. (1997). Children's motivations for reading and reading engagement. In J. T. Guthrie & A. Wigfield (Eds.), *Reading engagement: Motivating readers through integrated instruction* (pp. 14–33). Newark, DE: International Reading Association.

Wigfield, A. (2004). Motivation for reading during the early adolescent years. In D. S. Strickland & D. E. Alvermann (Eds.), *Bridging the literacy achievement gap in grades 4–12* (pp. 56–69). New York: Teachers College Press.

Wigfield, A., & Guthrie, J. T. (1995). *Dimensions of children's motivations for reading: An initial study* (No. 34). Athens, GA and College Park, MD: National Reading Research Center, Universities of Georgia and Maryland.

Wigfield, A., & Guthrie, J. T. (1997). Relations of children's motivation for reading to the amount and breadth of their reading. *Journal of Educational Psychology, 89,* 420–432.

Yancey, K. (2004). Using multiple technologies to teach writing. *Educational Leadership, October 2004,* 38–40.

3

Re/constructing Identities: A Tale of Two Adolescents

Josephine Peyton Marsh
Elizabeth Petroelje Stolle
Arizona State University

I'm more of a feminist ... [critical literacy helped me to see] the way that society wants us to be brought up and it just changed the way that I think about things ... I get into discussions with my friends and parents now about [movies and] stuff, how like people expect girls to be a certain way and they expect guys to be a certain way ... it[the critical literacy study] really changed my life.

—Carlie, seventh grade student

Carlie was a seventh-grade White adolescent girl who participated in an after-school critical literacy book club study that focused on how gender constructs and is constructed by texts. She was one of two girls in a group of six ethnically diverse middle-school-aged students who met weekly for 15 weeks to participate in critical literacy activities that focused on a variety of kinds of texts—short stories, novels, poems, magazines, television, and movies. We tell the story of her developing thinking about gendered identities later in this chapter.

We also tell the tale of Elsa, a ninth-grade Mexican immigrant, who participated in critical literacy activities focused on race and racial issues during small group literature discussions in her English classroom. While reading *The House on Mango Street* (Cisneros, 1984), Elsa saw life through the eyes of a young Hispanic girl struggling to construct and reconstruct her own racial identity. Within the discussion group, Elsa aligned herself with those who believe that race should not be a part of one's identity. She proposed colorblindness as the answer to racial tensions and inequities.

Thus, in this chapter, we present examples of spaces where two adolescent girls (Carlie and Elsa) began to re/construct (or as the case may be, confirm) their own gendered and racial beliefs and identities as they engaged in a critical reading and examination of redressive texts. We use *re/construction* to indicate that reconstruction and construction of identities happen continuously and simultaneously. For example, we may reconstruct stereotypical representations of gender identities and practices as we are constructing our own gendered identities.

Critical literacy, for Carlie and Elsa, opened spaces for them to examine social practices and identities (e.g., Martino, 1995; Young, 2000). For Carlie, participation in the critical literacy activities and discussions facilitated reflection on her personal beliefs about gender both during the book club discussions and alone as she read the selected texts. For Elsa, exposure to critical literacy activities helped to confirm her existing beliefs about race and racism. Critical literacy activities in schools often allow readers to deconstruct the language of texts and look at how language is used to silence and oppress some, while putting other people or beliefs into positions of power and status. In other words, critical literacy means examining the language of texts to uncover the hidden ideological meanings in these texts, or *reading against the grain*. Such an examination is driven by questions such as: Whose voice is heard? Whose voice is silenced or absent? Who is the author and what message is he or she trying to send the reader? How does the author's representation of gender and race relate to the reader's experiences and beliefs?

Critical literacy can also lead one to consider possible identities and social practices and facilitate a move toward social change (Janks, 2001; Luke, 2004; Morgan, 1997). We believe that inasmuch as social practices, inequities, and identities are socially and historically constructed, they can also be reconstructed and transformed (Ellsworth, 1989; Luke, 2004; Morgan, 1997). Re/construction adds a dimension to our thinking about critical literacy. It allows us to focus not only on the deconstruction of texts in an attempt to uncover ideologies and build awareness of inequities, but also to focus on reconstructing social structures and identities (Edelsky, 1999; Luke, 2004). Luke further advocates that educational researchers and practitioners document and analyze moments where spaces of liberation and emancipation are facilitated and where language and textual practices show some signs of re/construction. This documentation and analysis will help others put critical literacy into practice and create spaces for re/constructing social structures and identities. It was these kinds of spaces that we (Josephine Marsh and Elizabeth Stolle) looked for in data we previously collected for two different critical literacy studies (Young & Ricks, 2000; Stolle, 2004) to investigate what happened when we paired critical literacy activities with the reading of redressive texts. Redressive texts as defined by Luke (2004) are books, poems, television shows, movies, and other visual and aural readings that portray possible constructions of identity that question or resist dominant social ways of being and social structures. These sorts of texts can provide readers with opportunities to explore gender and race through fictitious characters. They also offer a space for readers to explore their own social and cultural beliefs and identities as they relate to fictitious characters.

Before we tell the tales of Carlie and Elsa, we provide a brief overview of the theoretical concepts that framed our analysis. As suggested by Gee (1999, 2004), we used socially situated identities, Discourse, and cultural models as analytical tools or thinking devices to conduct our analyses.

SOCIALLY SITUATED IDENTITIES, DISCOURSES, AND CULTURAL MODELS

We use the term *socially situated identities* (Gee, 1999) to represent our understanding that individuals have multiple identities that they take up as they move in and out of different social contexts and situations. Like Gee, we use the term "core identity for whatever continuous and relatively 'fixed' sense of self underlies our contextually shifting multiple identities" (p. 39, emphasis in original). Thinking about identities in this way means that although we may have a core identity, it shifts as we interact in different social contexts and as we participate in different social practices. For instance, both authors have identities as researchers, teachers, mothers, wives, and daughters, and the actions and thoughts associated with these identities shift as we move within different social contexts like school and home. In other words, we construct and reconstruct our identities as we attempt to make our way through varying environments and situations over time. The notion of Discourse helps us to further understand our multiple identities. In order to continually shift identities, we must adapt our behavior and thinking to the norms of the Discourse community in which we want to claim membership.

Discourses

Gee (1999) explains that in order to represent *who* we are and *what* we are doing, we use more than language. We act, interact, think, value, talk, write, and read "in 'appropriate' ways with the 'appropriate' props at the 'appropriate' times in the 'appropriate' places" (p. 17). These socially accepted associations are what Gee terms big *D* Discourses. When others recognize an individual as a specific *who* participating in a particular *what*, then that individual belongs to a recognizable Discourse community. Gee (1999) likens a Discourse to a "dance" that individuals perform, manipulate, and never quite duplicate. However, ultimately the "masters of the dance" choreograph the Discourse by what is recognized as legitimate possibilities for the dance (p. 19). We used the notion of Discourse in this analysis to identify and consider the book club and literature discussion group members' practices. Identifying what is appropriate and recognized within the groups helped us understand how the participants functioned within each particular Discourse community. We were also able to uncover some of the other Discourses to which the participants claimed membership.

Cultural Models

Cultural models are the beliefs, values, and attitudes that inform what we say and how we act, read, and interact (Gee, 1999; Strauss & Quinn, 1997). In this way, cultural models influence how we identify ourselves and others. Our cultural models change as we read, experience, observe, and adapt to new situations, never remaining static. Gee (1999) describes cultural models as movies or videotapes in the mind that inform our ways of being, doing, and thinking. These movies/videotapes help us determine what is normal and typical within a particular Discourse. However, what is normal and typical changes from Discourse to Discourse. By identifying cultural models, a window opens into an individual's identities. For this analysis, we wanted to uncover the cultural models or movies/videotapes the participants held in their minds regarding issues of gender and race that informed their re/construction of identities and ways of being. Additionally, we wanted to see how these movies/videotapes shaped the participants' responses and understandings of redressive texts during critical literacy book discussions, or how these cultural models were edited or re/constructed through the discussion groups.

BACKGROUND OF THE STUDIES

Carlie and Elsa participated in two distinct but similar critical literacy studies. Study 1(Young & Ricks, 2000) took place within a semester-long, after-school critical literacy book club for middle-school students. Study 2 (Stolle, 2004) took place in a ninth-grade reading classroom in which service–learning interns from a local university facilitated literature discussion groups twice a week for a semester. In both cases, we were interested in knowing if a focus on critical literacy during literature discussions made a difference in the participants' re/construction of gender and race, and how these re/constructions influenced the ways in which they represented themselves within the discussion groups, that is, their socially situated identities. For this chapter we analyzed a subset of the data that illuminated instances in which critical literacy practices were intended to create spaces for re/constructive thinking (Luke, 2004). We narrowed our analysis further to highlight Carlie and Elsa as they interacted within these spaces with other adolescents about redressive texts. From Study 1, we analyzed Carlie's response to the book *The True Confessions of Charlotte Doyle* (Avi, 1997). From Study 2, we focused on Elsa's interaction during a literature discussion that focused on racial issues represented in the book, *The House on Mango Street* (Cisneros, 1984).

Research Contexts

In Study 1, Josephine was a coresearcher and participant observer and helped facilitate critical literacy activities during the discussions. Along with a coresearcher, she selected redressive texts, books, and other readings that demonstrated possible constructions of gender and ways of doing gender differently for the participants to read and discuss. For example, they read *The True Confessions of Charlotte Doyle,* a story about the young protagonist, Charlotte, who blurred gender boundaries as she crossed the ocean on a ship full of men in 1832. The hope was that by selecting this sort of redressive text, the young adolescent participants would feel less threatened when asked to critically examine gender representation in these texts and compare them to their personal constructions of gender. Through the use of redressive texts, students were invited to explore their own gender identities as they reflected on the fictional characters' actions and resistance of gendered norms.

In Study 2, Elizabeth was an observer participant. She introduced university service–learning interns to critical literacy and then together they developed critical questions to ask during the literature discussions. Elizabeth specifically selected redressive texts and critical literacy activities that she hoped would encourage the high school students to enter into a discussion about racial identities and issues. The books portrayed characters resisting traditional racial stereotypes and struggling with racial identities. These portrayals invited readers into the minds of the characters and provided students with possible ways of thinking about race. For instance, in *The House on Mango Street*, the main character, a Hispanic girl named Esperanza, shares her experiences struggling with her own racial identity when she moves to a new neighborhood with her family.

We used the critical discourse analysis procedures outlined by Gee (1999, 2004) to uncover and interpret Carlie's and Elsa's re/constructions of gender and racial identities during critical literacy activities and their interaction with redressive texts. To do our analysis, we first identified data that represented instances in which critical literacy practices were intended to create spaces for re/constructive thinking. For example, in Study 1, we examined a time when Carlie dominated the book-club discussion as she excitedly talked about how Charlotte Doyle went against gender stereotypes. She explored her own gender identity through the character's actions and resistance to societal norms. In Study 2, we explored Elsa's opinions about racism that were shared during a critical literacy activity connected with *The House on Mango Street*. Through this discussion, Elsa revealed conflicting identities related to race and racism.

Next we put the transcript and interview data, using only the girls' words, into stanzas to help us explore and interpret the space we identified as possibly showing signs of re/constructing social structures and identities. Stanzas represented a common theme or topic and were made up of a connected set of lines (Gee, 1999). Each line consisted of one idea unit. For example, as you will read shortly, one idea unit was *defying gender stereotypes is awesome*.

After the stanzas were constructed, we read and reread the stanzas to determine Carlie and Elsa's cultural models. We then rearranged the stanzas and lines, grouping them according to the girls' cultural models. Next, similar to a previous study (Young, 2004), we eliminated the sound representations such as "um," "ah," and false starts from the text in order to create a clear, concise reading. In this new format, we read and reread through the stanzas again looking closely at Carlie and Elsa's pronoun usage.

As in the earlier research project (Young, 2004), Josephine found that I-statements were useful in uncovering the cultural models held by Carlie because I-statements appeared to articulate how Carlie wished to define herself or represent herself. I-statements such as *I thought, I understand, I've learned, I've become* provided knowledge and insight about what Carlie reported thinking as she read the book and the cultural models that influenced her understandings. They also demonstrated the ownership and confidence she had about her own thinking and beliefs about gender and identity construction. Carlie's use of the pronoun *she* also revealed her ideas regarding gender in her retelling of Charlotte's actions and choices. *She* became a useful word behind which Carlie explored and expressed her ideas about gender and identity. With this confidence and safety net, Carlie then imposed her beliefs about gender on others using *you* and the indirect (*you*) in the command form.

Elizabeth specifically looked at Elsa's language regarding race by looking at her pronoun usage to identify how she positioned herself and others in regard to her understandings of race and racism and how she perceived that race did or did not relate to her own identity. Elizabeth also focused on the group Discourse, uncovering what was acceptable and unacceptable to the "masters of the dance" (Gee, 1999, p. 19) within that Discourse regarding the exploration of race and racism. Through Elsa's use of three distinct pronouns: *I* in the form of I-statements, *you* and the indirect (*you*) in command form, and *they* in reference to a universal, ambiguous *they*, she revealed her cultural models and her own conflicting identity regarding the issues of race and racism. Elsa's use of pronouns worked to separate her from the issue of racism and demonstrated that racism was not part of her identity. Elsa represented herself as one who belonged to a specific Discourse where race didn't matter and color was not talked about. Within this Discourse, race was not part of one's identity because only the person mattered.

Finally, we read and reread the observational data to find evidence to support or disconfirm our notions about the cultural models and Discourses we uncovered and about the identified liberatory or re/constructive space.

STORY 1: RECONSTRUCTIVE SPACE, CULTURAL MODELS, DISCOURSES, AND CARLIE

For Carlie, a re/constructive space opened for her as she transacted with the novel, *The True Confessions of Charlotte Doyle*. This space allowed Carlie to explore her beliefs about gender and support the cultural models that influenced her gendered identities. Carlie's public discussion of the book appeared to be a retelling of her private thinking as she read the novel. During the book club discussion, she summarized incidents in the book that represented affirming and redressive representations of gender. Through her private reading and this retelling, Carlie was able to try on a different gender identity, one that resisted the gender norms of the times. The other book club members listened and rarely entered the discussion. The boys occasionally asked Carlie a question, made a comment, or asked for a clarification, but the discussion of this book truly belonged to her.

Two cultural models about gender informed much of Carlie's thinking about and interpretation of Charlotte's actions in the novel—that women and men should be treated equally, not differently, and that how one does gender is an individual choice that has consequences.

Treating the Sexes Equally

The first cultural model—women and men should be treated equally—became visible during an anticipation guide discussion prior to reading *The True Confessions of Charlotte Doyle*, when Carlie complained about the boys in her PE class who treated the girls like "little fragile freaks" or "flowers:"

> Like in PE the guys are safer with the girls
>
> They treat us like we're little fragile freaks
>
> You know, we can't be touched
>
> Like, if we're playing a rough and tumble game
>
> Or anything like that, you know,
>
> The guys treat us like we're little flowers that can't be …

The tone in Carlie's voice and her words indicated disdain for these practices. "Fragile freaks" does not appear to be a term Carlie admires. Rather, Carlie seems to indicate that when the boys do this to the girls, the boys are acting in a derogatory manner toward the girls, identifying them as weaker individuals needing special treatment. This leads us to infer that Carlie does not believe the girls need this special treatment and that boys and girls should be treated equally regardless of the situation or the roughness of the game. Extending this thinking, we believe Carlie does not see physical difference as a part of one's gendered identity. We can only assume that the boys treat the girls in a lighter manner due to their belief that they are bigger, stronger, and could hurt the girls. However, through Carlie's disdain and anger regarding the subject, it seems she feels competent to go up against these boys equally in physical play. Therefore, part of her identity is the confidence in her own physical strength, which may be contrary to society's assumptions about being female.

Another incident in Carlie's life that contributed to this cultural model or videotape in her head about equality was an experience her mother had with workplace gender discrimination. Her mother discovered that a man who was hired for the same job at the same time as she was earning a larger salary. According to Carlie, her mother was told the pay difference was due to the fact that she was a woman. Her mother quit her job immediately. Carlie retold her mother's experience during both the prereading and postreading discussions, personally connecting these instances with Charlotte's doing gender differently than society expected. Here we see an example of one's gendered identity taking precedence over one's identity as a capable employee. Carlie expressed that the man was "basically a slacker," and that her mother "was always on top of things." Through Carlie's annoyance, and the fact that she brought the incident up on two separate occasions, we see her disapproval of such practices, identifying individuals based on gender rather than competence within the workplace.

Carlie also related to the group a specific example of gender inequality that irritated her:

> And that's another thing that bugs me
>
> Is like, she's a girl and he's a guy
>
> Instead of she's a woman, he's a guy
>
> Or if she's a girl and he's a boy
>
> It's she's a girl, he's a guy

Here, Carlie proposes that the use of the word "girl" somehow indicates a lower status than "guy." This may stem from her associations of "girl" with immaturity and childhood, which parallels the word "boy." "Woman" and "guy" seem to indicate a sense of equality, referring to adulthood or maturity. Carlie feels the use of "girl" with "guy" puts females at a disadvantage, or lower status. Carlie would prefer to hear "girls" and "boys" or "women" and "guys," creating more equality in language. In this way, Carlie's prior experiences and background knowledge facilitated re/constructive thinking about gender as she read and constructed her identity.

Gender as an Individual's Choice

Similarly, Carlie believed that how one does gender is an individual choice and that consequences exist for making these choices. This cultural model is specifically seen through Carlie's retelling of the story. As she retells the story, she mainly uses I-statements along with the pronoun *she* to describe Charlotte's actions. Out of the 200 lines of transcripts composed into stanzas, 28 lines are I-statements and 43 lines use *she* in reference to Charlotte. First we looked at Carlie's I-statements and categorized them according to the verb following the pronoun *I*, whether it was active or cognitive (Young, 2004). Carlie used three times more cognitive I-statements such as

"I thought" and "I was like" than active I-statements. The cognitive I-statements used during the retelling of the book show that Carlie respected, related to, and approved of Charlotte's actions and choices:

> She's all prim and proper and everything.
>
> And the next thing you know,
>
> She's like all like weird
>
> And she's all on the ship
>
> And all like, part of the crew,
>
> And *I* thought that was totally awesome.
>
> *I* was like, that's awesome.

Here Carlie evaluates Charlotte's choices, calling them "awesome." She approves of Charlotte's defiance toward gender stereotypes and applauds her actions.

In the retelling of the story, Carlie's use of *she* also expresses her approval of Charlotte's actions. However, the use of *she* allows Carlie to distance herself from the gender discussion because she doesn't have to speak personally about her own life and her own gender issues. Throughout the transcripts, Carlie, like the other book club participants, does not refer to herself specifically when discussing gender. Rather, the participants discuss the character, like Carlie, using *she*, hypothetical individuals, or people they know. This kind of talk within the Discourse community provides a distancing that creates a freedom to explore gender through others. As Carlie articulates her ideas about the text, she excitedly dominates the discussion and retells the story. In her retelling, she performs a practice of the book club Discourse by expressing her own feelings and emotions as she talks about Charlotte blurring typical gender boundaries:

> One of the parts of the book that I thought was awesome
>
> Well not awesome,
>
> But you had to take time and think about it
>
> Was when she whipped the captain
>
> She like took the whip away from him and whipped him
>
> And then she felt just horrified with herself that she had done that
>
> And that I thought was like, "Wow"
>
> Cause, I mean like, she did something
>
> And yet, she hadn't really meant to do it
>
> That was pretty cool
>
> I wasn't surprised by it
>
> I just had to take the time and think why she was acting so,
>
> "Oh my gosh! What have I done?"
>
> Well, I thought it was because she saw the captain

She saw the captain through the crew's eyes for once

And how he was like, almost evil

And she just lost her temper with him

And she grabbed it (the whip) away from him

And gave him a little taste of his own medicine

You know, that she had just acted on impulse like she had never done before

And it was like, a totally new experience for her.

Here, Charlotte blurs gender stereotypes, making her own choices and impulsively acting out in violence. She chooses to whip the captain—something usually associated with being a certain kind of male, not female. This directly relates to Carlie's physical strength issue seen through the boys in PE class. Here Charlotte calls into question society's stereotype that girls are less physical or strong and represents her strength and drive, a far cry from a "fragile freak." Carlie's retelling of the story reveals an approval of Charlotte's defiance and implies an approval of all individuals who defy gender stereotypes. She seems to think that defying gender stereotypes is awesome. Talking about Charlotte, a fictional character, may give Carlie the ability to express some of her ideas about gender and an avenue to explore ways she would like to reconstruct her own identity. Using the fictional character and the pronoun *she*, Carlie can vicariously live Charlotte's experiences. This living out of the characters' achievements opens Carlie up to the possibilities of doing gender differently in her own life.

Carlie best summed up this belief that gender is an individual choice when asked what the book told her about being a girl. Carlie clearly conveyed her beliefs about Charlotte and rigid gender practices, using *you* and the indirect (*you*) as a command to impose her beliefs on others. She uses the command form to share her cultural model that gender is a personal choice. As she commands others regarding gender, she reiterates individual agency—an individual controls his or her destiny and his or her own identity:

You don't have to be what is expected of you

That's basically the message I got from the book

You don't have to put up a façade

For everybody else to see you as something that you are not.

If you want to be something other than what's expected of you,

Then (*you*) go ahead

And (*you*) do it,

(*You*) defy others if you want to…

As Carlie directs others to resist gender norms, she seems to forget the other piece of her cultural model—consequences exist such as Charlotte's punishment given by her father. Carlie disregards the power of punishments and social structures to influence practices of gender. After Carlie made her statement, the conversation turned to discuss the punishments one might receive for doing gender differently at the students' school. Specifically, the students explained what might happen to a boy who came to school cross-dressed as a girl. The students articulated that these punishments might include being shunned, teased, and disliked by others. Carlie said:

> Basically what would happen is that he might get beat up
>
> He'd be shunned by all the other kids
>
> No one would talk to him
>
> I mean, that's not very nice
>
> Basically do anything that we could to let him know he's not wanted
>
> To let him know that he is not wanted at this school
>
> And that he does not belong
>
> And that he is not supposed to act like that
>
> And basically that's what would happen
>
> I'm not saying the way other kids treat you is right
>
> I'm just saying that's what they'll do
>
> I don't necessarily agree just because somebody's doing a certain something
>
> That you should treat them a certain way
>
> But people do

Even as Carlie describes the possible consequences for resisting gender stereotypes, she eliminates herself from the problem of accepting others' gendered identities. Through her I-statements, Carlie distances herself from the problem by saying, "I'm just saying that's what they'll do" and "I don't necessarily agree." These sentences position Carlie within the group as someone who doesn't care what others do because she feels gender is an individual choice, but she is also cognizant of reality—others do not feel the same. Still, the conversation stays true to the Discourse practices of the book club, never getting too personal, never reflecting on how they personally contribute to the societal stereotypes that repress and oppress individuals who do not fall into society's acceptable gender categories.

Re/contructive Space?

Did critical literacy and redressive texts open up possibilities for re/constructing beliefs about gender and gender identities? Did the book club provide a place for Carlie to explore her own identities and contributions to societal issues? The answers are unclear.

It is apparent that Carlie quickly participated in the Discourse practice of the book club of not talking about one's self in relation to gender. She tended to blame others for gender inequalities, never looking at her own role in the re/construction of gendered practices and identities. She blamed the boys in PE, and ultimately the PE teacher. She blamed her mother's employer. She blamed the invisible *they* who use the terms "girls" and "guys." Yet, she was clearly excited about how Charlotte resisted the gendered practices of her day and spoke with admiration about Charlotte's actions. The reading and discussion of the novel facilitated her thinking about how gender influenced her life and the life of others. She made personal connections between the character's actions and her life experiences. But did it lead to a re/constructive space for her, one that would lead her to consider possible ways of being female? Perhaps.

We wonder if the Discourse practice of not being too personal hindered her and other members of the book club from opportunities to think re/constructively about gender identities. Although we believe that some opportunities for re/constructive thinking were lost due to this Discourse practice, Carlie self-reported during the final interview that the experiences in the book club helped her to think differently about gender and about texts. As stated in the opening quotation, Carlie said that the critical literacy activities helped her to analyze things more and think about what she was reading. She also said that she better understood the characters and where they were coming from. She thought that the experience helped her become "more of a feminist" and helped her to see "the way that society wants us to be brought up and it just changed the way that I think about things ... I get into discussions with my friends and parents about [movies and] stuff, how like people expect girls to be a certain way and they expect guys to be a certain way ... that has really changed my life." Carlie believed the critical literacy experience changed her life. So, we are led to believe that, at least for Carlie, the reading of redressive texts and participating in critical literacy began the process of re/constructing her own gendered identity and provided a space for her to explore her own ideas and beliefs about gender.

STORY 2: RE/CONSTRUCTIVE SPACE, CULTURAL MODELS, DISCOURSES, AND ELSA

Elsa also found her own re/constructive space. However, different from Carlie, Elsa's re/construction was a form of confirming her existing beliefs while discussing *The House on Mango Street*. Elizabeth's intent was to help students feel safe during discussions by opening the floor for students to examine issues of race within the text and to explore how race connects with one's identity. However, instead of exploring racial issues in relation to the novel, Elsa and the other students in her discussion group spoke about race outside of the text, relating race and racism to their own personal experiences. In fact, at one point in the text, the narrator comments about how one of her friends is moving because the neighborhood was getting bad: "... they'll just have to move a little farther north from Mango Street, a little farther away every time people like us keep moving in" (p. 13). Here the author, Cisneros, is referring to the fact that as minorities and people of different ethnicities and races move into the neighborhood, White, Anglo families move out. Elsa refused to recognize this as racism; she refused to interact with examples of racism within the text. Instead, she said with an edge in her voice, "So far it doesn't say what race a person is. It has nothing to do with race." If Elsa will not acknowledge the example of racism set forth in the text, we begin to ask, how can she explore the issue of race? Will the redressive text spur conversation about race and one's racial identity?

Within the discussion group, Elsa was a vocal member who seemed to stubbornly defend and define her identity as "not racist" while preaching to others about overcoming racism. Elsa did not use the discussion to explore the ways of doing race in the text and connecting those to the ways of doing race in her own life. Rather, Elsa separated race and identity, inferring that these two concepts have nothing to do with each other. Through discussion, Elsa built a façade that separated her from the issues of race and isolated race from one's identity. Her refusal to explore race and racial issues with her classmates may have stemmed from a feeling of prejudice she sensed from her classmates, thus deeming the space not safe for re/construction.

Elsa was one of two Hispanic students in a group of seven ninth graders (6 girls and 1 boy) that was facilitated by a White female university intern. There was also one Native American student in the group and four Caucasians. Before reading the novel, the students participated in a critical anticipation guide discussion. The university intern constructed the anticipation guide statements so as to draw the students into thinking about and discussing stereotypes, diversity, and prejudice. One true/false statement sparked controversy, *All Hispanics have an attitude problem,* and one student marked, *True.* Later in an interview, Elsa talked about this incident saying:

> One person in our group said that all Hispanics have an attitude problem
>
> And that really offended me
>
> Because I know that's not true.
>
> He said, some people,
>
> And I said, exactly,
>
> Not the whole race!
>
> You can't go around judging all Hispanic people
>
> Just because one person is mean to you.
>
> So, the race has nothing to do with it.
>
> I don't know,
>
> That just disappointed me.
>
> And my friend Jessy noticed that real quick when he said that.

This incident may have closed off any sort of re/constructive space. Instead of feeling free to examine her own role within the system, or how her own Hispanic heritage influences her identity, Elsa felt compelled to shut down the conversation, markedly identifying herself by saying, "I'm not racist." Here she aligned herself with a nonracist Discourse that preaches "race has nothing to do with it" and the need for equality. The intern sensed Elsa's defensiveness and tried to interject, assuring the students that the statement was not a personal attack. The intern proceeded to insert other ethnicities and religious affiliations into the statement, trying to point out that generalizations about any group can be damaging and false.

The group's response also may have contributed to the elimination of a re/constructive space. After the boy articulated his opinion, Elsa and the other female participants dominated the discussion with reasons why this statement could not be true. Rather than questioning the boy, allowing him to explore his feelings, opinions, and own identity regarding race, the girls attacked him, clearly indicating that his response was inappropriate and was not an acceptable step in this group's Discourse "dance." Following this incident, the dominant Discourse practices did not include any true self reflection, resistance, or exploration of one's own racial identity. Rather, the group understood that the appropriate responses denied any talk regarding one's exploration of personal racial tendencies and identity.

Racism Imposed

Elsa's cultural models represented conflicting notions about her own identity regarding racism—she believed: *Racism is imposed* and *Racism is an individual choice.* She saw racism as something inherited, or taught by others—an imposed piece of one's identity. She explained that parents teach their children who, in turn, teach their own children:

> It depends on how your parents are raised
>
> And how they're trying to raise you.
>
> It's just, it goes on and on.
>
> People trying to brainwash other people
>
> Saying that their race is better than another one.
>
> People try to brainwash you.
>
> So, some people still think it's right
>
> Because that's how they were brought up.
>
> It just keeps being done.

Elsa talks about children who are born into families that she identifies as racist. These families teach racism to the children, and racism becomes a continuum—"it goes on and on." Elsa's statements imply that children innocently born into racist families have less agency. Therefore, their racist Discourses are not 100% their own fault, but rather partly the fault of the generations before. But, Elsa also places blame on a distant group labeled *people*. These *people* try to brainwash other *people*. Again, racism is an imposition placed on the individual from some "other," but also a learned identity.

Racism as an Individual's Choice

Elsa's other cultural model that *Racism is an individual choice* conflicts with this notion of a learned racist identity. Within this cultural model, Elsa seems to suggest that one decides to take up a racist identity or not. Similar to Carlie, Elsa uses I-statements to articulate her own thoughts, positioning herself within the group as one who is not part of the problem. She says, "I don't want to hear it (racism)" and "I'm not racist." One section initiated by an I-statement allows the reader into her thinking process:

> The way *I* think of it is like,

Nobody's better than nobody.

Nobody's perfect in the world.

Either you're White, Black, Hispanic, any color

That doesn't matter.

So, my whole focus is, you know, the person.

Well, you like them, and that's your choice.

It's not like, Oh, he's Black, I'm not going to like him.

Oh, she's White; I'm not going to like her.

That doesn't make a difference to me.

That's not a problem in my life.

Here Elsa shows she has dealt with the problem, personally overcoming racism because "that's not a problem in my life." Through this accomplishment, Elsa separates herself from the issue of racism and erases herself from the equation. She no longer is responsible for examining her own contributions to the issue or her own racial identity. She makes a conscious choice to not look at color because in her eyes, race is not part of one's identity and does not make a difference. Therefore, Elsa believes she sits outside the problem, looking in. This distancing creates a sense of freedom to postulate her ideals and beliefs on others.

Elsa readily voices her opinions, commanding others to end racism by taking up a non-racist identity. By isolating the statements in which Elsa uses *you* and the indirect *(you)* in the command form, we see her cultural model at work. Elsa commands others to understand the world through her lens, which is one of complete equality and justice. In Elsa's words, overcoming racism appears to be a simple three-step process: Say, "Go away!"; Move on; and Don't judge.

You stop it (racism) by saying, "Go away. I don't want to hear it"

Times have changed now

You've got to move on.

(You) Don't judge a person based on their skin color

Instead of delving into the why, how, and what, Elsa performs a practice of the discussion group Discourse by keeping the discussion on a surface level. Within the context of this discussion about *The House on Mango Street*, Elsa's re/construction becomes confirmation. She does not explore issues of race or make connections between race and her own identity, or the identity of others. Instead Elsa confirms her self-proclaiming nonracist identity and challenges others to be like her. Although Elsa believes what she is saying, she views the issue through a narrow scope and misses the complexity of human emotion, historical experience, and society's social construction of race.

Elsa also uses the pronoun *they* to position herself and others. Elsa believes this ambiguous *they* exists within the world, perpetuating the problem of racism. Specifically, the topic of institutional racism emerged in regard to marking one's race on a standardized test. This frustrated Elsa because she doesn't see race as an issue, or something that should be associated with one's identity—why would we track a person's race? According to Elsa, we're all equal and color doesn't matter:

They'd say that White people are better

That's how *they* were brought up

They shouldn't be saying that (marking one's race on a standardized test)

They don't need to know (one's race)

All *they* should focus on is how well you are and what you learned

Using the pronoun *they* Elsa again excludes herself from the issue. With this distancing, Elsa eliminates the need for examination of her own role in constructing and re/constructing racial beliefs and identities. Instead, *they* need to examine themselves and should obey her *you* commands.

Re/constructive Space?

In looking at Elsa's cultural models of racism, she did not seem to re/construct the cultural models or videotapes in her mind regarding issues of race. In fact, from Elsa's point of view, there's no need for re/construction because within this particular Discourse community (the literature discussion group), the students' way of doing, acting, relating, believing, and speaking was based on the notion that race doesn't matter. When one student spoke outside of the Discourse practice and said that he agreed with the statement, *All Hispanics have an attitude problem*, the students within that group recognized this idea as unacceptable within the Discourse. They called him on this belief and from then on no one questioned or explored race or racial identities. Instead, the group, led by Elsa, seemed color-blind. Even when one student recognized institutional racism, noting that minority students fill the remedial classrooms because of low standardized test scores, Elsa explained this away by insisting that test makers shouldn't ask to know one's race. She insisted that color did not matter and stopped any exploration of the complexities behind minorities filling the remedial classrooms and how this experience related to these students' sense of identity. In Elsa's own words, "My whole focus is the person [not race]." So within this Discourse, all human beings are seen as fundamentally the same and differences are simply illusions. That is, the "masters of the dance" (Gee, 1999, p. 19) determined that being a student in this discussion group meant denying that race directly relates to identity.

We wonder how the Discourse practices based on the belief that race doesn't matter influenced opportunities for re/construction during discussions by Elsa's group. Elsa's voice was a powerful voice within the group. She held and voiced to the group conflicting views about racism as imposed or as an individual choice. She was able to completely separate herself from issues of race and in doing so, silenced some of the other students. Her interactions with the redressive texts and critical literacy seemed only to confirm her racial identity and beliefs about race.

In an interview, Elsa revealed what she learned from critical literacy:

Oh, just to be more and more independent. Just like my mom has always raised me to be independent, but I've decided to be independent to get things for myself because my mom's not always going to be there. So, I have to value myself for who I am and not think that just because other people are different color they're less than you.

So, in Elsa's own words, even after participating in critical literacy discussions, she believed we live in a meritocracy where an individual's hard work can make all the difference instead of understanding how race might play a significant role in an individual's achievements and identities.

DISCUSSION

As we view our findings in light of the notions of socially situated identities and re/construction, the complexity of critical literacy becomes apparent. In each of the studies presented, we attempted to provide students with re/constructive spaces through reading and discussing redressive texts and participating in critical literacy. Carlie may have come the closest to re/constructing gender and connecting this re/construction to her own gendered identity as she transacted with the text and retold her thought process to the book club. Elsa, on the other hand, used the space created by the literature discussion groups to confirm her prior beliefs and ideas about race and racial identities and ignored the texts that she read.

Carlie and Elsa positioned themselves outside of gender and racial issues during discussions about gender and race. This positioning outside of one's self became a Discourse practice in both the book club and the literature discussion group. Carlie used the pronoun *you* to impose her beliefs on others, whereas Elsa used the pronoun *they* to represent the invisible others who perpetuate racism. Both said that they were neither sexist nor racist, but both were not aware of their part in constructing or reconstructing practices of gender or race.

Both girls talked of gender or racism as one's individual choice. Carlie spoke of the consequences for doing gender differently but did not find them severe enough to stop someone from doing gender how they wanted. She pointed to the character, Charlotte, as an example of someone who made the choice to do gender differently and dealt with the consequences. Elsa acknowledged racism exists, but said that getting rid of racism was as easy as telling someone to stop it and making an individual choice not to be racist. It is apparent that neither girl recognized the power of social contexts and structures to define and construct identities and practices. This lack of acknowledgement of the power structures points to the need for critical literacy facilitators to do more instruction about social systems and structures prior to and in conjunction with the critical literacy activities. Although others (e.g., Alvermann, Commeyras, Young, Randall, & Hinson, 1997; Ellsworth, 1989; McIntosh,1998) have experienced resistance and disbelief to such re/constructions of gender and race, facilitators of critical literacy still need to contextualize and teach the social and historical contexts of gendered and racial constructions and beliefs for critical literacy to be most effective. Students like Elsa have fairly simplistic and idealistic understandings of these issues, so in order for students to work toward re/construction, facilitators need to help them become aware of the complexities of gender and race and how gendered and racial identities were constructed, are constructed, and continue to be reconstructed over time.

Using redressive texts along with critical literacy activities offers promise as an avenue to further explore the re/construction of gender and race and stop the perpetuation of inequities and prejudices. Doing so, along with instruction about social structures, can provide re/constructive spaces for students like Carlie and Elsa to explore possible identities and social practices and facilitate a move toward social change.

REFERENCES

Alvermann, D. E., Commeyras, M., Young, J. P., Randall, S., & Hinson, D. (1997). Interrupting gendered discursive practices in classroom talk about texts: Easy to think about, difficult to do. *Journal of Literacy Research, 2,* 73–104.

Avi (1997). *The true confessions of Charlotte Doyle.* New York: Harpertrophy.

Cisneros, S. (1984). *The house on Mango Street.* New York: Vintage Books.

Edelsky, C. (Ed.). (1999). *Making justice our project: Teachers working toward critical whole language practice.* Urbana, IL: National Council of Teachers of English.

Ellsworth, E. (1989). Why doesn't this feel empowering? Working through the representive myths of critical pedagogy. *Harvard Educational Review, 59*(3), 297–324.

Gee, J. P. (1999). *An introduction to discourse analysis: Theory and method.* London: Routledge.

Gee, J. P. (2004). Discourse analysis: What makes it critical. In R. Rogers (Ed.), *An introduction to critical discourse analysis in education* (pp. 19–50). Mahwah, NJ: Lawrence Erlbaum Associates.

Janks, H. (2001). Identity and conflict in a critical literacy classroom. In B. Comber & A. Simpson (Eds.), *Negotiating critical literacies in classrooms* (p. 137–150). Mahwah, NJ: Lawrence Erlbaum Associates.

Luke, A. (2004). Notes on the future of critical discourse studies. *Critical Discourse Studies, 1*(1), 149–153.

Martino, W. (1995). Deconstructing masculinity in the English classroom: A site for reconstructing gendered subjectivity. *Gender and Education, 7*(2), 205–220.

McIntosh, Peggy, (1998) White privilege: Unpacking the invisible knapsack. Available: http://www.utoronto.ca/acc/events/peggy1.htm

Morgan, W. (1997). *Critical literacy in the classroom: The art of the possible.* New York: Routledge.

Strauss, C., & Quinn, N. (1997). *A cognitive theory of cultural meaning.* Cambridge, UK: University Press.

Stolle, E. P. (2004) *Critical literacy with adolescents: What difference does it make?* Unpublished raw data.

Young, J. P. (2000). Boy talk: Critical literacy and masculinities. *Reading Research Quarterly, 35,* 312–337.

Young, J. P. (2004). Cultural models and discourses of masculinity: Being a boy in a literacy classroom. In R. Rogers (Ed.), *An introduction to critical discourse analysis in education* (pp. 147–171). Mahwah, NJ: Lawrence Erlbaum Associates.

Young, J. P., & Ricks, B. (2000). *Critical literacy and gender in an afterschool book club.* Unpublished raw data.

4

Adolescents' Multiple Identities and Teacher Professional Development

Alfred W. Tatum
Northern Illinois University

On one point, therefore, there can be no question—no hesitation: unless we develop our full capabilities, we cannot survive. If [black men] are to be trained grudgingly and suspiciously; trained not with reference to what we can be, but with sole reference to what somebody wants us to be; if instead of following the methods pointed out by the accumulated wisdom of the world for the development of full human power, we simply are trying to follow the line of least resistance and teach black men only such things and by such methods as are momentarily popular, then my fellow teachers, we are going to fail ignominiously in our attempt to raise the black race to its full humanity and with that failure falls the fairest and fullest dream of a great united humanity.

—W.E.B. Du Bois, 2001, p. 26

Once I had read enough, learned enough to identify that process, I then had to reconstruct myself as a decent and worthy child of God, painfully peeling away the layers of filth that covered me. This deniggerization, this de-savaging of my soul, began with Shakespeare; it continued in my voracious exploration of literature. Authors as disparate as Mark Twain and W. E. B. Du Bois, Carter G. Woodson and Victor Hugo, Malcolm X and Maya Angelou challenged me, inspired me, and taught me endless lessons. Through them I have found the soul I had thought forever lost.

—Carl Upchurch, 1996, p. xii

These two quotes suggest that literacy development extends beyond cognitive domains that focus on learning how to read text, that is, "educational texts, visual, printed and electronically mediated, [which] typically seem and claim to speak in one voice, for all possible perspectives and with competence and comprehensiveness" (Freebody, 2003, p. 180). Du Bois (2001) suggested that the development of African

Americans is connected to larger goals of humanity and that wisdom is required to move beyond things that are momentarily popular to develop full human power. Upchurch (1996), a once troubled African American teenager who spent his teenage years in and out of the criminal justice system after quitting school while in the fourth grade, suggests that his literacy development led to a reconstruction of self. He refers to the reconstruction as a "deniggerization" process that occurred after he read the words and ideas of authors, playwrights, and poets who taught him endless lessons that permeated his soul. He was then able to peel away painful layers of filth that covered him. He asserted that the layers of filth accumulated because of his feelings of invisibility connected to his upbringing in the Philadelphia ghetto where his identity was shaped. Later in his autobiographical text, he states:

> Everything I had experienced in my childhood was the opposite of what I needed to survive socially, intellectually, and psychologically at school ... I was socialized at home under the most negative emotional conditions; as a result, my socialization in school felt like an assault to my culture and values. (p. 17)

The major goal of this chapter is to discuss how students' identities and subjectivities interplay with their literacy development. The discussion centers on the identity/subjectivity of African American adolescents, particularly the ones living in impoverished communities in the United States and attending low-achieving schools. The discussion is anchored by a case study of teacher professional development conducted over a 19-month period in one of Chicago's lowest performing schools where I supported one seventh- and one eighth-grade teacher to honor students' adolescent and cultural identities as part of the literacy instruction they provided. Many of the students were in need of developing the human power Du Bois said needs to be developed and the social, intellectual, and psychological development that was missing in Upchurch's life. These teachers share how their students' literacy behaviors shifted and how their own beliefs about literacy instruction changed when they made pedagogical shifts that honored their students' identities. Before proceeding with details from the qualitative case study, I share the rationale for honoring the identities of adolescents, particularly students of color, and the potential this honoring has on their literacy development and life outcomes.

HONORING STUDENTS' MULTIPLE IDENTITIES AND LITERACY DEVELOPMENT

Identity development is critical for adolescents. Identity has been defined as the "presentation of self in a matrix of social relationships—a pattern of social assertion that significant others recognize and come to expect" (Davidson, 1996, p. 2). The concept of identity "is a complex one shaped by individual characteristics, family dynamics, historical factors, and social and political contexts" (Tatum, 1997, p. 2). Researchers have found that adolescents of color are more likely to be actively engaged in an exploration of their racial and ethnic identity than are White students, and that examinations of one's racial identity, often triggered by environmental cues, may begin as early as junior high school (See Tatum, 1997 for a more detailed explanation).

Although identity construction is central to one's literacy development, many teachers responsible for teaching adolescent students of color are unaware of their students' multiple identities and how these identities can be used or should be built on during literacy instruction. This holds true for teachers who share the same cultural and racial identity traits as their students because many of these teachers have had their own identity construction marginalized or overlooked by curricula orientations in schools that defined their education. For example, Gay (2000) explained, "If educators continue to be ignorant of, ignore, impugn, and silence the cultural orientations, values, and performance styles of ethnically different students, they will persist in imposing cultural hegemony, personal denigration, educational inequity, and academic underachievement upon them" (p. 25).

The lack of preparation in using knowledge of students' multiple identities during literacy instruction was visible in the school where I conducted this study. When asked to recall the aspects of his teacher education program that had prepared him to teach African American adolescents, Mr. Tuscany, a seventh-grade teacher, explained, "It was pretty much directed to students. I cannot pinpoint anything that would necessarily say it was for older students … [or] anything specifically culturally relevant." In the remainder of this chapter, I describe how I became involved in a project to provide professional development support that led two teachers to honor students' identities as part of the literacy instruction they provided.

THE RADNUS ELEMENTARY SCHOOL PROFESSIONAL DEVELOPMENT PROJECT

Believing that academic failure is not inevitable for African American adolescents attending public schools located in poor, urban communities, I had chosen to become a teacher of adolescents 7 years before my involvement in the Radnus Elementary School Professional Development Project. Early on in my teaching career, I sought ways to break down barriers that disenfranchised my African American adolescent students, many of whom were from economically disadvantaged homes and reading several years below grade level (Tatum, 2000). Eventually, I enrolled in a doctoral program that pulled me away from teaching adolescent students for close to 3 years. However, I continued to regard adolescence as a pivotal period for literacy development, particularly for those who struggle with print.

In the spring of 2001, I received an e-mail notice from a university listserv about a position that propelled me back into working with adolescents, not as a classroom teacher, but as a reading specialist, where I was responsible for providing professional development support to a group of teachers in Grades 6–8. I understood that helping teachers develop professionally in a low-achieving school was not a well-trodden area, and that the process would have to occur without a blueprint guaranteeing success. However, I applied for and accepted the reading specialist position in Radnus Elementary School, one of the lowest performing elementary schools in its district.

Radnus Elementary School was stamped with probationary status by its district's office of accountability. Eighty-two percent of the students were reading below grade level at the beginning of the 2001–2002 academic school year based on data from the Iowa Test of Basic Skills. Only 22% of the seventh-grade students and 21% of the eighth-grade students were reading at or above grade level. Being placed on probation caused tensions for many teachers and administrators who were uncertain about their futures in a school on probation. This uncertainty created considerable pressure to increase students' test scores. The high premium placed on increasing test scores influenced the instructional decisions the teachers made as reflected in their use of test preparation materials and publisher's skill-oriented worksheets. Teachers were using a *momentarily popular* approach to improve test scores.

THE FIRST PROFESSIONAL DEVELOPMENT APPROACH

I initially provided professional development support guided by a literacy framework largely derived from research on effective elementary teachers (Allington, 2002; Allington & Cunningham, 1996; Pressley, 1998). The literacy framework involved read-alouds, word study and vocabulary development, guided reading practices, independent reading, and writing. Although the literacy framework was research-based and had both the human and material resources to move it forward, it needed to be expanded. The teachers, who had been involved for 5 years prior to my involvement in professional development efforts that placed an emphasis on instructional strategies with little success in increasing test scores, did not believe in the efficacy of instructional strategies to resolve the dilemmas faced by teachers and students in a school with a chronic pattern of school failure.

AN ANATOMICALLY COMPLETE MODEL
OF PROFESSIONAL DEVELOPMENT

The initial literacy framework was expanded to provide what I characterized as an anatomically complete model of professional development support. In this model (Fig. 4.1), students' adolescent identities and cultural identities were centralized. Although I was the reading specialist for teachers in Grades 6 through 8, this model focused on adolescent identities and cultural identities for students in Grades 7 and 8 because of my interest with that age group, and the seventh- and eighth-grade teachers' consent to participate in the study. Radnus Elementary School had one seventh-grade teacher and one eighth-grade teacher. My work with these teachers, who are described later, is the focus of this chapter.

The head of the anatomically complete model was conceptualized based on the following:

1. Professional development support needs to be built on the knowledge of effective teachers of African Americans (Ladson-Billings, 1991; Lipman, 1995). Gay (2000) explains:

A very different pedagogical paradigm is needed to improve the performance of underachieving students from various ethnic groups—one that teaches to and through their personal and cultural strengths, their intellectual capacities, and their prior accomplishments. Culturally responsive teaching is this kind of paradigm .... It filters curriculum content and teaching strengths through cultural frames of reference to make content more personally meaningful and easier to master. (p. 24)

2. The concept of adolescent literacy is undergoing a productive reconceptualization (Alvermann, Hinchman, Moore, Phelps, & Waff, 1998). The focus on the literacy development of adolescents now moves beyond cognitive approaches and encompasses social and complex conceptions of literacy not limited to in-school literacy. Narrowly conceived cognitive approaches are insuffi-

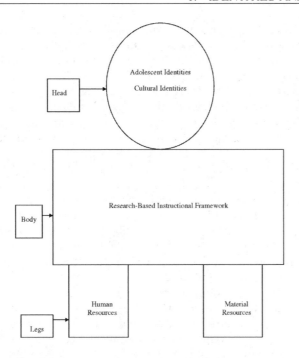

FIG. 4.1. Anatomically complete model of professional development support.

cient for a growing population of linguistically, culturally, and socioeconomically diverse students (Moje, Young, Readence, & Moore, 2000; Schoenbach, Greenleaf, Cziko, & Hurwitz, 1999).

Several texts have been written in the past couple of years that bring attention to the promise and potential of honoring students' inside- and outside-of-school identities as an approach to advance their multiple literacies, literacies that shape their lives (Hull & Schultz, 2002; Mahiri, 2004; Rymes, 2001). Effectively addressing the multiple literacy needs of adolescents requires a hybridization of literacy practices that balance the literacies that students develop out of school with literacies that develop in school (Finders & Tatum, 2005).

OUT-OF-SCHOOL LITERACY OVERLOAD AND IN-SCHOOL LITERACY UNDERLOAD

Many students of color suffer from what I refer to as an imbalance between "out-of-school literacy overload" and "in-school literacy underload." This imbalance often shapes a trajectory of negative life outcomes, particularly for African American adolescent males because in-school literacy instruction fails to answer the question, "What am I going to do with the rest of my life?" (Tatum, 2003a). Many students' academic performance and lives are shaped by the images of their communities and the associated possibilities they imagine for themselves as a result of the surrounding images. Ogbu (1998) referred to these images or products of sociocultural adaptation located within the minority community as *community forces*.

The community of Radnus Elementary School can be accurately described as low-income and inner city. The median income is about $23,000. There are signs in the front of convenience stores that read, "Government LINK cards accepted." The immediate area of Radnus Elementary is home to several liquor stores, several vacant carwash lots, and blocks of vacant lots where homes once stood. The lots are dotted with abandoned cars and are used as short-cut paths for children walking to school. Gang and drug warfare is part of the fabric of the community. These images, coupled with the class-based, race-based experiences taking place inside their homes, can lead many students to surrender their life chances before they come to know their life choices (Tatum, 2005). These factors and images contribute to the students' out-of-school literacy overload. This out-of-school literacy overload can be characterized as a discourse community that works like an identity kit that comes already equipped with ways of seeing, acting, thinking, and talking in the world (Gee, 1991).

Without a counterbalance of effective in-school literacy instruction that points adolescents toward new and better realities for themselves or moves them toward a new discourse (Gee, 1991), adolescents' identities and subjectivities are in large part shaped by the overload in their out-of-school literacies. On the other hand, students at Radnus Elementary School were experiencing an in-school literacy underload because of the teachers' focus on test scores and use of test preparation materials. Their chances for encountering "touchstone texts" (Neilsen, chap. 1, this volume), texts that can potentially help nurture students' identities and reshape the trajectory of their life outcomes, were significantly reduced. Observing the imbalance between the out-of-school literacy overload and in-school literacy underload, I conceptualized professional development support for two teachers informed by the community forces and school factors impacting the literacy development of the students.

THE TWO TEACHERS

Mr. Tuscany

Mr. Tuscany, an African American male, had been teaching for 16 years, 15 of those years at Radnus Elementary. He was teaching seventh-grade students for the first time during the year of the case study. The major challenge of teaching for Mr. Tuscany was motivating students and increasing their scores on standardized assessments despite some of their disruptive behaviors. There were also professional-based challenges. He explained, "Being on probation, we have tried numerous programs and you know [we] have to be open to allow people to come in [our classrooms] to observe." He felt bombarded by the various workshops when professional developers gave him things to try or to do in his classroom.

Mrs. Garden

Mrs. Garden was a veteran African American teacher who had been teaching for 26 years. She was teaching seventh- and eighth-grade students for the ninth year at the time of the study. When asked to describe the major challenges she had faced over the past 5 years teaching at Radnus, her first comment was, "God, we would never finish if I talked about the major challenges." She believed the biggest challenge was teaching kids who lack self-confidence, kids who cannot see beyond their neighborhood. Both teachers' comments and dispositions reflected that the students and their "families seemed to be immersed in [a] hostile educational and community [setting]" (Garcia, 2002, p. 139).

THE PROFESSIONAL DEVELOPMENT SUPPORT

My professional development support was designed to move the teachers toward instructional practices that would grant their students entrée into literacy instruction that extended beyond a sole indoctrination of basic skills aimed at minimum requirements on a standardized instrument. The support focused on several dominant themes for the teachers that included helping them to:

1. Engage their students with authentic text and in authentic discussions where the students could analyze their realities and discuss strategies for overcoming academic and societal barriers.
2. Use meaningful literacy activities that took into account students' adolescent and cultural identities.
3. Acknowledge that skill development, increasing test scores, and nurturing students' identities are fundamentally compatible.
4. Legitimatize African American students' culture and make it a reference for learning.

These themes anchored all of the professional development activities, which included whole-group staff sessions, grade-level meetings, postobservation conferences, sharing of professional readings in the form of books and articles, personal conversations, and various materials I shared with the two teachers. Throughout the professional development project, teachers were encouraged to think about the role of literacy instruction for the students they were teaching. Here I provide, as an example, a two-page letter I distributed to the teachers in April 2002 that expressed concerns for teaching students who lived in an environment where schooling has failed to live up to the promises of quality education for most of the members living in their communities. This letter (Fig. 4.2) provides a rich snapshot of the types of dialogue held throughout many of the professional development activities that focused on students' identities.

Teachers,

I was approached by a member of the faculty yesterday who encouraged me to think deeply about the issue of educating the children at Radnus. The issues of culturally relevant teaching versus teaching as a neutral discipline that ignores the issue of student's culture were discussed. (Why can't we just teach children as children?) We spoke honestly and candidly about the differences and did not leave with a consensus. However, during the course of the conversation high expectations, communication patterns with students and parents, curriculum selection, discipline, and the larger ecology that pollutes the educational experiences of our children were discussed. I offered that schooling for many of our children has become a ritualistic indoctrination of failure predicated by many circumstances beyond our control; however, there are certain aspects within the teachers' realms of control. I also offered that instructional approaches in and of themselves are limited because they fail to address other competencies that are beyond the reach of identifying details, making inferences, making predictions, etc. Education has always been more than the A, B, Cs.

Solely focusing on instructional approaches ignores the strengthening of students' identities. This is important because many of our students live lives in contradiction. It is communicated to them in their homes that schooling is the pathway to promises that they do not readily witness. A feeling of inferiority is endemic for many of our students. They still associate being smart and being wealthy as being white. Focusing on instructional approaches or a student's skill-base leaves these issues uncovered, ultimately leading to the reproduction of the status quo. We will fail miserably if we do not nurture our students' identities, push them towards academic excellence, and utilize their culture as a vehicle for learning to build cultural competence.

Here, I do not speak of the KKK culture – tell them they are born of African Kings, make sure they know about Martin Luther King, and discuss the seven principles of Kwanzaa. These K's have been used as add-ons or cultural feel goods but have led to the debasement of an authentic form of culturally responsive pedagogy. Culturally relevant pedagogy is a pedagogy of opposition that encourages students to read between the lines and beyond the pages and is designed to have students examine the society in which they live. But, in order for them to read between the lines requires that there is strong instructional support in a caring community to teach them to read. For many of our students, "it is less about what's on the lines and pages than what is between the lines and beyond the pages."

The idea is not to expose our children to cultural artifacts and historical facts about African Americans in isolation, but to expose them to a conceptualization that there is a positive uniqueness about being black in hopes that this uniqueness allows them to interact with other cultural groups more fully, an inevitability in society. "I Too, Am America." Make the teaching efforts explicit when exposing them to the *dialect* of Standard English (the *dialect* of power in these United States), and other forms of power in the United States. Our students' exposure must be wide and varied and grounded in the belief that these kids can learn just as much and more than any group of children.

FIG. 4.2. Letter distributed to teachers.

The following is part of the follow-up conversation with Mrs. Garden and Mr. Tuscany about the contents of the letter at a grade-level meeting during the first week of May 2002. I asked them to help me understand my thinking about literacy instruction in the context of Radnus Elementary School and its surrounding community.

Tatum: There were some things I put in [the letter] that hopefully you and Mrs. Garden can help me figure out. One of the things placed in the letter was the issue of culturally responsive teaching versus a neutral form of teaching … I want both of you to help me understand if our students' identities matter, and if there are cultural considerations for providing a better quality education.

Mr. Tuscany: I think culture definitely matters because there are particular surroundings that [the students] are involved with. By making it culturally relevant when we are teaching, if they do not understand exactly what we are teaching they still have something to draw from because it touches their lives.

Tatum: What about you, Mrs. Garden?

Mrs. Garden: I agree whole-heartedly. The reason I say this is because I think you were here when we started reading Dick Gregory's novel, *Nigger* (1995). The kids really enjoyed the book because they were familiar with the language … They said it was because they could relate to things.

Mr. Tuscany: I also feel by making it culturally relevant, it empowers the kids to a certain degree because it's not like [they] are sitting around knowing totally nothing about it. By making it culturally relevant, they can identify with something in there, which means they don't feel left out.

Tatum: We know they can relate. We know the students buy into it. But, are these the things making them better readers in your estimation? Is this going to lead to higher reading achievement? I think it is a dichotomy. We can invite them in and motivate them and empower them with ideas and feelings, but are we increasing their reading achievement?

Mr. Tuscany: To a degree. I think it is, for the simple fact it's going to allow them to get into it. When you want to achieve something, you practice towards that goal. If it is something that I don't like, I'm not going to practice, which means I am not going to reach my goal. If I like it or can get into it, then I am apt to do a little bit more, which in the end it is going to raise the achievement. I think it is going to lead to better achievement based on the simple fact that they will read it now.

Mrs. Garden: That's an excellent point, Tuscany. I think the primary reason they were having so much trouble with other texts, and I use that term openly, is maybe they didn't fully understand what they were reading. But since we have been reading a lot of books by a lot of different authors and bringing things that are culturally relevant to the students—I think now when I bring in stuff to them—now they say it's easy.

Mr. Tuscany: It's opened the door. At first the door was not opened. Now the door is opened.

The reflections of the teachers throughout the study suggested a reconceptualization in their literacy instruction that moved closer toward an intersection of improving students' reading scores and nurturing students' identities. Mr. Tuscany mentioned in March 2002 that his goal was "to make sure [the students] move at least one year." He also mentioned, "I just want to make them knowledgeable." After 7 months of placing emphasis on curriculum orientations and a culturally responsive approach to literacy teaching, Mr. Tuscany explained how the professional development support had affected his beliefs about teaching literacy: "I've always known that success was possible, but it's helping me believe that more success is possible ... I mean, you hear that this will work, that will work, but by doing it the way we are doing it [focusing on students' identities] we actually get to see some success stories." Mrs. Garden, in a separate conversation, explained how the professional development support had impacted her teaching of African American adolescents: "We are now dealing with culture in our school. We are dealing with issues that pertain specifically to us, and what we are going to do about it in this area. That's an eye-opener for them and me."

CURRICULUM ORIENTATIONS

I had the autonomy and financial resources provided through a grant to select curriculum materials to support Mrs. Garden and Mr. Tuscany, the only teachers at Radnus Elementary who did not use a basal reader during the 2001–2002 school year. I decided not to select a basal reader and opted for young adolescent (YA) literature for both the seventh and eighth grades, and a literature anthology, *African American Literature: Voices in Tradition* (1998) for the eighth grade. (See Fig. 4.3 for a list of the YA literature used.)

There were several reasons for this. I wanted to select curriculum materials that would lead the teachers toward the following:

1. Striking a balance between students' out-of-school literacy development and in-school literacy development.
2. Using a culturally responsive approach for teaching literacy to help reshape students' views of who they are and what they can become.
3. Using and discussing literature appropriate for adolescents.

During the professional development project, culturally relevant literature anchored the culturally responsive approach. I selected curriculum materials, a large percentage written by African American authors or with African American characters, that I thought could help the students think about ways to plan their futures and shape a positive trajectory for their lives, lives "not limiting the space in which the self can roam" (Achebe, 1988, p. 53). For example, *Slam* (Myers, 1996) was selected for Mr. Tuscany's class because it provided opportunities to discuss making sound academic decisions and examining the consequences when inappropriate decisions are made. Slam, the main character in Myers' novel, is consumed by

Babbitt, N. (1975). *Tuck Everlasting*. Farrar, Strauss & Giroux

Cushman, K. (1995). *The Midwife's Apprentice*. New York: HarperTrophy.

Gregory, D. (1995) *Nigger: An Autobiography*. New York, Mass Market.

Hamilton, V. (1990). *Cousins*. New York: Scholastic.

Hinton, S. E. (1967). *The Outsiders*. New York: Puffin.

Johnson, A. (1998). *Heaven*. New York: Aladdin.

Kunjufu, J. (1987). *Lessons from History*. Chicago: African American Images.

Lowry. L. (1989). *Number the Stars*. New York: Yearling.

Lowry, L. (1993). *The Giver*. New York: Yearling.

McKissack, P. (1992). *The Dark Thirty: Southern Tales of the Supernatural*. New York: Knopf.

Myers, W. D. (1993). *Malcolm X: By Any Means Necessary*. New York: Scholastic.

Myers, W.D. (1988). *Scorpions*. New York: HarperTrophy.

Myers, W. D. (1996). *Slam*. New York: Scholastic.

Naylor. P. R. (2000). *Shiloh*. New York: Aladdin

Sachar, L. (1998). *Holes*. New York: Yearling.

Taylor, M. D. (1976). *Roll of Thunder, Hear My Cry*. New York: Dial.

Washington, B. T. (2000). *Up From Slavery*. New York: Signet.

Woodson, J. (1994). *I Hadn't Meant To Tell You This*. New York: Laurel leaf.

Wright, R. (1994). *Rites of Passage*. New York: HarperTrophy.

FIG. 4.3. Curriculum materials selected for classroom instruction.

dreams that his basketball talents will remove him from the stings of poverty. His dreams are continually challenged. He neglects his studies at a magnet high school, is faced with the reality of his grandmother dying and his father's drunkenness, and has friends selling drugs. Slam is able to make great decisions on the basketball court, but is challenged to make good decisions off the court.

While discussing the curriculum materials selected for their classroom instruction, the teachers reflected on the usefulness of the materials for advancing their students' literacies. After 3 months of using the materials, Mrs. Garden said:

> Oh, those readings that you have given me—every book that you have thrown in my hand … have been a blessing. Especially the African American literature because I never had that approach with my students before. I always tried to feel that I had to do readings with this, that, or the other. And, those [other] readings are fine, but I think for our African American students that there are a lot of things going on that they are missing [but which they get] with the literature you are giving us now.

The two teachers found a culturally responsive approach to literacy teaching as one of the useful aspects for helping them to advance their students' literacies. Using students' adolescent and cultural identities as frames of reference allowed teachers to facilitate learning and address concerns specific to their students. Mr. Tuscany, commenting on the curriculum materials that anchored the culturally responsive approach, stated:

> Each of the topics we seemed to cover with our novels I thought were things that should be talked about with adolescents because of the things that were going on. I felt those were actually choices that one day may present themselves to them in their own lives. We went through gang-related things all the way through relatives, then we took them to new heights in terms of fantasy. Then we came back and went through a lot of genres. In *Toning the Sweep* (Johnson, 1993), we talked about relationships between a mother and a grandchild. All the way back down to trust and what you should do [about] inappropriate advances by somebody [a reference to the novel, *I Hadn't Meant to Tell You This*, (Woodson, 1995)]. So those were all suitable topic, topics that as a teacher I think you need to be comfortable to teach.

The curriculum materials also allowed students to connect their out-of-school and in-school literacies as Mr. Tuscany illustrates:

> I think back to *Cousins* (Hamilton, 1992). [The students] compared some of their relationships to a relative in terms of some of the things we were discussing .... Basically, things like that in their lives, their relationships with other family members, especially grandmothers.

Mrs. Garden, when reflecting on the curriculum materials, added:

> First of all, we started with the African American literature book, which is something considering we're teaching African American students. You also brought in independent reading books that dealt with African Americans, which is something we never had in the past. You gave the kids a sense of being. Going back to … Jesse Jackson's old saying—"I am Somebody." I think whether they say it, the kids started seeing it. I am somebody. This is my community. These are my people I associate with on a daily basis. [With this curriculum] they can be attuned with themselves and know [that] whatever is good for somebody else can be good for them.

STUDENT ACHIEVEMENT AND LITERACY SHIFTS

Mrs. Garden, in her final interview, shared the following:

> Mr. Tatum, Tonya came up to me and I'll never forget it as long as I live, the look on her face when she just held me. She locked me in a lock and held me and looked me dead smack in the face and said, "Mrs. Garden, we did it." I asked, "What are you talking about, we did it?" She said, "We made a lie out of my grandmother. My grandmother said that I would never be able to graduate and we did it."

Tonya was not the only success story. By the end of the study, 39% of the seventh-grade students were reading at or above grade level and 57% of the eighth-grade students were reading at or above grade level, up from 22% and 21%

respectively prior to my involvement. These were the highest percentages achieved over at least the previous 5 years at Radnus Elementary. From a cognitive perspective, the test data, along with teachers' reports of students' frequent independent strategy use, indicate that there was growth in students' reading abilities. However, the improvement in students' literacies extended beyond standardized test scores. There were shifts in students' literacy behaviors observed by the teachers that fit within a sociocultural view of literacy instruction, namely students' confidence levels, student expectations of themselves as literacy learners, students' connection of literacy to real-world learning, and students' positive responses to literature. This was suggested by teachers' comments that meshed with my observations.

Mr. Tuscany: I found that, through some of our discussions, the students wanted to take books home. In the past nobody—well, we weren't [reading] novels—but nobody wanted to do extra reading. When I asked them to read from A to B, that was it. But now I am finding them wanting to go on. They're already telling me, discussing the book with me, telling me what happened here and there.

Mrs. Garden: They're reading more. I have kids who have been literally nonreaders raising their hands to respond … [Student] was basically a nonreader for a couple of years in a row. He's even reading more now. He has confidence in himself since we brought about this Black—I don't know if it's the Black literature or the approach that I have with him with the Black literature.

Mr. Tuscany: Some of them I couldn't get to pay attention (at the beginning of the year). [Student] is doing better now. Before, he wouldn't cause me problems, but he wouldn't pay attention. Now I am finding them getting into the stories. Now they will try to defend their answers. "Look I found—it says so and so," and they take me back to the spot where they found certain things. I see their confidence level building.

The teachers shared their reasons why a culturally responsive approach to literacy teaching helped them advance their students' literacies. The most salient explanation converged on the idea that the approach provided an inviting pathway for student participation, namely, students' voices were awakened because the literature had familiar contexts that allowed them to make personal responses based on their experiences with the content of curriculum materials. This led to increased student participation, which in turn contributed to their literacy growth. Mrs. Garden stated, "The things that we're doing invites in the knowledge that they already bring to the table. So, I think that's how it's helping them."

The results from this study (See Tatum, 2003b for complete study) suggest that a professional development model that took into account students' adolescent and cultural identities by using texts selected with consideration for those identities helped the teachers advance the literacies of economically disadvantaged adolescents struggling with reading. Planning professional development supports based on considerations for multifaceted dilemmas related to students' identities (e.g., African American adolescent struggling readers), institutional constraints, and strong embedded historical realities that reached "beyond simply educating the child ... [to] shaping the child" (Rymes, 2001, p. 90) was central to the seventh- and eighth-grade teachers at Radnus Elementary. This broader view for providing professional development moved toward an examination of factors both outside and inside of schools that influence literacy outcomes.

Literacy instruction that takes into account students' identities, shaped by historical and current circumstances and a vision for the future, can be viewed as a seed of optimism. Ignoring students' historical and contemporary circumstances can render an uncritical approach to literacy development that allows traditional instructional approaches to remain largely unchallenged and unchanged. At Radnus Elementary, moving beyond an emphasis solely on instructional strategies influenced the teachers' desires to develop professionally and to invest energy to change curriculum orientations and place emphasis on students' identities. Throughout the professional development project, a high premium was placed on addressing the varied needs of adolescents and redressing some of the inadequacies in education experienced by adolescent students in low-achieving schools. As a result, efforts were made to have the teachers not only provide explicit strategy instruction, but to also include YA literature, strive to use a culturally responsive approach to literacy teaching, honor students' identities, create supportive classroom environments, and engage students in discussion where they could analyze their realities in the context of the curriculum.

This experience suggests that there is a need to reconceptualize the roles of professional development support targeted toward improving the reading achievement of African American adolescents. Professional development must fit with the current concepts of adolescents' multiple literacies and must include pedagogy that has been found to be effective with African American students. There are several potential benefits related to such a reconceptualization:

1. Professional development support for teachers of African American adolescents can be built on a conceptual basis that includes theoretical, instructional, and professional considerations.
2. A cohesive system of professional development support will include considerations for educating adolescents, educating African Americans, students' literacies, and teachers' literacies.
3. Professional development support can be analyzed for its effectiveness in narrowing the literacy gap between African American adolescents and other students.

This qualitative case study provided research-based evidence that when teachers honor students' multiple identities as a critical part of the literacy instruction they provide, students show growth in traditional cognitive domains as reflected in test scores. As more research on adolescent literacy research is conducted, it will be productive to include a focus on the complexity inherent in the multiple identities that adolescents bring to our nation's classrooms (e.g., cultural, gender, racial) and to examine how the honoring of these identities can be used to advance the literacies of all adolescents. Wrestling with the complexities associated with student's multiple identities may not be *momentarily popular* in school environments where quick solutions to raise test scores are being sought, but may hold out the most promise of not only advancing students' literacies, but shaping the lives of many students who are in desperate need of full human development.

REFERENCES

Achebe, C. (1988). *Hopes and impediments*. New York: Doubleday.

African American literature: Voices in tradition. (1998). New York: Holt Rinehart Winston.

Allington, R. L. (2002). What I've learned about effective reading instruction from a decade of studying exemplary classroom teachers. *Phi Delta Kappan, 83,* 740–747.

Allington, R. L., & Cunningham, P. M. (1996). *Schools that work: Where all children read and write.* New York: Addison Wesley Longman.

Alvermann, D., Hinchman, K., Moore, D., Phelps, S., & Waff, D. (Eds.). (1998). *Reconceptualizing the literacies in adolescents' lives* (1st ed.). Mahwah, NJ: Lawrence Erlbaum Associates.

Davidson, A. L. (1996). *Making and molding identity in schools: Student narratives on race, gender and academic engagement.* New York: SUNY Press.

Du Bois, W. E. B. (2001). *The education of Black people: Ten critiques, 1906–1960.* New York: Monthly Review Press.

Finders, M., & Tatum, A.W. (2005). Hybridization of literacy practices: A review of *What they don't learn in schools: Literacy in the lives of urban youth. Reading Research Quarterly, 40*(3), 388–397.

Freebody, P. (2003). *Qualitative research in education: Interaction and practice.* Thousand Oaks, CA: Sage.

Garcia, E. (2002). *Student cultural diversity: Understanding and meeting the challenge.* Boston: Houghton Mifflin.

Gay, G. (2000). *Culturally responsive teaching: Theory, research, & practice.* New York: Teachers College Press.

Gee, J. (1991). *Social linguistics and literacies: Ideology in discourses.* London: The Falmer Press.

Gregory, D. (1995) *Nigger: An autobiography.* New York: Mass Market Paperback.

Hamilton, V. (1992). *Cousins.* New York: Scholastic.

Hull, G., & Schultz, K. (2002). *School's out: Bridging out-of-school literacies with classroom practice.* New York: Teachers College Press.

Johnson, A. (1993). *Toning the sweep.* New York: Scholastic.

Ladson-Billings, G. (1991). Returning to the source: Implications for educating teachers of Black students. In M. Foster (Ed.), *Readings in equal education: Qualitative investigations into schools and schooling* (Vol. 11; pp. 227–243). New York: AMS Press.

Lipman, P. (1995). "Bringing out the best in them": The contribution of culturally relevant teachers in educational reform. *Theory Into Practice, 34,* 202–208.

Mahiri, J. (2004). *What they don't learn in school: Literacy in the lives of urban youth.* New York: Peter Lang.

Moje, E., Young, J., Readence, J., & Moore, D. (2000). Reinventing adolescent literacy for new times: Perennial and millennial issues. *Journal of Adolescent & Adult Literacy, 43,* 400–410.

Myers, W. D. (1996). *Slam.* New York: Scholastic.

Ogbu, J. (1998). Voluntary and involuntary minorities: A cultural–ecological theory of school performance with some implications for education. *Anthropology and Education Quarterly, 29,* 155–188.

Pressley, M. (1998). *Reading instruction that works: The case for balanced teaching.* New York: Guilford.

Rymes, B. (2001). *Conversational borderlands: Language and identity in an alternative urban high school.* New York: Teachers College Press.

Schoenbach, R., Greenleaf, C., Cziko, C., & Hurwitz, C. (1999). *Reading for understanding: A guide to improving reading in middle and high school classrooms—The reading apprenticeship guidebook.* San Francisco: Jossey-Bass.

Tatum, A. W. (2000). Breaking down barriers that disenfranchise African American adolescent readers. *Journal of Adolescent & Adult Literacy, 44*(1), 52–64.

Tatum, A. W. (2003a). All degreed up and no where to go: Black male literacy education and beyond. *Journal of Adolescent & Adult Literacy, 46*(8), 620–623.

Tatum, A. W. (2003b). *Advancing the literacies of African American adolescents: A case study of professional development.* Unpublished doctoral dissertation. University of Illinois-Chicago.

Tatum, A. W. (2005). *Teaching reading to black adolescent males: Closing the achievement gap.* Portland, ME: Stenhouse.

Upchurch, C. (1996). *Convicted in the womb: One man's journey from prisoner to peacemaker.* New York: Bantam Books.

Woodson, J. (1994). *I hadn't meant to tell you this.* New York: Laurel Leaf.

Wright, R. (1994). *Rites of passage.* New York: HarperTrophy.

II

Positioning Youth as Readers and Writers

CHAPTER 5

Adolescent Identities as Demanded by Science Classroom Discourse   85
Communities
Elizabeth Birr Moje and Deborah R. Dillon

CHAPTER 6

Utilizing Student's Cultural Capital in the Teaching and Learning Process: 107
"As If" Learning Communities and African American Students'
Literate Currency
Jennifer E. Obidah and Tyson E. J. Marsh

CHAPTER 7

Adolescent Agency and Literacy   129
David W. Moore and James W. Cunningham

CHAPTER 8

Fallen Angels: Finding Adolescents and Adolescent Literacy   147
in a Renewed Project of Democratic Citizenship
Helen J. Harper and Thomas W. Bean

Introduction to Part II: Positioning Youth as Readers and Writers

David W. Moore
Arizona State University

When community members participate with one another, they jointly produce story lines that position, or situate, themselves in particular ways (Davies & Harré, 1990). This section examines how youth are positioned as readers and writers in school. The chapters in this section point to the processes involved in youth seeing themselves in such ways as high achievers, questioners, and disappointments relative to academic literacy. The authors show such positioning occurring while youth participate in the particular discursive practices of their academic subjects enacted by their particular teachers, classmates, and themselves.

The first three chapters shed light on positioning processes as youth engage in science, persuasive writing, and poetry. These chapters portray a range of literate actions as youth express transformative insights about personal issues, inappropriately apply strategies to novel situations, and take up only the minimal proficiencies needed to pass a course. The closing chapter of this section advocates specific literacy positions for a renewed project of democratic citizenship, a form of social and political participation that extends far beyond classrooms.

The authors come to the contents of their chapters by different routes. Elizabeth Birr Moje and Deborah Dillon revisit their chapter from the first edition of this text, along with their supporting data, to forge new ideas about literacy and learning in content area classrooms. Moje and Dillon now focus on the interplay among the identities students bring to classrooms and the identities sanctioned by those classrooms. For instance, they examine the contrasting positions of a youth who enters a science class as a self-directed, inquiring problem-solver and encounters a teacher who endorses scientific organization, precision, and accuracy.

83

From the perspectives of literate currency and cultural capital, Jennifer Obidah and Tyson Marsh tell of African American youth participating in a learning community that intentionally positions each learner as if he or she were someone important. Obidah and Marsh showcase youth writing and responding to issues such as racism, education, violence, beauty, peer pressure, and self-mutilation. Participating in this learning community's positioning and tackling such compelling issues serve to reinforce and revitalize youths' identities not only as free but transformative.

David Moore and James Cunningham streamline and update their chapter from the first edition of this text to account for the role of agency in adolescents' literacies. They echo Tennyson's question: Do we move ourselves, or are we guided by an unseen hand? Keying on individuals' internal dialogues, Moore and Cunningham present youth deciding personal positions relative to their literacies in the midst of complex mediating contexts.

Helen Harper and Thomas Bean assert that new times require new literacies, that today's youth should approach print as overtly political readers and writers. Harper and Bean consider critical literate positions essential for renewing democratic life. They urge secondary-school educators and students to adopt a position of radical pluralism, one that analyzes and embraces social diversity as a framework for achieving freedom and equity.

Taken together, the chapters in this section suggest possible positionings of youth as readers and writers. These four chapters shed new light on the classroom conditions youth encounter and the decisions they make relative to the literacies in their lives.

REFERENCE

Davies, B., & Harré, R. (1990). Positioning: The discursive production of selves. *Journal for the Theory of Social Thought, 20,*(1), 43–63.

5

Adolescent Identities as Demanded by Science Classroom Discourse Communities

Elizabeth Birr Moje
University of Michigan

Deborah R. Dillon
University of Minnesota

Our purpose in this revision of our 1998 contribution to *Reconceptualizing the Literacies in Adolescents' Lives* is to examine adolescent identities in light of new research and theory generated in just the few years since we wrote the 1998 chapter. In particular, we are now interested in examining how content areas represent an environment, or context, that demands that students enact particular identities to make the most of opportunities to learn offered in the curriculum. Although we maintain that it is important that teachers understand the subjectivities young people bring to the classroom, it is equally important that teachers understand how any disciplinary subject area classroom—which constitutes a discourse community where people speak, read, and write in particular ways—demands that students think and act in certain ways to be successful (Lee, 2001). It is also important to understand how the space and relationships of the classroom itself—whether a science, social studies, mathematics, or English classroom—shape the identities that young people enact, particularly as different teachers demand or encourage different kinds of disciplinary and classroom (or student) identities. This chapter examines the interplay of the identities students bring to content-area classrooms and the identities demanded by content-area classrooms.

Our earlier version of this chapter focused on the subjectivities and identities of two young female science learners and examined the role of subjectivity and identity in content-area literacy and opportunity to learn (Dillon & Moje, 1998). In so doing, we examined the role of subjectivity and identity in content-area learning and opportunity to learn, focusing mainly on how the young women saw themselves and how their teachers, in turn, saw them. In our treatment of the young women's subjectivities and identities, however, we failed to examine how the classroom spaces, the relationships available within, and the developmental and historical time periods in which these young women were living, might have *produced* certain subjectivities and identity enactments in these young women. In addition, we did not examine how the spaces, relationships, and times enabled the teachers only to *recognize* certain kinds of identities in the young women's practices.

In this chapter, we take up where that earlier chapter left off, using our theory, research, and practice over the last 6 years to forge new ground and offer additional suggestions for how content-area teachers might promote the literacy learning of students from many different backgrounds. Specifically, we use the data from the 1998 chapter, as well as some new data in a few instances, to argue that to enhance student content-area learning and content literacy learning, in particular, more is needed than merely understanding who students are as acting subjects. We must also understand how academic disciplinary identities intersect with and contradict the identities youth enact in their everyday lives. Thus, we reexamine Carolyn and Heather—the young women featured in our earlier chapter—in light of the identities/subjectivities demanded by the classroom environment of a science content area. In the final section of the chapter, we discuss implications of this analysis for adolescent and secondary school literacy practice, research, and policy.

BACKGROUND ON THE 1998 CHAPTER

Our 1998 chapter drew from our research with students in two different classroom science contexts: a high school biology and a high school chemistry classroom.

The Biology Class

The biology class was designed for academic-track students at Jefferson High School, a large, comprehensive urban school in a midwestern state in the United States. The school enrolled approximately 2,200 students. The student population was primarily White and included individuals from families representing a range of socioeconomic levels and backgrounds (population is about 4% African American and Hispanic students, and about 29% of the students are from poor families). The community where the school was situated had a population of about 50,000 and was economically stable because of a diversity of small- to medium-sized manufacturing plants. The community also included a considerable number of white-collar jobs associated with various service professions and businesses. The 19 students in the observed class were 14 freshmen, 4 sophomores, and 1 junior; 10 students were male and 9 were female. Most of the students were from working-class families and were labeled as academic-track students. These adolescents were involved in sports, cheerleading, band, choir, and drama and they worked outside school.

The classroom teacher was Mr. Ruhl, a middle-class White man, who was 34 years old at the time of the study and had taught for more than 10 years. Ruhl had a BS in biology and taught basic and academic-track biology and genetics courses. He was viewed as professional in appearance and manner, yet he was known by students and faculty as a friendly, energetic, caring teacher who loved to joke with students. Ruhl also was known for his love of the subject matter of biology and his passion for and creativity in teaching real-life concepts associated with the curriculum. Ruhl's overall goal was for students to successfully learn important biology concepts by actively engaging in learning while receiving support from a caring teacher. Ruhl had been recognized for excellence in teaching by winning a community-sponsored Golden Apple Teaching Award and a Presidential National Science Foundation Teaching Award.

The Chemistry Class

The chemistry class was a college preparatory course taken by sophomores and juniors at Taft High School, which was located in the same midsize town as Jefferson High School, but in a more rural section of the town. The town's major employers included small industry, agricultural settings, and a university. The school population—both students and faculty—was composed primarily of European Americans from working- and middle-class backgrounds. The class represented was composed of 22 students—8 female and 14 male—most of whom had previously taken either general science or biology. At the time of this study, the chemistry teacher, Ms. Landy, was a 20-year veteran, in her sixth full year of teaching at Taft High School. Like her students, Landy was European American and had been reared in a working-middle-class background.

Landy's primary areas of responsibility and interest were chemistry, mathematics, and science research. Landy was passionate about chemistry and about science in general. She performed this passion for the discipline in her manner, her voice, and her dress (e. g., donning a white lab coat during lab activities). Moreover, Landy said that she cared deeply about students, and Moje observed evidence of her caring throughout the 2½ years of working with her. Landy worked hard to involve students in the activities in her classroom, and she spoke of her special commitment to making sure that girls and boys knew that girls could do science. To that end, she regularly called on both male and female students, asking them to read from the text, respond to questions, and work problems she posed.

We focused on the two particular young women—Carolyn and Heather—because our in-depth case studies from the larger classroom analyses supported the claim that they were achieving readers and learners. However, their achievements were not always visible to the teachers.

In particular, our earlier chapter illustrated that although the two science teachers featured were caring, exemplary teachers who were highly respected by their students, they missed opportunities to engage Carolyn and Heather in deep science and literacy learning. Using classroom observation and individual interviews, we illustrated how the identities these girls enacted in the classroom both constrained and enabled the teachers' views of them and, thus, opportunities to learn science and scientific literacy at deep levels. We concluded that teachers could learn a great deal by listening more closely to their students, by examining their own assumptions about who students are and what science and literacy learning entails, and how their curricula make possible particular kinds of learning while constraining and even prohibiting other kinds. At the end of the chapter, we posed a list of questions to guide teachers' planning, decision making, and assessment of their own instruction and of students' learning (see Fig. 5.1). Although these questions are still compelling and relevant to the development of deep content-area literacy instruction, our research in the intervening years has led us to reexamine the data and to pose new questions about the relationship between adolescents' identities and those identities demanded by content-area instruction.

- How can I listen to adolescents more carefully and critically? Specifically, what tools might we use as teachers (such as talking with peers, viewing transcripts and videotapes of lessons, engaging in action research on discursive practice) to better see, hear, and understand adolescents' lived experiences?
- How might my allegiance to the routines of a particular pedagogical approach limit my ability to see or hear what my students are doing and saying?
- How might my curriculum exclude the interests of and questions posed by various students?
- How can I help students seize a voice and claim a position?
- How do I negotiate the fine distinction between valuing what adolescent students have to say and moving them toward challenging, disrupting, and reconstructing their experiences and discourses?

FIG. 5.1.   Questions to guide teacher thinking about student subjectivities (Dillon & Moje, 1998, pp. 221–222).

NEW STANCES ON IDENTITIES IN THE CLASSROOM

When we refer to *subjectivities* and *subject positions*, we mean that people, whether adolescent or adult, are not objects. We use the phrase *occupying subject positions* to evoke the sense that these positions are temporary, fluid, and context dependent. In addition, the word *position* keeps us focused on how people position themselves or are positioned by others as a result of asymmetrical power relationships. Much of this positioning occurs in and through *discourse,* which Gee (1996) defined as "any stretch of language (spoken, written, signed) which 'hangs together' to make sense to some community of people who use that language" (p. 103). Positioning also occurs as people use literacy in certain ways (Street, 1994).

IDENTITIES AS ENACTED

People—regardless of age—are acting subjects, or defined selves, who engage in many different practices, depending on the spaces, times, and relationships in which they find themselves (Moje, 2004). People also act on what they believe others expect of them, based on the messages they get from others and from society at large. Thus, it can be argued that they *enact* identities that draw from their senses of self in spaces, times, and relationships (Moje, 2004) and from the ways that their identity enactments are recognized (Gee, 2000/2001).

As we have studied adolescents, it is clear that they occupy many different subject positions, and in fact, because of their age and dependence on parents and family, adolescents are often engaged in attempts to construct a position for themselves in the world. Just as adults' subjectivities are structured by broader social discourses, much of adolescent subjectivity is structured by discourse as well, and adolescents are positioned by others, even as they attempt to position themselves. Their attempts to position themselves by enacting particular identities also are shaped by discourse and structural constraints, although they do have room to make some decisions among various discourses. In other words, adolescents may make choices about whether to enact "good" student or "resistant" student identities within a set of discourses about what it means to be a student and what the consequences of resistance include (see Moore & Cunningham, chap. 7, this volume). Moreover, adolescents are, in many cases, positioned, or recognized, as powerless in relationships, although they often seize power through acts of resistance, especially in school settings. Unfortunately these acts of resistance often serve to reproduce the very structures that oppress them (Willis, 1977). As adolescents explore different subject positions, and as they are positioned by others around them—whether parents, peers, or teachers—they enact various identities.

Classroom discourses about what it means to "do" school—to think like a student—are particularly strong for adolescents as they position themselves by enacting certain kinds of identities. Students who rarely participate verbally in class can be variously recognized as shy, uninterested, or slow. Students who do participate, but participate by yelling out responses or by dominating conversations, can be recognized as troublesome. Thus, through various discourses constructed over many years in school (Rogers's "histories of participation," 2002, p. 267), students learn how to participate in different classroom and school activities.

These recognitions and their subsequent positionings, translated into classroom identities, are not, however, uniform or static. A young woman who enacts one identity in chemistry class may enact a different identity in art class, depending on the relationships available in the different contexts, on arrangements of space, on access to material and human resources in the different spaces, and on what she has come to understand about how to do the different content areas over her history of participating in such content-area learning throughout her schooling.

In addition, for many adolescents the shift to middle, junior, or senior high schools represents their first formal exposure to disciplinary discourses, that is, discourses about what it means to think, act, and talk like a scientist, mathematician, or writer (Gee, 1996; Hicks, 1995/1996; Lemke, 1990; Michaels & O'Connor, 1990). These discourses represent a new world for many students; through their classroom conversations, uses of oral and written texts, and experiences, adolescents are enculturated into membership in different disciplinary communities at the same time that they learn content concepts. It is valuable to explore how the different subject positions that adolescents take up or are assigned influence their literacy and learning practices and allow or deny them access to different social and academic discourses and experiences. In doing so, however, one must also acknowledge the spaces and relationships that mediate the identities youth enact in these different subject positions. Although we implied a fair amount about the spaces and relationships within science classrooms in our earlier version of this chapter, we did not explicitly attend to the identities that are required for learning in those classroom spaces.

LEARNING AS SHIFTS IN IDENTITY ACROSS DISCOURSE COMMUNITIES

A number of scholars have argued that learning anything requires shifts in identity (Gee, 2001; Lave, 1996). In addition, a number of scholars have argued that shifts in identity often occur when people are pushed across—or choose to cross—cultural or discursive communities (Guerra, 1998; Pratt, 1991). Thus, it could be argued that secondary schools and classrooms represent spaces in which young people are asked to make rather weighty identity shifts as a part of their learning. It has been argued that the academic disciplines operate as cultural and discursive communities, with particular ways of knowing, doing, believing, reading, and writing privileged above other ways (Gee, 1996; Lee, 2001; Lemke, 1990; Moje, Ciechanowski, et al., 2004). Learning in the disciplines can thus be considered learning to shift ways of knowing, doing, believing, reading, and writing—a type of identity shifting that young people are asked to do not just from out of school to in school, but also across the many class periods of a typical school day.

To complicate things, disciplinary learning is not just about the ways of knowing and communicating in the discipline, but also about any given teacher's or peer group's ways of knowing and communicating. For example, although we focus on science classrooms in this chapter, we illustrate two different representations of science as a discipline or profession because these representations are not only of the discipline and profession, but also of classrooms, which are structured by the particular teachers and students who inhabit them and by the discourses of control and evaluation that surround them. In other words, it cannot be said that secondary school classrooms replicate with exactness some set of agreed-on disciplinary or professional conventions of a given content area. Each classroom, via its participants' unique takes on science and on each other, constructs a particular version of scientific discourse norms and practices.

With the recent attention to the identity and discourse shifts required in the disciplines, disciplinary curriculum interventions have promoted strategies for explicitly teaching students the communicative norms and practices of the disciplines while also building on the norms and practices youth bring from their everyday lives (Goldman, 1997; Hudicourt-Barnes, 2003; Lee, 2001; Moje, Peek-Brown, et al., 2004). How deeply these different curriculum interventions look into the multiple and complex identities both enacted by students and demanded by their curricular practices remains an unanswered question, one particularly relevant for adolescent literacy theory because it is often through literate and other communicative practices (e.g., oral and visual representations) that disciplinary identities are displayed and reproduced. Thus, it is important to examine the *interplay* among adolescents' identities enacted as they occupy the various subject positions demanded for learning by different classroom content areas.

ADOLESCENTS' IDENTITIES AND CONTENT-AREA IDENTITIES: A REEXAMINATION

With this logic as a guide, we reexamine Carolyn and Heather—the young women featured in our earlier chapter—in light of the identities/subjectivities offered by their particular science classrooms. We use the following three questions:

1. How are the subjectivities these young women bring to the classroom like or distinct from those of science as a profession, a discipline, or a classroom curricular activity?
2. How are their identities recognized by teachers and other students?
3. How do these identities make possible or constrain the learning of science in the classroom?

To address the first question of how the subjectivities and identities of these young women were both similar to and distinct from the subjectivities and identities demanded in content learning, we thought it would be helpful to review first our analysis of the two young women's subjectivities from the 1998 chapter.

CAROLYN'S SUBJECTIVITIES AND IDENTITIES ENACTED: 1998

Dillon summarized the multiple subject positions and identities Carolyn enacted using the following categories: (a) Independent Young Woman: Good Daughter; (b) Happy-Go-Lucky Student/Involved Group Member; Compliant Group Member; Uninvolved Group Member; (c) Serious Future Veterinarian/Average Biology Student. To provide a more detailed portrait, we include here a lengthy portion of the 1998 chapter in which Deborah analyzed Carolyn's subjectivities as enacted in the biology classroom:

> Carolyn was an attractive, vivacious 14-year-old, who seemed like she was in the most popular group in her freshman class. Carolyn was blonde with medium-length curly hair, which she played with or flipped around as she talked. She was always neatly dressed in clothes considered fashionable, and she usually had a playful smile on her face. Throughout my interactions with Carolyn, I observed her taking up several different subject positions. For example, I learned about her family life and how she positioned herself as daughter. My observations of Carolyn during biology class helped me to see how she positioned herself as a newcomer to high school, as a young woman, and as a student. Carolyn appeared to have a good time in biology, and her giggles could be heard daily across the room. She expressed a genuine interest in learning and doing well in biology; participated actively in small group but not whole-class lessons; and often exhibited a sense of loneliness and a need to interact with others to learn, have fun, and feel a part of the class. These subject positions were meshed together into a complex composite portrait of Carolyn—full of contradictions. Carolyn was at times the independent daughter, seemingly self-assured and knowledgeable about her future plans. The next moment she was a giddy freshman, excited by the possibilities high school held for her socially, yet scared, wondering if she would be accepted and find her place in this large school setting. As a student she expressed a desire to learn the content, but her actions indicated that having fun in class was her primary goal. Carolyn's desire to be accepted socially and academically presented a challenge for her as a young woman. In the following sections, we see Carolyn as an independent, young woman who lived through the divorce of her parents. In contrast, we see her life in school where she asserted herself one moment, was silenced the next, manipulated a situation to garner attention, and then capitulated after encountering conflict. (Dillon & Moje, 1998, pp. 197–198)

HEATHER'S SUBJECTIVITIES AND IDENTITIES ENACTED: 1998

In 1998, Moje's analysis of Heather's subjectivities, as enacted in and out of the chemistry classroom, showed contradictions similar to those of Carolyn's. Moje wrote:

> Throughout my relationship with Heather, I observed her taking up, integrating, and casting aside many different subject positions. For example, Heather seemed to simultaneously occupy the positions of a young woman, an outsider to life in high school, a student, and a thinker. Perhaps because I studied her foremost as a student, I can delineate more easily multiple positions within her student subjectivities, including that of chemistry student, English student, successful or "super smart student," struggling student, expressive student, questioning student, resistant student, and complacent student. These subject positions were never occupied singly or uniformly: Even though she expressed both resistance and complacency and saw herself as successful as a chemistry student although struggling as an English student, Heather did not shed one subjectivity as she occupied another subject space. Instead, for example, she often displayed both resistant and complacent student subjectivities in the same activity. (Dillon & Moje, 1998, p. 210)

Drawing from her interviews and observations, Moje summarized the multiple subject positions and identities Heather enacted according to the following categories: (a) Young Woman and Outsider: Alienation and Resistance (b) Student: Struggling/Successful; Resistant/Complacent, (c) Thinker and Questioner.

This in-depth view of just some of the subject positions Heather and Carolyn occupied in a given day or week elucidated for us the complexity of examining and understanding the identities students enact in classrooms. We used these in-depth examinations not only to bring the voices and experiences of these young women to the fore, but also to raise questions for teachers about how their students' experiences might shape their science teaching. But our findings about the complexity of Carolyn's and Heather's identities often left unexamined the contexts in which they were enacting those identities.

IDENTITIES/SUBJECTIVITIES ENACTED AND DEMANDED

Drawing from conceptions of identity as enacted and learning as shifts in identities, we now turn to the question of what identities were enacted in and demanded by the science discourse community of the particular classrooms these young women experienced. (For ease and clarity of presentation, we each write in the first person in the following sections, with Dillon writing about Carolyn, Mr. Ruhl, and the biology classroom and Moje writing about Heather, Ms. Landy, and the chemistry classroom.)

Ruhl's Classroom

In Ruhl's classroom, the epistemology that Ruhl articulated was "science as struggling to understand core pillars of knowledge" (Dillon, O'Brien, Moje, & Stewart, 1994). The primary mode of instruction was small-group work where students completed study guides or engaged in labs. Classroom routines included a few whole-class minilessons and lectures by Ruhl, small-group work, and lab work completed by pairs of students. The predominant mode of learning was group work, and most days when students entered class they were directed to immediately work with four to five peers unless a new unit was introduced or Ruhl felt the need to make a special presentation on a particularly difficult concept. Cooperative learning groups used study guides designed by Ruhl; these guides helped students work through biology concepts deemed important by Ruhl. In examining the study guides, I found that Ruhl lifted key concepts from the text and arranged ideas in ways where questions were posed and students needed to skim the text to find answers. Group work was designed to ensure that students worked as a team to use pieces of information from various sources to construct answers or engage in lab work to learn about concepts and then address questions on the guide sheet. There was a system to completing the study guides: One worked at a steady pace and completed the guides in class or on one's own at home. Ruhl also employed mastery learning, offering students multiple options to test their biology knowledge on various forms of end-of-unit tests (Dillon, O'Brien, & Volkmann, 2001).

Thus, a combination of mastery learning and cooperative small groups formed the basis for learning—and the participant structures—in the classroom, with

Ruhl's primary goal being the creation of a "positive atmosphere of warmth, openness, and encouragement [because] most of my kids won't grow up to be scientists, but they will be tomorrow's citizens." Ruhl created the study guides and used small-group work because he cared about what students learned and how they learned in his class. He sought ways to ensure successful learning by creating support structures (e.g., the study guide, peers to help each other, and the teacher to intervene when material was particularly difficult). The predominant scientific discourses/identities demanded were those of "working collaboratively to complete tasks," "putting two heads together to solve problems versus working individually," "drawing information from more than one source," and "doing lab work that is hands-on like the work that scientists engage in."

Landy's Classroom

Landy's epistemological stance toward class science was "science as organization" (Dillon et al., 1994). Therefore, the scientific discourses/identities demanded were those of "organized," "precise," "careful" student/thinker/scientist. The chemistry classroom interaction patterns and participant structures generally followed an initiation–response–evaluation/follow-up (I–R–E/F) format (Lemke, 1990) conducted in whole-group settings. At times, Landy would introduce a concept with a short lecture, but more often, she directed students to read a section from their textbooks. These readings often served as introductions to a concept. Approximately once or twice a month, depending on the length of a particular unit, Landy would ask students to participate in a laboratory activity. Landy clearly pointed out to students that they were not conducting experiments, because they were not discovering or researching new ideas; rather, they were using the activities to help them understand how scientists had come to make certain claims. In that sense, then, there was no pretense that students were doing science; the identities demanded in the classroom were those of *science students*, individuals who, according to Landy, needed to learn organizational skills (Moje, 1996).

Although students were not discouraged from asking questions (and, in fact, many did), they were not encouraged. Instead, they were routinely positioned via classroom practices of problem demonstration, IRE/F recitations, and seat work as demonstrators of knowledge learned through lecture or reading, with Landy and/or the textbook positioned as source of knowledge and Landy as evaluator of knowledge demonstrated (Moje, 1997). This positioning as demonstrators of knowledge, woven together with the spatial and relational arrangements in the class and with Heather's own adolescent development and histories of participation, figured strongly in how Heather enacted her identities in the chemistry classroom.

IDENTITIES RECOGNIZED

Ruhl's Biology Classroom

Carolyn believed that she didn't do well in her previous biology class because the teacher's style didn't match her needs: The class was predominately a lecture course with multiple choice tests. She needed a teacher who allowed her to work with others, to learn content in multiple ways other than only lectures, note taking, and tests. And she wanted to do well in biology because she knew that this content was important to her future goal of becoming a veterinarian. However, her goals for learning (e.g., having fun while learning with others) often did not match the science identity that was expected in Ruhl's classroom space/environment. Specifically, her goals didn't always match the learning routines of small group members that Carolyn found herself working with, or the focused, active learning behaviors Mr. Ruhl expected to see when he observed whole-class or small-group interactions.

Discourses Deemed Important in Ruhl's Biology Classroom. During whole class lessons, Mr. Ruhl took students' questions as a sign of their interest in and seriousness about learning in biology. Carolyn rarely asked a question or participated in interactions between students or Mr. Ruhl. She listened during lectures but rarely took notes. She also rarely asked Mr. Ruhl a question after class or in small-group sessions. The following whole-classroom session and informal moments after class provide an example of Carolyn's lack of participation:

> Joe talked with the students about a film on mollusks that they would be viewing. He introduced the concept and then opened the floor to questions.

> **Kerry:** Do clams change shells?
> **Ruhl:**   Let's think about that. Can anybody tell me why they do or don't?
> **Tim:**   They're [the clam] attached to the shell.
> **Kerry:** So the shell grows with it [the clam]?
> **Ruhl:**   Yes [He held up a shell and demonstrated with his hands how the rings add on as the clam grows.]
> **Mike:**   They get wavy when they get bigger.

> The class then breaks into small groups to work on the starfish lab. After the lab and before class ends, Kerry approaches Mr. Ruhl.

> **Kerry:** I'm interested in science—I want to go into science.
> **Ruhl:**   Good! You want to take as much math and English as possible then. [Observer Comment: Ruhl believed that writing skills and math were important skills for scientists along with content knowledge.]
> **Joey:**   I am going into science, too.

An examination of this classroom excerpt indicates that Carolyn did not interact with Ruhl or her peers during whole-class discussions; a review of other whole-class sessions indicates a similar pattern of lack of involvement. Unlike Kerry and other peers who asked or answered questions during the lecture—actions valued in Ruhl's science classroom—Carolyn was silent. Carolyn was not observed talking with Ruhl about her desire to do well in biology and her interest in a career linked to science. Thus, identity enactments did not position her to be recognized as a serious, interested biology student.

Relationships and Classroom Spaces That Shape Identity Enactments. When Carolyn worked with Tim and Mike in a starfish lab, linked with the whole-class discussion previously presented, Carolyn took on (and was later assigned by Mike) the position of reading sections from the book and study guide, while the boys in the group performed the dissection. Tim assumed the role of dissecting the starfish and

Mike gave him directions on what to do. The two young men engaged in the talk and actions that linked them to being like scientists, but Carolyn did not.

Mike: (to Carolyn) You read it [lab guide/study guide] and tell us what to do. (He picked up the starfish and shoved it toward Carolyn's face).

Carolyn: Get it away from me please.

Mike: Okay. Afraid of it?

Carolyn: No, I just don't want it in my face.

Mike: (grabbing the scissors) Those are mine. I'm going to dissect. (He shouts to Tim who is walking away to work with another group) Tim—stay here. You want to be in our group?

Tim: As long as I get to do some cuttin.'

Mike: You can cut in our [group]. (He turns over the role of dissecting to Tim and he assumes the role of reading the directions from the lab guide/study guide.) Okay, I've got to read page 409 to 411 (from the textbook) carefully. (He clears his throat and begins to read aloud from the book.)

Carolyn: Are those things (pointing to the starfish) crammed? (She laughs at her own comment. Mike continues reading. A few moments later Ruhl walks by.)

Carolyn: I just happen to be one of the lucky ones to be paired up with Mike.

Tim: Doctor Mike. Dr. G?

Mike: Okay, read that thing. "As you work, picture starfishes ...." page 410—I've got it right here. "Use figure one below" [as you dissect]. I hope I don't have to cut this time because I cut that whole worm open last time.

Carolyn: Wait—did you read both of these pages?

Mike: Yeah. What?

Tim: Wait a minute (realizing that he might cut something before knowing what to cut). We've got to try to locate the following structures.

Mike: We've got to cut it open, we can't see in it.

Tim: Well alright then.

Mike: Alright dude, cut it open (he hands the scissors to Tim. Mr. Ruhl walks by at this moment and engages Tim and Mike in a conversation.)

Ruhl: Why is echinoderm a good name for this phylum?

Tim: (quickly responds) Because echino means spiny things.

Ruhl: Right.

An analysis of the interactions in the lab demonstrate that Carolyn is positioned as having a role of observer, not active contributor. She is not included in the interactions of "doctor" or scientist that Mike and Tim assign to each other. When she does try to intervene to ensure that a mistake is not made in the dissection before first reading about what needs to be cut, she appears to be dismissed. From Mr. Ruhl's standpoint, Carolyn did not seem to be involved in the dissection lab and from her peers' perspectives she was viewed as "scared," and potentially disinterested, passive, and dispensable.

However, Carolyn did try to be involved in labs and viewed many tasks as important to her long-term goal of working in a science-related field. She would often state, "I'll do the dissecting—I have to learn to do this because I am going to be a vet" to peers when she worked with them on various activities. As time went on in the semester, I saw Carolyn work with peers who allowed her to enact different identities. For example, in a grasshopper dissection lab, Carolyn selected group mates and made it clear from the outset that she would be doing the dissection. The first task of the group was to find the simple eye of the grasshopper but the students had trouble finding it in their grasshopper. Mr. Ruhl stopped by to help the group.

Joey T.:	I don't think I want to go into biology [based on the dissection lab].
Carolyn:	I have no choice (laughs).
Ruhl:	Are you trying to see the simple eye?
Joey:	Yeah, we're trying to take it out.
Carolyn:	Owww.
Ruhl:	The compound eye is pretty easy, isn't it? Let me get you a dissecting scope so they can see the simple eye.
Carolyn:	Let's dissect (she has decided to do the dissecting.)
Ruhl:	(watching Carolyn begin) Well, you're going to want to systematically dissect away certain parts.
Joey:	Do we cut off the head to do this?
Ruhl:	Yes, that might make it a little easier. (He moves away from the group for a moment.)
Carolyn:	Cut off the head? I take these, right? [referring to scissors to cut].
Joey T.:	No, use a razor blade.
Carolyn:	The razor blade makes my hand closer to it [the grasshopper] and my fingernails [might touch it] (she laughs).
Ruhl:	You might try using this. (Ruhl comes back with the dissecting scope and hears the last part of her statement.)

In this excerpt, Carolyn indicated that she wanted to do the dissection because she needed this experience to prepare her for her chosen vocation. She quickly situated herself with the grasshopper and the scissors so she could dissect. Her peers supported this action. She also started dissecting—without knowing exactly where to begin. This appeared to be her way of making sure that the dissecting task was not taken away from her because often she was positioned as an observer in other groups. However, her comment about needing the experience of dissecting was not heard by Mr. Ruhl. Furthermore, what Ruhl did observe was a rush to cut instead of a careful analysis of the task and the use of appropriate dissecting practices. Thus, Carolyn—in her haste to assume the role of dissector—was not recognized by Ruhl as a serious biology student. Instead, Ruhl observed an impetuous young lady who was afraid of her nails touching a grasshopper.

Overall, the three excepts reveal how Carolyn's identity enactments were produced. Particular spaces, interactions, and relationships in the biology class (whole- or small-group sessions or one small group over another group) produced an engaged versus a less engaged Carolyn. These excerpts also reveal how particular moments that teachers observe and the discourses they overhear can shape their perspectives of learners and thus the identities that students are allowed to enact in classrooms.

Landy's Chemistry Classroom

In many ways, Landy's classroom, where students were positioned as "demonstrators" of knowledge, was both a perfect place for Heather to "hide out" and a problematic space given her subjectivities of struggling and successful student and thinker and questioner. As explained in the 1998 chapter, Heather had suffered a close-head trauma in her eighth-grade year in school. She had missed a fair amount of school and had slipped, in her estimation, from one of the "super smart students" to someone who had trouble remembering information on a short-term basis. This excerpt from the 1998 chapter summarizes Moje's analysis of Heather's subjectivity:

> In addition to seeing herself as an outsider to high school life and as a resistant student, Heather constructed a number of student subjectivities in relation to the disciplines she studied. Heather saw herself variously as a successful student and a struggling student. She believed that prior to her junior year she had been "super smart," not "in terms of grades, but maybe in terms of ability." Although Heather's doctors had pronounced her fully recovered, she said that they "couldn't have tested everything," because she did not feel like her memory was what it used to be. Thus, Heather's accident and its aftermath represent another aspect of Heather's construction of subjectivity, in this case her student subjectivity. Before her accident, Heather felt confident about her memory and her learning abilities; after her accident, Heather said that she had trouble remembering things and concentrating. Although chemistry and trigonometry seemed easy to her, she said that she had to pay more attention in her classes, although I observed her talking and writing notes during chemistry. When asked to explain what made chemistry class easy, she replied, "I don't know, everything works out perfectly. Like the periodic table, it's all set up. It's so perfect …. It all seems really logical, I don't know. Heather repeated this theme of logical perfection in chemistry throughout our discussions. In fact, at one point Heather said that "Chemistry has just like one interpretation. That's all like what it says in black and white. That's the only meaning." Heather was not enrolled in honors chemistry (or any other honors course) in high school, even though she had taken 2 years of algebra, one of the main requirements for honors chemistry. In fact, after the first semester, Landy encouraged one female student to move to the honors class, but she did not approach Heather about switching, despite Heather's excellent performance on homework and examinations. Heather seemed unconcerned, despite her self-identification as a "super smart" kid in middle school. Heather's talk about her accident, however, reflected a discomfort—one she never acknowledged consciously—with her changed student status. (Dillon & Moje, 1998, pp. 212–213)

Having to demonstrate understanding with precision could have been a daunting task for Heather, and yet, her love of chemistry as "perfect" because "everything works out," enabled her to perform with great success (Heather always earned a grade of A in the class). Oddly, however, Heather did not openly enact a "demonstrator" identity in the class. Instead, she enacted a quiet, complacent, sometimes apathetic identity, writing notes during lessons and answering only when called on. Why? An analysis of Heather's identity enactments in light of the particular classroom space, her relationships with Landy and the other students, and the particular developmental period of her life helps to shed light on this question.

Space, Structures, Literacy Practices.   Several aspects of the physical and social space of the classroom—and the participant and literate structures employed within—mitigated against Heather enacting an active and enthusiastic demonstrator of knowledge identity. In fact, the spaces and structures may have *produced* a complacent student identity for Heather. (Note that Moje's 1998 representation suggested the Heather *constructed* a complacent identity. Our current analysis, informed by our developed theorization of the relationship between subjectivity and identity, puts the onus for that construction on the spaces, times, and relationships in which Heather was situated, rather than on Heather as individual acting subject, although we do acknowledge the histories of participation she brought with her.)

For example, the participant structure that Landy favored—whole-class activity, focused either on problem solving or a recitation-based lecture—allowed Heather to remain virtually silent during class. As documented in fieldnotes, Heather only participated vocally when called on, although she was, for the most part, attending to class activity. At times, she wrote notes to her friend who was also in the class, but she remained attentive to the class activity. This structure, then, neither silenced nor evoked her participation, but allowed her to hide, saving her "burning questions" for her own solitary contemplation, where she might not have to risk exposure of her uncertain student subjectivity.

By contrast, as illustrated in the 1998 analysis, on the rare occasion when students were asked to work in small groups (usually to carry out laboratory investigations), Heather often complained that the work was "stupid," perhaps because the more intimate participant structure demanded a different kind of identity from Heather, one less of complacence and more of questioner, interpreter, and active science learner. And yet, also as illustrated in the 1998 chapter, the lab investigations often did not ask much of students except, in Heather's words, "to go through the motions." The participant structure of lab investigations, then, produced a space that demanded more verbal or vocal enactments of Heather, but the content of the lab investigations did not replicate for Heather the identities of active investigation and questioning that seemed to Heather like they should accompany such a structure. The participant structure and content structures were at odds in such activities, producing a resistant identity, as illustrated by Heather's comment in the following exchange among students:

> **Heather:** I'll say again, I think we're just going through the motions.
> **David:** It's better than taking notes.
> **Joseph:** It's to give us variety.
> **Heather:** Personally [she shrugs], I prefer taking notes ....
> [After another brief exchange over terminology, she starts heating the crucible; there's a long silence. Then she turns to Elizabeth.]
> **Heather:** ... I don't like this lab; it's a stupid lab.

Literacy events and practices were similarly focused on organization, precision, and accuracy, rather than on questioning, challenging, or even synthesizing. For example, three dominant literacy practices of the classroom included (a) notetaking on readings and oral lectures, facilitated by the Survey, Question, Read, Recite, Review (SQ3R) strategy; (b) writing summaries of assigned expository text readings; and (c) students taking turns solving demonstration problems at the board while the remainder of the class commented on and copied the problems into their class notes. Each of these strategies, although important to facilitating information transfer, produced a complacent student identity in Heather. Her task as a reader of the chemistry textbook was not to question or wonder as she did when she read other texts at home; her task was to extract and organize information. Of critical importance to understanding how these literacy practices played a role in Heather's identity enactment is Heather's admission that she was grateful to Landy for providing such strategies, which helped her organize and remember information, a critical factor in her struggle to regain the sense of self and identity as "super smart" that she felt she had lost in her accident.

Discourses of the Classroom Space.   Although the content of the lab investigations and the literacy practices may not have meshed with the small-group participant structures Landy occasionally employed, they did fit neatly into the scientific identities demanded by the discourses of this *particular science classroom.* That is, although Landy readily acknowledged that science, as a discipline and profession, was about much more than organization, precision, and accuracy, she chose to emphasize those aspects of scientific work in her classroom because she saw adolescent students as in need of organization (Moje, 1996). Thus, the lab investigations—which took students "through the motions" of doing science by following a series of written steps, but which did not promote active questioning and theorization—fit the identities of demonstrators of knowledge (and processes) demanded in this science classroom. What they called into question, however, was Heather's complacent student identity, particularly when the lab investigations were married with a participant structure that put Heather in the position to talk and raise questions, but did not provide the content for questioning and theorizing that Heather enjoyed in subjective positions outside of school (see the discussion of Heather's out-of-school reading of philosophy, her self-label of "doubting Thomas," and other aspects of Heather's subjectivity as "thinker/questioner" in Dillon & Moje, 1998).

Relationships in the Classroom Space.   Heather's relationship with Landy also may have played a role in her identity enactments in the classroom. Heather spoke regularly about Landy's strengths as a teacher, citing her "confidence," "humor," and "spontaneity." An analysis of Landy's discursive practices (Moje 1997), which were shaped by discourses of science, instruction, and motherhood, further underscores Landy's dominance in the classroom. Informal interviews with all of the students in the classroom indicated a uniform recognition of Landy as a master teacher. Students routinely claimed that she was smart, knowledgeable (for some, "all knowing"), and fun. They claimed to do their work "for her." Landy was clearly a well-liked, but also dominant, presence in the classroom space.

Heather's construction of self as confused, struggling to remember, and doubtful was at odds with Landy's recognized identity as organized, precise, and accurate. It could be argued, then, that Landy and Heather's relationship (note, not Landy alone, but the relationship) was also in part responsible for producing a complacent student identity enactment in Heather. Such a claim is supported by events in the second semester of the school year, during which a student teacher—an individual with less personal and professional cachet in the classroom than Landy enacted—began to teach the class. In the words of another student, Heather became a "question maniac," pestering the student teacher with questions often designed to reveal the student teacher's mistakes, at other times to push the student teacher to what Heather seemed to sense was the edge of her knowledge about the subject. This dramatic shift in Heather's identity enactments reveals the importance of understanding how classroom relationships, both teacher–student and student–student, can produce different kinds of identity enactments.

In sum, Heather's confusion about herself as a former "super smart student" constructed a self-doubting and confused subjectivity that clashed, in some ways, with Landy's strongly confident identity enactments in the classroom. Although Heather looked up to Landy and greatly admired her, she was also hesitant to pose her theoretical and ontological questions about the world ("How do we know there are atoms in a table?") to such a certain and sure individual. What's more, Heather's "doubting Thomas" subjectivity did not represent the kind of science identity that was demanded of the science discourse of organization, precision, and accuracy in that particular classroom space/environment. Although she read philosophy at home for fun, Heather did not read with enthusiasm the texts of her science class, nor did she ask "burning questions" in the class.

HOW IDENTITIES PROMOTED OR CONSTRAINED THE LEARNING OF SCIENCE

Carolyn's Biology Identity and Learning

In many ways, the classroom culture in Mr. Ruhl's class allowed Carolyn to construct multiple subjectivities and enact multiple identities within limits because small-group work was the primary mode of learning and Carolyn could self-select group members. When the option of selecting group members was removed, Carolyn's position was more easily determined by peers. This is particularly evident when comparing the interactions between Carolyn and her peers Mike and Tim as they worked on the starfish lab with her interactions with other peers during the grasshopper lab. Mr. Ruhl did not see Carolyn's abilities as a science student during the starfish lab because Mike and Tim's identities and their scientific discourses (e.g., capable biology students) overshadowed Carolyn's few contributions. In the grasshopper lab, Carolyn assumed a strong identity as a leader and the dissector for the group, but her discourse, actions, and interactions with peers did not indicate a student who was serious about learning. Ruhl's direct observations of Carolyn's dissection of the grasshopper did not provide evidence that Carolyn was a serious biology student. The laughter and banter between students he heard from across the room when he worked with other groups also indicated off-task behavior. Thus, Ruhl often viewed and positioned Carolyn and the peers in the second group as less academically able. Overall, Ruhl's use of teaching techniques or participant structures such as cooperative learning can allow opportunities for students to share ideas that lead to deeper learning, but group relationships and classroom spatial structures within these can also shape the enactment and recognition of identities in dramatic ways.

Heather's Chemistry Identity and Learning

In the chemistry classroom, Heather achieved good grades and, as a result, Landy did not recognize Heather as struggling and in need of her special nurturing. Simultaneously, Heather did not enact an identity as interested in the chemistry class or in performing exceptionally well on homework and tests. As such, however, Landy did not recognize her as having a serious student identity. Consequently, she did not reach out to Heather by encouraging her to take honors courses or the senior science research course as she did to other students who were active "demonstrators" of science knowledge. Instead, in many ways, Heather slipped through the cracks. She was not empowered as a science student because, despite Landy's care for and commitment to students, Landy was not able to make chemistry "burn on" Heather's mind, to encourage the enactment of a questioning science identity in Heather.

In the 1998 chapter, (Dillon & Moje, 1998) we wrote that "the lack of a relational, embodied science experience positioned Heather as successful in the class, but outside of the real work of the discipline. Thus, although Heather was not disempowered by inequitable treatment from Landy, she was disempowered because she could make no personal, embodied connection to the content" (p. 221). Our theorization of identity enactments and demands in content classrooms, however, suggests an even more nuanced explanation for Heather's experience in the chemistry classroom. In short, Heather's daily subjective experiences shifted from confused and lacking in confidence to thinker and questioner. But the classroom discourses of science focused on accuracy, precision, and organization in the demonstration of science knowledge in reading and writing tasks. There was little room for a confused, doubting, or resistant identity to be enacted in the science discourses and literacy practices privileged in the chemistry classroom space. In addition, Heather's sense of Landy as powerful and confident inspired both feelings of support and inadequacy. In the face of such confidence and certainty, Heather was unwilling to perform a doubting or questioning identity. Thus, the discourses of the classroom, the spatial arrangements, the relationships available, and Heather's histories of participation and development produced identity enactments in Heather as complacent, at times even apathetic, about science learning. Heather enacted these complacent identities even as she enjoyed the feeling of power that the logical, organized, chemistry activities gave her, especially over what she saw as a failing memory, compromised by her physical injuries. In many ways, Heather's basic science learning was facilitated by the space, time, and relationships of the classroom, but her more extended, expanded, and advanced learning may have been compromised.

Moreover, Heather's literacy practices in the classroom were shaped by these discourses and her consequent identity enactments. Heather saw uses of literacy in chemistry as ways of summarizing and retaining information for the purpose of demonstrating knowledge and receiving a grade within a complacent and distant student identity enactment. Heather's comment that writing in chemistry was about summarizing someone else's ideas because "her opinion would not change everything that science was based on" illustrates how she took up the discourses of science and scientific literacy in the classroom. In her enactment of a detached and distanced science student identity, Heather failed to learn about the power of literacy practices to answer the questions she was afraid or unmotivated to ask or to use literacy to make her voice heard in regard to critical issues of science that affect society, "life or death" issues that may have jolted her from a complacent identity to an active or questioning one.

IMPLICATIONS FOR TEACHING

This reanalysis in light of developing theories of subjectivity and identity raise obvious questions about what any of this means for adolescent/secondary school literacy teaching and learning. Many educators may be reading this chapter, thinking, "It was bad enough in 1998 when they suggested that we should develop a better understanding of who our 150 or so students are as acting subjects. Now they want us to think about who we are, as well, and how our interactions with students and the structuring of our classroom environment engenders certain kinds of identity enactments in students? Are they crazy?"

We acknowledge the possible "craziness" in applying these theories and empirical analyses to everyday teaching situations; we struggle with the "what does this mean for my teaching" question ourselves. To wit, we thought it would be useful to write about how we see these analyses as informing our own teaching, albeit of preservice teacher education and literacy doctoral students, rather than of high school students. Although the content of preservice teacher education courses is quite different from the content of secondary school content-area courses, we use our musing on our own teaching to offer some questions—as we did in 1998—that might be helpful for teachers in working to explore and expand the identities demanded and enacted in their various content classrooms. We conclude with policy implications as a result of these reanalyses of our data.

Three important findings stood out to us as we reanalyzed these data in light of the space/time/relationship theory of identity and in light of Gee's conception of identities as *recognized* (Gee, 2000, 2001). First is the finding around *identities demanded* in different education settings. We found ourselves thinking a great deal about the identities we demand of our students in preservice courses, especially in relation to the identities we enact. In particular, we demand an identity as *professional* from our students. What do they know about how to enact a professional identity? How does that mesh with the various subjectivities that they bring to the classroom? For Elizabeth, this has particular implications. She tends to think of students in terms of their content-area subjectivities (because her class is an interdisciplinary arrangement that seems to highlight disciplinary differences), but she has thought less about the move that she asks them to make from a student subjectivity (and often, student as receiver of information or demonstrator of knowledge) to a professional subjectivity (in which they take responsibility for the learning of others).

We were also struck by the importance of examining identity enactments of the teacher as well as the students. As teacher educators, we strive to enact identities as professionals. Like Landy, we dress in suits to convey a sense of the professional; we stress punctuality and preparation and strive to enact those qualities via intricately designed lectures, assignments, and small-group discussion activities. At the same time, however, we also stress the importance of self-questioning and reflection as an aspect of professionalism in teaching, and we try to model such qualities by openly critiquing our own teaching moves in front of our students. How do our students read these strikingly different identity enactments? Do we confuse students by enacting two very different takes on identity? And how do these enactments support or contradict the enactments that we intentionally and unintentionally demand of them? We don't pose these questions as a way of laying out serious problems in our teaching, but we do intend to use these questions to rethink various activities and interactions that we have with students, as well as how we enact particular forms of teaching as we engage in the disciplinary discourses of education.

Finally, the finding regarding the role of participant structures leads us to be even more committed to providing multiple participant structures for students to engage in our various courses. Concomitantly, however, we see the need to assess the *content* of activities we have designed for various structures. Is it worth a small group's time to discuss information that can be easily pulled from a text? Is a lecture the best place to engage students in a discussion of what literacy is? Similarly, drawing from Deborah's analysis of how Carolyn was *recognized* within various participant structures, we find ourselves searching for strategies to better assess who students are in relation to the different participation structures we develop for our classes. We also have begun to examine the different kinds of literate practices demanded, offered, and recognized in our courses. How do the participant structures of our classes support or constrain not only identity enactments, but also literate practices associated with different identities? Should we engage in structures that make reading and writing tasks of the class more public? Should we engage in structures that provide opportunities to model feedback on reading and writing practices? Should we try to change the literate practices and participant structures of our classes to facilitate multiple ways of engaging with print and other forms of representation, as well as multiple ways of "doing" a professional teaching identity?

QUESTIONS TO GUIDE CONTENT-AREA PLANNING AND TEACHING

Simple answers to addressing the classroom mediation of identity enactments and learning are not forthcoming because, as our analyses and musings indicate, teaching and learning are situated in particular times, spaces, and relationships. Acknowledging the local nature of teaching and learning does not, however, translate into a stance of teaching and learning as idiosyncratic. Generalizations can be made at global levels about the local nature of teaching and learning. For example, these data demonstrate that teaching, like learning, demands and recognizes shifts in identities (cf. Lave, 1996). In addition, disciplines or content areas, like any other discourse community, demand certain kinds of identities—and concomitant literacy and other communicative and social practices—from their members. Identities bump up against each other in these different classroom and content-area relationships, spaces, and times. Thus, responsive and planful teaching requires that we examine the identities we enact as teachers, those we demand from students, those required for conventional proficiency in our disciplines, and those that move students beyond the conventional, providing them with the ability to traverse multiple disciplines and communities. And each of us, as teachers, can engage in this relational, spatial, and temporal work in our own local and particular contexts, drawing from the wisdom generated by deep and broad analyses of teaching and learning. Thus, rather than providing answers, we pose a list of questions for teachers to consider as they plan for their own classrooms:

1. What identities do you enact in your classroom?
2. How do these mesh with your own subjectivities or with other identities you enact in other spaces (e.g., at home; with your partner, children, friends)?
3. How many of your classroom identity enactments are a "performance" enacted to convince your students of something (i.e., that you are "in control," that you hold knowledge they do not hold, etc.)?
4. How much of your classroom identity enactments stem from your relationships with students?
5. What identities do you think your discipline demands of students if they are to be proficient learners?

   a. Are there any you've left out (e.g., Landy's focus on organization, despite her recognition that science involved much more, such as creativity, messiness, and uncertainty).

    b. Why did you leave those identities out?

    c. What is the role of literacy in enacting these identities (e.g., scientists making records of investigations, authors revising their writing without prompting, mathematicians working problems in multiple forms of representation, historians reading primary sources, etc.)

6. What identities do you recognize your students as typically enacting? (Or, if a novice teacher, what identities do you predict adolescent students will enact?)

7. What do you know about other identities your students enact in other spaces or relationships (e.g., highly successful student in your classroom, struggling in another classroom; talkative in your classroom, silent and alone at lunch)?

8. How do the identities your students enact (or the subjectivities they reveal to you) mesh with those demanded in your classroom? Of your discipline?

IMPLICATIONS FOR POLICY

In the present social and political education environment, teachers, administrators, researchers, parents, and even adolescent students have become more aware of the implications of local, state, and federal policies for the lives of teachers and learners. We want to turn the tables and pose some implications of this work for policy decisions. First, the identity work that goes on in classrooms is vast, particularly in classroom settings where people come from diverse backgrounds and experiences. We suggest that more attention needs to be paid in teacher education programs to the subjective experiences of teachers and students—whether socially, culturally, or historically mediated—that shape how they enact identities when they come together to teach and learn. This is not a simple call for another educational psychology or social foundations course, but for more opportunities—through community-based service learning programs, through field-based practicum programs, or through beginning teacher induction programs—for prospective and inservice teachers to study their own subjectivities and identity enactments, to examine rigorously the identities their students display, and to spend time building, analyzing, and expanding the relationships with their prospective students.

Second, our findings support current educational movements such as small learning communities, small schools, block scheduling, interdisciplinary teaming, or class-size reductions, particularly at the middle and high school levels. Each of the aforementioned policy initiatives provides opportunities for teachers not only to develop relationships with students, but also to more closely interrogate the influence of those relationships on student learning.

Third, our findings support policies in teacher education and beyond aimed at developing better understandings of what constitutes learning and literate practice in the disciplines. Our work underscores past research that illustrates proficient secondary teaching to be dependent on more than ample content knowledge. Strong content-area teachers such as Landy and Ruhl have clear stances on the nature of knowledge in their disciplines. Strong content-area literacy teachers—again, Ruhl and Landy fit the bill here—employ literacy practices that mesh well with their views on knowledge in their disciplines and that support students' growth in those literate and content or disciplinary practices. And yet, we have demonstrated that both of these teachers, as strong and explicit as they were with students about what students needed to learn in their respective content areas, also communicated only partial views of the nature of their disciplines. This partiality had implications for the identities their students enacted and for the literacy practices learned. Thus, teacher education and beginning teaching programs would do well to invest prospective and inservice teachers with tools for examining disciplinary discourses and literacy practices, toward the development of pedagogical content and process knowledge that will serve all of their students in deep disciplinary learning and the development of sophisticated literacy practices across the disciplines.

Finally, although federal adolescent literacy policies that focus on decoding of print may be useful for some young people who have not yet mastered print codes in academic reading and writing, such policies are not enough to move the vast majority of young people from basic literate proficiency (e.g., extracting a main idea from a single, short passage) to sophisticated textual and intertextual processing and practices. Such processes and practices includes literate acts such as reading across multiple print texts; integrating ideas from print with visual, oral, and performed texts; synthesizing and communicating findings or ideas in written, oral, pictorial, iconic, and performed forms; and critiquing, expanding, or reconstructing ideas garnered from multiple sources, all within particular domains and discourse communities. These processes and practices are dependent on young people learning to try on, play with, and reconstruct a host of identities within and across disciplines and other social settings. To do so, they need access to multiple forms of texts and to the time and support for thinking through and working across those texts. A steady diet of test preparation and testing for the purposes of measuring student "achievement" will not support the nuanced development of literate identities in the disciplines. Consequently, we call for broader programs of adolescent literacy instruction, ones that provide time for development, freedom for disciplinary exploration, and opportunities to learn the range of skills, strategies, and identities that young people need to develop to navigate many different discourse communities, both within secondary school settings and beyond.

REFERENCES

Dillon, D. R., O'Brien, D. G., Moje, E. B., & Stewart, R. A. (1994). Literacy learning in secondary school science classrooms: A cross-case analysis of three qualitative studies. *Journal of Research in Science Teaching, 31,* 345–362.

Dillon, D. R., & Moje, E. B. (1998). Listening to the talk of adolescent girls: Lessons about literacy, school, and life. In D. E. Alvermann, K. A. Hinchmann, D. W. Moore, S. F. Phelps, & D. R. Waff (Eds.), *Reconceptualizing the literacies in adolescents' lives* (pp. 193–223). Mahwah, NJ: Lawrence Erlbaum Associates.

Dillon, D. R., O'Brien, D. G., & Volkmann, M. (2001). Reading and writing to get work done in high school biology. In E. B. Moje & D. G. O'Brien (Eds.), *Constructions of literacy: Studies of teaching and learning in secondary classrooms* (pp. 51–75). Mahwah, NJ: Lawrence Erlbaum Associates.

Gee, J. P. (1996). *Social linguistics and literacies: Ideology in discourses* (2nd ed.). London: Falmer.

Gee, J. P. (2000/2001). Identity as an analytic lens for research in education. In W. G. Secada (Ed.), *Review of research in education* (Vol. 25, pp. 99–126). Washington, DC: American Educational Research Association.

Gee, J. P. (2001, December). *Reading in "new times."* Paper presented at the National Reading Conference, San Antonio, TX.

Goldman, S. R. (1997). Learning from text: Reflections on the past and suggestions for the future. *Discourse Processes, 23,* 357–398.

Guerra, J. C. (1998). *Close to home: Oral and literate practices in a transnational Mexicano community.* New York: Teachers College Press.

Hicks, D. (1995/1996). Discourse, learning, and teaching. In M. W. Apple (Ed.), *Review of research in education* (Vol. 21, pp. 49–95). Washington, DC: American Educational Research Association.

Hudicourt-Barnes, J. (2003). The use of argumentation in Haitian Creole science classrooms. *Harvard Educational Review, 73*(1), 73–93.

Lave, J. (1996). Teaching, as learning, in practice. *Mind, Culture, and Activity: An International Journal, 3*(3), 149–164.

Lee, C. D. (2001). Is October Brown Chinese? A cultural modeling activity system for underachieving students. *American Educational Research Journal, 38*(1), 97–141.

Lemke, J. L. (1990). *Talking science: Language, learning, and values.* Norwood, NJ: Ablex.

Michaels, S., & O'Connor, M. C. (1990, Summer). *Literacy as reasoning within multiple discourses: Implications for policy and educational reform.* Paper presented at the Council of Chief State School Officers Summer Institute on Restructuring Learning, Educational Development Center, Literacies Institute, Newton, MA.

Moje, E. B. (1996). "I teach students, not subjects": Teacher–student relationships as contexts for secondary literacy. *Reading Research Quarterly, 31,* 172–195.

Moje, E. B. (1997). Exploring discourse, subjectivity, and knowledge in chemistry class. *Journal of Classroom Interaction, 32,* 35–44.

Moje, E. B. (2004). Powerful spaces: Tracing the out-of-school literacy spaces of Latino/a youth. In K. Leander & M. Sheehy (Eds.), *Space matters: Assertions of space in literacy practice and research* (pp. 15–38). New York: Peter Lang.

Moje, E. B., Ciechanowski, K. M., Kramer, K. E., Ellis, L. M., Carrillo, R., & Collazo, T. (2004). Working toward third space in content area literacy: An examination of everyday funds of knowledge and discourse. *Reading Research Quarterly, 39*(1), 38–71.

Moje, E. B., Peek-Brown, D., Sutherland, L. M., Marx, R. W., Blumenfeld, P., & Krajcik, J. (2004). Explaining explanations: Developing scientific literacy in middle-school project-based science reforms. In D. Strickland & D. E. Alvermann (Eds.), *Bridging the gap: Improving literacy learning for preadolescent and adolescent learners in grades 4–12* (pp. 227–251). New York: Carnegie Corporation.

Pratt, M. L. (1991). Arts of the contact zone. *Profession, 91,* 33–40.

Rogers, R. (2002). Between contexts: A critical analysis of family literacy, discursive practices, and literate subjectivities. *Reading Research Quarterly, 37*(3), 248–277.

Street, B. V. (1994). Cross cultural perspectives on literacy. In J. Maybin (Ed.), *Language and literacy in social practice* (pp. 139–150). Clevedon, England: Open University.

Willis, P. (1977). *Learning to labor: How working class kids get working class jobs.* New York: Columbia University Press.

6

Utilizing Student's Cultural Capital in the Teaching and Learning Process: "As If" Learning Communities and African American Students' Literate Currency

Jennifer E. Obidah
Tyson E. J. Marsh
UCLA

Literate Currency

In the first edition of *Reconceputalizing the Literacies in Adolescents' Lives*, I (Jennifer Obidah) examined African American students' use of what I termed *literate currency* (Obidah, 1998).I used this term to describe the multiple and interactive forms of literacy that students bring into the classroom and that their encounters with the myriad people and processes of everyday schooling. As noted in the first edition, students' literate currency encompasses more than the literacy acquired in schools. Although significant elements of literate currency are acquired as students engage in the schooling processes, literate currency is also gleaned through their personal, familial, and social interactions, both within and outside of schools.

In Fig. 6.1 the terms *peer literacy, school literacy, home/community literacy,* and *popular culture literacy* are a few examples of the many sources of the information adolescents utilize, simultaneously, to make sense of the worlds in which they live. Moreover, their responses to school subjects also draw on information from this variety of sources that ultimately constitute their literate currency. Thus, literate cur-

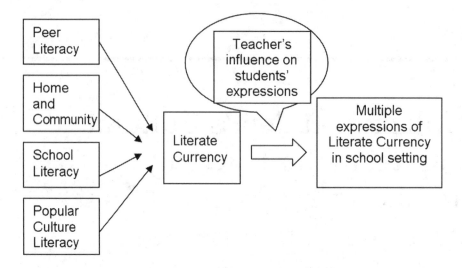

FIG. 6.1.   Cultural capital as literacy currency utilized in "As-if" learning community.

rency is maintained and transformed through interactions of multiple realities. It is part of discourse, which Gee (1989) describes as "a socially accepted association among ways of using language, of thinking, and of acting, that can be used to identify oneself as a member of a socially meaningful group or 'social network.'"(p. 18.) An important part of Gee's notion of discourse is that it is composed not only of every act associated with being a member of a social network, but the interaction of these acts with greater social institutions and constructions of the particular social network to which we belong. In this way, literate currency is a vehicle utilized to manifest discourses that predominate in instances of human interaction. We contend that the challenge for teachers is to create spaces in their classrooms where students' literacy currency can be showcased and built on to enhance their academic endeavors. Thus, in Fig. 6.1, we also highlight the significant influence that teachers have on students' abilities to express themselves and what modes of expression of their literate currency they ultimately employ in the classroom context.

For African American students, the knowledge matrices that comprise their literate currency make no divide between what they knew already about certain subjects—these subjects as they pertained to their identity—and the who, when, what, where, and how relative to their acquisition of such knowledge. Knowledge acquired in school that informed students about their African American identities was equally as valued as the knowledge acquired through other experiences and interactions. These students did not automatically relinquish one set of knowledge at the moment they were exposed to another. Rather, students inculcate and combine sets of knowledge to form a continuum of literate currency. Along this continuum, school knowledge enters and interacts, with an end result of either disapproving long-held beliefs—held by both the students and society in general—or, doing nothing to challenge or critique these beliefs, aiding their perpetuation.

In this chapter we continue to focus on literate currency that alerts us to students' larger discourses about their identities as African Americans. We focus specifically on the creative writings of four African American female students who participated in an after-school program in an urban, inner city high school. This class was led by Tyson Marsh, a young African American male who is also the co-author of this chapter. Through the use of students' voices portrayed in their writing, we present a counterstory to their student identities, which for the most part were stories of failing students in a failing inner city public school. We offer the insights gleaned from students' poetry and prose as a lens through which teachers can reconceptualize students who may be perceived as failing if their value is weighed only through their outcomes in traditional academic settings and schooling processes.

First, we discuss African American students' literate currency in the larger theoretical framework of cultural capital (Bourdieu, 1977; DiMaggio, 1979; Harker, 1984; Swartz, 1997). We couple this framework with Perry's (2003) notion of the creation of "as if" educational communities, which she posits as a distinct aspect of African American culture developed in response to subordinate framing in American society. Within the context of possibility, we offer the students' poetry and prose as critical portrayals of the issues that matter most to them. Interwoven with the students' writings are analyses of the texts and their potential as lenses for teachers' insights. As in the first edition, we conclude by asserting that when teachers make space for dialogues that include students' literate currency in their classroom, their actions begin a reciprocal process of teaching and learning between teacher and students. This process leads to end products of higher levels of student engagement, interest, desire to learn, and, ultimately, academic success.

CULTURAL CAPITAL

Bourdieu takes as the fundamental problem of sociology the means by which systems of domination persist and reproduce themselves without conscious recognition by members of a society. Bourdieu's conceptualization of the social system is one in which both society and its systems of maintenance (legal, political, educational, and so forth) are founded on hierarchies governed by similar beliefs, values and legitimized rules (Bourdieu, 1973, 1977, 1986). Within this social system are different forms of capital—symbolic, cultural, social, and economic—through which Bourdieu conceptualizes the attributes, possessions, and/or qualification that can be exchanged for goods, services, or esteem (Harker, 1984; Swartz, 1997). Specific to framing our discussion of literate currency is Bourdieu's notion of *cultural capital*.

Bourdieu (1973) posits cultural capital—the general background, knowledge, dispositions, and skills that are passed from one generation to the next and that can be exchanged for economic capital—as a mediating force in the reproduction of societal inequality. He argues that even though each social class has a distinct cultural capital, schools as social institutions place greater value on the cultural capital of the dominant classes. Members of the dominant classes are in possession of the cultural capital (familiarity with and the knowledge of the dominant social norms) to provide them subtle and obvious benefits in the schooling process. Thus, they rationally invest the time, effort, and money that will allow them to profit from the academic and economic markets. Because schools simultaneously devalue the cultural capital of groups on the lower rungs of the socioeconomic ladder, these students with nondominant cultures (Carter, 2003) are not privy to these subtle benefits. In short, students who do not already possess the cultural capital that is valued in schools are inherently disadvantaged within the educational process, and students whose cultures mirror the cultural capital endorsed by the schooling system are overly advantaged in the race for academic merits (grades, diplomas, and degrees).

Interestingly, Bourdieu argues that these rewards simultaneously legitimate the schooling process as meritocratic and unbiased at the same time that they perpetuate a hierarchical and unequal educational system. Moreover, the normalization of a dominant culture makes the associated values and beliefs systems appear accessible to everyone equally when, in fact, inaccessibility is an important element upon which a culture remains dominant and of higher value in a capitalist society.

Bourdieu (1973) also suggests that disadvantaged children failing more often in school is a result not only of an initial lack of cultural capital but an unconscious estimation on their part of their objective chances of success. In this light, Kohl's (1994) work on students' not-learning can serve as an example of students' consciousness of the lowered expectations that schools and educators hold for them in terms of their eventual academic success. The result of this process is that the uneven distribution of cultural capital is doubly reproduced inasmuch as the consequent failure of the children from the subordinated classes appears to be an individual failure and not a systemic failure.

In summary, although educational success appears in society as an asset available to all, Bourdieu's arguments underscore the unequal schooling prevalent in America's schools. Although Bourdieu's arguments lend valuable insight into prevailing educational inequality in our society, his theories are often criticized as overly deterministic and pessimistic of the possibilities that dwell within human agency (DiMaggio, 1979). Indeed, the overdetermination of school success and failure suggests a system that leaves little if any opportunity for contestation, struggle, or transformation. Nevertheless, it is clear that in many cases students, parents, teachers, and community members struggle against dominant processes of reproduction and legitimation. It is therefore possible to imagine educational spaces and practices that are not automatically oriented toward reproduction. Perry's (2003) account of African Americans' creation of "as if" communities of learning is one such example.

AFRICAN AMERICANS' "AS IF" EDUCATIONAL COMMUNITIES

In a critical analysis of the establishment of an African American education philosophy, Perry (2003) posits a philosophy comprised of the following elements: education for freedom, racial uplift, citizenship, and leadership. Amidst a reality of unequal educational opportunity for African Americans in the pre-Civil Rights era of America's history, African Americans worked intentionally to oppose the prevailing ideology of Black intellectual inferiority. In Black segregated schools, pedagogies of resistance were "designed to counter the status of African Americans as a racial caste group." (Perry, 2003, p. 89). For example, in addition to these schools' curricular practices were behavioral and ritualistic practices that exhorted Black youth to "hold your head up high, throw your shoulders back, walk like you are somebody" (Perry, 2003, p. 90). This matrix of practices embedded an ideology on which "as if" educational communities were formed. There were learning communities that sought to educate students "as if (they) were free." (Perry, 2003, p. 90). African Americans were less than 100 years removed from the elimination of the institution of slavery in America, and even though slavery had been declared constitutionally illegal, the mindset of White Americans at that time was still convinced of the inferiority of African Americans. This ideology of Black inferiority supported by the converse belief of White superiority was important to the maintenance of a system of dehumanizing enslavement of a group of people. Those who enslaved other humans had to believe that their actions were just, and this justification was based on the premise that African Americans were less than human and did not deserve to live as free citizens.

Thus, even after slavery ended, African Americans had to continue their struggle to prove their humanity, their worthiness to be free. This struggle was fraught with legal roadblocks such as Jim Crow laws, political roadblocks that hindered their ability to vote, and educational roadblocks that severely limited their access to equal education. In such contexts that sought to maintain their symbolic enslavement, Perry (2003) asserts African Americans' development of a counterideology exemplified in the notion of "as if we were free" learning communities.

Perry (2003) noted how the teachers and leaders in segregated African American communities stressed that the youth should "refuse to allow our social location, our positional identity, to find expression in our bodies" (p. 90). Rather, despite the obstacles maintained by social structures that severely limited their ability to participate as full citizens in society, African Americans as a community encouraged their youth to live their lives to the fullest extent, to envision opportunities for themselves beyond their immediate circumstances, and, importantly, to fight against the obstacles placed in their way "as if" they deserved and were free to exercise the unalienable rights of life, liberty, and pursuit of happiness granted to all Americans under the Constitution. In short, an education within this framework encompasses much more than learning academic subjects; education is the valuing of students' humanity despite any beliefs to the contrary that may exist in society.

While we are not advocating segregated schools, we assert the need for "as if" educational communities for African American students, in schools where these students are valued as human beings and as learners, where their teachers hold high expectations for their academic and life success. We assert this need in light of the disproportionate academic failure experienced by this student population. Moreover, we posit teachers' creation of spaces for students' literate currency as spaces within schools where dominant processes that belie such perceptions of learning, high expectations, and success for these students can be interrupted, reconfigured, and made problematic. We contend that within "as if" educational communities, African American students' cultural capital and literate currency can be drawn on to counter deficit notions of African American literate achievement. Furthermore, such spaces can empower students in a way that assists them in developing confidence and agency, "as if" they can rewrite their oppressive reality and the reality of their community. In the remainder of this chapter, we tell the story of one such learning space in an after-school program at an urban inner city high school. The class was taught by and is conveyed in the next section by Tyson Marsh.

ACKNOWLEDGING STUDENTS' LITERATE CURRENCY: ONE TEACHER'S STORY

B. Heard

My Black People, speak up and be heard

Words Written take shape as modern day ammunition

As spoken words invoke our ancestral traditions

Constructing verbal weapons of mass destruction

Flattening any obstruction in our quest for freedom and peace

With a force powerful enough to part the seas

Freeing Black bodies from the depths of the middle passage

Reincarnating the nameless that died in the name of collateral damage

United We Spit … some shit to be reckoned with.

Metaphors in multiple dialects

500 year old halitosis, breathing breath hot enough to melt through the metal doors of

massa's masochistic, misogynistic, materialistic, sick social reproductive mansion, well into the next millennium.

—T. Marsh

As an educator, I have employed poetry and spoken word as tools to enable me to connect with my students while providing them with an avenue to paint their portrait of the world in a language that is their own. In coconstructing an enrichment class with a fellow graduate student, we sought to weave together music, spoken word, written word, and film to engage our students while assisting them in developing a critical consciousness and voice. Reflecting on our own educational experiences, we felt that through reading, writing, and sharing poetry as well as other forms of critical expression, our students could connect the knowledge they obtain in school with the cultural knowledge and capital that they acquire from their parents, community, peers, and popular media. In this way, we made a space for students to articulate their literate currency in a school setting.

Golden State High School

Located across from the city courthouse, Golden State High (a pseudonym) is surrounded by a large chain-link fence with each entrance secured by a chain lock and staffed with a security guard. Walking into the main building of the school, you are immediately requested to show your identification to the security guard, and if you do not possess one, you are referred to the office, which is right inside the door. Once you have signed in, you are permitted to proceed through the building and into the yard just outside two heavy metal doors. Immediately across from the entrance to the main building are several modular classrooms that contain the overflow of students the concrete structures of the school were not built to hold. The classroom windows are covered by a heavy black material that prevents prying eyes and natural light.

On any given day there are youth outside, talking, laughing, and sometimes hiding from security guards and teachers if the requisite bell signaling a temporary release from classroom activity has not yet rung. As your eyes wander across the yard, there seems to be an endless slab of asphalt with two trees whose roots crack the asphalt. As you walk across the yard, a plane flies low overhead and the deafening roar of its jet engines drowns out all other sounds. All verbal communication halts until the sound subsides. The campus is inconveniently located in the flight path to the busy runways at Los Angeles International Airport. On the part of the asphalt landscape designated as the recreation area are twelve basketball hoops, none of which have nets and some of which have no hoop. Despite this, during the day these basketball courts are occupied by throngs of young people dressed in PE clothes, doing their stretches and playing a game of basketball, or they are in Army ROTC uniforms, conducting drills and marching to the commands of their drill instructor.

Situated in the Los Angeles Basin, Golden State High School is one of the two high schools in the district that serve a predominantly Chicano/Latino and African American working class community. Physical appearance aside, Golden State High is the district's flagship school, boasting graduates that include professional athletes and rap artists as well as local politicians. Yet, under the auspices of the No Child Left Behind Act, Golden State is also considered to be a low-performing school. In an effort to improve the school's academic standing and students' college attendance and graduation rates, the district has partnered with the Graduate School of Education and Information Studies at the University of California, Los Angeles under a federal GEAR UP (Gaining Early Awareness and Readiness for Undergraduate Programs) grant.

The GEAR UP Program

In supporting a 5-year effort to enhance college awareness and readiness, the GEAR UP Program at Golden State High School offers after-school tutoring in core subjects, parent support, counseling, professional support for teachers, educational field trips, and a multitude of activities that serve to familiarize students with college campuses. The primary focus of the GEAR UP Program is to provide students with the knowledge and cultural capital needed to successfully pursue a college education. However, staff members recognized that the students already possessed a cultural capital that held a considerable amount of value but that, nonetheless, may not be embraced in the traditional classroom setting. As a result, enrichment courses focusing on the visual and performing arts and critical writing and expression were designed to draw and build on the cultural literacy and knowledge that students brought with them to school.

In drawing from and reinforcing the cultural capital of the students, these courses were designed to validate their culturally specific ways of knowing while encouraging them to maintain and develop their literate currency as tools that maintain their academic identity as future college students. Approximately 60 students participated in these courses, 15 of whom enrolled in the course that I cotaught with a fellow graduate student. The class was titled Political Education, Art, and Critical Expression (PEACE).

The PEACE Class

The class took place for 1 hour and 45 minutes, 4 days a week, and was available only to students who enrolled and attended daily. In addition to assisting students in developing a critical consciousness and voice, the PEACE Program syllabus evolved out of students' dialogues and writings. As a result of the emphasis we placed on student voice, we quickly came to the realization that the primary educational resources we incorporated in the class should come from the students. For our first class, we

shared our own poetry and a poem by Chrystos, a Native American female poet, ti-
tled "I Walk in the History of My People." Although we had initially intended to include film, the allotted time for the course limited us to including an assortment of
music and poetry that the students brought from their home collections. Students
were invited to bring in any form of media that inspired them; examples of these include the music of Lauryn Hill, Nas, and 2 Pac and poetry by Maya Angelou as well
as student family members. As the course came to an end, the students requested that
we take them to see the film *Fahrenheit 911* by Michael Moore.

For our first week of classes, we asked student to bring in music that they identified with, and we worked with each student to develop a list of verbs, adjectives,
and nouns to describe them. We then asked student to write about who they are as
individuals, using their respective descriptive vocabulary lists. In the following
weeks, we repeated this exercise to build on students' identities with respect to their
family as well as local and global community membership. As the course continued, students shared their written works with one another and assisted one another
in fine-tuning their writing.

Through the course of the summer, students began to use their knowledge and
experience to educate one another on critical issues of their choice. As a final project
we produced a compact disk featuring student poetry, spoken word, stories, and reflections. In addition, as the course was brought to a close in the summer, students
were given the opportunity to perform their poetry for their peers at a culmination
ceremony. In preparation for this event, for the final week of class, the students
worked on their poetry and developed skits to accompany each poem that would be
performed. Also, at the end of the summer, the class held a poetry and spoken word
night during a field trip to the University of California at Berkeley, where all 60 students involved in the summer supplemental courses participated. By the end of the
course we felt, along with the students and staff, that our goal of empowering students to freely utilize their literate currency in academic pursuits was
accomplished.

In the following pages, we draw on the poetry, spoken word, and written works
of the students who participated in the PEACE class. We demonstrate that when
given the opportunity to express themselves through self-selected mediums of
choice, students are able to voice their multiple literacies as they address the critical
issues that they face as urban youth of color within the contexts of their school, community, family, and peer settings.

Throughout this process, we demonstrate that in order for these students to vo-
calize their literate currency within an academic setting, a comfortable and safe
space is a prerequisite. Also, we posit that each of our students is unique and that
their voices are shaped by a combination and fluid interaction of their individual
subjectivities, specifically, their racial identity, gender, and socioeconomic status
(Anzaldua, 1987; Freire, 1970; hooks, 1989; Lorde, 1984). In acknowledging this, we
conclude by putting forth the argument that in order to be effective critical educators, we must acknowledge and challenge the misperceptions and assumptions we
impose on our students as individuals and agents of the education system.

Although African American and Chicano/Latino male and female students participated in the classes, here I focus only on the poetry and prose of the six participating African American young women. No African American males participated
during the first session of the poetry class, the session that is the focus in this chapter, although they participated in later sessions.

LITERATE CURRENCY: ARTICULATING STUDENTS' VOICES

Who Am I?

In an effort to break down any tensions or discomforts between class participants, and to create an opportunity for students to get to know one another, we began our first class by posing and discussing the question "Who am I?" Before embarking on a free write, we worked with the class to develop a list of verbs, adjectives, and nouns that students might use to describe themselves. As teachers we opened up ourselves by sharing very personal pieces that we wrote to model what we were encouraging our students to do. After reading our personal poems, we played music that exemplified the wording and phrases that other young spoken-word artists and rap artists had chosen to describe themselves. Finally, we gave students 15 minutes to freely write a response to the prompt "Who am I?" The following two responses are examples of what our students wrote:[1]

Who Am I?

Who am I?

I really don't know,

I'm trying to find me

I'm going through a maze

When will I get to the end?

Confusion is constantly on my mind

I hate all the pressures that are brought upon me

Too many decisions than I'd rather there be

I just can't stand it

Don't know what to do

To feel what I feel

Trying to find me has been very hard

But its right there, I just keep passing it by

And it's so close, all I have to do is reach out and grab it

And I will find the true me

That God put me here to be

—NF

In this piece, NF demonstrates her struggle to "find me." The only identification markers discussed in this piece are those of confusion, pressure, struggle and a belief in God. However, it is evident that NF has grappled with this question before, and despite her efforts, she is hesitant to pinpoint her identity. Moreover, she acknowledges that it is

---

[1] We asked students how they would like themselves identified in this chapter. They preferred that we use their initials, which grant them some autonomy while also allowing them to be recognized and validated in this text.

not an easy task to embrace one's identity. My initial perception of NF was that she was a very confident African American young woman who seemed very sure of who she was as an individual, and clearly this was not always the case. In essence, in her interaction with others, NF presented herself "as if" she were confident and sure, yet she struggled with her identity. By allowing NF to express herself in the safe environment we created and in a manner in which she felt comfortable, she was able to grapple with this question. She eventually allowed her literate currency to surface and assist her in reflecting on and confronting some of the potential sources of her struggle.

Next is another student's response to the prompt, "Who am I?"

I'm Just Me

I'm just me, I can't be anyone else

I am who I am don't you see

I can't be no one else

When I look in the mirror,

I only see myself

I may say something, but it's only out of reaction

It's like a feelin,

Kinda like a natural reaction

Each thing we chose, whether it be a song or a poem,

Everyone spoke and responded

Each thing helped us get connected to one another, to help us know each other better

Everyone sure felt something, whether it was an emotion or a reaction

You feel like you wanna say something, or punch something,

It was just a reaction

Everyone connected like a puzzle type thing

I think what we say and hear helps us

You never want to feel like a dawg with a muzzle on

No one can hear you speak

But if you can hear me and I can hear you

Now you hear me and I can hear you

Everyone listened and spoke to everyone

No matter you say, no matter what you said, no matter what you meant

We heard your opinion because you shared it

We basically all agree

We can't be everyone they want you to be

And I agree, I'm just me

And I hope you get to know me

I'm me, just me and that's all I'll ever be.

—DF

DF's poem demonstrates confidence in acknowledging, "I am just me, I can't be anyone else." However, on our initial interaction with DF, she seemed very shy and quiet. In matching this piece to the various personalities that make up our classroom, one would expect that it be written by one of our more outspoken students. For DF it appears that through writing poetry she is able to find and express her authentic voice "as if" she is secure and confident in her identity, which is very different from the voice she employs at school. Within the context of the classroom, DF's very quiet demeanor might misrepresent her as shy and often disengaged. However, she is the exact opposite of that when she is able to express herself in written poetic form. As is shown later, poetry also serves as an ideal avenue for DF to discuss her literate currency, as well as her understanding and expression within what could be termed as African American cultural capital.

With respect to these written pieces, both of the students seem to articulate who they are through their poetry and in a manner that allows them to be themselves. Whereas NF presents herself as confident and secure, her poetry demonstrates her difficulty in pinpointing her identity. Although DF appears to be quiet and shy, she writes in the exact opposite way. In the interest of maintaining an "as if" learning community, we encouraged NF to be truly the confident person she outwardly portrayed but inwardly struggled with, and we supported DF in showing her amazing confidence and wisdom in the context of school. In short, we not only worked on students' poetry; we worked with students on identifying obstacles of self-esteem, lack of confidence, and so forth to make sure that they realized their full potential in and out of school.

What Shapes Your Voice?

We felt it was critical to address the question "What shapes your voice?" early in the course. In posing this question, we focused on factors named by the students. In essence, by presenting them with this question, the students would be able to shape the course curriculum, taking it in the direction that best served their needs and subsequently facilitated the development of their voice. First, this is CG's response to the prompt:

> What shapes my voice is my influence. My influences vary from my entertainment, peers, environment, culture, to my mom. I am impacted in opinion, by what I grew up being taught to believe. My grandfather tells me, "The White man is going to bring us down. He wants to tear us down and eliminate us." Being told this I remain on the defense when it comes to politics. My life has a purpose, whether I know the intentions of my surroundings or not, these will shape my voice.

Employing paragraph format as her medium of expression, CG reveals that her literate currency is shaped by "entertainment, peers, environment, culture," as well as her mother. Most notably, CG draws on the words of her grandfather, demonstrating the possibility that her literate currency is also informed by the cultural capital of previous generations of family members. CG also writes, "Whether I know the intentions of my surroundings or not, these will shape my voice." This claim invokes the idea that CG is conscious of her identity and voice as being shaped by forces that occupy the multiple environments and spaces CG occupies.

In answering the prompt, "What shapes your voice?" DF chose poetry as her mode of expression:

I Write

I write …

I write about many things

I write about the things that I hear, see, or think.

I write about dramatic experiences that has happened 2 me

I've never written about the cage birds that sing.

I write about economic opportunities

And about where life will take me

I write about my friends and family

Teachers and schools, race and ethnicity

I write …

Multiple factors shape the voice and literate currency of DF. As previously demonstrated, DF employs poetry as a tool to write what she hears, sees, or thinks into reality. However, DF goes one step further to indicate that the "the dramatic experiences" she encounters have influenced her affinity for expressing herself in poetic form. In addition, DF alludes to the role that "Teachers and schools, race and ethnicity" have had in informing her literate identity. DF demonstrates in this piece that it is a combination of these literate interactions that manifest themselves in her thoughts and writing. Finally, DF employs complex literary symbolism in making the claim that she has "never written about the cage bird that sings" (which alludes to the literary work of Maya Angelou). This reference indicates the presence of a consciousness on which DF builds her own literate currency. Clearly, for DF and CD, their awareness of race and ethnicity are always present.

As the class progressed, we as the educators developed an understanding of the multiple factors that shape and inform the literate currency that PEACE class students possess and the modes in which they feel most comfortable expressing their literate currency. The following works by students demonstrate how, when facilitated, this currency can be used to assist students in developing and expressing their critical consciousness. We explore how these students use their modes of expression to discuss complex issues that might not surface in the forms of discourse employed within the traditional classroom context.

LITERATE CURRENCY, CRITICAL CONSCIOUSNESS, AND DISCOURSES OF STRUGGLE AS A FUNCTION OF "AS IF" EDUCATIONAL COMMUNITIES

As stated by McLaren (2003), "A critical and affirming pedagogy has to be constructed around the stories that people tell, the ways in which students and teachers author meaning, and the possibilities that underlie the experiences that shape their voices" (p. 245). With the initial goal of creating a space where students could develop their voice and consciousness, the PEACE program also hoped to facilitate a sense of validation and dialogue around the realities and struggles that our students faced. Gradually, the PEACE class evolved into a poetic space and community where students supported each another, shared stories, and connected with one another's struggles and lived experiences. In this process, we recognized the power of poetry as an instrument of empowerment wherein students validate their language, thoughts and cultural literacy.

We demonstrate these points by presenting a series of selected poems and spoken word pieces that embody the success of our poetic community in allowing students to freely express their feelings and perspectives about the obstacles and struggles they face on a daily basis. Students comment on large societal issues such as racism—how they experience this issue in society and in classrooms with teachers. They also write/speak on issues synonymous with the adolescent stage of life—peer pressure, a desire to fit in, and self-mutilation. Finally, we conclude with one student's poem on education—what it means to be educated, where education happens, and finding strength in identifying as an educated youth. Although some of the following pieces may appear in many ways disheartening, the performance of each of these pieces to a group of supporting peers served to purge the emotional pain and, in the process, birthed a stronger student voice and demonstrated the power of "as if" educational environments.

I Hate My Life

I hate my life

There, I finally got it out

I'm such a nerd a geek, a freak, I hate it all

Yeah I don't dress in the latest and greatest clothes,

And no I don't show the precious gifts given to me by my parents' precious souls

To about 101 different guys,

Why would I want too, I'm not wanting those things

I just don't want to be a geak or a freak anymore

I wanna be unique but pretty

I want guys to notice me instead of talk about me

In front of me, behind me

I can't stand it anymore

I wanna die and ease my teenage mutant looks

Feelings, stresses, peer pressure is what they use against me.

I'm slowly becoming nothing but a disappearing shadow in the midst of noise

And I turn around but why?

Wont I become a hypocrite of the very things I've always said I despise

In my mind, popularity is the thing to seize

The very essence of who I am is calling out to me

Come out is what its saying, but I don't want it out

Why can't you people just accept me for who I am

I'm normal, just like all of you

The difference is, I refuse to think like you

G-Strings, money and the thang, cursin'

Y'all sexual vibe to feed y'all's pathetic minds

Up to no good

Becoming grown, before your parents know your grown

And if you were to be given two seconds into the real world, you'd suffocate because you weren't ready, you weren't grown, it wasn't your time

Are you all hatin' on me cuz y'all know who y'all supposed to be and you see it in me?

Too bad you had to learn the hard way.

But don't try to level my thinking so that I think your poisonous crumbs are food

You know the things you did, you did them

When you did it you let it control its own dumbness

And it made sense for a while because of my untrained knowledge,

But now, I don't want god to make me lose my grip,

So what I said before, when I said I wanted to die

I take that back because your definition of normal ain't something I comprehend.

—VR

Throughout this piece, VR employs symbolism, layered meanings and multiple literary styles as she express her literate currency. She begins by admitting her own desire to be popular, despite her choice to resist obstacles that will harm her and disallow the emergence of her true self. VR continues to struggle with her unwillingness to fit in among her peer group. She acknowledges the option of sacrificing her authentic identity to become something that she is not in an effort to be popular. VR articulates the different ways in which she feels her peers act in order to fit in while they mock her because she chooses not too. VR describes the pain that results from not giving in: "I wanna die and ease my teenage mutant looks." Clearly, VR longs for people to value her for who she is as a unique young woman, and she struggles with both the cost of succumbing to peer pressure and the cost of refusing to give in.

Interestingly, as she continues to write, the tone of the poem changes: VR engages her peers as well as herself in a critical dialogue about her quest to be valued for who she is as she challenges what is considered to be normal. She triumphantly concludes her poem with, "So what I said before, when I said I wanted to die/I take that back." When VR presented this poem in spoken word, she received a standing ovation from her peers. Evidently, the poem reached her audience and pushed them to reflect on their actions as well as their own struggles. In this process of reflection, writing, performance, and validation, VR was empowered to embrace her identity and individuality. Outside of an "as if we are free" framework, VR may not have been able to discuss these issues that are central to some of the struggles within African American communities. As demonstrated in this piece, VR is able to focus on other issues that affect African Americans "as if" there is more to being African American than a perpetual struggle with racism.

The following piece performed by FB represents the power of "as if" educational communities as well as a very personal and complex struggle with which these adolescents struggle. Unfortunately, it is an issue not often provided an outlet in a traditional classroom setting:

FB

I like to cut myself

sometimes when I'm alone

I like to watch as the

Blood arches on and on

Then a call from my best friend

Is awaiting me on the phone

"What's goin' on", with worry in her tone.

Inside I'm shouting, "JUST LEAVE ME ALONE!"

So I tell her there's "Nothing Wrong" and I hang up the phone

There's nothing wrong with me at least I think

I just let this knife continue to cut me

Except the knife don't feel like no blade

It feels like sippin lemonade in the shade

When I start cutting my blood is the rain.

—FB

When FB performed her piece in front of 60 of her peers, the room was in complete silence and, as she finished, a tremendous yet solemn applause followed. I immediately recall feeling concerned and ready to take action in hearing this piece. In fact, after the poem was read, I approached the GEAR UP Project Director to discuss it with her. As a result of this conversation, I discovered that FB had written this poem about a close friend who was struggling with self-mutilation. In FB's piece, however, it is evident that her friend's actions had equally impacted her to the extent that she took on her friend's voice in a cry for help. This poem articulates the potential of our learning community to spark discussion around issues, aside from racism, that also affect African American youth.

While the GEAR UP staff respected her friend's anonymity, they assisted FB in providing her with resources and tools to help her friend. Importantly, the performance of this poem transformed FB's struggle to articulate a cry for help into spoken word. Finding her voice at that moment allowed FB to share a burden and educate the audience about the seriousness of self-mutilation. It was almost as if FB chose to share this piece to reach out and help her fellow classmates or someone they knew that may be experiencing this heart-wrenching struggle. Moments like the one created when FB shared her poetry inform my work as an educator and compel me to continue to seek more ways in which to make human-to-human connections with my students. The following piece, performed by DF, also pushes us to reflect on how much we can learn from our students regarding how they perceive themselves in the world around them:

Sing Me A Story

Sing me a story of a young black girl

Sing me a story of this cruel cruel world

The world she has to live in

Breathe in, and sing in

Sing me a story of a girl who gets mistreated and beaten

Beaten to the point where she can't move, or do what she wants to do

Mistreated to the point where she gets raped

And has a baby that she considers a mistake

So she decides to take matters into her own hands

And leaves god, for another man

A man who can do what no man can

A man that can treat her like a lady and like a friend

A man who isn't in a rush to get her into bed

I wanna hear someone singing that story

Sing me a story of a young black man trying to make it

As we get older times are getting shady

But we few black people suck it up and take it

After all, its not many of us left

Sing me a story of a young black man

Who can walk into a room and not be judged by the content of his skin

Even after Martin Luther King said his speech

We're still saying, well he doesn't look like me

Now you've heard that story, So I want you to sing me that story.

—DF

In this poem DF demonstrates the literate currency she has acquired living life as a young Black woman. Using her poetic voice, DF outlines a struggle that could encompass the lived experiences and perceptions of a number of young women of color in America's inner cites. DF articulated the struggles of young Black girls within their own respective communities while taking on the role of an educator encouraging listeners to reflect on both their struggle and privilege. Whereas DF's piece focuses on educating the listener, the tone of the following piece provokes empathy in those who also deal with societal racism:

Racism

Want to take a walk ... To think about racism ...

What's the big deal ... color ... I am somebody ... alone in the evening, alone on the streets

Alone not being the point, the point being I can't do what I want cuz I'm the wrong skin color. Even color has its strength, one cannot stand alone, but it's no place for me. Racism ... is that what I was wrong to be, me being me, where I was wrong to be, who am I, how can I protest my skin, have you ever wondered why cant racism be stopped, why cant we just love one another, and not hate because someone looks different, I do not know this answer, but I do know that racism has to stop!

—NF

In this spoken word piece, NF delineates her desire to have a discussion about a social phenomenon that has clearly impacted her identity development and opportunities. NF states that racism affects her ability to "do what I want" and she questions the continued presence of racism. Within the first few lines of the prose, NF articulates her inability to enjoy certain privileges enjoyed by other American citizens who are not perceived as "the wrong color." In presenting this work to her peers, NF demonstrates her impatience as well as her strength as she challenges the inactivity of the greater society to address the persistence of racism. In her prior writings, NF struggled to locate her identity as well as the factors that inform her identity. In this piece she identifies racism as an active agent influencing her voice. This poem represents her gradual understanding of the factors that inform her world.

Over the course of the poetry/spoken word class, NF gradually developed a consciousness about factors in society, such as racism that, in part, shape her identity. Although it is questionable as to whether or not NF would feel safe expressing this poem to a more diverse audience, I contend that "as if" learning communities serve the purpose of guaranteeing a safe venue for students' writings. In another writing, AB brought the issue of racism out of the larger societal context and into the educational setting:

Government Property

Trying to get rid of the humiliation, my teacher ask me how to say it. But what they fail to see is that there is no humiliation or embarrassment because I am proud of my name ... No it doesn't mean anything crazy or spiritual like strong, intelligent, or beautiful. It simply means "east." I'm from the east and I think that's the way my soul blows when I have any self doubt ... It comes from Zaire in which my great grandfather was king of.

—AB

In this piece, AB discusses the importance of her name as representing an aspect of her identity. As AB reflects on her teacher's inability to pronounce her name, she demonstrates that although her name is African, she holds no shame as it serves as a symbol of her cultural heritage. AB alludes to the manner in which her name might be romanticized or ridiculed by her peers and teacher, representing something symbolic, spiritual, or in reference to a state of being. With authority, AB articulates that her name "simply means 'east'" and that she is proud of its origins in Zaire. Performing this piece with confidence, AB invokes her literate currency while acknowledging the literate currency of her great-grandfather who was a king of Zaire. Clearly, AB is proud of her heritage as she states, "That's the way my soul blows when I have any self doubt." Although she is several generations removed from the proclaimed reign of her great-grandfather, she still feels she has a connection to the place of her origin. In this poem, AB effectively establishes her name, as well as her identity, as a source of pride, particularly in times of self-doubt. To AB, her literate currency and cultural heritage are drawn on for strength and endurance.

As demonstrated in students' poems and prose, modes of literate currency expression can serve as platforms in which students encourage others to channel their struggles for the purpose of meaningful engagement and self-exploration. This is also articulated by FB in the following prose:

FB

I go deeply into my mind, my body is the pen and the ink is my blood. As the ink starts to flow, I start to let go and the words in the back of my mind start to unwind and I found that this is me writing down combinations and illustrations that come from my head, leaving the close minded dead. With all the things I have said, I have come to beg your participation in this illustration in my mind and I encourage you to let those thoughts of yours to be shared. You may believe that no one cares but the strength of a young voice can change our daily affairs.

—FB

As her words materialize into written form, FB becomes the instrument that leaves the mark of her experiences in the minds of others. Notably, FB embraces the written word as a form of literate currency that enables her to "let go" as "the words in the back of (her) mind start to unwind." As FB orated before her peers, she translated her conscious and subconscious thoughts into written and spoken text. While FB expresses her comfort with spoken word and poetry, she invites her peer audience to participate in the shaping of her mind and, thus, the construction of her view of the world. In addition, FB pleas for her peers to find and express their voice as it "can change our daily affairs."

In speaking this piece, FB embodies a teacher/student who seeks to teach and learn from the words and experiences of her peers. Strikingly, it is through this form of expression that FB feels the world can be transformed. As an educator, it is inspirational to hear these words of encouragement and possibility from a student. Perry (2003) notes that the creation of such possibilities is a key aspect of "as if" educational communities. FB represents not only a critical voice, but one that has found a way to articulate hope for the future, and it is within this hope that we educators still have much to learn. We conclude this section with a final poem by DF. She locates students' struggles within an education system that does not, often enough, facilitate the written, spoken, performed, and illustrated expression of students—words and actions that possess the power to rewrite and redefine the students, their teachers, and ultimately, what it means to exist "as if we are free."

Education

Occasionally found in schools

But originate on the streets

What people don't understand is you don't learn

Everything you know in school

Like how to love, how to speak

And if you believe it then that's what you think.

Education is just another term for learn.

And many people believe that learn is a term

To educate yourself or say "I am educated"

Education, a tool some used in other civilizations

To determine their leaders and highest ranks. But

Most of their knowledge was not found where it is

Suppose to be

In school where it was found occasionally

I learned mostly everything from t.v., movies, and listening

To people on the streets

Where it was friends, family, or no one at all to me

Just another stranger on the street

What I heard is how I wanted to speak

What I saw is how I wanted to be

I learned I need and should value many things

By actually watching movies and

Thinking, make decisions, and really considering

My life and how I wanted to be.

I just want to say you do learn many things

But still, education, to me, is born on the streets

And just migrated to classroom seats.

I believe many people who value education

Made a decision, a decision to listen, a decision to learn

A decision to take education seriously

Once again, education is found in schools, occasionally.

—DF

According to DF, "education, to me, is born on the streets and just migrated to classroom seats." As students occupy these seats, they bring with them a literate currency that is informed by their peer, pop cultural, family, and community literacy, all of which play an active role in shaping their identity. However, in taking these seats, these students open themselves up to school literacy that can either draw and build on or diminish their existing literacies, in what Meacham (2001) describes as a crisis at literate crossroads. However, as stated by Meacham, "The crossroads response to crisis is movement, connection, and communication between worlds, toward the achievement of new possibilities amidst crisis" (pp. 183–184). As educators, we are at the center of this crisis, and it is up to us to determine whether or not the connection between the literate worlds of students manifests itself as crisis or communication.

As an instructor for the PEACE class, I reflect on my own educational experiences, which led me to believe that the only viable option for educational transformation is allowing students' realities to enter my classroom. Through their poetry, spoken, and written words, my students have taught me that in order to be an effective critical educator, I must first be willing to once again become a student who listens, values, and appreciates the literate currency that they possess and incorporate it into the process of schooling. I must create the "as if" learning communities of achievement and excellence for my students. In failing to do so, I contribute to a structure and system that enables education to only occasionally take place in schools.

CONCLUSION

To sum up, in this chapter, we have situated African American students' literate currency within Bourdieu's (1986) conceptualization of cultural capital. We have drawn from Perry's (2003) notion of "as if" learning communities in order to articulate the importance of creating a space where the expression of African American students' literate currency, and thus cultural capital, can occur. In visualizing the PEACE class as an "as if" learning community, we have endeavored to create a space in which the literate currency of our students can be expressed through creative writing. As demonstrated here, in creating this space, our students' literate currency manifests itself in poetic and paragraph form and, in some cases, serves to counter preconceived notions of their literate abilities.

By allowing our students to express themselves without limiting their mode of expression, we were able to gain powerful insight into their lived realities while gaining critical insight into the multiple aspects and complexities of their identities. In sharing their work, our students were able to communicate their literate abilities to both PEACE class facilitators and to one another. This afforded us the opportunity to gain a more holistic picture of our students as individuals and as class participants. As a result, we were able to engage our students in writing that connected them to themselves, their peers, their community, and the larger world. Through this connection, as an "as if" learning community, we were able to discuss issues such as self-mutilation, notions of beauty, racism, violence, culture, and education. More importantly, we were able to reinforce our students' identities and confidence through writing while revitalizing their hopes and possibilities "as if" they are not only free, but agents of transformation.

REFERENCES

Anzaldua, G. (1987). *Borderlands/La frontera: The new mestiza.* San Francisco, CA: Aunt Lute Book Company,

Bourdieu, P. (1973). Cultural reproduction and social reproduction. In R. Brown (Ed.), *Knowledge, education and cultural change* (pp. 71–112). London: Tavistock.

Bourdieu, P. (1977). Symbolic power. In D. Gleeson (Ed.), *Identity and structure: Issues in the sociology of education* (pp. 112–119). Driffield, UK: Nafferton Books.

Bourdieu, P. (1986). The forms of capital. In J. G. Richardson (Ed.), *Handbook on research for the sociology of education* (pp. 241–258). New York: Greenwood Press,

Carter, P. L. (2003). "Black" cultural capital, status positioning, and schooling conflicts for low-income African American youth. *Social Problems, 50*(1), 136–155.

DiMaggio, P. (1979). Review essay on Pierre Bourdieu. *American Journal of Sociology, 84*(6), 1460–1474.

Freire, P. (1970). *Pedagogy of the oppressed.* New York: The Continuum International Publishing Group.

Gee, J. (1989). What is literacy? *Journal of Education, 171,* 5–17.

Harker, R. K. (1984). On reproduction, habitus and education. *British Journal of Sociology and Education, 5*(2), 117–127.

hooks, b. (1989). *Talking back: Thinking feminist, thinking black.* Boston, MA: South End Press.

Kohl, H. (1994). I won't learn from you: Confronting student resistance. In B. Bigelow, L. Christensen, S. Karp, B. Miner, & B. Peterson (Eds.), *Rethinking our classrooms: Teaching for equity and justice* (Vol. 1, pp. 134–135). Milwaukee, WI: Rethinking Our Schools.

Lorde, A. (1984). *Sister Outsider: Essays and speeches.* Berkeley, CA: The Crossing Press.

McLaren, P. (2003). *Life in schools: An introduction to critical pedagogy in the foundations of education.* Boston, MA: Pearson.

Meacham, S. J. (2000-2001). Literacy at the crossroads: Movement, connection, and communication within the research literature on literacy and cultural diversity. In W. G. Secada (Ed.), *Review of research in education, (Vol. 25, pp. 181–208). Washington, DC: American Education Research Association.*

Obidah, J. E. (1998). Black—My story: Literate currency in everyday schooling. In D. E. Alvermann, K. A. Hinchman, D. W. Moore, S. F. Phelps, & D. R. Waff (Eds.), *Reconceptualizing the literacies in adolescents's lives* (pp. 51–71). Mahwah, NJ: Lawrence Erlbaum Associates.

Perry, T. (2003). Achieving in post-civil rights America: The outline of a theory. In T. Perry, C. Steele, & A. G. Hilliard III (Eds.), *Young, gifted and Black: Promoting high achievement among African American students* (pp. 87–108). Boston, MA: Beacon Press.

Swartz, D. (1997). *Culture and power: The sociology of Pierre Bourdieu.* Chicago: The University of Chicago Press.

7

Adolescent Agency and Literacy

David W. Moore
Arizona State University

James W. Cunningham
University of North Carolina—Chapel Hill

This second edition of *Adolescent Agency and Literacy* comes at an opportune time. National and state politicians in the United States now have secondary schooling on their agendas, and this foretells increased high-stakes, test-based accountability systems that emphasize reading. We contend that such systems will be counterproductive—and possibly deplorable—to adolescents and their literacies if the role of agency is ignored or misunderstood. During life in general and literacy learning in particular, adolescents exert their agency, or "self-direction" (Holland, Lachicotte, Skinner, & Cain, 1998, p. 4), facing choices, making decisions, and considering possible consequences. Acknowledging this dimension of adolescents embraces their humanity and bolsters secondary-school literacy initiatives.

We address agency in this chapter because accountability-based reading reforms, which emphasize high standards, clear expectations, and strict consequences (Conley & Hinchman, 2004), fail to address this important aspect of the literacies in adolescents' lives. These reforms portray adolescents as little more than passive figures for educators to control rather than as active, independent, and richly detailed human beings for educators to advise and assist. These reforms emphasize external forces and ignore adolescents' internal worlds. Because adolescents are not clay, such reforms are doomed to be rendered less effective by the decisions adolescents are not expected to make or not supposed to make—but do make.

As university professors involved in literacy education, our collaboration goes back more than 20 years (Cunningham, Moore, Cunningham, & Moore, 1983). We have spent countless hours together hammering out educational issues. When the opportunity emerged to contribute to the first edition of this book, we decided to concentrate on agency because we believed it deserved more attention than it had been receiving. We primarily consulted the writings of philosophers and social theorists who addressed this topic because agency, like values or moral obligations, is not amenable to scientific experiment.

In this second edition, we clarify many of our original ideas by streamlining their presentation and refining their examples. We also update our original treatment, describing some new thinking about agency's contribution to academic identities. We retain our central contention that agency plays a crucial role in the literacies in adolescents' lives.

A CASE OF PERSUASIVE WRITING

Our discussion of adolescent agency and literacy begins with a case study of a high school persuasive writing lesson presented by Nespor (1987). The classroom actions presented here provide a clear point of reference for considering adolescents' agency relative to their academic reading and writing. Additionally, this case portrays actual classroom life; it is not a fictional account. It presents a common, naturally occurring classroom experience. This case also describes a literacy event in rich detail, devoting several pages to narrating what happened, and it portrays student as well as teacher actions.

Nespor's (1987) classroom literacy event centers on a 2-week-long persuasive writing assignment in an 11th-grade English class. Nespor observed and audiotaped the classroom interactions, interviewed the teacher and students several times, and analyzed the compositions the students produced during the assignment. Nespor's account of the event highlights the thoughts and actions of the teacher, Mr. Shaw, and three of his urban middle-track students, Arthur, Margaret, and Benny.

In his school district, Mr. Shaw was considered a proficient teacher of composition. He had a deep personal interest in writing, having written short stories and novels. He indicated that teaching English was a way to keep in contact with writing. The 11th-grade English class Mr. Shaw taught was meant to culminate a planned writing curriculum that students began in 9th grade, although he indicated that students came to him with little common writing experiences because teachers presented the curriculum so differently. Mr. Shaw considered the college-bound students in his class, who comprised about half, to be more motivated to improve their writing than the other half who were not college bound.

Mr. Shaw used one-on-one consultations, or conferences, to work intensively with the students who chose to seek his help with their writing. To occupy the rest of the class while he held individual consultations, Mr. Shaw assigned a heavy load consisting of vocabulary work, book reports, journals, grammar units, and essay-writing assignments. This work load meant that students needed to keep busy during each class period, which typically consisted of 40 to 45 minutes of loosely monitored work time.

Mr. Shaw had two broad goals for his writing instruction: proficiency with structural, or mechanical, features of writing for non-college-bound students; and proficiency with structure plus style, or embellishment, features for college-bound students. At the beginning of new writing assignments, he taught the structural elements of a particular genre to the whole class. Then he expected serious (i.e., college-bound) students to develop writing style by consulting with him individually about their drafts.

In the particular event Nespor (1987) described, Mr. Shaw spent 4 days preparing students for a persuasive essay assignment. He gave explicit structural guidelines for the task (i.e., present a general statement and a topic sentence in the first paragraph, produce three paragraphs for the body of the paper, link each paragraph with clear transition terms, include three supports in each paragraph, close with a paragraph explaining the importance or implications of the argument). Students practiced forming arguments about a topic by writing a few sentences each for 55 different topics (e.g., killing baby seals for fur), and they practiced using transitions and connectives by completing search-and-match fill-in-the-blank worksheets.

After the preparatory exercises, Mr. Shaw specified the persuasive writing assignment. He compared the production of the essay with a mathematics problem, giving the students a formula for solving the problem and the expectation to follow the plan in order to receive full credit. His formula, called the *three-three structure*, was a variation of the familiar five-paragraph essay. The first paragraph was to introduce the paper, each of the next three paragraphs was to contain three supports for its assertion (hence the name *three-three*), and the fifth paragraph was to explain the importance or implications of the argument. Mr. Shaw provided models of essays and essay outlines, a list of acceptable topics, brainstorming sheets, frameworks for outlining and proofreading, a sequence of products to be submitted before composing the final paper, and criteria for assigning grades.

The three students Nespor (1987) focused on enacted Mr. Shaw's persuasive writing assignment differently. Arthur saw writing as the production of stories, a strategy that had worked comfortably for him in the past, so he approached the persuasive writing task as he had approached others. He selected flying as his topic because of personal interest rather than controversial content for which supporting arguments could be more readily constructed. He did not outline a draft because, "Once I get it flowing, I can just put it down and it usually goes together okay" (Nespor, 1987, p. 216). He did not confer with others about his writing because his past independent efforts had been successful.

The way Margaret completed the persuasive writing assignment differed from Arthur's method. Margaret knew about the structure and function of different genres from previous English classes, she had produced persuasive pieces in a speech class, and she realized that Mr. Shaw wanted the essay to argue a specific point and be in the best written form possible. Rather than work alone like Arthur, Margaret conferred with Mr. Shaw about her confusion producing three supports in each of the three required paragraphs, and she obtained proofreading help from a peer to produce appropriate transition signals.

Benny earned an F on his persuasive essay largely because he transferred the form of the persuasive essay he produced the year earlier to the form Mr. Shaw expected this year. Benny previously had followed a thesis–antithesis–synthesis format for a persuasive essay, so he disregarded Mr. Shaw's format for three paragraphs supporting a single argument. When Benny showed Mr. Shaw his outline, their frames clashed. Mr. Shaw thought Benny's plan for an antithesis paragraph contradicted what the prior paragraph stated. After Benny was unable to explain this apparent contradiction during several consultations, he simply quit working on the paper. His decision to take an F on this paper was mediated by his knowing that he still would pass English, and he needed to concentrate on his chemistry and American history courses, which were challenging English for his attention.

Nespor (1987) interpreted the literacy event enacted by this teacher and his students through a *school task* perspective that emphasized students and teachers conceptions of academic work. In the particular event summarized here, Margaret earned a high grade on this assignment in part because she was proficient with Mr. Shaw's setup. However, when Arthur and Benny connected their prior experiences, knowledge and beliefs, and current academic situations to Mr. Shaw's assignment, they produced disjunctions and did not succeed like Margaret.

We find Nespor's (1987) school task perspective on this event to be reasonable as far as it goes. However, using a different conceptual frame—interpreting this case from the perspective of agency—focuses on a dimension that we believe deserves literacy educators' attention and action.

AFFIRMING AGENCY

The human dimension of agency emphasizes individual freedom. It focuses on autonomy, accounting for some of individuals' unique thoughts, beliefs, and feelings. Agency addresses humanity's free will and self-determination. It involves personal decision making. When people assert their agency, they carry out their intentions, acting according to their own purposes. In the case of Mr. Shaw's writing assignment, Arthur's, Margaret's, and Benny's actions could have been explored as instances of the students uniquely interpreting their situations and distinctively making choices within those situations.

Acknowledging agency draws attention away from emphases on classroom settings that constrain or enable students's actions. Such emphases often portray the social environment (Panel on High-Risk Youth, 1993) and teaching–learning processes (Lee, Bryk, & Smith, 1993) as flowing in a unidirectional, top-down pattern. They depict learners as unreflectively acting according to race, class, gender, and work roles (Bowles & Gintis, 1976). Overemphasizing classroom settings—along with federally mandated accountability systems—shortchanges adolescents' purposeful thoughts and actions within the settings, obscuring students' interpretations and personal decisions that help shape the worlds they inhabit.

The dimension of agency probably is most apparent when people enact it, making choices and realizing responsibility for them. Sometimes people say, "I wish I had acted differently," realizing that another course of action could have been chosen. Human agency is most obvious when people manifest self-reliance and personal responsibility. In the following exchange, Carla tells of herself assuming control of and responsibility for her academic literacy:

Interviewer: Do you have a special study technique?
Carla: Well, I have my little techniques, but I think the best way to study is just to let your mind know that you are going to do something; that you are going to pass this test. (Farrell, 1994, p. 125)

Cunningham has noted the responses of a few friends and family members to a true anecdote he shared with them that points out different beliefs about the existence of agency. The anecdote involves a pair of identical twin boys who were raised the same (dressed the same, shared a room, had the same teacher(s) every year in school, etc.). In their late teens, one of these twins began a life of crime that has resulted in him being in and out of jail. About the same time, the other boy committed himself to a life of honesty and hard work that he has maintained through several jobs and promotions. When asked to explain why the twins turned out so differently, one person told Cunningham that it could not be a true story, another said that the boys could not really have been raised identically, and a third said that there was probably some injury in the womb to the one who turned out badly. A fourth person attributed the two young men's differences to the source that the law-abiding twin himself attributed it to: personal decision making.

This anecdote reveals how people typically invoke genetic or environmental factors as the only forces shaping human action. Some of Cunningham's friends and family members apparently consider agency to be immaterial or nonexistent, thinking that humans are mostly—if not entirely—determined by some complex of genetics (nature) and environment (nurture), the latter including prenatal care as well as sociocultural factors such as race, economic class, and gender. At least one of his circle, however, seems to acknowledge a role for agency, or self-direction, in human affairs.

Many philosophers have argued for freedom of the human will.[1] Such philosophers of agency generally base their advocacy of human freedom on three grounds: (a) dismissing freedom eliminates all moral responsibility for human action because one is not responsible for doing what one was compelled to do; (b) dismissing freedom denies the commonsense perception that people are constantly making decisions that they could decide another way; and (c) dismissing freedom eliminates hope for changing life situations because whatever will be, will be, and there is no need to try to take positive action or oppose evil. While agreeing with these negative reasons, we consider internal dialogues to be sensible positive reasons for upholding agency, especially when interacting with adolescents. However, before explaining internal dialogues, we introduce arguments against agency in order to contextualize our explanation.

DENYING AGENCY

Although we find agency to be a compelling dimension of humanity, not everyone does. Many influential philosophers deny agency by emphasizing internal and external forces as the determinants of thought and action. The theology of the Reformation (1517–1564) and the science of the Enlightenment (1605–1789), which have permeated Western thinking over the past three or four centuries, place causal determinism over agency. Causal deterministic thinking assumes that everything that exists or occurs has been brought about by an earlier state or event, or by God.

Causal determinism has gradually come to dominate the thinking in most academic disciplines, especially the sciences. The argument about whether genetics or environment contributes more to human activity reveals this domination because the argument itself is based on the assumption that human activity is causally determined. All that is left to argue about is which of two causes, nature or nurture, is more determining.

---

[1]The main time-honored philosophers of agency have been René Descartes (1596–1650), Thomas Reid (1710–1796), Jean-Jacques Rousseau (1712–1778), Soren Kierkegaard (1813–1855), Charles S. Peirce (1839–1914), William James (1842–1910), John Dewey (1859–1952), George Herbert Mead (1863–1931), and Jean-Paul Sartre (1905–1980). Philosophers of agency from the 1970s through the 1990s included Mortimer Adler, Elizabeth Anscombe, Roderick Chisholm, Robert Kane, Robert Nozick, Richard Taylor, Peter van Inwagen, and David Wiggins.

Western philosophers, literary critics, and social scientists instituted a withering denial of agency in the second half of the 20th century with the ascendancy of two types of causal determinism: structuralism (see, for example, Chomsky, 1968; Culler, 1975; Jakobson, 1961/1981; Lévi-Strauss, 1958/1963) and poststructuralism (see, for example, Althusser, 1965/1969; Barthes, 1970/1974; Baudrillard, 1973/1975; Derrida, 1967/1976; Foucault, 1984; Kuhn, 1970; Lacan, 1971/1977). This denial of agency seems to reflect as well as contribute to everyday public opinion. Structuralists and poststructuralists differ on many issues, but both groups of thinkers have denied agency by decentering the subject.

The term *decentering the subject* has a very specific technical meaning in academic discourse. When something is centered, it is placed in the core of a conceptual network where it is thought to have special, central influence. To center a principle is to assume that it explains most of what relates to it. For example, Marxism centers economic class as the principle that drives human action; Freudianism centers sexual development as the major factor in human personality and adjustment. To explain oppression, critical social theorists center principles of race in critical race theory, gender in feminism, and discourse in Foucauldian analyses (Leonardo, 2004).

In Nespor's (1987) case study, Arthur's decision to write a story about flying to fulfill Mr. Shaw's persuasive writing assignment could be interpreted from a structuralist viewpoint. In such an interpretation, Arthur's previous schooling could be said to have caused him to unthinkingly privilege narration over exposition and pleasantry over controversy. The idea of centering Arthur as an individual, a subject, who encounters choices, makes decisions, and anticipates consequences would not be emphasized and probably not even acknowledged.

Structuralism leaves little or no room for agency because it explains human thought and action with a centered principle rather than with a centered individual. Structuralists see every unit of language, society, and culture as part of a whole structure, and they see that structure giving meaning to the parts. Consequently, structuralists have tended to remove people from the center of their lives, denying the role of individual decision making as a core explanation of human action.

Poststructuralists generally have completed the work of decentering the subject that structuralists maintained. Poststructuralism is a kind of structuralism because it, too, places great emphasis on principles that influence people's lives. However, it is a reaction against structuralism because it does not center any one particular principle; it envisions a turbulent mix of constantly shifting principles. Poststructuralists do not recognize a centered principle that is the core influence of any network.

Most poststructuralists have decentered the subject to the degree that every individual is seen as the site of nonintegrated influences and forces. A poststructuralist account of Margaret's persuasive essay in Nespor's (1987) case study could be presented as her response to an enormously complicated matrix of sometimes conflicting forces and influences. The matrix might include all the persuasive discourse she had previously read or heard, all the positive experiences she had seeking help from teachers and peers, and all her familial and social encouragements to succeed. The idea of Margaret exerting her will and choosing how to write her persuasive essay usually would not enter a poststructuralist account of her actions.

The impact of structuralism and poststructuralism on contemporary thinking in the academy has been so broad that many scholars now assume the idea of agency is dead as an intellectually respectable notion. Each person is held to be a postmodern individual produced by unique and contradictory social, cultural, and linguistic histories. In this view, adolescent readers and writers are seen as sites of all prior influences rather than as individuals capable of deciding among choices, or even creating new choices. What adolescents think and do is said to be causally determined by the networks of which they are a part, so adolescents' thoughts and actions are said to vary only when the networks vary.

A PERSPECTIVE ON AGENCY

The denials of agency just presented obviously have not convinced us to dismiss this dimension. Instead, we accept some social theorists' claims of a constant interaction between human agency and causal, structuralist determinism (see, for example, Archer, 2003; Schilling, 1992; Sztompka, 1994). We view agency and structure as inextricably linked, not necessarily in opposition. We recognize social enactment theorists' far-reaching claim that structure and agency are interdependent, each contributing to the other (Giddens, 1979, 1991). According to social enactment theory, agency is realized within limits, and individuals' choices reinforce or transform those limits over time. People both produce and are products of their social environments. The central message here is that people simultaneously (a) decide how they will act, (b) are influenced and limited in their decisions by their contexts, and (c) contribute to contexts that influence and limit how they will act.[2] This section offers a perspective on agency that we believe justifies emphasizing it when addressing the literacies in adolescents' lives.

You probably have known people who experienced terrible personal hardships, yet who interpreted the hardships positively and overcame them in ways you would not have predicted. Such people internally make the best of appalling situations. Viktor Frankl, a Holocaust survivor who wrote eloquently about his concentration camp experiences, put it this way, "Everything can be taken from a man but one thing: the last of the human freedoms—to choose one's attitude in any given set of circumstances, to choose one's own way" (Frankl, 1962, p. 65). He goes on with this compelling account, "There were always choices to make. Every day, every hour, offered the opportunity to make a decision, a decision which determined whether you would or would not submit to those powers which threatened to rob you of your very self, your inner freedom" (pp. 65–66). As these quotations illustrate, people are free to interpret the events of their lives (Colapietro, 1989; Wiley, 1994). This freedom of interpretation keeps peoples' past and current situations from determining their futures. It is the essence of human agency.

The remainder of this section sketches a perspective on agency that has the potential to enrich views of people in general as well as adolescents and their literacies in particular. First, we describe how the internal dialogue of the human mind permits the presence of agency. Next, we expand this description by explaining how social experiences that operate through language and caring relationships develop agency.

---

[2]We present agency in somewhat universal terms, with no attempt to qualify how different groups might experience and enact it differently. We realize that discursive practices constitute people certain ways (Davies & Harre', 1990); however, we could not locate sufficient information to fully portray different discursive practices systematically shaping youthful groups' enactments of agency.

Presence of Agency

Agency is present amid the internal dialogues of the mind. It exists as people continually negotiate links among their past, present, and future selves. It becomes apparent when people orchestrate their own and others' voices across time.

A compelling case for human agency existing amid the internal dialogues of the mind has been derived from literary characters' exchanges (Bakhtin, 1975/1981; Morson & Emerson, 1990). Dostoevsky, a premier Russian novelist of the mid-1800s, is widely admired for the dialogues he presents between, among, and within his characters. These dialogues not only show how people are constrained and shaped by their personal histories and environments, but they show how people enact agency when faced with decisions. Dostoevsky deftly represents people composing their responses to their environments, showing how people author their own lives.

The internal dialogue of the human mind continually coordinates different internal voices, and it answers questions that the self poses to itself (Bakhtin, 1975/1981). Some voices and answers are authoritative, some are internally persuasive, and most lie somewhere between these poles. The authoritative voices have been assimilated from the speech one has heard from others. The internally persuasive voices have been created in previous internal dialogues; they are voices the self has found convincing. Because agency both results from and influences internal dialogues, and because these dialogues are always somewhat unpredictable, the self is never finished. This unfinalizability is important to take into account especially when working with youth who act recalcitrant.

Development of Agency

The internal dialogues that account for human agency arise differently from person to person. Among other things, they develop according to social experiences and dialogic relationships.

Social Experiences.   Agency develops when people internalize their social experiences that operate through language (Wiley, 1994). "In the process of communication the individual is an other before he is a self" and "out of this process thought arises, i.e., conversation with one's self in the role of the specific other and then in the role of the generalized other" (Mead, 1964, p. 312–314). Stimulated by interactions with others, people come to develop internal dialogues among their past, present, and future selves. These exchanges among temporal selves constantly are negotiated in the internal conversation of thought.

Social experience also contributes to agency by posing necessities that are at odds with one another. Something as mundane as being invited to two different functions that occur at the same time contributes to an internal dialogue. "The possibility of choice in a situation in which there are contradictory requirements provides people with the possibility of acting agentically" (Davies & Harre', 1990, p. 59).

One mark of children developing higher mental functions is when they shift from being controlled entirely by the environment to independent planning and self-regulation. This independence occurs with the onset of inner speech (i.e., internal dialogue), which is derived from social experience and linguistic interactions with others (Vygotsky, 1934/1986; 1981). In essence, agency develops as people communicate with others, internalize strategies from their interactions, and apply these strategies to plan and regulate their own thinking and actions.

Dialogic Relationships.   Social experiences that operate through language provide especially rich conditions for agency when they are dialogic. In dialogic relationships, people recognize themselves and others as having a unity of being (Buber, 1937/1958). People do not analyze others' specific, isolated qualities; they accept each others' entire selves. They have high regard for whatever they and others have to offer. They share a sense of caring, commitment, and responsibility. When the voices contributing to inner conversations are dialogic, they are respected and consulted diligently. Authentic dialogues—as opposed to two ongoing monologues—occur.

Dialogic relationships among voices, whether external or internal, are crucial for agency to develop. To be personal, one of us (Cunningham), whose father has been dead for many years, still relates to him caringly, hearing his voice, feeling his presence, and experiencing the freedom gained from being loved by him. Such an internal, dialogic relationship develops agency, promoting its maturation.

REANALYSIS OF A CASE OF PERSUASIVE WRITING

As we attempted to show in the previous section, agency is a sensible contrast to the causal determinists' claim that external forces alone drive human thought and action. The internal dialogues that permit agency also play important roles. To demonstrate how this perspective contributes to understanding adolescents' literacies in academic contexts, we first reanalyze Nespor's (1987) case study, suggesting instructional moves with agency in mind. Then, in the next section, we show how agency contributes to youths' identities as school-based readers and writers.

Inspired by Hinchman (1998), we reconstruct Nespor's (1987) case by imagining the possible inner lives of three adolescent writers. Speculating about the thinking of Arthur, Margaret, and Benny helps us portray how agency might connect to and operate within adolescents' literacies. Of course, we have no knowledge of these three persons other than what Nespor presented. And even if we knew more, as Hinchman (1998) warned readers, "[Our] elaborations [are] not likely to match anything known by the … actual participants " (p. 187). Internal dialogues, after all, are not open to direct observation.

Arthur

From what Nespor told us of Arthur, we imagine that his internal dialogue during Mr. Shaw's 2-week-long persuasive writing assignment might have consisted of several internally persuasive voices. At least one of his inner voices probably said that success in writing is more likely when one tells a story about something one knows and cares about. The voices that argued against the values of conferring with fellow students and outlining surely were internally persuasive, too. An especially powerful voice may have said something like, "We should complete our assignments and pass. Beyond that, school (or English class or writing) isn't worth the effort." Together, these voices may have coalesced into the decisions that Arthur made and the actions he took or failed to take.

Showing the *Arthurs* of the world that they habitually close out the counsel of others might address agency productively. Although some of the counsel such students refuse might be well ignored, some of it might be helpful, coming from people who are knowledgeable about life and concerned about youth. We cannot ensure a change in Arthur's academic ambitions, but we can help him take responsibility for his lack of those ambitions. He will be free to change when he explicitly addresses issues about accepting advice, whether he chooses to or not.

Margaret

One dramatization for Margaret would depict her internal dialogue as having consisted largely of authoritative voices: her parents, her community or ethnic group, her previous teachers, possibly her religion, and Mr. Shaw. In this account, Margaret makes the decisions and takes the actions she does because her internal dialogue is dominated by a few unquestioned, authoritative voices. Or to put it another way, she is inscribed by the discursive practices of femininity and model student.

Although teachers generally are thankful for the *Margarets* of the world, attempts to learn whether such students' cooperation results from unquestioned acceptance is important. When we encounter people whose thinking habitually excludes both reason and personal experience, we may become concerned about them, however academically successful they might be. No one is truly educated who listens only to the voices of authority. What if the authorities are mistaken? Agency is maximized when internally persuasive voices join with authoritative voices in dialogic relations.

Benny

The major voice in Benny's internal dialogue apparently was the authoritative voice of his English teacher from the previous year who spoke with power regarding the form a persuasive essay should take. Another inner voice for Benny, however, was Mr. Shaw's authoritative voice, evidenced by Benny's decisions to outline the paper, show that outline to Mr. Shaw, and consult several times with him about it. The personally persuasive voice that prevailed then said something like, "You can only put so much effort into one class before you start hurting your performance in your other classes. If you can afford to, don't work any more on this assignment. More effort may not help your grade in this class, and it will hurt your grade in other classes."

Benny failed to orchestrate his internal dialogue in such a way that each voice was clearly heard and a conscious decision rendered about the writing formats. Once last year's English teacher had spoken, this year's English teacher was assumed to be saying the same thing without really being heard. For Benny to have overcome his problem understanding what Mr. Shaw wanted, he could have permitted the two authoritative voices to confront each other in his thinking. Had he still not understood the format, he could have asked Mr. Shaw the kinds of questions his previous English teacher might have asked to understand the similarities and differences in the two formats. In this case, Benny might not have had to choose between an F on this assignment or lower grades in chemistry and American history.

As these reanalyses show, connecting agency with adolescents' literacies sheds light on why students like Arthur and Benny performed poorly with the

2-week-long persuasive writing assignment. Perhaps we are told just too little, but Mr. Shaw's teaching seemed to allow few social experiences. Whether or not this was so, it seems instructive for such teachers and students to ask about the extent of social exchanges and to determine whether interactions with one another are in monologic or dialogic terms.

AGENCY, ACADEMIC LITERACIES, AND ACADEMIC IDENTITIES

As these reanalyses suggest, youth who enact agency readily affect their performance on writing assignments. In this section we expand what was just presented and depict youth exercising agency relative to their academic identities, their constructions of themselves as studious, intellectual kinds of people who connect with school (Jackson, 2003; Welch & Hodges, 1997).

In contrast to those who emphasize historical, institutional, and sociocultural forces shaping youths' identities (see, for example, Gee, 2001; McCallister, 2004), several theorists have been asserting that agency contributes to identities in general (Holland et al., 1998) and literate identities in particular (Hagood, 2002; McCarthey & Moje, 2002; Norton & Toohey, 2001). These writers align with theorists like Vygotsky, who claim that youth develop self-consciousness and self-reflection through social exchanges. As youth internalize various views of themselves from their interactions, they begin to compare, contrast, and play with them, seizing opportunities for combinations and modifications. They eventually take on and act out identities that position themselves various ways. In some cases these actions foster academic identities; in other cases they are impediments.

Fostering Academic Identities

Deciding whether or not to revise an essay differs substantially from deciding whether or not to drop out of school, and decisions about dropping out involve decisions about identity. Luis, a young man who shifted his attention among the streets, athletics, and academics, eventually decided to pursue academics (Hynds, 1997). When asked why he persisted with academics over other pursuits, Luis related an incident with a police officer who graphically described the grisly conditions of the state juvenile detention facility. This was a crucial moment; it disrupted Luis' flow of life experiences. He reports that at that point he decided to stop his criminal behavior, break away from many of his friends, and identify with those in mainstream academics. Decisions such as this one by Luis become critical life-defining incidents that exemplify the control humans have over their identities as well as their destinies.

By claiming an academic identity, Luis makes a pivotal decision that shapes his future literacies which, in turn, shape him. He reads school texts independently, studies seriously for tests, completes homework, and enrolls in reading-intensive courses. While pursuing academics this way, he visibly sets himself apart from others, no longer identifying with his former friends.

Along this same line, an urban college preparation program, Advancement Via Individual Determination (AVID; http://www.avidonline.org/), affects youths' identities by placing previously low-achieving students with high-achieving students (Mehan, Hubbard, & Villanueva, 1994). Teachers in this program stress the value and possibility of attending college, and they emphasize literacy skills such as note taking, test-taking strategies, and general study tips. Students have contributed to their enablement in this program by independently assuming academic identities without losing their ethnic identities, a practice termed *accommodation without assimilation*. The students manage both identities by bringing nonacademic friends into academic settings, planning to attend college in Mexico, and conforming to the dominant language and culture in academic settings while maintaining the language and culture of their home, peer group, and historical community in nonacademic settings. These linguistic- and ethnic-minority students independently construct border-crossing strategies and settings that allow them to pursue college preparation.

Newly immigrated students who enroll in high school often arrive with academic records the school staff cannot interpret and with language proficiencies that obscure their ability to perform mainstream academic tasks (Harklau, 1994). Consequently, school counselors typically misplace newcomers in low-track classes. Rather than succumb to the ineffectual environments of these classes, many students choose to negotiate upper track placements with their teachers, counselors, and school administrators. The students take it upon themselves to demonstrate academic identities through politeness, punctuality, and interest in school work to convince officials that they should be allowed to jump tracks to more academically challenging literacy-rich experiences.

In another situation, two youth produce—at least for themselves—meaningful discussions about what they read in their Advanced Placement English class (Moore, 1998). Heather and Alex maintain a privileged identity in class often without the explicit consent of their teacher or peers. They independently ask and answer questions of each other, bring to class and read aloud passages not tied to the official curriculum, frequently question the teacher about vocabulary terms and obscure passages, encourage each other to pursue particular lines of thinking, and insert and hold onto personal interpretations of texts not endorsed by the teacher. Alex and Heather exert their agency to identify themselves as classroom leaders who produce situations that promote deep and personal discussions of what they read.

Impeding Academic Identities

The examples presented in the previous segment portray students exerting agency as part of identifying themselves as academically literate individuals. But the educational research literature also contains many stories of adolescents who identify themselves differently.

Students have been shown to resist small-group writing discussions and brainstorming sessions because they identify those who participate in these practices as weak (Finders, 1996). For instance, Cleo explains her refusal to comply in small-group sharings with these words:

> I hate it when you have to share ideas in a group. People can steal your ideas. If anyone gets me an idea, I have to reject it. It has to be mine. I don't share my real ideas. (Finders, 1996, p. 109)

Dottie is one who chooses to resist peer responses during writing. Stressing the need for an audience and for a community of writers, her teacher requires classmates to sign written responses to daily journal entries. However, Dottie resists this practice by changing ink pens, writing a response to her own entry, and signing another student's name. Dottie's frequent comment, "It's none of their damn business," (Finders, 1996, p. 116) expresses her private loner identity.

When Tiffany's teacher reads orally to the class, Tiffany complains about it, rests her head on her desk, closes her eyes, scowls, and yawns. Yet during a private interview, Tiffany recalls minute details of the book, relates scenes from it to her life, and connects the book to others she has read. Her classroom enactment fits the rebellious identity she chooses to convey publicly, while privately she receives her teacher's instruction like an accepting learner.

As with Tiffany, Timony actively constructs identities in a manner that is "continuous, ever-shifting, and evolving" (Hagood, 2002, p. 255). Timony avidly reads a variety of texts that his teachers know about, although they worry that reading material such as *Rolling Stone* magazine might contribute to his occasional complacence and unruliness. Timony presents himself variously as an avid reader, bad student, and disturbed teenager, keeping these manifestations moving as he goes through school. Timony's exercise of agency to portray himself as a bad student and disturbed teenager worries his teachers, although he actually positions himself closer to mainstream academics than they realize.[3]

Adolescent second-language learners have been shown to assert agency in ways that defy classroom expectations (McKay & Wong, 1996). For instance, Michael responds to the novel *Dragonwings* resourcefully. Michael draws a scene showing Chinese-style buildings labeled in Chinese with euphemisms for brothels. He depicts two boys, labeled in English as two of his friends, approaching two curvaceous women lounging in the doorways of the brothels. Michael's placement of his friends in the scene; his focus on brothels, which were tenuously connected with the novel; his use of Chinese writing, which his teacher cannot read; and his competent drawing satisfy his academic and personal inclinations. These actions express Michael's multiple preferred identities such as *popular friend, sexually knowing male, Chinese nationalist insider*, and *visual artist*. They go against identities imposed on Michael such as *serious scholar, model minority*, or *rudimentary English writer*.

Many literacy-based studies of youth choosing to adopt identities that impede their academic success follow the resistance tradition pioneered by Willis (1977) and Ogbu (1978). According to this tradition, students choose to identify themselves as rebels because they believe traditional school practices represent corrupt race-, class-, or gender-based power structures or because they consider these practices irrelevant to their current concerns and future aspirations. And when students decide to rebel, they disrupt or withdraw from academic pursuits, frequently leaving school, thereby rejecting opportunities for academic development (Alpert, 1991).

CONCLUSION

Educators need not work to create agency. Youth already enact agency, with or without permission or instruction. Educators who acknowledge this condition support youths' wise use of this power.

---

[3]Rather than call presentations of self *identities*, Hagood (2002) notably refers to them as *subjectivities*, highlighting individuals' (i.e., subjects') constant agentive transformations according to particular contexts. Hagood links the idea of subjectivity with Foucault's *technologies of the self*, mechanisms by which individuals transform themselves in order to attain desired conditions.

As teachers, teacher educators, researchers, and parents, we realize that adolescents choose whether or not to read, write, and participate in school. A fitting response to this situation is to work to better understand the choices adolescents have, seek ways to give them more and better choices, help them become more aware of their choices, and assist them in making informed decisions. Along these lines, educational beliefs, practices, policies, and programs deserve attention.

Beliefs

Educators who acknowledge agency believe that adolescents make important decisions about their identities, the kinds of people they are and will be. These educators believe that youth are in a state of becoming, that they are taking up positions in the world now as well as in the future. Such beliefs help disrupt the notion that youths' identities are fixed, that adolescents can be pigeonholed now and in the future. When you were 16 years old, were you the same as when you were 12? If you are at least 20 years old, are you the same as when you were 16? Agency conveys the possibility of people directing their lives differently over time. It points to the notion that youth now and in the future decide how literacies will fit into their lives.

As Fecho, Davis, and Moore (chap. 10, this volume) assert, those who close their eyes to adolescent decision making often assume that language processing deficits—and not the decisions being made—are what limit youths' access to academic literacies. Working to remediate deficits rather than to inform choices too easily misguides instruction, leading to mistaken interventions. Focusing on agency does not imply that teaching students such things as cognitive strategies or writing patterns with textbooks is irrelevant; rather, it means that attention to agency is crucial.

Practices

When educators share the belief that people are active decision makers in the course of their lives, students have opportunities to evolve a greater sense of personal agency. Asking, "If you are not responsible for your actions, then who is?" might rouse adolescents to contemplate existential issues about the choices they make. Educators can help clarify the maxim that actions have consequences, so thinking through what one decides to do is crucial. Talking about readings from authors like Frankl (1962) and aphorisms like this one from Abraham Lincoln, "Your own resolution to succeed is more important than any one thing," might seem banal to some, yet life-changing to others. Inquiry into how reading and writing fit individuals' lives can be fostered throughout the school year. Such practices provide opportunities to develop conscious, informed decision making. Believing that adolescents who avoid or resist academic literacy are making rational decisions at the time might enable educators to work more effectively with these individuals rather than against them (Blackburn, 2004).

Acknowledging agency involves providing honest and compelling information about the ways reading and writing play out when individuals outside of school perform their jobs, run their households, act as citizens, and lead personal lives. One way to inform adolescents' decisions about reading and writing is to have people from many age groups, from many social and economic settings, and from community and work forces voice their experiences with and convictions about literacy.

These people could serve as guest speakers to classes as well as interviewees in individual or group situations on and off campus.

Informing adolescents' decisions about reading and writing can be accomplished by positioning literacy in the widest possible context. From a racial perspective, for example, adolescent African Americans (e.g., Scott, 1993) have attested to the impact authors such as Malcolm X had on their commitments to social justice. Information sessions along these lines, especially at the beginning of the semester, can help set a tone and common reference point for decision making throughout the year.

Along with informing decisions, acknowledging agency entails substantial use of instructional dialogue. Classroom dialogues can vary widely in that they may be whole-class, small-group, or paired; teacher-directed or peer-led; about literary or content texts; and preceding or following other kinds of instruction with the text. The large body of theory and research on classroom discussion (Burbules, 1993; Holden & Schmit, 2002) has much to say about using dialogue in literacy instruction.

Educators can make use of classrooms as rightful sites for negotiation, places for a give-and-take about the meanings of texts as well as about the values of literacies. The class discussions most likely to promote agency are suggested by the realization that "both relativism and dogmatism equally exclude all argumentation, all authentic dialogue, by making it either unnecessary (relativism) or impossible (dogmatism)" (Bakhtin, quoted in Morson, 1981, p. viii). When teachers or students limit the floor in a classroom dialogue to authoritative voices, they legislate dogmatism. When teachers or students exclude authoritative voices from a classroom dialogue, they legislate relativism. Authentic dialogue permits both authoritative and personally persuasive voices to interact.

Noting the ways voices are orchestrated during classroom discussions also points to agency. Having each person participate as one voice in a literature discussion circle might improve group dynamics, but it will not necessarily develop self-direction. To aid this development, students might become responsible for orchestrating classroom talk, rotating the responsibility for keeping the discussion moving and on point. At other times, students might conduct a discussion while others observe it, then all might assess it, writing or speaking about its dynamics analytically or critically. The idea here is to observe the types of exchanges that occur and inquire into how youth appropriate or resist them.

Another instructional practice that addresses agency involves multiply-voiced teacher presentations. Teacher lectures, demonstrations, and multimedia productions can be dialogic. For a teacher presentation to be dialogic, the struggle that led to the meaning of the presentation is revealed, often through a brief think-aloud or a direct explanation of the process. The different voices that participated in the struggle are heard. Much has been written and said about the need to teach students how to think (Bransford, Brown, & Cocking, 1999). When teachers make multiply-voiced presentations in which their internal dialogues result in meaning, they are modeling for students how self-direction shapes their thinking and learning.

Policies and Programs

The temptation for educational policy makers to utilize top-down, accountability-based mandates considered suitable for everyone in every school might result from not realizing or caring that adolescents enact self-direction. If legislators, school officers, and others in positions of authority were to acknowledge youths' enactments of agency as developed through social experiences and dialogic relationships, perhaps they would be less committed to tests and more committed to communities. Perhaps they would favor policies that foster programs where youth and adults are embedded in cultures of commitment that are developed according to schools' and classrooms' particular circumstances. Perhaps they would support programs that accentuate youths' exercise of agency when forming identities, programs where youth can interrogate existing conditions, then construct literacies that fit the conditions.

A FINAL WORD

Connecting agency with the literacies in adolescents' lives might help educators form productive conceptual networks when considering beliefs, practices, policies, and programs. For instance, research lines focusing on literary response (Trousdale & McMillan, 2003) as well as psychological topics such as resilience (Rouse, 2001), motivation (Ford, 1992; Walls & Little, 2005), volition (Corno, 1993), self regulation (Borkowski, Carr, Rellinger, & Pressley, 1990), and self-efficacy (Bandura, 1989) follow different theoretical and methodological traditions, but they can be linked to each other. They all share a tendency to center the student in his or her literacy learning and call attention to individuals' freedom and decision making. Thinking about agency might be useful for combining insights from these literatures, from what was presented here, and from other sources, then forming a tapestry of ideas that contribute to productive reconceptualizations of the literacies in adolescents' lives.

REFERENCES

Alpert, B. (1991). Students' resistance in the classroom. *Anthropology and Education Quarterly, 22,* 350–366.

Althusser, L. (1969). *For Marx* (B. Brewster, Trans.). London: Allen Lane/The Penguin Press. (Original work published 1965)

Archer, M. S. (2003). *Structure, agency, and the internal conversation.* Cambridge, UK: Cambridge University Press.

Bakhtin, M. M. (1981). Discourse in the novel (C. Emerson & M. Holquist, Trans.). In M. Holquist (Ed.), *The dialogic imagination: Four essays.* Austin, TX: University of Texas Press. (Original work published 1975)

Bandura, A. (1989. Human agency in social cognitive theory. *American Psychologist, 44*(9), 1175–1184.

Barthes, R. (1974). *S/Z* (R. Miller, Trans.). New York: Hill & Wang. (Original work published 1970)

Baudrillard, J. (1975). *The mirror of production* (M. Poster, Trans.). St. Louis, MO: Telos Press. (Original work published 1973)

Blackburn, M. (2004). Understanding agency beyond school-sanctioned activities. *Theory into Practice, 43,* 102–110.

Borkowski, J. G., Carr, M., Rellinger, E., & Pressley, M. (1990). Self-regulated cognition: Interdependence of metacognition, attribution, and self-esteem. In B. F. Jones & L. Idol (Eds.), *Dimensions of thinking and cognitive instruction* (pp. 53–92). Hillsdale, NJ: Lawrence Erlbaum Associates.

Bowles, S., & Gintis, H. I. (1976). *Schooling in capitalist America.* New York: Basic Books.

Bransford, J. D, Brown, A. L., & Cocking, R. R. (Eds.). (1999). *How people learn: Brain, mind, experience, and school.* Washington, DC: National Academy Press.

Buber, M. (1958). *I and Thou* (R. G. Smith, Trans.). New York: Charles Scribner. (Original work published 1937)

Burbules, N. C. (1993). *Dialogue in teaching: Theory and practice.* New York: Teachers College Press.

Chomsky, N. (1968). *Language and mind.* New York: Harcourt, Brace & World.

Colapietro, V. M. (1989). *Peirce's approach to the self: A semiotic perspective on human subjectivity.* Albany, NY: State University of New York Press.

Conley, M. W., & Hinchman, K. A. (2004). No Child Left Behind: What it means for U.S. adolescents and what we can do about it. *Journal of Adolescent and Adult Literacy, 48*(1), 42–50.

Corno, L. (1993). The best-laid plans: Modern conceptions of volition and educational research. *Educational Researcher, 22*(2), 14–22.

Culler, J. D. (1975). *Structuralist poetics: Structuralism, linguistics and the study of literature.* Ithaca, NY: Cornell University Press.

Cunningham, P. M., Moore, S. A., Cunningham, J. W., & Moore, D. W. (1983). *Reading in elementary school classrooms.* New York: Longman.

Davies, B., & Harre', R. (1990). Positioning: The discursive production of selves. *Journal for the Theory of Social Behaviour, 20*(1), 43–63.

Derrida, J. (1976). *Of grammatology* (G. C. Spivak, Trans.). Baltimore, MD: Johns Hopkins University Press. (Original work published 1967)

Farrell, E. (1994). *Self and school success.* Albany: State University of New York Press.

Finders, M. J. (1996). "Just girls": Literacy and allegiance in junior high school. *Written Communication, 13*(1), 93–129.

Ford, M. E. (1992). *Motivating humans: Goals, emotions, and personal agency beliefs.* Newbury Park, CA: Sage.

Foucault, M. (1984). *The Foucault reader* (P. Rabinow, Ed.). New York: Random House.

Frankl, V. E. (1962). *Man's search for meaning: An introduction to logotherapy.* Boston: Beacon Press.

Gee, J. P. (2001). Identity as an analytic lens for research in education. In W. G. Secada (Ed.), *Review of research in education* (Vol. 25, pp. 99–125). Washington, DC: American Educational Research Association.

Giddens, A. (1979). *Central problems in social theory.* Cambridge, MA: Cambridge University Press.

Giddens, A. (1991). *Modernity and self-identity.* Stanford, CA: Stanford University Press.

Hagood, M. (2002). Critical literacy for whom? *Reading Research and Instruction, 41,* 247–266.

Harklau, L. (1994). "Jumping tracks": How language-minority students negotiate evaluations of ability. *Anthropology and Education Quarterly, 25,* 347–363.

Hinchman, K. A. (1998). Reconstructing our understandings of adolescents' participation in classroom literacy events: Learning to look through others' eyes. In D. E. Alvermann, K. A. Hinchman, D. W. Moore, S. F. Phelps, & D. R. Waff (Eds.), *Reconceptualizing the literacies in adolescents' lives* (pp. 173–192). Mahwah, NJ: Lawrence Erlbaum Associates.

Holden, J., & Schmit, J. S. (Eds.). (2002). *Inquiry and the literary text: Constructing discussions in the English classroom.* Urbana, IL: National Council of Teachers of English.

Holland, D., Lachicotte, W., Jr., Skinner, D., & Cain, C. (1998). *Identity and agency in cultural worlds.* Cambridge, MA: Harvard University Press.

Hynds, S. (1997). *On the brink: Negotiating literature and life with adolescents.* New York: Teachers College Press.

Jackson, D. B. (2003). Education reform as if student agency mattered: Academic microcultures and student identity. *Phi Delta Kappan, 84,* 579–585.

Jakobson, R. (1981). *Selected writings (Vol. 3): Poetry of grammar and grammar of poetry* (S. Rudy, Ed.). New York: Mouton. (Original work published 1961)

Kuhn, T. S. (1970). *The structure of scientific revolutions* (2nd ed.). Chicago: University of Chicago Press.

Lacan, J. (1977). *Écrits: A selection* (A. Sheridan, Trans.). New York: W. W. Norton. (Original work published 1966, 1971)

Lee, V. E., Bryk, A. S., & Smith, J. B. (1993). The organization of effective secondary schools. In L. Darling-Hammond (Ed.), *Review of research in education* (Vol. 19, pp. 171–268). Washington, DC: American Educational Research Association.

Leonardo, Z. (2004). Critical social theory and transformative knowledge: The functions of criticism in quality education. *Educational Researcher, 33*(6), 11–18.

Lévi-Strauss, C. (1963). *Structural anthropology* (C. Jacobson & B. G. Schoepfe, Trans.). New York: Basic Books. (Original work published 1958)

McCallister, C. (2004). Schooling the possible self. *Curriculum Inquiry, 34,* 425–461.

McCarthey, S. J., & Moje, E. B. (2002). Identity matters. *Reading Research Quarterly, 37,* 228–238.

McKay, S. L., & Wong, S-L. C. (1996). Multiple discourses, multiple identities: Investments and agency in second-language learning among Chinese adolescent immigrant students. *Harvard Educational Review, 66,* 577–608.

Mead, G. H. (1964). The objective reality of perspectives. In A. J. Reck (Ed.), *Selected writings* (pp. 312–314). Chicago: University of Chicago Press.

Mehan, H., Hubbard, L., & Villanueva, I. (1994). Forming academic identities: Accommodation without assimilation among involuntary minorities. *Anthropology and Education Quarterly, 25,* 91–117.

Moore, D. W. (1998). Some complexities of gendered talk about texts. *Journal of Literacy Research, 29,* 507–530.

Morson, G. S. (1981). Preface. In G. S. Morson (Ed.), *Bakhtin: Essays and dialogues on his work* (pp. vii–xiii). Chicago: University of Chicago Press.

Morson, G. S., & Emerson, C. (1990). *Mikhail Bakhtin: Creation of a prosaics.* Stanford, CA: Stanford University Press.

Nespor, J. (1987). Academic tasks in high school English class. *Curriculum Inquiry, 17,* 203–228.

Norton, B., & Toohey, K. (2001). Changing perspectives on good language learners. *TESOL Quarterly, 35,* 307–322.

Ogbu, J. (1978). *Minority education and caste.* New York: Academic Press.

Panel on High-Risk Youth. (1993). *Losing generations: Adolescents in high-risk settings.* Washington, DC: National Academy Press.

Rouse, K. A. G. (2001). Resilient students' goals and motivations. *Journal of Adolescence, 24,* 461–472.

Schilling, C. (1992). Reconceptualising structure and agency in the sociology of education: Structuration theory and schooling. *British Journal of Sociology of Education, 13,* 69–87.

Scott, K. (1993). *Monster.* New York: Atlantic Monthly Press.

Sztompka, P. (1994). Evolving focus on human agency in contemporary social theory. In P. Sztompka (Ed.), *Agency and structure* (pp. 25–60). Langhorne, PA: Gordon and Breach.

Trousdale, A. M., & McMillan, S. (2003). "Cinderella was a wuss": A young girl's responses to feminist and patriarchal folktales. *Children's Literature in Education, 34,* 1–27.

Vygotsky, L. S. (1981). The genesis of higher mental functions. In J. V. Wertsch (Ed.), *The concept of activity in Soviet psychology* (pp. 147–188). Armonk, NY: M. E. Sharpe.

Vygotsky, L. S. (1986). *Thought and language* (Rev. ed., A. Kozulin, Trans.). Cambridge, MA: MIT Press. (Original work published 1934)

Walls, T. A., & Little, T. D. (2005). Relations among personal agency, motivation, and school adjustment in early adolescence. *Journal of Educational Psychology, 97,* 23–31.

Welch, O. M., & Hodges, C. R. (1997). *Standing outside on the inside: Black adolescents and the construction of academic identity.* Albany, NY: State University of New York.

Wiley, N. (1994). *The semiotic self.* Chicago: University of Chicago Press.

Willis, P. (1977). *Learning to labor.* New York: Columbia University Press.

8

Fallen Angels: Finding Adolescents and Adolescent Literacy in a Renewed Project of Democratic Citizenship

Helen J. Harper
Thomas W. Bean
University of Nevada, Las Vegas

As of November 1, 2005,

141 teenaged American soldiers

have been killed in Iraq:

19 eighteen-year-olds and

122 nineteen-year-olds

killed in the line of duty

(www.fallenheroesmemorial.com).

If the ultimate test of American citizenship is a willingness to fight and die for one's country, and if youth are expected to answer the call, then the young men and women who have fought and died in Iraq, Afghanistan, and elsewhere have passed the test and paid the ultimate price for life in a democracy. The phrase *fallen angels* in the title references Walter Dean Myers' (1988) novel by the same name. Myers' *Fallen Angels* chronicles the experiences of young African Americans soldiers serving in Viet Nam. Although an award-winning young adult novel, it has been banned in some schools because of its graphic depiction of war.

In this chapter we consider how adolescents and adolescent literacy can contribute to the renewal of democratic life. We contend that adolescent literacy, with its acknowledgment of multiple literacies, multiple texts, popular culture, in-school and out-of-school literacies, and identity issues, offers a vehicle for expanding conceptions of democracy and citizenship in the 21st century. Our notion of adolescent literacy draws on the work of Alvermann, Hinchman, Moore, Phelps, & Waff (1998); Bean & Readence (2002), and others in reconceptualizing literacy as social, radical, and critical practice. In considering the role of adolescent literacies in democratic life, we argue for a radical democracy that supports a pluralistic society in which critique, difference, and dissent renew and enliven political discourse and action, where the tensions between the common good and individual freedom, between unity, solidarity, and difference are, by necessity, ever-constant (Cunningham, 2002; Parker, 2003).

We recognize that literacy, public education, and democracy have been aligned in America since the time of Jefferson, but in these new times the shifting phenomenon of the adolescent and, more specifically, the recent acknowledgement of adolescent literacies have not yet entered the inscription of democracy in contemporary life. In part, this is because the field of adolescent literacies is a relatively new area of study, but perhaps more fundamentally because democratic citizenship has been aligned with adults, not adolescents. In a liberal democracy that names citizenship in relation to voting and adulthood, adolescents have been seen as citizens-in-training; so, too, their literacies: as literacies-in-training. However, in these new and troubled times, both democratic citizenship and adolescent life are changing, as is their connection. Youniss, Bales, Christmas-Best, Diversi, McLaughlin, and Silbereisen (2002) suggest that contemporary political and social circumstances demand that youth participate in the creation of social and political change:

> We enter the 21st century contending with the end of the Cold War's legacy of political uncertainty, expecting youth to play a significant part in the search for new principles that will bring about stability in the world political order. In forging the future, youth will have to collaborate with adults but on terms more fitting of the historical circumstances that lie ahead than those of the past. (p. 121)

Schools are an obvious site of such collaboration. Schools offer a public space where adolescents and their teachers can consider, critique, and act on a host of topics and issues ranging from American history, foreign policy, equity and social justice, to the influence of pop culture on contemporary democratic life. In doing so, they are rethinking and remaking democratic life in their own times. The project of democracy and citizenship needs public spaces like schools, and, much like contemporary theories concerning adolescents and their literacies, citizenship requires a thoughtful consideration of individuality, collectivity, social difference, and identity (Delanty, 2001; Parker, 2003).

This project has become even more important for adolescents and their teachers since 9/11. In *The Abandoned Generation*, Giroux (2003) argued that: "Already imperiled before the terrorists attacks on September 11, democracy appears even more fragile in the United States in this time of civic and political crisis" (p. xiiv). In addition, he noted that this fragile democracy devalues children and youth in the public sphere: "Increasingly, children seem to have no standing in the public sphere as citizens, and thus are denied any sense of entitlement and agency … [and] if not represented as a symbol of fashion or hailed as a hot niche, youth are often portrayed as a problem, a danger to adult society or, even worse, irrelevant to the future" (p. xiv).

We believe that adolescent literacy, with its emphasis on social difference, identity, multiple texts, and literacies of youth, adds new and unacknowledged dimensions important to the forging of democratic citizenship in the 21st century. In addition, we believe that such work must include the explicit teaching of radical democratic citizenship as opposed to instilling patriotism (Edelsky, 2004; Parker, 2003; Westheimer & Kahne, 2004).

We begin this chapter by considering the historical intersection of democracy, literacy education, and efforts to build on Dewey's (1916) notions of progressive education as well as Rosenblatt's (1938/1968) transactional literacy. While acknowledging the substantial contributions of Dewey, Rosenblatt, and others, we consider recent critiques of their liberal-humanist pedagogy and argue for a more radical democratic literacy education. We then examine selected work in adolescent literacies to inform and renew the project of radical democracy and citizenship and the literacy it requires. We offer the caution that this is a complex history, with philosophical and pedagogical ideas that are rooted in the fields of philosophy, political science, critical theory, sociology, and cultural studies, among others. We conclude this chapter with selected examples and concrete ways in which teachers of adolescents and adolescent literacies can take up a project of radical democratic citizenship.

DEMOCRACY AND LITERACY EDUCATION

Democratic life and literacy education have long been connected in America and elsewhere. For instance, in the United States, Thomas Jefferson suggested that citizenship in a democracy required literacy skills and that public education would assure such skills. Since that time, the notion that citizens who can engage in the literacy practices of the nation will ensure a stronger and freer democracy has been accepted as a given. Indeed, democracy and literacy have had a commonsensical, taken-for-granted, apple-pie-like quality and connection. But such easy acceptance belies the wide-ranging, shifting, and often contradictory or ambiguous meanings that now and in the past have characterized democracy, freedom, and literacy. Greene (1988) suggested that in contemporary American life, freedom, for example, is not definitive nor often meaningful:

> The United States presents itself as the apostle of freedom. It resides in our tradition, the world is told. It lies at the core of the American dream ... [it] is a taken-for-granted possession. Born into it, the young are expected to defend it, whether or not it means anything in their personal lives. (p. 26)

Similarly, the idea of democracy carries many and at times conflicting meanings. Cunningham (2002) outlined multiple forms of democracy including liberal democracy, radical democracy, participatory democracy, deliberative democracy, and democratic pragmatism. And democracy shifts according to the political power structure and related social climate. Thus, Edelsky (2004) noted that democracy during the McCarthy era looked and meant something considerably different from how it looked and what it meant in the 1960s. We add that democracy has come to mean something quite different again in the 21st century. Radical and progressive educators, among many others, have become increasingly alarmed by the ways in which democracy has been defined and aligned with corporate culture and commercial values (Apple, 2000; Giroux, 2003; Osborne, 2001). Apple (2000) pointed out that the American citizen is often equated with the American consumer, with freedom redefined as a set of consumption practices.

The literacy required of democratic citizenship shifts according to the understanding of democracy dominating at the time. Literacy education in colonial America, for example, relied on transmission methods: rote learning, repetition, and recitation with an ongoing emphasis on the development of moral character. Such pedagogy was to ensure that a law-abiding, virtuous, and rational citizenry could read the arguments put forth by the natural aristocracy of the republic in order to vote and participate in the economy appropriately (Shannon, 2001). Much of this view of democracy and literacy education remains in contemporary life and in the education of adolescents, but alternative and more expanded notions of democracy and literacy education began to gain prominence in the 19th and 20th centuries.

In America the 19th and 20th centuries brought increasing numbers of non-Anglo-Saxon immigrants, demands for greater participation of women and others in political and social life, and an economy rapidly shifting from agrarian to industrial and later to postindustrial modes of production. The scope of government involvement increased substantially, particularly in the private sector, in order to address the challenges these changes presented and, perhaps, to answer the call of so-called ordinary people. This expanded notion of the state and of democracy required an education system that would produce not only an electorate that would understand and vote in an informed and rational manner, but a state collective that would insure citizens had a fair and equal opportunity to develop their potential, to participate as citizens, and to share in the nation's prosperity. Quality education had to be available to all in an increasingly diverse America and available to the increasing numbers of adolescent students attending and completing secondary education. Indeed, adolescence is a 20th-century phenomenon that developed in part by changes in child labor laws, by social and economic circumstances more generally, and certainly by the related rise of developmental psychology (Lesko, 2001). Adolescent culture was increasingly distinguished from childhood and adulthood, as was secondary education.

Progressives of the early 1900s argued that schools, both secondary and elementary, should become models of democracy, sites in which democracy was understood not as a set of political structures but as a way of life. Dewey (1916) claimed that democracy was a mode of living and experiencing life more than a form of government. Citizens in Dewey's democracy required an education that would promote the cooperative development, testing, and refinement of new ideas and new institutions for the good of society. His model of schooling was that of the open, collaborative, and scientific community. Such a community demanded that citizen-students develop "intellectual, social and communicative virtues essential to collective, cooperative inquiry" (Riley & Welchman, 2003, p. 96). In part, this meant school literacy lessons that enhanced dialogue across social and economic class divisions to ensure a more critical, active, and communal democracy than colonial Americans ever envisioned.

Rosenblatt (1938/1968) expanded on the link between literacy and democracy. She connected reader-citizens in the "free exchange of ideas [which in the case of literature] will lead each student to scrutinize his [sic] own sense of the literary work in the light of others' opinions" (p. 110). She argued that "literature by its very nature invokes participation in the experiences of others and comprehension of their goals and aspirations" (p. 93). For Rosenblatt, enlarging one's own response in light of others allowed for a broader, more critical perspective to understanding life and literature, and for fostering understanding and empathy for others. Although this was viewed as an important practice to counteract the self- conscious, self-absorbed traits of many adolescents, it was considered absolutely necessary for more powerful literacy study and, in the mind of Rosenblatt, for a stronger and more equitable democracy.

Although much from Dewey and Rosenblatt continues to underscore what democracy requires of literacy education for today's adolescents and others, ongoing economic and social inequalities, dramatic technological changes, philosophical shifts and political upheavals have led some to pose a more radical democracy and, consequently, a more radical literacy education. Critiques of Dewey and Rosenblatt have focused on these progressives' liberalism, which many see as failing to make class, gender, and racial inequalities sufficiently problematic to create viable social change (Freire & Macedo, 1987; Maher, 2001). Although progressives emphasized collaboration, interaction, dialogue, empathy, and a sense of the common good, they tended to ameliorate difference by enhancing social harmony. Maher (2001) noted that "these progressive pedagogues failed to problematize their goals of 'unity' and the benign inclusiveness of diversity" (p. 27). In response to the increasing social difference and diversity apparent in the late 1900s and early 2000s, some conservative individuals and movements have insisted that a strong and unified democracy necessitates a single common culture. This common culture can be ensured in part by sanctioning English as the only national language and by exposing citizens to a predetermined and highly selective American literary canon (Bloom, 1987; Hirsch, 1987). In contrast, others offering a new and more radical progressivism have emphasized incommensurate social difference as a necessary part of the democratic collective. These scholars advocate a radical literacy education that has an overriding concern for participation, social equity, and plurality in democratic life (Dimitriadis & Carlson, 2003; Carlson, 2002; Mouffe, 1992, 1995; Nadesan & Elenes, 1998).

Radical social thought rejects the notion of a single universal truth or common culture. It emphasizes the point that dissent and difference are not problematic in a democracy but constitute its very foundations. Mouffe (1992) proposed that:

> We must accept the inevitability of conflict and antagonism as fundamental and constitutive elements of political life. Therefore, instead of perceiving those traits as problematic, as an obstacle to a movement of total stability and homogeneity, they should be perceived as the healthy traits that allow for constant transformation and prevent that movement of stability as a menace to the liberties of the members of a society that do not coincide with what the "general will" at a certain historical moment might be. (p. 371)

Dewey (1916) himself acknowledged that disagreement and dissent drive growth in a democracy. A stronger emphasis on a pluralistic and radical democracy demands the fostering of and engagement with social difference. It is the noisy democracy of many voices, many perspectives, and a more active citizenship. Radical educators have pressed further on Dewey's belief that schools should be models of democracy, public spaces where social inquiry can be undertaken. Such inquiry now is said to require the critical literacy of reading the word and the world promoted by Freire (1998), Giroux (2003), McLaren (1995), and Shor and Pari (1999), among others. Social inquiry also speaks to a critical and poststructural approach to the constituting effects of language and discourse. In what Carlson (2002) called *new progressivism,*

> language is now understood to play a generative and formative role in shaping both our reading of texts and the texts themselves. Language thus becomes the central concern of a new progressivism in education, and the role of language in constituting the world along particular lines … [for] until people are able to "re-think" self, world and other, they have not really changed, no matter how much more information they have access to, no matter how many textbooks they read (pp. 179–180).

In new progressivism, a critical view of language moves literacy education away from simply encoding and decoding the words of the natural aristocracy, away from developing moral character and patriotism, and away from improving cross-cultural communication and empathy in the development of collaborative civic projects. Rather, a critical view of language opens the world and the word to critique and dissent—to how the world is made and can be remade in language. This more dynamic and overtly political stance welcomes productive critique that fosters and analyzes social differences organized discursively in democratic life. It is a literacy that considers the social, cultural, and hegemonic dimensions of language use. It is consciously political, acknowledging the transformative power of language, and, as Powell (1999) reminds us, it also nurtures compassion and care.

We believe that research and scholarship in a promising reconceptualization of adolescent literacy, despite its relative infancy in the larger field of literacy, names, supports, and furthers this more radical notion of democracy and literacy. We turn now to its contribution.

ADOLESCENT LITERACY AND THE PROJECT OF RADICAL DEMOCRACY

Compared to the now lengthy history of content-area literacy and secondary reading (Moore, Readence, & Rickelman, 1983), reconceptualizations of adolescent literacy occupy different terrain (Alvermann et al., 1998; Readence, Bean, & Baldwin, 2004). New thinking about adolescent literacy acknowledges the changing nature of texts and adolescents; it encompasses postmodern dimensions including multiple literacies, multiple texts, popular culture, and issues of adolescents' identities in shifting global contexts (Bean & Readence, 2002). It is derived from ethnographic research indicating that many adolescents now interact with the widest array of print and nonprint media of any time in history (Alvermann, 2002; Moje, 2002: Moje et al., 2004). These diverse forms of information include traditional books and magazines, as well as more avant-garde forms of text including postmodern young adult novels, graphic texts, and more technology-based texts such as instant Internet-based messaging, digital ad boards, and a host of other newly developing media (see O'Brien, chap. 2, this volume). Adolescents who are engaging in these wide-ranging texts and textual practices are now seen as diverse, sophisticated, and multifaceted learners.

Adding to this picture, Lesko (2001), in her sociocultural analysis of adolescence, contested common essentialist views of youth as biologically driven bundles of "raging hormones" barely capable of rational or critical thought (e.g. Wallis, 2004, p. 61). Lesko (2001) proposed a more complex postmodern view of adolescence that challenges biologically deterministic portrayals:

> Youth are simultaneously young and old, learning and learned, working and in school. This idea of time (that is, of past, present, and future) as holding seemingly opposing identities simultaneously is, I believe, a necessary dimension of a retheorizing of adolescence. (p. 197)

Rather than viewing adolescents in relation to the future as citizens-in-training with literacies-in-training, or to the past as former children, with Lesko's guidance it is possible to rethink adolescence as organized simultaneously in the past, present, and future. Such a perspective captures the complexity and possible agency of adolescent life. At the very least, this view permits educators to interrogate the binaries that produce adult and adolescent identities and that position adolescence as a deficient Other to adulthood (Hagood, 2002).

The complexity and diversity found in the lives and literacies of 21st-century adolescents demand a shift from classroom-based, single-text forms of learning to an environment that involves students in reading across multiple forms of texts and discourses and in making intertextual connections that acknowledge complexity, difference, and diversity. Such a literacy education refuses to narrow pedagogical experience to one sanctioned or preferred textual practice or, for that matter, to one form of pedagogical intervention. It refuses to homogenize adolescents, which means a literacy education that acknowledges, encourages, and embraces social difference. Such an education is in keeping with the needs of a radical and pluralistic democracy. But as Dimitriadis and Carlson (2003) cautioned, difference need not be reified:

> Of course this could also lead to an isolation of various affinity and identity groups and a failure to come together around any shared visions of democratic public life. Perhaps a better response among progressives would be to support heterogeneity within schools, with space allowed for the constitution of groups around difference and identity, and also for the crossing of borders and the construction of hybrid, non-essentialist identities … Democratic communities of learning in the twenty-first century must be communities of difference without normalizing centers; and public education, we believe, must play a role in building and sustaining such communities. (pp. 23–24)

Radical literacy education then works to engage difference and diversity without stabilizing it, to construct communities of difference that have no normalizing centers. This is not easy to do, but it is nonetheless imperative considering the complex and fluid lives of youth. Radical literacy supports a democracy that demands plurality along with an education that acknowledges the shifting and multiple reading and writing practices of the nation's youth. Moreover, such a democracy and such an education takes adolescent life and their literacies seriously, naming them as citizens active in the inscription and transformation of democracy.

Yet within this radical plurality, this democracy of many voices, Dimitriadis and Carlson (2003) also commented on the need for understanding the common good. Conceiving democracy as a radical plurality, as fueled by difference and dissent, suggests that schools as public spaces must become sites not only for the performance of social, cultural, and other forms of difference, but also for the analysis of difference within a framework of democratic life and the common good. This notion of the common good, we argue, rests not on a common culture but on a common commitment to the principles of a modern, pluralistic society, and the assertion of liberty and equality (Mouffe, 1992). Ongoing struggles over how social existence is to be organized are an inevitable part of democratic life, but we agree with Nadesan and Elenes (1998) that these struggles must be reconciled with a shared commitment to freedom and equality. A commitment to equality and freedom names democratic citizenship. In this rendering, affiliation to home and homeland (and to state or national identity) are not the central feature of democratic citizenship.

At least for some adolescents, home and homeland are becoming less definitive in their lives. Research and scholarship in adolescent literacies finds that the current generation of adolescents occupies a world in which the Internet and other technologies create a borderless, seamless landscape. Langhorne (2001), a political scientist noted:

> Global markets, global manufacturers and purveyors of knowledge, and global consumers, already either horizontal in shape or lacking any physical shape at all, have arrived as new participants, stirring like a rising mist on a summer's morning round the soaring trunks of the trees in an old wood. They move inexorably across global space and time without respect to physical geography, political frontiers, or night and day. (p. 39)

Developing technologies are allowing people to interact virtually anywhere at any time with anyone from across the globe who has access to similar technology. The Internet and the globalization of popular and mass culture permit adolescents to be in continual motion, expanding their social networks beyond the local neighborhood and its high school. Affiliation patterns may well be dispersed among many social groups or communities. Local or state affiliation may be only one site of identification among many, so it cannot be assumed to be transcendent. Developing technologies may well be changing civic identity and engagement. Although traditional notions of citizenship have been developed for embodied individuals located and invested in specific sites, cyberspace creates disembodied, disembedded subjects. Cyberspace deterritorializes individuals and may be a space for renegotiating the nature of citizenship and rules of civic engagement (Kenway & Langmead, 2000).

In addition, research and scholarship in the field of adolescent literacy reveals that youth are using their new literacy practices to construct multiple dynamic identities or subjectivities across virtual and real communities (Alvermann, 2002; Hagood, 2002; Lankshear & Knobel, 2002; Moje et al., 2004). Rather than seeing this as a problem, multiple and shifting identifications and affiliations offer many lenses through which to consider issues of the day. The diversity of adolescents in terms of their virtual and real communities and related literacy practices offers pluralistic terrain for securing potentially more perspectives and potentially greater equity and fairness in democratic life.

However, the vast quantities of information and multiple communities possible in the textual practices of adolescents require critique. The project of democracy becomes centered on citizens who not only manipulate huge quantities of information but who effectively question the value and underlying beliefs that underpin any form of discourse. We argue that critical postmodern literacy has never been more important in the project of democracy. Adolescents require a democratic framework of and commitment to equity and freedom as well as a predisposition to question the ideological underpinnings of any text or textual practice and the identities they promote.

In summary, recent scholarship aimed at reconceptualizing adolescent literacy supports radical, pluralized notions of democracy because adolescents are:

- active participants in democracy with agency and voice (Moore & Cunningham, chap. 7, this volume);
- complex, multifaceted, and multitalented users of diverse literacy practices (Bean, 2006; Luke & Elkins, 1998; Moje, 2002; Moje et al., 2004);
- active learners capable of critiquing policies and issues that impact their lives (Lesko, 2001; Parker, 2003; Stevens & Bean, 2002; Westheimer & Kahne, 2004);
- diverse citizens with multiple and fluid affiliations, capable and interested in issues of democracy and social justice (Bean, 2006; Sturtevant et al., 2006);
- global citizens increasingly aware of multinational risks including war, environmental disasters, and global capitalism (Giroux, 2003; Lankshear & Knobel, 2002).

Given these characteristics of adolescents and their literacies, we believe that teachers and students who reconceptualize literacy education as a project of renewed democracy have access to exciting pedagogical possibilities.

A RENEWED PROJECT OF DEMOCRATIC CITIZENSHIP: PROMISING ADOLESCENT LITERACY PRACTICES

A growing number of initiatives are aimed at developing critical and radical democratic citizenship in secondary and college students (Stevens & Bean, 2002; Shor & Pari, 1999; Weiner, 2002). We are impressed by these efforts and in particular by several experimental workforce education programs recently established that place students in sites where they can enact critical democratic citizenship (e.g. Behrman, 2003). For example, Sturtevant et al. (2006) highlighted the experiences of a Latina student interning in a bilingual community clinic as part of a workforce general education diploma program. Confronting the daily challenges that second-language-speaking patients encountered with the forms and policies of the clinic, the student created a CD-ROM for Spanish-speaking patients that explained medical procedures and medicare documents. The efforts of this student were understood within a frame of responsible citizenship. Certainly the students and teachers in this program should be applauded. Although we regard individual social action as an important and valuable activity, we suggest that students, like this one, would benefit from a larger and more collective analysis of systemic problems of equity and fairness in relation to democratic rights and principles. Teachers and students might want to consider how the politics of language and literacy arise in a medical office and how *patient* has been understood in local and more general medical discourse as White and English-speaking. In addition, it is important to consider what this rendering of *patient* means for a pluralalistic and radical democracy and American citizenship This might lead to broader political action beyond the production of a CD-ROM.

Westheimer and Kahne (2004) note the importance of critical analysis along with the importance of real, collective, political action with students. Not surprisingly, Westheimer and Kahne's study of two democratic school projects found that high school students preferred collective community-based activism with a focus on the *doing of* democracy to traditional classroom-based programs and the *learning about* democracy through appeals to individual action and moral character. Clearly, democratic school projects must take seriously adolescents and their desire for real and active involvement in democracy. Moreover, as suggested at the outset of this chapter, there is a need for youth working together with adults to forge democratic life for 21st-century democracy.

It is also important to acknowledge the growing number of teachers (Bean & Harper, 2004) who are drawing on the genre of young adult novels and on adolescents' out-of-school reading material to address, among other things, democratic commitments to freedom, equity, and issues of social justice. The following young adult novels are just a few of those now available that have been used in such a manner. Each of these novels considers serious issues including war, poverty, racism, displacement, and loss. As such, they offer powerful sites for critical literacy and careful consideration of how democracy plays out to benefit some and exclude others:

- Ellis, D. (2000). *The Breadwinner*. Toronto, Ontario, Canada: Groundwood.
- Flake, S. (2001). *Money Hungry*. New York: Hyperion.
- Kass, P. M. (2004). *Real Time*. New York: Clarion.
- Myers, W. D. (2004). *Shooter*. New York: HarperCollins.
- Naidoo, B. (2000). *The Other Side of Truth*. New York: HarperCollins.
- Woodson, J. (2002). *Hush*. New York: Putnam.

These novels and other print and nonprint texts popularized by adolescents can be approached with an eye toward examining democratic principles and commitments. For example, in Naidoo's (2000) award-winning novel, *The Other Side of Truth*, Sade, the main character, flees Nigeria for England following an assassination attempt on her father and the killing of her mother. She is positioned as an outsider in the British school she attends while trying to locate her father, an exiled journalist imprisoned in London. This and the other novels listed are powerful sites for critical discussion of democratic principles including resistance and dissent. In our discussions with our students about this novel, we raise questions that attend to key elements of radical democratic citizenship. For example, we have posed the following discussion question:

> Sade joins her imprisoned Dad's hunger strike to protest the denial
> of Nigeria to attend the Commonwealth Conference. To what degree
> is this act of resistance likely to gain media attention and alter the
> status-quo for Nigerian citizens and refugees like Sade and her family?

In reading and discussing these novels or other popular genres, critical questions can address the systemic problems and issues of race, class, and gender and other forms of social difference in relation to democracy. Related questions of textual representation, identity, freedom, equity, security, and of local, state, and global practice and policy can also be considered with many popular texts. The novels cited here feature settings from across the globe, thereby drawing on and expanding the border crossing already apparent in the literacy practices of many adolescents. This would seem crucial for a pluralistic democracy. Moreover, educating adolescents for the global community is becoming increasingly crucial, with a growing body of research showing the diminished capacity of individual nation-states to solve world problems like poverty, violence, and environmental disaster, among others (Tsolidis, 2002).

Parker (2003), a political scientist with an abiding interest in developing high school students' collective involvement in democratic life, provides some support for teachers in his book: *Teaching Democracy: Unity and Diversity in Public Life*.[1] Parker recommended involving youth in a rich array of associations and governance where they plan, decide, implement, and evaluate outcomes in policies and practices both in and out of school. Parker's pedagogical model, which places tremendous emphasis on dialogue, exposes students to divergent opinions and debate on important issues in what he calls *deliberative forums*. Parker recommends selecting problems that interest students (e.g., dress codes, on-campus skateboard bans, bullying), and ones that lend themselves to pluralism so that multiple, competing perspectives are possible. To organize classroom discussion and action, Parker uses an intellectual framework for problem and policy analysis similar to ones used by professionals working in public agencies:

1. Identify and explain a public problem and map stakeholders and their views.
2. Develop and analyze policy alternatives to include goals, consequences and trade-offs.
3. Decide what action to take.

For example, the booklets include one on "Remedies for Racial Inequality," as well as a host of other lesson topics. Text materials for global problems can be found in *Choices for the 21st Century* briefing booklets published by the Center for Foreign Policy Development. See http://www.choices.edu available from Brown University, Providence, Rhode Island.

We add *take action* as a fourth step. Parker's curriculum design ensures that in analyzing issues students, individually and collectively, engage in contrasting points of view through debate, seminars, and deliberations. Parker (2003) writes, "Seminars and deliberations represent the distinction between the world-revealing and the world-changing functions of conversation" (p. 129). We agree, but open dialogue—world-changing conversation—and the receptive listening that is necessary to the process can be difficult. Located in social space and time, the speaker and audience are rarely neutral or objective observers on any issue of substance. Social and linguistic power can affect who and what is heard or ignored. Most importantly, ra-

---

[1]Useful text materials for Parker's citizenship curriculum are available from the *National Issues Forum* (NIF) booklets. Information on these booklets can be found at http://www.nifi.org/about/index.aspz and information on ordering teacher's guide material can be found at http://www.nifi.org/forums/publications.aspx. For example, the booklets include one on "Remedies for Racial Inequality," as well as a host of other lesson topics. Text materials for global problems can be found in *Choices for the 21*[st] *Century* briefing booklets published by the Center for Foreign Policy Development. See http://www.choices.edu available from Brown University, Providence, Rhode Island.

tional decision making itself needs to be problematized. In particular, the basis and the process on which a decision is rendered needs to be explored. In the case of projects of democratic renewal, democratic principles, practices, and commitments need to be made explicit, if not themselves debated in the course of school/community advocacy. Nonetheless, Parker's model offers pedagogical structures that might help organize or complement pedagogical activities in democracy projects. And, although he doesn't speak to adolescent literacies per se, Parker does take adolescents and their democratic participation seriously.

Of course, considering the diversity in adolescents' lives and literacy, we anticipate that students would require a variety of projects, materials, modalities, and pedagogical strategies to insure that the intersection of literacy and democracy comes alive analytically and practically. In our estimation, the capabilities and sensibilities found in the multiliteracies of a growing number of 21st-century adolescents have the potential to refigure a stronger and more pluralistic democracy. Although, perhaps at this point, this potential has yet to be fully realized in practical, pedagogical terms. We welcome efforts to create innovative pedagogical projects for adolescent citizens, particularly considering the competing interests and demands placed on teachers' time and energy. Creating curriculum that brings social difference, diversity, and complexity to classrooms devoted to the renewal of democracy, although often exciting, is not easy.

CONCLUDING THOUGHTS

By referring to *Fallen Angels* (Myers, 1988), the young adult novel referenced at the beginning of this chapter, we acknowledged adolescent soldiers who have made the ultimate sacrifice in the name of democracy. Their sacrifice, at a time when children and adolescents seem to be disappearing from public visibility, speaks to the need to reinscribe adolescents as active participants into the everyday of democratic life.

Democracy and literacy have been closely aligned in American life, although both the definition of democracy and literacy and their connection have shifted and changed. We argue that a radical pluralism, one that critically fosters and analyzes social difference within the framework of democratic commitments to equity and freedom, is fundamental to democratic life. Tensions between individual freedom and social unity, and between cultural and state affiliations, will be and need to be ever-present (Cherland & Harper, in press).

Research and scholarship in the field of adolescent literacy suggests the diversity, fluidity, and complexity of adolescent identities and points to the changing nature of the texts and textual practices in adolescent life. Although unintended, newly developing literacies can be seen to name and support a more radical vision of democracy. By infusing adolescent literacy experiences and practices with a critical and democratic focus, we believe, teachers are contributing not only to their students' success but, potentially, to the reconfiguring of literacy and democratic life in the 21st century. Much still needs to be considered pedagogically and theoretically, and this chapter represents only the beginning of our own efforts. At the very least, the research on adolescents and their literacies speaks to the need to rethink the relationship of adolescents to literacy and democracy in both theory and practice. Surely the times and lives of adolescent soldiers demand such work.

REFERENCES

Alvermann, D. E. (Ed.). (2002). *Adolescents and literacies in a digital world*. New York: Peter Lang.

Alvermann, D. E., Hinchman, K. A., Moore, D. W., Phelps, S. F., & Waff, D. R. (1998). *Reconceptualizing the literacies in adolescents' lives*. Mahwah, NJ: Lawrence Erlbaum Associates.

Apple, M. (2000). *Official knowledge: Democratic education in a conservative age* (2nd ed.). New York: Routledge.

Bean, T. W. (2006). A scholar's response to preparing adolescents for critical citizenship. In B. Sturtevant, F. B. Boyd, W. G. Brozo, K. A. Hinchman, D. W. Moore, & D. E. Alvermann (Eds.), *Principled practices for a literate America* (pp. 138–141). Mahwah, NJ: Lawrence Erlbaum Associates.

Bean, T. W., & Harper, H. J. (2004, March). *Notions of freedom in multicultural young adult novels*. Paper presented at the 48th Annual Conference of the Comparative and International Education Society, Salt Lake City, UT.

Bean, T. W., & Readence, J. E. (2002). Adolescent literacy: Charting a course for successful futures as lifelong learners. *Reading Research and Instruction, 41*, 203–210.

Behrman, E. H. (2003). Reconciling content literacy with adolescent literacy: Expanding literacy opportunities in a community-focused biology class. *Reading Research and Instruction, 43*, 1–30.

Bloom, A. (1987). *The closing of the American mind: How higher education has failed democracy and impoverished the souls of today's students*. New York: Simon and Schuster.

Carlson, D. (2002). *Leaving safe harbors: Toward a new progressivism in American education and public life*. New York: Routledge Falmer.

Cherland, M., & Harper, H. J. (in press). *Advocacy research in literacy education*. Mahwah, NJ: Laurence Erlbaum Associates.

Cunningham, F. (2002). *Theory of democracy: A critical introduction*. New York: Routledge.

Delanty, G. (2001). *Challenging knowledge: The university in the knowledge society*. Ballmoor, Buckingham, England: Open University Press.

Dewey, J. (1916). *Education and democracy*. New York: MacMillan.

Dimitriadis, G., & Carlson, D. (2003). *Promises to keep: Cultural studies, democratic education and public life*. New York: Routledge Falmer Press.

Edelsky, C. (2004). Democracy in the balance. *Language Arts, 82*(1).

Ellis, D. (2000). *The breadwinner*. Toronto, Ontario, Canada: Groundwood.

Flake, S. (2001). *Money hungry*. New York: Hyperion.

Freire, P. (1998). *Pedagogy of freedom: Ethics, democracy, and civic courage*. New York: Rowman & Littlefield.

Freire, P., & Macedo, D. (1987). *Literacy: Reading the word and the world*. South Hadley, MA: Bergin and Garvey.

Giroux, H. (2003). *The abandoned generation: Democracy beyond the culture of fear*. New York: Palgrave-MacMillan.

Greene, M. (1988). *The dialectic of freedom*. New York: Teachers College Press.

Hagood, M. (2002). Critical literacy for whom? *Reading Research and Instruction, 41*, 247–266.

Hirsch, E. B. (1987). *Cultural literacy: What every American needs to know*. Boston: Houghton Mifflin.

Kass, P. M. (2004). *Real time*. New York: Clarion.

Kenway, J., & Langmead, D. (2000). Cyberfeminism and citizenship: Challenging the political imaginary. In M. Arnot and J. Dillabough (Eds.), *Challenging democracy: International perspectives on gender, education and citizenship* (pp. 312–329). New York: Routledge/Falmer.

Lankshear, C., & Knobel, M. (2002). Do we have your attention? New literacies, digital technologies, and the education of adolescents. In D. E. Alvermann (Ed.), *Adolescents and their literacies in a digital world* (pp. 19–39). New York: Peter Lang.

Langhorne, R. (2001). *The coming of globalization: Its evolution and contemporary consequences*. England: Palgrave.

Lesko, N. (2001). *Act your age! A cultural construction of adolescence*. New York: Routledge Falmer.

Luke, A., & Elkins, J. (1998). Reinventing literacy in "New Times." *Journal of Adolescent & Adult Literacy, 42*, 4–7.

Maher, F. (2001). John Dewey, progressive education, and feminist pedagogies: Issues in gender and authority. In K. Weiler (Ed.), *Feminist engagements: Reading, resisting, and revisioning male theorists in education and cultural studies* (pp.13–32). New York: Routledge.

McLaren, P. (1995). *Critical pedagogy and predatory culture: Oppositional politics in a postmodern era*. New York: Routledge.

Moje, E. B. (2002). Re-framing adolescent literacy research for new times: Studying youth as a resource. *Reading Research and Instruction, 41,* 211–228.

Moje, E. B., Ciechanowski, K. M., Kramer, K., Ellis, L., Carillo, R., & Collazo, T. (2004). Working toward third space in content area literacy: An examination of everyday funds of knowledge and discourse. *Reading Research Quarterly, 39,* 38–70.

Moore, D. W., Readence, J. E., & Rickelman, R. J. (1983). An historical exploration of content-area reading instruction. *Reading Research Quarterly, 18,* 419–438.

Mouffe, C. (1992). Feminism, citizenship, and radical democratic politics. In J. Butler & J. Scott (Eds.), *Feminists theorize the political* (pp. 369–384). New York: Routledge.

Mouffe, C. (1995). Politics, democratic action, and solidarity. *Inquiry, 38,* 99–108.

Myers, W. D. (1988) *Fallen angels.* New York: Scholastic.

Myers, W. D. (2004). *Shooter.* New York: HarperCollins.

Nadesan, M., & Elenes, C.A. (1998). Chantal Mouffe: Pedagogy for democratic citizenship. In M. Peters (Ed.), *Naming the multiple: Poststructuralism and education* (pp. 245–264). London: Bergin and Garvey.

Naidoo, B. (2000). *The other side of truth.* New York: HarperCollins.

Osborne, K. (2001). Democracy, democratic citizenship, and education. In J. Portelli & P. Solomon (Eds.) *The erosion of democracy in education: From critique to possibilities* (pp. 29–61). Calgary: Detselig Press.

Parker, W., C. (2003). *Teaching democracy: Unity and diversity in public life.* New York: Teachers College Press.

Powell, R. (1999). *Literacy as a moral imperative: Facing the challenges of a pluralistic society.* New York: Rowman & Littlefield.

Readence, J. E., Bean, T. W., & Baldwin, R. S. (2004). *Content area literacy: An integrated approach* (8th ed.). Dubuque, IA: Kendall/Hunt.

Riley, P., & Welchman, J. (2003). Rousseau, Dewey, and democracy. In R. Curren (Ed.), *A companion to the philosophy of education* (pp. 94–112). Oxford, UK: Blackwell.

Rosenblatt, L. (1968). *Literature as exploration.* New York: Modern Language Association of America. (Original work published 1938)

Shannon, P. (2001) Turn, turn, turn: Language education, politics and freedom at the turn of three centuries. In P. Shannon (Ed.), *Becoming political, too: New readings and writing on the politics of literacy education* (pp.10–30). Portsmouth, NH: Heinemann.

Shor, I., & Pari, C. (1999). *Education is politics: Critical teaching across differences, K–12.* Portsmouth, NH: Heinemann.

Stevens, L. P., & Bean, T. W. (2002). Reading in the digital era: Strategies for building critical literacy. In C. C. Block, L. B. Grambrell, & M. Pressley (Eds.), *Improving comprehension instruction: Rethinking research, theory, and classroom practice* (pp. 308–317). San Francisco, CA: Jossey-Bass.

Sturtevant, E., Boyd, F. B., Brozo, W. G., Hinchman, K. A., Moore, D. W., & Alvermann, D. E. (2006). *Principled practices for a literate America.* Mahwah, NJ: Lawrence Erlbaum Associates.

Tsolidis, G. (2002). How do we teach and learn in times when the notion of "global citizenship" sounds like a cliché? *Journal of Research in International Education, 1*(2), 213–226.

Wallis, C. (2004, May). What makes teens tick. *Time, 163*(19), 56–65.

Weiner, E. J. (2002). Beyond remediation: Ideological literacies of learning in developmental classrooms. *Journal of Adolescent & Adult Literacy, 46,* 150–168.

Westheimer, J., & Kahne, J. (2004). What kind of citizen? The politics of educating for democracy. *American Educational Research Journal, 41,* 237–269.

Woodson, J. (2002). *Hush.* New York: Putnam.

Youniss, J., Bales, S., Christmas-Best, V., Diversi, M., McLaughlin, M., & Silbereisen, R. (2002). Youth civic engagement in the twenty-first century. *Journal of Research on Adolescence, 12*(1), 121–148.

III

Mediating Practices in Young People's Literacies

CHAPTER 9

Self-Fashioning and Shape-Shifting: Language, Identity,   165
and Social Class
James Paul Gee

CHAPTER 10

Exploring Race, Language, and Culture in Critical Literacy   187
Classrooms
Bob Fecho, Bette Davis, and Renee Moore

CHAPTER 11

New Literacies, Enduring Challenges? The Influence of Capital   205
on Adolescent Readers' Internet Practices
Phillip Wilder and Mark Dressman

CHAPTER 12

Literacies Through Youth's Eyes: Lessons in Representation   231
and Hybridity
Kathleen A. Hinchman and Kelly Chandler-Olcott

Introduction to Part III: Mediating Practices in Young People's Literacies

Kathleen A. Hinchman
Syracuse University

Merriam Webster Online (2005) lists two definitions for the word mediate: "to occupy a middle position; to act through an intervening agency, exhibiting indirect causation, connection, or relation." The term is said to be "of Middle English origin, from the Late Latin *mediatus* intermediate, from the past participle of *mediare*."

Gee (1996) helps us to consider why mediating practices in literacies is important when he explains that:

> There are many different "social languages" connected in complex ways with different discourses. There are many sorts of literacy—many literacies—connected in complex ways with different Discourses. Cyberpunks and physicists, factory workers and boardroom executives, policemen and graffiti-writing urban gangmembers engage in different literacies, use different "social languages," and are in different Discourses (p. viii—ix).

Both of Merriam-Webster's definitions are useful when we explore how we conceptualize practices in young people's multiple literacies. What aspects of the social world mediate youth's literacies? How do youth's literacies mediate their social worlds? What other aspects of the social world are implicated in these transactions? How does school help and hurt such mediations of youth's literacy practices?

Gee introduces this theme in chapter 9, "Self-fashioning and Shape-shifting: Language, Identity, and Social Class." Specifically, he explains that youth's identity, social class, and language mediate one another. More successful individuals are those who can adapt to new situations adeptly, positioning themselves for success in today's quickly evolving academic and business worlds. Gee uses three discourse analysis tools to show disparities in how youth from different social backgrounds are prepared for such shape shifting.

In chapter 10, "Exploring Race, Language, and Culture in Critical Literacy Classrooms," authors Bob Fecho, Bette Davis, and Renee Moore explore the complex issues that are brought to the foreground when teachers and students in three quite different critical literacy classrooms explore how language and culture mediate one another. Fecho describes a classroom exploration in response to a Nikki Giovanni poem, Davis explores "classtalk" orchestrated to explore code switching, and Moore explains her classroom study of race, language, culture, and opportunities in language use.

Phillip Wilder and Mark Dressman explore social and cultural reproduction as youth use computer technology in a cultural geography class in chapter 11, "New Literacies, Enduring Challenges? The Influence of Capital on Adolescent Readers' Internet Practices." Wilder and Dressman observe students in two course sections, one taught for students in a college preparatory program and the other taught for those who struggle with reading. Their exploration tells a fascinating story of channeled opportunity, but at the same time, of opportunities for students, educators, and families to step outside such channeled expectations to create their own, other-than-expected place in the social and cultural world.

In chapter 12, "Literacies through Youth's Eyes: Lessons in Representation and Hybridity," Kathleen Hinchman and Kelly Chandler-Olcott consider anew the thesis that we have much to learn by exploring youth's insights about that which mediates and is mediated by their literacies. They review five studies for the purpose of theorizing what a more hybrid academic literacy pedagogy would look like if it were anchored in youth's multiliteracies.

As a group, these chapters represent insights regarding the ways in which youth's literacy practices are mediated by and mediate widely varying aspects of the worlds in which they live. They help us to see how schools help or hinder youth's efforts to succeed in developing the skills they need.

REFERENCES

Gee, J. P. (1996). *Social linguistics and literacies: Ideology in discourses* (2nd ed.). Bristol. PA: Taylor and Francis.

Merriam-Webster. (2005). *Merriam-Webster online*. Retrieved July 20, 2005 from www.m-w.com

9

Self-Fashioning and Shape-Shifting: Language, Identity, and Social Class

James Paul Gee
University of Wisconsin-Madison

SELF-FASHIONING AND SHAPE-SHIFTING PORTFOLIO PEOPLE

In this chapter, I first discuss the idea of "self-fashioning" and its role in modern society. I will then turn to a discourse analysis of how teenagers from different socio-economic classes fashion themselves in and through language. I end with a discussion of some of the implications of my remarks for schools and society.

Leading scholars like Bauman (2000), Beck (1992, 1995), Giddens (1991) and Taylor (1992, 1994) have each made the point that in today's high-tech, global, fast-changing world, people are expected, more than ever before, to fashion themselves, rather than follow the dictates of relatively fixed roles. More and more, they are supposed to make up for themselves (using whatever cultural resources they have available, of course) what it means to be a male or female, a student or a professor, a teenager or an elder, an Italian American or African American, a husband or wife, a Catholic, Protestant, Jew, or Muslim.

In fact, in the "new economy," identities have become consumer niches (Rifkin, 2000). The modern economy doesn't want just any old "Latinos" or "Asians" or "middle-class people." No, the economy wants different types of Latinos, Asians, and middle-class people who constitute different niches for the consumption of different products and services and to whom politicians can campaign in specific ways (Bauman, 1992).

There are well-off people who buy neobugs from Volkswagen, others who buy Mercedes, and yet others who get Hummers. These are different types of people, displaying, reinforcing, and creating their identities through the objects and services they buy.

It is not enough today to be a student. One has to be a distinctive type of student with distinctive experiences and achievements (e.g., having helped build houses for poor people, albeit on a Caribbean island) in order to get into a "good" college. The college one attends is no longer one's "education:" it is a badge of one's merit and identity. He's a Harvard man, she's a Yale woman, and poor John, he's a State guy.

So identities today take work. A person is expected to craft them out of available social and cultural resources. A person is expected to take on new identities through life, dropping some, changing others, and taking on new ones. This is partly because of the changing nature of work and skills today (Gee, Hull, & Lankshear, 1996; Greider, 1997; Kanter, 1995; Reich, 1992). In today's world, thanks to the fast pace of change due in part to the workings of science and technology, any knowledge and skills one has may soon go out of date. New knowledge and skills arise at an ever-faster pace. New types of jobs open up and old ones disappear or go overseas. People can't expect to stay in the same job—moving ever gradually up the ladder—their whole lives any more.

A person today is invited to see him or herself as a portfolio of skills, experiences, and achievements, something like a walking resumé. People must be prepared to rearrange their skills, experiences, and achievements—to describe themselves in new ways, not in terms of one fixed role or identity—to display themselves as fit and ready for new jobs, identities, and roles as these emerge in their futures. Indeed, it has been said that what workplaces today owe their workers are not permanent jobs, but the opportunity to learn something new on the job, something to add to their portfolios for identity changes in new workplaces in their futures. People must be prepared to recreate themselves and prepare for multiple jobs—indeed multiple careers—across their lifetimes.

If they seek economic success in our "fast capitalist" world, young people today often need to view themselves as what I have elsewhere called *Shape-Shifting Portfolio People* (Gee, 2004; see also Kanter, 1995). They have to be prepared throughout their lives to acquire new knowledge, skills, experiences, and achievements and to be able and willing to redefine these to make themselves ready for new jobs, new roles, and even new careers. People must be willing and able to fashion and refashion who they are. This is not necessary just for work, but in almost all aspects of life today. What it means to be married and how men and women relate to each other, for instance, change more quickly than the span of one lifetime now (Giddens, 1992). So does the meaning of being religious, being a citizen, being a consumer, being an environmentalist, and so forth.

Before I proceed to discuss self-fashioning and Shape-Shifting Portfolio People further, two words of caution: First, the demand for self-fashioning is not new, just greatly advanced and accelerated in our times. Greenblatt (1980) argues that the demand for self-fashioning started in the Renaissance and has accelerated ever since. Second, I am not arguing that the demand to become a Shape-Shifting Portfolio Person is good (ethically); I am arguing that it is an identity to which young people today are "summoned" by our modern world. It is also an identity that, if left only to the rich, will simply further acerbate serious equity divides already in existence in our society. Thus, we need to think both about how to allow less well-off young people to share in the resources of the modern world and, at the same time, how to moderate the ill effects of ever-increasing demands for shape-shifting for success in our contemporary world. Now back to my mainline concerns.

There is, of course, a great backlash to all this today. We see this backlash across the world in the rise of fundamentalism of all types, Christian, Islamic, Jewish, Hindu, and others. People perplexed by the complexity of the modern world—and in some cases oppressed by the self-fashioning options that other, richer people have adopted—react by seeking certain immutable truths, truths they would like to impose on others and on the world as a whole. Indeed, this sort of backlash is only liable to grow worse as the modern world continues to create complexity and a lack of justice for the poor.

It is probably the case that some readers having been saying for a while now: You're only talking about rich kids and rich adults. Poor people don't get these shape-shifting luxuries and opportunities. Well, yes and no. First, consider no. Many of today's young people who are not well-off or Anglo display a keen sense of the importance of how the modern world works. Let me give but one example. Consider a young man named Almon, a young man written about by Lam (2000).

Almon emigrated to the United States at the age of 12 from Hong Kong. After 5 years in the United States, Almon was frustrated by his skills in English. School only offered him ESL, bilingual, or remedial courses, courses that stigmatized him as a "low-achieving student." Almon felt that it was going to hard for him to develop his "career" (his own word) in the United States because of his English skills.

Eventually, Almon got involved with the Internet, created his own personal home page about a Japanese pop singer, and compiled a long list of names of online chat partners in several different countries around the world. He started to write regularly to e-mail "pen pals." Almon's Internet writing eventually improved his writing in school significantly.

After his experiences with and on the Internet, here is how Almon talked about himself and his future:

> ... I'm not as fearful, or afraid of the future, that I won't have a future .... I didn't feel I belonged to this world .... But now I feel there's nothing to be afraid of. It really depends on how you go about it. It's not like the world always has power over you. It was [names of a few chat mates and e-mail pen pals] who helped me to change and encouraged me. If I hadn't known them, perhaps I wouldn't have changed so much .... Yeah, maybe the *Internet* has changed me. (Lam, 2000, p. 468)

Almon had chosen to settle his home page in the "Tokyo" section of *GeoCities* (an international server) where a global community of Asians gathers around Japanese pop culture. Almon's online chat mates were located in a wide variety of places, such as Canada, Hong Kong, Japan, Malaysia, and the United States. They were mostly girls because he felt the girls' type of dialogue forced him to learn more English, partly because they talked about more topics and in a more personal and reflective mode.

Almon's story is typical of what I have been talking about, despite the fact that he is not rich, Anglo, or "mainstream." He thinks in terms of his career and future and evaluates his current skills and experiences in that light. He gains his most important skills, experiences, and identities, including even school-based skills, outside of school (indeed, school stigmatizes and deskills him).

Lam (2000) argues that the genre of electronic dialogue, as a form of communication that relies heavily on writing, "constitutes a highly visible medium for the scripting of social roles" (p. 474), that is, for identity fashioning. She points out that many of

Almon's postings to his female interlocutors "sound both very personal and very much like role play" (p. xx). Almon not only gains new skills and develops new identities on the Internet, he also learns to shape-shift, to enact different social roles.

There is no doubt that Almon, regardless of his economically based social class, is building a portfolio and learning to think of himself in entrepreneurial terms (as witnessed by the creation of his own Web site and in his sense of free agency and control over his own destiny) and in shape-shifting terms. Connected to a young Asian diaspora, Almon is not at the margins (except in the eyes of the school), but at the center of the new global world.

But now for the "yes": Yes, what I have been saying can often apply more to the rich than the poor. But that is the very nature of the world I am talking about. Being able to shape-shift brings big rewards; not being able to shape-shift brings big costs. The rich get richer selling their ever-new or newly defined skills on ever-changing markets and the poor get poorer as they are left further and further behind, watching their old jobs go overseas or disappear altogether. The middle class is imperiled, ever pressured to rise or fall.

The dilemma is that well-off kids and kids like Almon are getting their shape-shifting identities and many of the skills for their portfolios outside of school. Poor kids—White or Black or anything else—are often left to trust the schools to give them shape-shifting abilities and skills for their emerging portfolios. But, schools rarely give them these.

I do not intend in this chapter to document the fact that schools today are often out of kilter with the contemporary culture in which young people live outside of school. This matter is discussed fully in Gee (2003, 2004). What I do focus on is how language is used by teenagers from different social classes in such a way that well-off teens speak out of a Shape-Shifting Portfolio identity more readily than do less well-off teens. Thus, social class is reflected in language use as it orients or not toward being a Shape-Shifting Portfolio Person.

FASHIONING THE SELF THROUGH TALK

I turn now to a summary of several studies we carried out that looked at how teenagers from different socioeconomic classes used language to fashion certain sorts of identities in interviews (the research team consisted of Annie Allen, Katherine Clinton, and Valerie Crawford: see Gee, 2000a, b; Gee, Allen, & Clinton, 2001; Gee & Crawford, 1998; see also Gee, 2002). In the first part of our interviews, we asked the teenagers questions about their lives, homes, communities, interests, and schools. This is the "life" part of the interview. After these questions, the teenagers were asked to discuss two much more abstract "academic-like" questions: "Does racism exist?" and "Does sexism exist?" This is the "racism/sexism" part of the interview.

Each teenager was interviewed by a different research assistant on our project who was familiar with the teenager and his or her environment. The teens all viewed the interviewer as a "school-based" (indeed, college-based) person. We used such an interviewer and included the more abstract questions in the "racism/sexism" part of the interview precisely because we were interested in whether and how each teenager would use language to accommodate (shift) to a school-based identity.

Our evidence that all of our teens viewed the interviewer as school-based ties to the following considerations: All the teens well knew the interviewer came from the university; knew the interviewer was interested in how their middle schools did or did not facilitate going on to the college-prep part of their local high schools and, later, to college; and oriented to the interviewer's university identity by asking her questions relevant to this identity. In the working-class school, our interviews were part of other projects, known to the students, designed to help students access the sort of education that would increase their chances of later going on to college. Our judgment that the working-class teens viewed the interviewer as school-based is not just based on the interviews themselves, but on the many interactions the interviewer had with the teens outside the interview (including shadowing and ethnographic work).

We humans mutually shape and negotiate, with our interlocutors, the socially situated identity (and its attendant style of language) we will display, often moment by moment (Malone, 1997). Thus, when we talk about identities here, we are, unavoidably, talking about something that is coconstructed by the teen and the interviewer.

We used three discourse analysis tools to investigate how the teens we interviewed used language in the interviews. The first tool, discussed in this section, considers statements where the teenager uses the word "I" to refer to him or herself. We call such statements "I-Statements." Such statements about oneself clearly seem to be relevant to how people fashion themselves—enact a particular type of identity—in talk with others. The second and third tools, discussed next, are key motifs in each of the interviews and narrative analysis of narratives that appeared in the interviews.

Our analysis considered the following kinds of I-Statements: (a) "cognitive statements" about thinking and knowing (e.g., "I think ...", "I know ...", "I guess ..."); (b) "affective statements" about desiring and liking (e.g., "I want ...", "I like ..."); (c) "state and action statements" about states or actions of the speaker ("I am mature," "I hit him back," "I paid the bill"); (d) "ability and constraint statements" about being able or having to do things ("I can't say anything to them," "I have to do my paper route"); and (e) a category of what we call "achievement statements" about activities, desires, or efforts that relate to "mainstream" achievement, accomplishment, or distinction ("I challenge myself," "I want to go to MIT or Harvard").

We used lexical classifications for predicates to decide into what category each I-Statement fell (what we called "achievement statements" are not a lexical category—these are discussed later). A predicate is the verb ("I think ..."), adjective ("I am happy"), or noun phrase ("I am a student") that accompanies the "I" subject. Using the lexical classification of the predicate (which is straightforward and discussed in most introductory linguistics texts) eases problems of interjudge reliability and multiple coding.

Table 9.1 shows the distribution of different types of I-Statements in terms of the percentage of each type out of the total number of I-Statements the interviewee used (thus, e.g., 32% of all Sandra's I-Statements were "Affective Statements," such as "I don't like them"). Note that there are two sets of numbers for Brian—we explicate why this is so at the end of this chapter.

The numbers in Table 9.1 are not meant to be significant in and of themselves. We use such numbers to guide us in terms of hypotheses that we can investigate further in other ways, including through close scrutiny of the actual details and content of the teenagers' language.

In Table 9.1, we have subtotaled the scores for "Affective," "Ability–Constraint," and "State-Action" I-Statements, on the one hand, and the scores for "Cognitive"

TABLE 9.1

Percentage of Different Categories of I-Predicates Out of Total I-Predicates

	WORKING CLASS			UPPER MIDDLE CLASS			
	Sandra	Kevin	Maria	Brian	Emily	Ted	Katie
AFFECTIVE	32	21	28	7/5	8	12	13
ABILITY–CONTRAINT	7	7	7	5/6	1	4	2
STATE–ACTION	39	49	40	44/36	24	18	7
Subtotal (A)	78	77	75	57/48	33	28	22
COGNITIVE	22	23	23	28/34	54	50	65
ACHIEVE	0	.5	2	15/18	13	22	13
Subtotal (B)	22	23	25	43/52	67	72	78

and "Achievement" I-Statements, on the other ["Achievement I-Statements" are not a lexical category of English. They represent statements where the speaker is directly talking about accomplishments that relate to mainstream success. We coded a statement as an "Achievement I-Statement" only if all three coders agreed that it was]. We call the first combination Category A and the second Category B. When we make such combinations, we find something interesting and suggestive. The working-class teens are high in Category A and low in Category B, whereas the upper-middle-teens are low in A and high in B.

Why should this be so? It is, we argue, our first indicator of what in these studies eventually became our major claim: The working-class teens fashion themselves through language as immersed in a social, affective, dialogic world of interaction, and the upper-middle-class teens fashion themselves through language as immersed in a world of information, knowledge, argumentation, and achievements built out of these.

What the teens actually say in each category is more important than how many times they say certain sorts of things. In our studies (e.g., Gee, 2000a, b; Gee, Allen, & Clinton, 2001; Gee & Crawford, 1998), we found that working-class and upper-middle-class teenagers talk about quite different things when they speak in the first person, even when they are using the same I-Statement category (e.g., Cognitive or Affective). For example, consider a few typical examples of Cognitive I-Statements and Affective I-Statements from the "life part" of Sandra's and Maria's (working class) and Emily's and Karin's (upper middle class) interviews:

COGNITIVE I-STATEMENTS

Sandra (Working Class):

I think it is good [her relationship with her boyfriend];

I think I should move out [of the house];

I didn't think it was funny [something she had done that made others laugh];

Maria (Working Class):

I guess they broke the rules;

I think I'm so much like a grown up;

I don't think they'd let me.

Emily (Upper Middle Class):

I think it's okay for now [living in her current town];

I think I have more of a chance of getting into college;

I think she's the coolest person in the whole world [a trip leader she admired].

Karin (Upper Middle Class):

I think they [her parents] want me to be successful;

I think of that as successful;

I don't really know anyone who doesn't understand me;

AFFECT/DESIRE

Sandra (Working Class):

Like I wanted to say, "Kinda kinda not. How could you kinda kinda not?";

I don't want to sit next to her, I don't want her huggin me or something;

(They [her friends] give me the answer) I want to hear;

Maria (Working Class):

I like hanging around with my aunt;

I like hanging around with big people;

I want to get out of my house;

Emily (Upper Middle Class):

Now I want to go to Europe;

I want to go to MIT;

I like backpacking and outdoor stuff.

Karin (Upper Middle Class):

I don't really care what other people think of me;

I feel pretty accomplished;

I'd like to be comfortable with my work [what she will do in the future].

The working-class teens' cognitive statements (here and throughout our data) almost always assume a background of dialogue and interaction. For example, Sandra makes clear elsewhere in her interview that other people don't like her boyfriend and that there is a debate about who should move out of the house. Or, to take another example, when Maria says, "I think I'm so much like a grown up," she has made it completely clear that this is a response to an ongoing struggle with her parents, who will not give her the independence she wants.

The upper-middle-class teens' cognitive statements are explanatory claims within an explicit or assumed argumentative structure, rather than directly dialogic and interactional. We can point out, as well, that the upper-middle-class teens are very often focused on direct or implied assessment and evaluation of self and others. For example, when Emily says, "I think it's okay for now [living in her current town]," nothing in her interview suggests that this is in reaction to anything anyone else has said or thought. At this point in her interview, she is discussing whether, in her own opinion, her old town or her new one is a better place from which to launch a successful career as a "worldly" (i.e., her word for cosmopolitan) person (in light of the fact that she views the kids in her new town as wealthy, but "sheltered"). It is simply her assessment of her own autobiographical trajectory toward her own goals for success. When Karin says, "I think they want me to be successful," nothing in her interview suggests that this is in response to any doubts or debates about the matter. Karin, in fact, repeatedly says how supported and well understood she is by her parents.

If we consider the teenagers' Affective I-Statements (see examples) and I-Statements about their actions (not given), we see that the upper-middle-class teens very often talk about relationships and activities in ways that seem to have a direct or indirect reference outside of themselves to achievement, success, and/or distinction in the adult world and in their futures. The working-class teens, on the other hand, seem to talk about activities and relationships in and of themselves and without such a side-long glance at their implications for the future. For example, considering two of our upper-middle-class teens, Emily's interview makes it clear that going to Europe and backpacking (see her Affective I-Statements), and other similar activities mentioned throughout her interview, are like items on a resume that will help toward getting into schools like MIT; Karin's remarks, here and throughout her interview, are heavily focused on what her present desires, feelings, and activities portend for the future in terms of achievement and success.

To see this point about activities further, consider a representative sample of Maria's (working class) and Karin's (upper middle class) I-Statements that refer to actions (some of Karin's actions are actually classified in the category of Achievement I-Statements). We list actions involving speech separately:

KARIN (Upper Middle Class):

Action

I went a lot over the summer (to Boston)	I go sometimes to Faneuil Hall
I go to the Community center	On weekends I hang around with friends
I've met people with different racial ethnicity	I go to school
I play a lot of sports	I do soccer and gymnastics and tennis
I go to gymnastics two nights a week	I do tennis in Holiston
I did well at that	I always make sure that I do it [homework]

Speech

I'd say an event that changed my life (was) ….	I usually let them know
I'd say over half of the people	I heard (about Rodney King)
but I've heard many …	I'm not saying that they didn't choose that

MARIA (Working Class):

Actions

I look at her	I see something pretty
I see (teenagers) walking places	after I come from New York
when I do something right	I wash the dishes
I'll do the dishes	I watch (the videos)
I go up to this one kid	I did my project on AIDS
I would help her cook	I go crying to her

Speech

I talk to her a lot	I'm like "I don't want to"
I always tell her	I ask once a week
I ask on Monday	I'm going to ask
I ask and they'll say no	I'll just go "fine"
I was like "I'm going to kill myself"	I was like "what am I doing?
I'm like "why did I do that"	I don't talk to her as much

It is clear that Karin's actions and activities are often tied to institutions and personal achievements, and that Maria's are not. In fact, the closest Maria comes to activities that appear to refer outside themselves to institutions or achievements is her remark that "I did my project on AIDS." Interestingly, she introduces this as a way to talk about her relationship with and attitude toward her younger sister, whom she considers much less mature than herself ("Last year I did my project on AIDS … we had condoms on our board and my sister used to be like all yelling and she was all laughing").

When Karin talks about speech events, her verbs of saying are, in many cases, "cognitive," that is, estimates or claims (e.g., "I'd say over half the people …", "I'd let them know." Most of Karin's few speech events are in the society section of her interview and part of arguments she is making to a fictionalized audience). Maria devotes far more of her interview to depicting herself as a speaker, and her speech events are much more interactional and dialogical (even when speaking to herself, she is responding to what has happened in an interaction).

One other indication that the working-class teens are more focused on the world of interaction than the upper-middle-class teens is the fact that they narrativize far more than the upper-middle-class teenagers. The percentage of lines in each teenager's transcript that are involved in a narrative are given in Table 9.2 ("line" here and elsewhere in this chapter means "lines" in the "lines and stanzas" sense, basically "clauses" or "tone units," see Gee, 2005).

We conclude this section by summarizing the differences we have pointed to thus far. The upper-middle-class teenagers are focused on knowledge claims, assessment, evaluation, their movement through achievement space, and the relationship between the present and the future. The working-class teens are focused on social, physical, and dialogic interactions. We see some indication here, as well, of what we will see further on: The upper-middle-class teenagers' interviews express, directly and indirectly, an alignment (and trust) among family, school, community, adult, and teen in terms of norms, values, and goals. The working-class teens express, directly and indirectly, much less alignment (indeed, in many cases active disalignment) among family, school, community, adult, and teen in terms of norms, values, and goals.

We turn now to a second tool, namely a study of the key motifs that run, like threads, throughout each teenager's interview. We find motifs as follows: One member of our research team goes through the transcript of an entire interview to look for recurring issues and themes in the teenager's talk. Each line is marked as to whether it directly discusses a theme or motif found in other lines (or is connected to such a theme or motif by, for instance, setting it up or elaborating it). Lexical items that are semantically related are one key way to find motifs (e.g., consider the motif "violence and conflict" in Jeremy's interview: Many different lines contain related lexical items like "fight," "beat," "punch," "get mad," "stab," "gangs," "war," etc.). We attempt, as far as we can, to exhaust all the lines in the interview. A second member of the research team independently verifies the motifs and assignment of lines, and we then discuss them further as a group. For our analysis here, we have used teenagers for whom there is nearly complete agreement on motifs and assignments of lines.

As an earlier publication discussed Sandra's and Emily's motifs (Gee & Crawford, 1998), we will restrict ourselves here to Brian and Karin (upper middle class) and Jeremy and Maria (working class). We list for each teenager the percentage of lines in their transcript devoted to each motif and then give typical examples of each motif. The category "other" represents lines that discuss something that did not recur in any significant amount. In some cases the same line could have been placed in more than one motif (e.g., for Jeremy, speech events in and with the family

TABLE 9.2

Percentage of Lines in Each Transcript That are Involved in a Narrative

Sandra	Jeremy	Maria	Brian	Emily	Ted	Karin
57%	35%	36%	19%	17%	12%	8%

could have been labeled as either "speech" or "family"). We label each line only once and pick the narrowest category (so for Jeremy, here, we pick "speech").

Because our interviews had a second part (what we called earlier the "society part") that was based on more abstract, academic-like questions, we might expect that the interviewees will, especially in this part of the interview, engage in a lot of fairly impersonal or abstract "viewpoint and argument giving" ("argument" here is used in the sense of a set of grounded claims, not in the sense of a dispute). This is, in fact, true for the upper-middle-class teens, although not for the working-class teens. The working-class teens often discuss social and personal events and feelings in the society part of the interview, just as they do in the life part. At the same time, the upper-middle-class teens by no means restrict their more impersonal "viewpoint and argument giving" to the society part of the interview, but engage in such talk in the life part, as well. We argue later that the upper-middle-class teens "viewpoint and argument giving" lines actually do often reflect personal motifs or themes, but in a fairly "impersonal" language.

Next we list the motifs of each of our four teens, with typical examples of each (in these examples, and elsewhere in this chapter, we run transcript lines together in order to save space). The numbers shown represent percentage of lines devoted to each motif out of the total number of lines in each teenager's transcript:

UPPER MIDDLE CLASS

Brian

Viewpoint/Argument Giving	=	39
Future plans and prospects	=	22
Self-assessment	=	20
Activities	=	17
Other	=	2

Argument/Viewpoint: I think that society stereotypes, like take a look at some of the movies we make

We were actually the bad guys in that situation, because we made treaties with them [Native Americans] and we broke the treaties

Future plans and prospects: I have a bunch of possibilities

I want to go to either MIT, Harvard, Princeton, Stanford or maybe Dartmouth

Self-Assessment: I'd probably be right on the line [between the "in" group and the "out" group]

Well, I'm kinda happy where I am

Activities: I have a report that I need to work on

I'm kind of busy with them [two music clubs] because I've been updating my records and stuff

KARIN

Viewpoint/Argument Giving	=	44
Affiliation with School and/or Adults	=	21
Achievement	=	12
Activities	=	10
Being Supported and Understood	=	8
Other	=	5

Argument/Viewpoint: I believe that every person has equal chances to become what they want to be, but they need the education though

I think that everyone should be treated equally and feel comfortable with their own background

School/Adult Affiliated: They [her parents] know how important education is

Because things that you learn now could help you later, and so you need to remember them

Achievement: I feel pretty accomplished

You have to remain on the top, and you have to keep working hard, there can't be a year that you slack off or anything

Activities: Every summer, we have tennis tournaments at the yacht club

We've also been to Dartmouth

Supported/Understood: She [her mother] does understand me a lot

I don't really know anyone who doesn't understand me

WORKING CLASS

JEREMY

Violence and Conflict	=	44
Activities	=	19
Speech in Social Interaction	=	15
Family	=	11
Sexism Viewpoint/Argument	=	7
Other	=	4

Violence/Conflict:	They can hit you, but you can't hit back
	So I just hit them back
Activities:	Go outside and play sports
	We go play that—it's like an army game
Speech in Social Interaction:	I wanted to swear at both my parents so many times, cause they get me mad a lot of the time
	I hated all my teachers last year, they were all jerks, you couldn't like ask them questions
Family:	I'm usually not bad around my parents
	Because like my dad always taught me not to steal

MARIA

Personal Experience of "difference"	=	35
Conflict/Control Issues with Parents	=	29
Being Mature and Responsible	=	20
Desire for Independence	=	10
Argument	=	2
Other	=	4

Personal Experiences of "Difference:"	He would come by us and would say it's the United States or whatever and you have to talk English
	I never felt it [racism] until I came here, with Jeremy
Parent Conflict/Control:	I've had a lot of problems with my mom and my stepdad
	I just don't understand why he [her stepfather] can't tell her [her mother] the good things AND the bad instead of just the bad
Maturity/Responsibility:	That's why I think I'm so much like a grown up
	I already know what's wrong and what's right and I know like the rules

Independence: Cause I always tell her [her mother] that I want
                                 some independence

                                 Someday soon I'll be out of the house and I'll
                                 have my own car

There are many differences in the motifs these teenagers use across their interviews. We deal here with only two. First, as we mentioned earlier, the upper-middle-class teenagers devote far more of their interviews, in both parts, to stating their viewpoints and constructing arguments for them in relatively distanced and impersonal ways. It would seem, at first sight, as if the upper-middle-class teens, then, take a more detached, less involved view of what they are talking about than the working-class teens.

But a deeper look at the interviews seems to show that when the upper-middle-class teens are engaged in "viewpoint/argument" talk, they are often rhetorically clothing their own very personal interests and concerns in a more distanced language. At the very least, they are probably very much aware of the connections between their "distanced arguments" and their personal interests, values, and favored themes or motifs. For example, consider first Jeremy (working class) and Brian (upper middle class) on racism, and then a piece of "viewpoint/argument" talk from Karin (upper middle class):

JEREMY

Interviewer: … Is there racism [in society]?

… like colored people I don't, I don't like. I don't like Spanish people most of 'em, but I like, I like some of 'em. Because like if you, it seems with them, like they get all the welfare and stuff. Well, well White people get it too and everything but, I just- And then they think they're bad and they're like- They should speak English too, just like stuff like that.

BRIAN

Interviewer: Why do you think there are relatively few Hispanic and African American doctors?

… well, they're probably discriminated against, but, but it's not really as bad as—as people think it is, or that it once was. Because, uh, I was watching this thing on T.V. about this guy that's trying to—How colleges and and some schools have made a limit on how many White students they can have there, and a limit—and they've increased the limits on how many Black and Hispanic students they have to have. So, a bunch of White people [rising intonation] are getting—even if they have better grades than the Black or Hispanic student, the Black or Hispanic student gets in because they're Black or Hispanic. So, I think that that kinda plays an effect into it.

KARIN

Interviewer: ... just say that it's a really really poor neighborhood um or a ghetto school, and, um, do you feel like somebody who goes to school there would have a chance, um, to succeed or become what they want to become?

Not as good as they would in a good school system. It depends on- I know that they probably don't. If they don't have enough money, they might not have enough to put into the school system and not- may not be able to pay the teachers and, um, the good supplies and the textbooks and everything. So maybe they wouldn't- they probably wouldn't have the same chance. But, I believe that every person has equal chances, um, to become what they want to be.

Jeremy (working class) personalizes his response and subordinates his argumentative "facts" to his by no means distanced viewpoint on minorities (we say "by no means distanced" because, in his interview, Jeremy directly expresses, on several occasions, hostility to minorities, particularly in their role as what he perceives as gang members, and nonnative speakers of English). Brian, the upper-middle-class teen, does not, at first, seem to personalize his response in the same way. In fact, elsewhere in his interview he says he has experienced little or no ethnic diversity in his school or town. However, Brian's interview is replete with worries about "making it" in terms of going to a top college and having a successful career. In this sense, we can say that Brian's response is, in reality, quite personal nonetheless (note also the rising emphatic intonation on "a bunch of White people"). Although he most certainly could have stated his concerns as directly related to his own fears of affirmative action negatively impacting on his plans and desires, he chose not to. Thus, his response sounds less personalized than Jeremy's, but, in fact, it isn't.

Karin (upper middle class), after having spent a good deal of time discussing how good her school is and how important this fact is to her future, is then asked about the connection between poor schools and success. She first offers an argument, consistent with her views on her own school and future, that such schools will lower children's chances of success. However, she then contradicts her own argument when she says that she believes that every person has equal chances to become what they want to be. Given the fact that Karin spends a great deal of her interview talking about her hopes and fears for a successful future, it is easy to interpret her remark "they probably wouldn't have the same chance" as meaning the "the same chance as ME." Karin's "distanced" argument has come too close to rendering the grounds of "worth" and "distinction" (of the sort she seeks) a matter of "chance," or, worse yet, injustice.

Maria (working class), too, like Jeremy, personalizes her talk about racism. Maria's motif of "personal experiences of difference" represents the fact that she spends a good deal of the society part of her interview (but some of the life part, as well) talking about her personal experiences with and knowledge about the Puerto Rican community and racism (she herself is Puerto Rican, the only "minority" among the teenagers we focus on in this chapter). In fact, her remarks (see previous examples in motifs) that "He would come by us and would say it's the United States or whatever and you have to talk English" and "I never felt it [racism] until I came here, with [Jeremy]" are about the very Jeremy discussed in this chapterr!

In fact, the upper-middle-class teenagers (as they all say in their interviews) have little actual experience with cultural diversity, too little to talk about it in the personal way in which Jeremy and Maria do. Bernstein (1974) would say that Jeremy and Maria are speaking in a "restricted code." But, ironically, this is so because their experience of social and cultural diversity is *not* restricted and the upper-middle-class teens' experience is. In fact, the upper-middle-class teens' language appears more "elaborated" in large part because they distance themselves from "everyday" social interaction, mediate almost everything they say through their relationship to (and fears about) achievement and success, and sometimes "cloak" or "defer" their "material interests" with abstract argumentative talk in which they fail to directly mention their own personal interests and concerns. Far from being a novel point about Bernstein's distinction, this is much the same point Labov (1969) made in his classic paper "The Logic of Nonstandard English" (a paper otherwise unfair to Bernstein, who was not talking about "dialects," but, rather, ways of semantically encoding experience).

When we turn to the other sorts of motifs in the interviews, we reach the same sorts of conclusions we reached on the basis of our I-Statement analysis. The two upper-middle-class teenagers' themes are focused on assessment, achievement, and affiliation with adults and their institutions. The two working-class teens' motifs are focused on social interaction and conflict with peers and adults (Maria's maturity and independence themes are closely linked with her conflict with her parents and her desire to spend more time with her peers). The activities the upper-middle-class teens mention are adult and achievement oriented; the activities the working-class teens mention are peer oriented and centered in "everyday" teenage life.

NARRATIVE

Our third tool is narrative analysis (see Gee, 2005). We do not have space here to engage, to any great extent, in close narrative analysis (see Gee, 1997 for an extended narrative analysis from this data), although narratives are crucial for understanding people's "deep sense-making" in interviews (Mishler, 1986). We can, however, give one brief example.

We have already seen that the upper-middle-class teens narrativize much less than the working-class teens. But, then, let us turn, at last, to why there are two sets of numbers listed for Brian in Table 9.1. The first set of numbers is for Brian's interview as a whole. The second set is the scores Brian receives when we remove the only extended narrative in his interview. In fact, Brian was the only upper-middle-class interviewee who gave us an extended narrative, whereas such narratives were common among the working-class teens (this narrative is not reflected in Table 9.2). The difference in Brian's numbers is illuminating when we come to see two things about his interview: First, when we remove his one extended narrative, he (of course) patterns yet closer to his fellow upper-middle-class teens, and, second, and more importantly, his single extended narrative is precisely about moving from being an "outsider" to being an "insider" among these teens. We print Brian's narrative in terms of its lines and stanzas, followed by some of the interviewer's follow-up questions and Brian's answers. We have bolded Brian's repeated use of the habitual aspect marker "used to":

Interviewer: ... did anything happen that changed your life significantly?

Oh um, when I was in like fifth and sixth grade, I **used to** take like hyper-spasms at recess. Like I **used to** get like mad and run around like a freak. And I was like the most hated kid in the grade, because I was such a spaz and I **used to** run around, and I **used to** be like—I **used to** be like—Like I'd play tetherball at recess. So whenever like I lost, and somebody like cheated, I **used to** get so mad

I **used to** run around and everybody **used to** gather around like laughing at me and stuff. But then—but then like—then after awhile, I just like realized why the hell am I doing this, everybody hates me, so then I stopped. And then—and then, its not really any problem now. I'm just kind of—I dunno.

Interviewer: Did it kind of come to a head, where like it went really bad one time, and it was after that you just realized that—

No, not really, I just—in fifth grade I was pretty bad, but in sixth grade I just slowly, slowed down. And then seventh grade I didn't have any and then I haven't had any this year.

Interviewer: So, did you feel like it was cause you just—you hate losing? I mean when—I mean you were younger and—

No, no, the thing I hate is, I hate unfairness in games, and I just really hate it.

Interviewer: If somebody cheats?

Yeah and I got so mad, because whenever I played, they knew that I would take like, hyper-spasms, so they all gathered around and then when I—and then when I tried to hit the ball, they would like grab my shirt or something. So I was like [burned???].

Brian describes himself as a pariah ("hyper-spasms," "get mad and run around like a freak," "most hated kid," "a spaz"). His repeated use of the habitual aspect marker "used to" stresses that his pariah behavior and status was an enduring and ingrained trait, part of his "habitus" in Bourdieu's (1984, 1998) terms. He was driven to a state of frenzy by "cheating" or "unfairness in games."

Brian's "redemption" is described as a moment of sudden, personal, individual, rational realization. All at once, based on his personal effort, he "stopped" (note that the "unfairness" need not have stopped). But when the interviewer asks if, indeed, Brian's transformation was so sudden, he indicates that it was not (it appears to have taken a year or two).

We have seen that Brian, in his interview, is, like our other upper-middle-class teenagers, deeply invested in assessment of self and others, the connection between today's activities and tomorrow's success, and movement through "achievement space." Brian's narrative is his "origin" story, how he transformed himself through his own individual efforts and through rational calculation into an "acceptable" and "worthy" person (with the "right" habitus). Such "redemptive moments" are, in fact, typical of many male autobiographical stories in Western culture (Freccero, 1986). In stressing individual effort and rationality overcoming emotion, Brian is enacting classic values of U.S. middle-class, capitalist culture.

At the same time, the "old Brian" (the one that "used to") learns that one cannot show too much emotion in the face of competition, even in the face of unfair competition. In middle-class, Anglo-centered culture, the person who shows heightened emotion, or too much emotion, "loses" (Kochman, 1981). And, yet, if one has learned to let go of one's anger at unfairness in competition, it is not likely that the larger inequities of our society (things such as racism, classicism, and sexism) will engender much passion in Brian, and, indeed, they do not in his interview. Brian's transformation story—his only extended narrative—is, then, too, the story of an upper-middle-class child rationalizing (in several senses of the word) his assumption of an upper middle-class habitus (Bourdieu, 1984, 1998), a process that actually took extended norming and socialization.

CONCLUSIONS

The upper-middle-class teens fashion themselves in and for these interviews as well on their way to being Shape-Shifting Portfolio People. This is something at which they get a good deal of practice at home, in school, and in out-of-school activities. The working-class teens do not attempt to display themselves this way. Rather, they display themselves as immersed in a world of action and feeling untied to vaunted futures of achievement, transformation, and status. And, indeed, at one level, this is understandable and all to the good: they are reacting intelligently to an "on the ground" reality that is less supportive, offers many fewer economic resources, and is much more risky than the lives of the upper-middle-class teens. At the same time, they may be being left behind in the race for success in a fast-changing world, success that might allow them a greater capacity to challenge or change the darker aspects of our new capitalist reality.

We spent enough time in the school our working-class teens attended to know that this school offered them few resources to prepare them for self-fashioning futures. In fact, many of the students were advised to attend the local Vocational Education High School because their teachers and advisors believed this would lead to "better jobs." Unfortunately, we later discovered that most of the major employers in town would not hire graduates of the Vocational Education High School because its training and technological resources were considered entirely out-of-date for modern workplaces.

As I don't have time here to detail what the school our working-class teens attended was like, suffice it to say that when we shadowed students in their classes, there was a great emphasis on skill-and-drill, following directions without question or challenge, and low-level, rather than conceptual, understandings. And this was prior to the full expression of the testing and accountability regime that has now fully devoured this and many other schools.

In the school our upper-middle-class students attended, the emphasis was on conceptual understanding, self-expression, and self-presentation on the part of the students. Neither school, I should add, stressed political or critical understandings.

One social studies teacher in the upper-middle-class school claimed to do so and, indeed, seemed to do so in his classes, but when we asked his students what they took away from his classes, they told us that listening to his stories of turmoil in far-away countries made them more "worldly" and, thus, better prepared for careers in a global world from which, they acknowledged, they were sheltered. None of them espoused the teacher's political agenda.

It is not my argument here that schools themselves are producing a "Great Divide" between well-off kids who are going to be Shape-Shifters less and less tied to local action and feeling and less-well-off kids who are not prepared to transform themselves beyond the grounds of local action and feeling in a global world. This divide is produced by families and the society at large. The schools simply abet it (Gee, 2003, 2004).

The schools our upper-middle-class teens attended did not critically confront them with the social, economic, and cultural differences and inequities of the world in which they and we live. The schools the working-class teens attended did not confront them with the realities of the high-tech, global, fast-changing world they would enter, a world with few good blue-collar jobs of the sort their parents had had. And, in any case, as is typical today, they weren't in the same schools.

So, in the end, what's all this got to do with literacy? Of course, the shape-shifting orientation of our upper-middle-class teens is one they associate with school-based literacy practices—supplemented greatly by many home-based activities, hobbies, and trips that support school success—and the success these literacy practices can bring them for getting into good colleges and pursuing good careers. On the other hand, I have pointed out in other work that many of our working-class teens associated school-based literacy practices with a lack of personal caring and social bonding between themselves and school-based adults, including their teachers (Gee, 1997).

But, for me, the real issue is what literacy practices can do to help ease the divide discussed in this chapter. In my recent work, I have taken a tip from young people playing video games and using other forms of digital literacies (Gee, 2003). Many young people today don't just play video games, they use the software that comes with the games to modify and customize the games, to redesign them. They are not just consumers of this form of digital literacy, they are proactive producers.

The same sort of thing is true of other aspects of many young peoples' interactions with digital literacies today, for example, in respect to the Internet (remember Almon, earlier). Furthermore, in games, chat rooms, instant messaging, and Web sites, they enact and play with a variety of different, even esoteric, identities and social relationships, some virtual, some real, and many somewhere in between. Self-fashioning becomes a form of play, an opening, in fact, to think about identities in society and the values connected to different identities.

As young people become active producers and designers, they pick up a wealth of technical knowledge of the sort that is crucial to many spheres in our modern, global, high-tech world. They sometimes pick up a critical capacity to critique design and ask questions about how various modern media are designed to affect people in specific ways. In this more recent work, I have found that many schools, especially urban schools, do not resource their students with modern technologies or integrate these into their curricula. The action, once again, is often more at home and in the community than it is at school.

Nonetheless, I believe that it is within the realm of modern digital literacies that the divide I have discussed in this chapter can either be made much worse or begin to be remedied. Here is the space where students, schools, and homes can make contact with the possibilities for fashioning new identities in the modern world that will either harm us or heal us. Here, identity can be about the play of self-discovery and not just the hard work of staying on the fast track to financial success in the world.

REFERENCES

Bauman, Z. (1992). *Intimations of postmodernity*. London: Routledge.

Bauman, Z. (2000). *Individualized society*. Cambridge: Polity Press.

Beck. U. (1992). *Risk society*. London: Sage.

Beck, U. (1995). *Reflexive modernization*. Stanford, CA: Stanford University Press.

Bernstein, B. (1974). *Classes, codes and control* (Vol. 1., 2nd rev. ed.). London: Routledge and Kegan Paul. (Original work published 1971).

Bourdieu, P. (1984). *Distinction: A social critique of the judgement of taste*. Cambridge: Harvard University Press.

Bourdieu, P. (1998). *Practical reason*. Stanford: Stanford University Press.

Freccero, J. (1986). Autobiography and narrative. In T. C. Heller, M. Sosna, & D. E. Wellbery, with A. I. Davidson, A. Swidler, & I. Watt (Eds.), *Reconstructing individualism: Autonomy, individuality, and the self in Western thought* (pp. 16–29). Stanford, CA: Stanford University Press.

Gee, J. P. (1997). Thematized echoes. *Journal of Narrative and Life History, 7*, 189—196.

Gee, J. P. (2000a). New people in new worlds: Networks, the new capitalism and schools. In B. Cope & M. Kalantzis, (Eds.), *Multiliteracies: Literacy learning and the design of social futures* (pp. 43—68). London: Routledge.

Gee, J. P. (2000b). Teenagers in new times: A new literacy studies perspective, *Journal of Adolescent and Adult Literacy, 43*, 412—420.

Gee, J. P. (2002). Millennials and Bobos, *Blue's Clues* and *Sesame Street*: A story for our times. In D. E. Alvermann (Ed.), *Adolescents and literacies in a digital world* (pp. 51—67). New York: Peter Lang.

Gee, J. P. (2003). *What video games have to teach us about learning and literacy*. New York: Palgrave/Macmillan.

Gee, J. P. (2004). *Situated language and learning: A critique of traditional schooling*. London: Routledge.

Gee, J. P. (2005). *An introduction to discourse analysis: Theory and method* (2nd ed.). London: Routledge.

Gee, J. P., Allen, A-R, & Clinton, K. (2001). Language, class, and identity: Teenagers fashioning themselves through language, *Linguistics and Education, 12*, 175—194.

Gee, J. P., & Crawford, V. (1998). Two kinds of teenagers: Language, identity, and social class. In D. Alvermann, K. Hinchman, D. Moore, S. Phelps, & D. Waff (Eds.), *Reconceptualizing the literacies in adolescents' lives* (pp. 225—245). Hillsdale, NJ: Lawrence Erlbaum Assocates.

Gee, J. P., Hull, G., & Lankshear, C. (1996). *The new work order: Behind the language of the new capitalism*. Boulder, CO: Westview Press.

Giddens, A. (1991). *Modernity and self-identity*. Cambridge: Polity Press.

Giddens, A. (1992). *The transformation of intimacy*. Cambridge: Polity Press.

Greenblatt, S. (1980). *Renaissance self-fashioning: From More to Shakespeare*. Chicago: University of Chicago Press.

Greider, W. (1997). *One world, ready or not: The manic logic of global capitalism*. New York: Simon & Schuster.

Kanter, R. M. (1995). *World class: Thriving locally in the global economy*. New York: Simon & Schuster.

Kochman, T. (1981). *Black and white styles in conflict*. Chicago: University of Chicago Press.

Labov, W. (1969). The logic of nonstandard English. *Georgetown Monographs on Language and Linguistics, 22*, 1—31. Reprinted (1972) in *Language in the Inner City* (pp. 201—240). Philadelphia: University of Pennsylvania Press.

Lam, W. S. E. (2000). L2 literacy and the design of the self: A case study of a teenager writing on the Internet. *TESOL Quarterly, 34*, 457—482.

Malone, M. J. (1997). *Worlds of talk: The presentation of self in everyday conversation*. Cambridge: Polity Press.

Mishler, E. G. (1986). *Research interviewing: Context and narrative*. Cambridge, MA: Harvard University Press.

Reich, R. B. (1992). *The work of nations.* New York: Vintage.

Rifkin, J. (2000). *The age of access: The new culture of hypercapitalism where all of life is a paid-for experi-ence.* New York: Jeremy P. Tarcher/Putnam.

Taylor, C. (1992). *The ethics of authenticity.* Cambridge, MA: Harvard University Press.

Taylor, C. (1994). *Multiculturalism: Examining the politics of recognition.* Princeton: Princeton Univer-sity Press.

10

Exploring Race, Language, and Culture in Critical Literacy Classrooms

Bob Fecho
University of Georgia

Bette Davis
William Carey College

Renee Moore
Broad Street High School

The specific circumstances may have been different, but for each of us—Bob, Bette, and Renee—our explorations into issues of race, language, and culture began with what Bob has called teachable/researchable moments. Bob's moment hinged around a class reading of a Nikki Giovanni (1971) poem, "Beautiful Black Men." Feeling the poem to be a celebration of African American slang, language, and culture, Bob imagined that day's lesson with his high school class of African American juniors to be a romp through a discussion of vibrant imagery before moving to other work. However, what slowly emerged on that day were concerns and questions raised by his students about how they felt Giovanni was mocking Black dialect and, on learning that she was African American, how she was even betraying the African American community. Spurred by his own working-class concerns about language, his students' issues raised by the Giovanni poem, and a growing popular and academic zeitgeist around the ways language and culture transacted, Bob urged his class to begin collecting examples of dialogue around them so that the class could explore the power of language up close and with personal connections and context.

For Bette, her teachable/researchable moment is less a particular instance in time and more a collection of events centered around a teaching activity she has called "classtalk," spontaneous or framed discussions that focus on issues of language and grow from her needs as a teacher and the expressed needs of her students. In particular, Bette recalled a moment in a college freshman composition class she was teaching where students had come to the course with higher levels of critical language awareness than she might have anticipated. However, a few African American students expressed negative attitudes toward their most intimate language, even as they spoke it. In *Voices of the Self*, Keith Gilyard (1991) characterized such views as "eradicationist." Other African American students adamantly defended their home codes, at times voicing some aversion to code switching. Many of these comments surfaced during online exchanges with students in other regions of the United States participating in a Bread Loaf School of English online discussion about language issues. Specifically, one student whom Bette calls *E* complained online about having to switch to the linguistic code of the culture of power for any reason. From this planted seed branched a diversity of rich and insightful dialogue and exploration by Bette and her students into issues of race, language, and culture.

Renee's teachable/researchable moment surfaced in the late hours of the evening as she was grading papers. In a frustrated outburst in her teaching journal, Renee wrote the following about her rural Southern, mostly African American high school English classroom:

> The first semester is over and it is time for serious reflection and preparation. We [the English Department] have decided to launch the new grading scale. We will use it to penalize students uniformly for the most common grammatical errors after we distribute the departmental grammar handbook .... I approach this with a good deal of anxiety. Will it achieve the desired results, or will we simply frustrate the students and make life miserable for everyone? One grim omen has been the grammar diagnostic that I used at the start of the school year. This past week, I had my accelerated 9th-grade class take the same test again as a post-test. I've only made it about halfway through the scoring, but the results so far are depressing; most of the students' scores improved only slightly, several stayed the same, and some dropped! This is after a solid semester—two grading periods—of intense grammar instruction! So what now?" (12/23/91)

On the eve of holiday break, Renee resolved to launch herself and her students into a systematic study of race, language, and culture, one that was not about penalties, but about opportunities.

These incidents are significant because, in many ways, they are microcosms of what happens daily in urban, suburban, and rural classrooms across the United States. Students and teachers had run smack against problems of language and seemingly innocent transactions had left them bewildered, angry, frustrated, and betrayed. What was evident was that home codes, street codes, generational codes, and mainstream power codes had collided in our classrooms and had shattered opinion in many directions, none of which could be counted on to focus our discussion, yet all of which offered tantalizing possibilities for learning. As Lindfors (1998) indicated, inquiry is impositional and, although daunted by these language transactions, our students and we were also shaken from our complacency and compelled to investigate these issues.

Given this backdrop, two African American women and a European American man argue that all students, even those for whom school replicates their home codes, need to learn about the cultural complexities of language and to become critically aware of the role language plays in all our lives. However, for students whose home codes differ markedly from the mainstream power codes, such approaches to language learning are crucial. What we mean by language learning is that students need to be invited into the academic conversations about the social and political issues inherent in language—that unless learners have clear understandings of the import of code switching, for example, they will make ill-informed decisions regarding the impact of language on their lives. Therefore, creating a classroom where critical inquiry is the foundation presents one pedagogy of possibility wherein students and teacher can delve into the nature of the mainstream culture while coming to some greater understanding of the diverse cultures present in the room. Furthermore, if student agency is to be respected, then such classrooms need to be sites where multiple perspectives become the fabric of the curriculum.

This chapter builds upon the foundation of the chapter Bob wrote for the first edition of this book, but it is expanded and deepened by the addition of the work of Renee and Bette. As such, we construct our argument by first creating a theoretical framework based on the work of Delpit, Rosenblatt, Freire, Gee, Bahktin, and Gordon. The aim of this framework is to provide a lens for considering both our research and our pedagogy. Furthermore, we build on this theoretical framework as we discuss the teaching, research, and policymaking implications of our work. Between this framework and our implications, we—Bob, Bette, and Renee—provide brief, but rich sketches of the teaching and research that occurred in our classrooms, particularly focusing on literacy events that complicated our discussions of language and the roles it plays in our lives.

THEORETICAL FRAMEWORK

At the time of our work, we were all English teachers with over 50 years of combined teaching experience. Yet we were all at metaphysical places where our traditional charge of teaching students what some have called standard English was conflicting with what we knew about how language played out in our classrooms, and in the lives and communities of our students. Therefore, we were teachers with conflicted goals. We wanted our students to be fluent in mainstream power codes because we, as Delpit (1995) noted, had seen too often how ignorance of those codes nullified otherwise bright and vibrant lives. On the other hand, those who too readily embrace mainstream power codes run the risk of forsaking their culture and the dialect that ties them to that culture. Most importantly, we wanted our students to understand the beauty and power inherent in a deep grasp of mainstream power codes, but we also wanted them to find the opportunities to express the beauty and power of their home and other personal codes. The rub, however, was, and remains, that limitations of time, resources, and an overarching curriculum required that we make terrifying choices among these options.

The theoretical keystones of our framework are three concepts for which Delpit (1995) argued:

1. All students must be taught mainstream power codes because not to do so will further marginalize those who are already marginalized from access to social, economic, and political power venues.

2. Teachers must find ways to legitimize, validate, and celebrate the home and other personal codes students bring to the classroom. Not to do so is to create a gulf among the child, his home, and the school.

3. Students need to be taught the mainstream power codes in ways that critique those codes and open them to further expansion and greater inclusion. Only through critique will the codes become more representational and equitable.

It is our belief that any sound pedagogy in a literacy classroom is built on these concepts. Also, these concepts take on greater significance when they transact with the work of Rosenblatt (1995), Freire (1970/1993), Gee (1996), Bakhtin (1981), and Gordon (2000). The work of the first three theorists is familiar to the field of education. Rosenblatt's (1995) transactional literary theories, Freire's (1970/1993) theories of praxis and dialogue, and Gee's (1996) theories of learning and acquisition all expand or illuminate Delpit's three concepts.

However, with the work of Bakhtin being less accessible to teachers and the work of Gordon being less well known in educational literature, we felt an expanded discussion was warranted. In the case of Bakhtin (1981), we think the concept of what he calls *heteroglossia* provides the larger picture of support for Delpit's three concepts. Bakhtin used heteroglossia to describe an ongoing transaction between centripetal, or unifying forces of language, and centrifugal, or diversifying forces of language. On one hand, the centripetal forces, largely through dominant social control, are constantly trying to stabilize and ultimately reify language. On the other hand, the centrifugal forces, primarily through personal interpretation, are always diversifying language, possibly to the point of anarchy. Neither extreme is desirable, and Bakhtin argues that it's the balance of these tensions—their points of transaction—that makes for a healthy, living language. We believe such a scenario is exactly what Delpit's three concepts realize—classrooms at the nexus where home and personal codes transact with mainstream power codes toward the reshaping of new codes.

Furthermore, this transaction of theories needs to be seen through the existential lens provided by Gordon (2000), a Caribbean American philosopher. He posited that all attempts at meaning making are existential acts and that the more one is marginalized from mainstream power codes due to random events of birth, the more one needs to make meaning of the chaos he or she encounters. In particular, he averred that Blacks, due to the long-term and ongoing effects of racism, have particular need to write about and make sense of their lives, to find purpose beyond the reality. As Gordon cited, autobiography has dominated Black literature because, on one hand, it refuted racist arguments that Blacks were not fully human and lacked point of view. To write about one's life is to speak for one's humanity and perspective. On the other hand, such literary work also provided insight into the nature of being Black, particularly in an oppressive culture. Therefore, literacy practice is an existential act, that is, when we teach students to transact with language, we give them tools on which all future meaning will rely.

When backlit by Delpit's concepts, Gordon's existential perspectives and Bakhtin's concept of heteroglossia create an urgency for language learning in classrooms. Reading is less a handy academic tool or skill and more a primal necessity for negotiating one's sense of self and place in society. Furthermore, the import of cultures transacting with literacy and language to support identity creation become prominent; the idea that we use reading, writing, speaking, and listening as a means to position ourselves in relation to the greater world around us, regardless of how rational or irrational our transactions with that world may seem, takes hold.

THREE ATTEMPTS TO RECONCEPTUALIZE
LANGUAGE LEARNING

Bob's Classroom

As a high school teacher in an urban northeast classroom, I was first daunted and then challenged by Delpit's complex charge—to create a classroom that taught the mainstream power codes, honored home and other personal codes, and invited students to critique their learning through those codes. Encouraged by the work that emerged from my students who had called Giovanni's poem into question, in subsequent years I sought to develop deeper, more systematic investigations into language. The key was to envision a classroom where critical inquiry could be enacted, one in which language became an object of study open to question by students but remained mindful of the traditions and conventions that currently held sway. By investigating and calling into question the language around them, my students would be given opportunities to both understand and accept the mainstream power codes, also coming to know the many dialects in use in the classroom and the extent to which those language codes affected their lives. The intent was to neither teach mainstream codes nor dialect directly, but instead to create academic situations in which students could look at the way language transacted with their lives and the lives of others and then speculate what future encounters with language might hold in store. At base, I would be inviting students into the political, social, and academic discussions about language that seem to exist in the courts, legislatures, corporate boardrooms, and academic conferences across the United States—everywhere, it seems, except language arts classrooms.

Faced with a mix of students whose success in school varied widely and wishing to incorporate Grades 9 through 12 in all language arts classrooms, my small learning community within a larger high school sought focus within this diversity. We found it by centering around one essential question—how does learning connect you to your world—from which I keyed on language and created a curriculum that evolved through three inquiry projects. The first third of the year focused on raising issues and questions about the nature of language. Using literature as a base from which to work, students read texts such as Wilson's (1986) *Fences*, Gibsons's (1957) *The Miracle Worker*, and *Girl* by Kinkaid (1993), in each case being mindful of what each had to say about language and the ways in which language was used to further the needs of the story. Through discussions and activities centered by these works, themes that would drive the curriculum for the whole year began to emerge.

It was during this opening project that language was first connected to race when a discussion ensued, invited by the text of *Fences*, about the appropriateness of the racial invective *nigger*. Any teacher of African American students knows that although nigger is the worst racial slur and should be shunned by all White speakers, it is used by many Black adolescents as an inclusive greeting. My middle-class African American colleagues generally tend to frown on any use of the word in any context, as do many of the parents of the students I taught—yet, others of both groups model usage of the word. So when one student expressed concern that the main character used *nigger* too often and another student called that hypocrisy because his perception was that all the students used the word, we had stumbled into our first public display of the range of opinion that existed in the classroom regarding language.

With issues and questions emerging at a steady pace, it occurred to me that my students needed to somehow make a personal connection to these ideas about language. Consequently, the second third of the year was consumed by an autobiographical inquiry into language. Using models such as the movie of Christy Brown's (1989) *My Left Foot* and literary works like Angelou's (1970) *I Know Why the Caged Bird Sings* and Wright's (1945) *Black Boy*, students then wrote autobiographies, four chapters in length, of which at least one chapter had to deal with a way in which language had affected their lives. It was during this project that students broke through many of the barriers presented when an Eastern European American man teaches an African American student population. If revelations about language and connections to personal life had been lacking as the year started, they came out with depth and richness through the autobiographical writing. Language themes relating to family turmoil, profanity, racism, disempowerment, empowerment, and popular culture permeated the writing. Ways in which students were victimized by words ("The first sentence of the letter just made me put my head down and cry") or used words to victimize others ("I was also satisfied that he was hurt because of my words") were imbedded in thoughtful and descriptive tales of urban life.

Four major themes began to dominate our discussions that would propel us into the year-ending investigation. Through writing, debate, and mutual inquiry, concerns about the nature of standard English, Black English,[1] slang and profanity, and code switching continued to weave throughout the warp created by our investigation. These four themes eventually led to individual investigations into language. Students developed questions such as "What happens when the language of rap music is studied for what it says about Blacks in America?" and "What happens when an African American speaks standard English?" Armed with questions that they generated, students set about collecting data through interviews, journal keeping, note making, and electronic recording. In research reports and essays, students made tentative assertions, raised intriguing questions, and made empathetic pleas based on their analysis of the data.

For many students dealing with investigations into slang and profanity, the pervasiveness of these language forms seemed overwhelming. As one student put it, "Everywhere you look, you see profanity. Everywhere you go, you hear profanity. Profanity is everywhere, even in your home." She then used the assertion, based on the feelings of mothers she had interviewed, to argue that something so unavoidable should ultimately be embraced. Another student who had chronicled student–teacher classroom confrontations, concluded by noting that, "Until now, I really never cared about how profanity affects others ... but I believe it's not appropriate in the classroom or toward teachers." In either case, although the assertions differed, the arguments were based in part on the information gathered through the personal investigation into language.

The student inquiries into code switching often showed sophistication in terms of what students knew about shifting language based on audience and social expectations. As one student noted in discussion about her study:

---

[1]Although Bob now prefers using terms like *mainstream power codes, home codes, and Black Vernaculars*, he has elected to remain with the terms *standard English* and *Black English* in this section because these are the terms that were used in his class at the time of the study.

> When I'm with my mother and we get to talkin', we just having' our own time, we're speaking' Black English. Like if I go around my grandmother's way, they're White, and she has a certain way of speakin'. And I talk a different way around her. When I'm with my friends I talk slang ... Right here [in school], I'll talk standard ... What I really speak is Black English. 'Cause that's what I'm used to—Black English and slang. That's what I mainly grew up around.

It is clear by these words that some students are fairly savvy about code switching and do so with some degree of intention and purpose. All too frequently, however, students also expressed resentment that they needed to shift into language forms that, for one reason or another, did not seem to represent them as they wanted to be represented to the world.

Most often, the resented switch was into standard English, and studies into the impact of standard and Black English abounded. Each term brought its share of controversy, passion, and divided opinion to the table. Perhaps this range is best embodied by the following observation, also taken from a discussion of the student's personal inquiry:

> My aunt on my dad's side, she speaks standard English all the time. And when I go over there, she corrects me all the time. "It's not you *ain't*, it's *you're not*. If I had a dime for every time you said *you ain't*, I could be the richest woman on this earth." And she even makes fun of how we speak. [unclear] and laughs about it. I don't think it's really funny, for real for real. I think she's lost her whole background. It seems like when I see her, I don't see a Black aunt, I see a White aunt. That's what I see. A creation of learning back in her day.

It may not be true that this student's aunt "lost her whole background," and it is prudent to consider that what constitutes Blackness or Whiteness is not limited to language. But this student showed strong evidence of using her investigation into language to gain deeper and more complex understandings of the way language played out in her life.

What stood out most from these discussions based on the student investigations into standard and Black English was the range of opinion about both concepts. Within my classroom, students found facets of both that were beneficial and problematic. Rarely were we able to gain much consensus on either topic, except to agree that both were not going away and would continue to affect the lives of us who studied them.

Although the frame around which we worked remained of my doing, the students had developed questions for inquiry, gathered and analyzed data, and arrived at conclusions that suited their needs and concerns. Over the course of the year, a loose and superficial set of queries had coalesced into areas of inquiry that were investigated through a variety of questions that were both challenging and meaningful to the student inquirers. As Delpit (1988) and Freire (1970/1993) both recommended, the codes of power were brought under scrutiny by those who have something to gain, but also something to lose, through acquisition of those codes. In naming the nature of the impact language held on our lives, we had brought our inquiry, if not to a conclusion, then to some plateau from which we could momentarily contemplate the view.

Bette's Classroom

"The spontaneous dialogues helped me a lot," a former student responded when, some 3 years after her course with me, I asked her what single feature of the class had contributed most to her development as a writer. These not-always-so-"spontaneous dialogues," which students and I call *classtalk*, have become a fixture in my courses at a small private liberal arts college in South Mississippi, where I have taught for 9 years.

Many years before, when I taught public high school in the same town, I had begun exploring new ways of enhancing students' language development. This exploration grew out of my frustration that too many of my students left my class writing the same way they had when they entered. And while my experiments led to a variety of approaches that helped students create more substantive texts, we have continued to struggle in adapting language for various contexts. In addition, many reluctant writers in my classes have expressed to me their sense of inadequacy as speakers and writers, recalling how they had been silenced or ridiculed in school settings because they spoke and wrote in dialects that did not conform to academic standards.

Thus, two crucial questions guided our search:

1. How do we create a class community wherein students, their teacher, and their peers value the dialects they all bring to the classroom?
2. How do we assist one another in adapting our written language codes for a variety of audiences and purposes?

Fortunately, through study with Dixie Goswami, professor of English emerita at Clemson University and director of the writing program at Bread Loaf School of English, I learned of the benefits of teacher research in addressing these questions. Four important theory-based assumptions underpin this study. To start, I believe that well-facilitated conversations in a multicultural classroom can help "ensure the kind of equal-status interactions from which positive attitudes across. . . differences can grow" (Cazden, 1988, p. 135). Closely connected to this idea is my notion that contextualized talk is the primary mode of language acquisition, that we learn language through ongoing transactions with others (Bakhtin, 1981). I also believe that classtalk can provide a less threatening means of elevating students' critical language awareness (CLA), raising their consciousness of the power and politics of language (Clark & Ivanic, 1998). Throughout *Other People's Children*, Delpit (1995) expresses a similar view, stressing that children need to be instructed in the codes of the "culture of power." Finally, conversation provides a way to build on shared experience in developing written texts. If students are going to acquire "the language of education" (Martin, 1983, p. 9), they must be able to bring the knowledge and the language they gain in their homes and communities to school.

In addressing inquiry questions, I have documented selected classtalk events in a freshman composition class. The total class population included 10 low to upper income European American students and five low to middle income African Americans. By recording these sessions, I was able to gain an understanding of the range of response to these issues and to observe connections among the dialogues and theories cited earlier.

As mentioned in our introduction, my class became particularly engaged in discussion of language issues when an African American student (*E*) from our online discussion expressed his resistance to switching to standard American English. Although this transcript excerpt of our conversation in response to *E's* comments is long, I am including it in its entirety because it not only gives a sense of the range of perspective this classtalk brought to the surface, but it also holds potential for shaping future teaching and learning practices.[2]

> **WS**: I can identify with his opinion. But I still feel that everybody ought to learn standard English and use it in the proper situations. But I still do not approve ridiculing people who speak a different dialect. It's important to have a common dialect among a similar group of people, because this is one aspect of what makes up culture.
>
> **DP** (African American male): I wouldn't change my language for no one. Cause I'm gonna talk the way I talk anyway. [Some girls giggle.]
>
> **BR** (European American female): I think people should be allowed to express themselves in their own way. But I do believe that if you're going to school you should learn standard English. I'm not African American, but I was raised in a family with a strong Southern drawl, so when I started to school my teachers corrected me about my speech, and I don't feel that learning standard English took away from my culture or background …. [some students, African American and European American, indicate agreement].
>
> **GT** (African American female): Yeah, he said something about losing his dignity when he change his dialect. But it don't have nothing to do with losing your dignity. It's just normal for you to change your speech according to who you talking to. And it's not just Blacks—it's Whites, too.
>
> **AN** (European American female): E needs to understand that everyone does not live in his community. Everybody is not Black and they don't know the dialect. Standard English is a universal language, and the majority of people understand it. While E was growing up, he shoulda wanted to learn—like the big words—like if it was a word he didn't know, they told us to go look it up …. [Exchange of stares among a few African American students; longer interval before next speaker.]
>
> **WS** (African American male): He is saying there is a point where we cross over …. It's not like we have to be White. And I disagree about a universal language—I don't think there is one universal language. [Silence, but some African American students nod in agreement.]
>
> **BD**: I think we're on our way to some important insights. All of you have made very significant points. Let's get back to them and think further about this whole matter. We're running out of time, but I want you to do some further thinking—careful and honest thinking on paper—about these questions. I'd like to see your responses, but you don't have to share them with anyone else. It's your choice. [I write questions on board, saying them aloud as I write]: Are using "standard English" and using big words the same thing? Try to give examples to back up your response. Do you always find it easy to code switch in situations requiring a formal—or standard—usage which you don't

---

routinely use? Here I mean speaking or writing. Is standard English a "universal language?" Are you comfortable with your language practices? If so, what factors make you comfortable? If not, what makes you uncomfortable? How might we—teacher, student peers, and you—work together to enhance your effectiveness in using language?

In sum, most students admitted to having some trouble code switching from informal to more formal language, although some said it was easier to accomplish in writing than in speaking. All, including the student who initially made the claim, denied that standard English was a "universal language, " while most expressed some discomfort with their language practices.

AS, who had made insightful contributions to the conversation, described what she considered to be her deficiencies as well as how we might best address them:

> I need to do more brainstorming before I write and take more time to get my verb tense right. Also when I slow down I catch myself when pronouncing things wrong. I believe reading the articles aloud in class make us pay more attention to the proper language, also we can read our papers aloud to each other and correct each other mistakes ....

The written responses, like the conversation, reflected some tensions often conducive to introspection and potential change: the African American male "identifying" with E, asserting the necessity of using "standard English ... in the proper situations, " but insisting, "it's not like we have to be White;" the gradual acknowledging of the discomforts of code switching. All these perspectives would help direct our further inquiry.

In addition, through close and recurring analyses of these classtalk events, including observations of student coresearchers and of colleagues, as well as my own, I have noted the following most important developments in our inquiry:

1. Students across racial and economic backgrounds display a strong sense of the role of audience and purpose in language choice. Therefore, they agree generally on the necessity of occasional code switching, or register shifting.

2. Although students recognize the strong impact of family and social traditions on individual language patterns, they also see that appropriating the language of another culture does not necessarily mean adopting an entirely new set of values.

3. Through carefully facilitated talk, students work toward their own understandings of complex language matters—understandings that challenge assumptions based on ignorance and bigotry. They confront the reality that such assumptions transcend race, as noted in BR's comments about her "Southern drawl," although this accent does not necessarily imply "nonstandard " usage. Students of all ethnic and economic backgrounds come to resist the notion that either race, region, or any dialect necessarily reflects intelligence or that "English is the universal language."

This elevated awareness contributes to "equal-status interactions" and "positive attitudes" that Cazden (1988) considers important to language growth.

As students gain new insights on the complex and controversial issues surrounding language, some of them, like *AS*, assume greater roles in questioning and revising their own linguistic practices. Even where such agency is not evident among students, appropriations of particular new language patterns—new ways representing ideas in speech and writing—surface. Students whose dialects often deviate from mainstream quickly add terms such as *context, code switching*, and *appropriation* to their vocabulary, applying them effectively in their conversations and written texts. Obviously, they acquire some of these new codes from the teacher, but they learn others from peers. Granted, these new patterns do not always include verbs or pronouns; however, they offer encouragement for further inquiry. And although we cannot discount the effects of other class events—the readings, direct instruction, the actual writing process, the careful observation—our inquiry calls attention to the potential of class conversation in heightening awareness of language issues, fostering positive attitudes toward dialect diversity, and promoting students' agency in adapting their language for various contexts.

Renee's Classroom

As I started a decade-long inquiry to construct a response both to Delpit's challenge and my own concerns about the needs to teach mainstream power and home codes in my rural Mississippi high school classroom, I used a variety of means to get a range of perspectives on what such a classroom should look like. In collegial discussions, my former department head pointed out, "Everybody likes this teaching grammar through writing stuff because all it requires is doing a little 5-minute review of something we assume the students already know; then showing them how they can use it to improve a particular piece of writing. But somebody has to do the dirty work of teaching the concepts the first time, and that's the job nobody wants." In truth, most of us were teaching grammar skills as if every time were the students' first time being exposed to the topic. After these generally unsuccessful lessons, we would commiserate over how little the students knew or remembered from the last time they had studied the topic.

Continuing to inquire, I selected the group of students and parents who would work with me in the research process. I chose as my research assistant a high school senior, Sheila (not her real name), whom I had taught for the 2 previous years. I had a more difficult time choosing the students who would make up the focus group for my research interviews. I wanted a mix of males and females and of ability levels in grammar and usage. Also important were their parents or significant adults, who would make up the adult focus group. I deliberately chose students whose parents I knew would be more cooperative and likely to participate until project's end.

With the help of my online partners from Bread Loaf Teacher Network, I engaged my students and parents in discussions of the question, "What makes a good English teacher?" I knew from previous experience that students from our small, closely knit community often expressed themselves more freely to distant online peers than they would to me or to their classmates. In a typical response, CA, a student from Mississippi noted:

> A good English teacher is a teacher that has a good relationship with their students. Not only do they teach their students but they talk to the students about things other than the things that are supposed to be taught. Good teachers take time out and speak to students like they are your friends. They never give up on any student no matter how much a student does not understand the work, the teacher always keeps their patience and tries to help the student no matter what.

I was surprised at the commonality in opinions among my rural students and their more urbane, online counterparts in East Orange, New Jersey.

My parents' group also provided rich perspectives. When I asked one parent during a Saturday morning conversation, "Why are our students so resistant to learning and using standard English?" he looked straight at me and said:

> "English has a way of degrading you. Talkin' is s'posed to be natural. I feel angry. I'm angry about this. This deals with my self-esteem. They always tell us we're shiftless; we're lazy. I passed ENG 101 class at junior college, but the teacher flunked me and wrote on my last paper that is was because I "talked funny." English is a weapon of oppression. Just another tool to keep me in my place. Even if I master the language ... [trails off]."

His passionate response caught my attention because he had so eloquently captured the language dilemma with which I was struggling within the classroom, and indeed had struggled throughout my own education and professional life.

I also began to mine the rich body of work on language, race, and culture, studying such educators as Geneva Smitherman (1983), Ladson-Billings (1992), and Delpit (1995) among the over 70 research sources into which I tapped. In particular, Ball's (2000) study of female African American teachers reminded me of the importance of community. As Ball noted, "Discourse practices that take place within [the African American community] contribute to the building and sustaining of a sense of community and support a pedagogy that takes advantage of the cultural and linguistic knowledge that students bring to the learning environment" (p. 1008).

I put all these perspectives to work as I began to construct a vision of my classroom that employs an approach to language teaching I call Culturally Engaged Instruction (CEI). Over the course of my research, I've come to see CEI as *empowering language arts instruction in a dynamic practice shaped by informed and collaborative analysis of the particular cultural experiences, strengths, and learning goals of a specific group of students within a particular community.* Using CEI as my guide, I refined my preassessment process and developed individualized communications skills portfolios for each student, which required the participation of a significant adult member of the community. I have always used some kind of preassessment, but I also realize that my earlier preassessments had been too long and had too many separate parts, making the analysis very time consuming. I had learned it was more important that the students and I be able to draw some immediate conclusions from this early assessment, so we could begin working in a more personalized way sooner in the school year. Based on my hypothesis, an early, accurate, and detailed knowledge of the students is vital for culturally engaged instruction. Certainly, such knowledge is important for all good teaching; CEI is simply good teaching for a particular population of students.

My preassessment process revolved around having students demonstrate through performance their abilities in reading, writing, listening, and speaking. Only reading and writing are tested in the district or statewide assessments; however, I included the oral skills not only because they are part of the state framework, but also because they are highly valued communication skills within the local African American community and the ones in which the students tend to be strongest.

We began with a short, carefully chosen reading passage by or about an African American, preferably someone with whom they were not familiar. First, we did a timed reading to determine their speed. Then, they were allowed to read the article in full, set it aside, and free write what they remembered from the article. Next, I had them listen to an audiotape of a professional speaker on a motivational or inspirational topic, such as how to be a better reader. They were required to take notes during the tape. Scanning these later gave me an idea of their skills at listening comprehension. Finally, they used their notes from both exercises to draft an essay. I made sure to give the essay an I-Search twist, such as "What, if anything, did you get from the reading and or the lecture that might help you this school year?" These essays became our writing and grammar samples. All this took a few days to complete.

After the first week of school, we started analyzing the results together and developing personal learning plans (PLPs). The PLP was the first requirement in the communications skills portfolio for my class. I spent at least one full class period introducing the portfolio. There were several points in the portfolio that were negotiable, both initially and as the school year progressed. The final step was for them to take the PLP and the portfolio checklist home.

Each student had to identify a significant adult of his or her choice (e.g., parent, neighbor, teacher, church member, etc.) who was willing to act as a mentor for the duration of the school year. The mentor's role was to encourage the student to keep up and complete his or her portfolio. Students had to explain the portfolio to the mentors and get them to sign a contract. I contacted the mentors as soon as I knew who they were to introduce myself, answer questions, take suggestions for adjustments in the PLP or portfolio, and open the door for communication throughout the year. All these steps helped us create a culturally engaged learning environment.

Applying what I have learned from my research specifically to the teaching of grammar instruction has led to several meaningful changes in my classroom practice. First, I made a decision to talk with my students honestly and often about why we are required to study and master standard American English. Second, I used what I have learned about the students throughout the language instruction, starting with the extensive preassessment. Taking the time to learn about them and using that information as we learn about language and how to use it has incredible benefits for all of us.

Over time, I realized I was searching for a more empowering approach to language arts instruction. I wanted to teach the language arts in such a way that each student not only became technically proficient or skillful, but also became cognizant of the effects of language on others. Just as important, I wanted my students to understand how language arts/communication skills could be used to project one's own ideas and to assess more critically the ideas of others.

Conclusion

What, then, is the nature of an English classroom where language is the subject of critical inquiry? What occurs there? What do students do? What is the teacher's role? What issues get raised, discussed, and explored? What is the atmosphere that is conducive to such inquiry, and how is that atmosphere created? What is the work of such a classroom, and how is that work negotiated? In theory, according to Freire (1970/1993), such a classroom would engage students and teacher in a dialogue about the nature of the world, would help students to problem pose and problem solve for themselves, would encourage the oppressed to name a world that is other than the world of their oppressors, and would develop a means for inquiring into the world as a co-investigation between teachers and students. Delpit (1988) would add that such a classroom must acknowledge, celebrate, and use the culturally inherent expertise of the students in the classroom, while informing those students about the codes of power so they may both utilize and critique those codes. These studies give us three separate, yet similar visions of what those combined theories could look like in practice.

IMPLICATIONS

As Bob has argued elsewhere (Fecho, 2004), making separate recommendations for separate stakeholders is problematic for a number of reasons. To begin, such practice implies that a suggestion for one stakeholder applies only to that stakeholder and no others, thus creating a kind of tunnel vision. Nor does this stance of separate recommendations encourage dialogue across stakeholders; instead, each assumes that if they take care of their concerns, all the pieces will come together. And, too often, in listing separate stakeholders, some key group is left out. All groups need to take responsibility for collaborative solutions. Therefore, in this section, we will argue that the implications of our work have mutual relevance for teachers, researchers, policymakers, and all other groups who hold vital interest in the education of our children.

Recognizing the Political Nature of Language Study

It is our contention that educators shouldn't go on teaching mainstream power codes to students of varied cultures and dialects as if acquisition of that privileged dialect had no impact on student cultural and familial identity; to do so is tantamount to burying our collective heads in the chalk dust. As teachers of children from cultures other than our own, we need to understand the importance of the home language, the language of peers, and any other language codes our students have acquired in their education both in and out of school. We should acknowledge that choices in subject–verb agreement and other seemingly neutral grammar constructions have at least partial connection to personal identity and an eventual impact on the way that students see themselves as members of racial, ethnic, regional, and class-based communities.

Yet, by admitting that we place students in awkward situations when we ask them, even at very young ages, to choose between the language of the home and that of school, we open ourselves to pedagogies of possibility that might enable such choices to be done with more grace and less loss. All stakeholders need to acknowledge the oppressive nature of mainstream power codes while affording students the opportunity to become fluent in those codes. In doing so, we can create pedagogy and educational policy that responds to Delpit's challenges and creates schools that are more inclusive of a wider range of cultures, as well as devising research that will help us to better understand how to do so wisely.

Recognizing the Need for Agency on the Part of All Stakeholders

As we showed through our classrooms, the voices of students, teachers, parents, researchers, and community members generate rich and multiple perspectives when entered into dialogue with each other and the voices of policymakers. This is a very Bakhtinian notion. Although we acknowledge the need for policy on language that helps to stabilize it and the ways it is learned, current policy is, instead, reifying language and language learning, encasing them in cement. Educators need to make room for centrifugal tension provided by local input into how we learn language, what counts as the range of language, and what meaning and import is derived through language. We're not asking for an either/or situation, but instead seek a dialogue around language and language learning that honors the input of more than one stakeholder.

By listening to our students and opening ourselves to the wider educational community, we—Bob, Bette, and Renee—created classrooms where students were engaged in language learning rather than merely complying with the process. They came to see language learning as something for which they had input and options, and we have come to further appreciate the multiple insightful perspectives students bring. If the educational community continues to operate as if no choices about language and language learning exist, we will continue to foster the false belief that some students cannot learn the mainstream power codes, when in reality these students often elect, either consciously or subconsciously, not to use those codes, despite their capacity to learn those codes. When all stakeholders grasp the existential nature of this work and provide students with the opportunities for making sustained, substantive meaning through language, then students will have greater agency in how they shape their identity through language. Furthermore, they will bring a critical eye to the printed and other texts of their lives, reading the language used therein in terms of their own identities and intentions.

Inquiry Is a Vital Pedagogical Tool

We mean this statement in a variety of ways. To begin, all stakeholders can acknowledge that adolescents are capable of conducting substantive inquiry and critique in general and, in particular, of doing so into the nature and impact of language in their lives. This notion flies in the face of stereotypes of adolescents as being disinterested in language and language learning or even capable of conducting systematic and extended exploration. Furthermore, all stakeholders need to acknowledge the power and possibility of teachers inquiring into their own classrooms, of seeing where they teach as transactional spaces where they can create new texts of their teaching practice as well as shape the existing educational canon. In addition, it would help if all concerned widened paradigmatic views on what counts as research and who gets to inquire.

Again, we call for a Bakhtinian dialogue on inquiry, one that acknowledges a need for a range of perspectives and a multiplicity of views, one that is polyphonic, one that understands that no view is privileged. In doing so, we hope to create conditions that would support a range of inquiry projects conducted by a range of stakeholders. So, of course, there is an expectation that students will inquire into a range of texts and raise questions through their inquiry. But the same expectation holds for teachers. The three of us were able to inquire into our classrooms because we were part of vibrant, supportive educational communities—the Bread Loaf Teachers Network in the cases of Bette and Renee and the National Writing Project in the case of Bob. Unfortunately, too few teachers have access to such communities and we need to envision school, district, and state networks that would support inquiries within and across stakeholders in order to begin to see inquiry as the work of all rather than the privilege of a few.

Providing Time and Opportunity for Language Inquiry

A final and crucial implication for practice is that crossing boundaries—whether they be racial, expectational, or personal—takes concerted time and opportunity. Depth of classroom inquiry and discussion evolves over the course of the year. Serious and lengthy discussions around race and language come only as a result of continued forays into and retreats from the topics over time. Students begin to question their own gaps between belief and action only when they have had ample opportunity to examine those beliefs and actions.

In effect, two inquiries take place simultaneously. The first of these is centered about the named subject of investigation; in all our classrooms, these were our inquiries into language. At the same time, a second and more tacit inquiry is being conducted. All members of the class are looking into the seriousness and safety of the class; the students and teachers are taking the measure of each other to see how much they can risk of themselves, what can be put on the table for discussion, and what might be rejected. The movement is in small increments across the whole of a year and needs time and multiple opportunities to prosper. Any classroom that expects students to risk their anonymity and the security it brings needs to understand that such risk is the product of an inquiry into the supportive ethos of the class. This inquiry can be conducted only over time and with much possibility of gathering more supportive evidence.

EXTENDING THE DIALOGUE

Although we three who authored this text all have our beliefs fall within a certain range of mutual acceptance, we recognize that a range does exist. For example, terms such as *mainstream power codes*, *homes codes*, and *street codes* get unpacked in different ways by each of us and have different implications for the user. As Bakhtin (1981) noted, language is half ours and half that of others, and speakers are forever striving to clarify meaning. In this text, we have only scratched the surface of our understandings of these ideas and, although we share some common vision, we also each bring our individual experience to bear.

Because we see that language and language acquisition are complex and nuanced, we realize that a completely unified stance would be foolish and perhaps even hypocritical, given our belief in dialogue. For example, although this chapter does argue that adolescents have many valid reasons for struggling with and resisting mainstream conceptions of language and literacy, the three of us remain in dialogue about those reasons. One line of reasoning offers that because language is first learned in the home and then in the neighborhood, it is very much tied to identity. When associations with mainstream power codes also are linked to a history of oppression, learners from marginalized cultures may show reluctance to acquire language that too closely ties them to visions and conceptions of the oppressor. If Gee (1996) is to be believed, acquisition of a discourse involves mutual acquisition of the mores and values of the progenitors of that discourse. This possibility of having to alter one's core belief in order to speak acceptably in mainstream settings either consciously or subconsciously can act as a deterrent toward literacy and language acquisition by learners whose language markedly differs from the mainstream.

Of the three of us, Bob is more inclined to accept this line of reasoning as being the key factor as to why marginalized students—for example, poor and rural Whites, urban African Americans living in racially isolated neighborhoods, Latino/Latinas trying to negotiate language and cultural differences—might resist code switching into dominant discourse. Bette, although accepting of this argument to a point, feels other mitigating factors such as habit and access need to be factored into the equation. Renee, somewhat less vocal on the issue, seems to fall somewhere between these views. However, no matter what our range of thoughts on these concerns, we do agree that educators should no longer—or should have ever—chalk up these struggles with mainstream power codes as an inability to learn.

Nor, however, can educators ignore the dominance of mainstream power codes in our society. Delpit (1995), although she called on educators to appreciate the language and literacy of the home, implored us to find ways to engage students in these codes of power in order to avoid continued marginalization. Teachers of students whose home languages differ markedly from the standard need to acknowledge those differences and to incorporate discussions about such differences into the fabric of the classroom. If students are aware of these differences that exist between the languages of their lives and the privileged mainstream dialect, they can make appropriate choices about accessing that privileged dialect and controlling the effects of such access on their sense of self and sense of membership in larger identifying cultures of race and class. However, again as Delpit (1995) cautioned, we must be careful that we teach in ways that don't blindly reify these codes, that students and teachers alike understand that no language code is innately superior or inferior, that all are forms of dialect, and all bring richness to our daily language use and learning.

A classroom where inquiry is the primary approach to learning is best suited, in our opinion, for allowing such investigation, discussion, and choice to take place. It allows for a conception of adolescent language learning that is complex, one that acknowledges what Bakhtin (1981) described as being multivoiced. In such a class, teachers and students call the mainstream power codes and their own language use into question in order to develop newer and deeper understandings of the import of language in their lives. In doing so, they gain insight into the complicated ways their personal language is a multivocal mix of a range of codes. Until students are actively engaged in such critique about the language and literacy that is so much a part of their lives, they will be at the mercy of those educational tools rather than masters of their complex, but much rewarding craft. As this chapter represents the second published installment of an ongoing dialogue about these issues, we encourage the larger educational community to join the circle and be heard.

REFERENCES

Angelou, M. (1970). *I know why the caged bird sings*. New York: Random House.

Bakhtin, M. (1981). Discourse in the novel. In M. H. C. Emerson (Ed.), *The dialogic imagination: Four essays by M. M. Bakhtin* (pp. 259–422). Austin, TX: University of Texas Press.

Ball, A. (2000). Empowering pedagogies that enhance the learning of multicultural students. [Electronic version] *Teachers College Record, 102*(6), 1006–1034.

Brown, C. (1989). *My left foot*. United States: Miramax Films.

Cazden, C. (1988). *Classroom discourse: The language of teaching*. Portsmouth, NH: Heinemann.

Clark, R., & Ivanic, R. (1998). *The politics of writing*. London, UK: Routledge.

Delpit, L. (1988). The silenced dialogue: Power and pedagogy in educating other people's children. *Harvard Educational Review, 58*(3), 280–298.

Delpit, L. (1995). *Other people's children: Cultural conflict in the classroom*. New York: The New Press.

Fecho, B. (2004). *"Is this English?" Race, language and culture in the classroom.* New York, NY: Teachers College Press.

Freire, P. (1993). *Pedagogy of the oppressed.* New York: Continuum. (Original work published 1970)

Gee, J. P. (1996). *Social linguistics and literacies: Ideology in discoursesi* (2nd ed.). London, UK: Routledge Falmer.

Gibson, W. (1957). *The miracle worker.* New York: Knopf.

Gilyard, K. (1991). *Voices of the self.* Detroit: Wayne State University Press.

Giovanni, N. (1971). Beautiful Black men. In D. Randall (Ed.), *The Black poets* (pp. 320–321). New York: Bantam.

Gordon, L. (2000). *Existentia Africana: Understanding African existential thought.* London, UK: Routledge.

Kinkaid, J. (1993). Girl. In T. Wolfe (Ed.), *The Vintage book of contemporary American short stories* (pp. 306–307). New York: Vintage.

Ladson-Billings, G. (1992). Liberatory consequences of literacy: A case of culturally relevant instruction for African American students. *Journal of Negro Education, 61*(3), 378–391.

Lindfors, J. W. (1999). *Children's inquiry: Using language to make sense of the world.* New York: Teachers College Press.

Martin, N. (1983). *Mostly about writing.* Upper Montclair, NJ: Boynton / Cook.

Rosenblatt, L. (1995). *Literature as exploration.* New York: The Modern Language Association.

Smitherman, G. (1983). Language and liberation. *Journal of Negro Education, 52*(1), 15–23.

Wilson, A. (1986). *Fences.* New York: New American Library.

Wright, R. (1945). *Black boy: A record of childhood and youth.* New York: Harper Brothers.

11

New Literacies, Enduring Challenges? The Influence of Capital on Adolescent Readers' Internet Practices

Phillip Wilder
Mark Dressman
University of Illinois at Urbana-Champaign

In professional-managerial circles around the world, there is little doubt that digital, computer-based technologies have rapidly transformed the ways in which work gets done. From the capacity of word processing programs to allow for the infinite, almost effortless revision, printing, sorting, and storing of texts, to the use of a vast array of software programs to simulate, model, and predict outcomes, to the use of the Internet and World Wide Web as tools for communication and persuasion, these technologies have had a dramatic effect not only on the productivity of businesses, governmental and other organizations, and academia, but on the social relations that bind these organizations and on the ways in which the individuals who use them imagine their own roles as workers. Indeed, it can be argued that for those persons who have fully embraced the use of computers in their lives and work, their very sense of being in the world, the very ontological platform or condition in which all their activity is embedded, has been radically altered, if not shaken loose, from the conditions that came before (Lyotard, 1984).

This rapid transformation of the world for computer users has been helped along in large part not only by the technologies themselves but by the apparent ease with which they can be acquired and assimilated into the activities of daily life. The invention of user-friendly Apple™ computers in the late 1970s, shortly thereafter of

Windows™ programming software in the 1980s, and most recently of versions of PowerPoint™ and programs for composing Web pages such as Front Page™ mean that the investment of time and expertise necessary for their acquisition has been reduced to a point at which anyone can "pick up" (Dressman, 1997, pp. 89–90) these skills with little or no formal instruction and become, it would seem, a fully capitalized player in the world of cyber technology. Indeed, as Haythornthwaite and Wellman (2002; cited by Leander, 2005) noted, "It is the boringness and routineness that makes the Internet important because this means that it is being pervasively incorporated into people's lives" (p. 7).

In educational circles, the promises of technology have recently been the subject of much theorizing, particularly in the area of secondary literacy. Under the rubric of New Literacies, researchers and theorists of children's and adolescents' literacy have described scenarios in which students who were previously disenfranchised by their school's curriculum might find, in digital, computer-based media such as instant messaging, chat rooms, the World Wide Web, and personal Web pages, the opportunities to use literacy in highly empowering and sophisticated ways (Bean, Bean, & Bean, 1999; Bruce, 2002; Gee, 2000). These scenarios are predicated on the breakdown of traditional distinctions between modes of consumption and production as well as the dissolution of class-, gender-, and race-based modes of differentiation within the "virtual" (in all that term's possible meanings) world of the Internet—a highly democratized world in which one's identity and one's capacity to become whatever one wishes to be are limited only by the conditions of one's access and one's own productive capacity, and not, it seems, by one's social, cultural, economic, political, or educational history (Gee, 2004; Lankshear & Knobel, 2002; Luke, 2000).

A Brave (Completely) New World?

And yet, for all its apparent ubiquity and for all the obvious social benefits and opportunities that digital computer technology offers within educational spheres, we are struck not by the revolutionary impact of technology on the lives of the students with whom we work, but rather by the ways in which educators and many students routinely fail to capitalize on its promises. In a previous study (Dressman & Wilder, in press), for example, we examined the effects that a grant of 30 wireless laptops, a printer, a digital camera, supporting software, and tens of thousands of dollars of funding for educational materials, field trips, and teacher release time and inservice had on the reform of curriculum in an alternative middle school that served approximately 40 to 50 students per year. We found that despite the good will of the district, school director, faculty, and the enthusiastic response of students to the use of wireless laptop technology, little change in most areas of the curriculum occurred, save perhaps for that of the tech-savvy science teacher, and despite intense efforts on the part of Mark and Phil to work with teachers, the director's strong encouragement of cross-disciplinary, project-based learning, and the overwhelming enthusiasm and engagement of the students with the laptops' wireless connectivity to the World Wide Web.

Our observations of how students made use of high-speed wireless connectivity for academic and personal purposes also raised issues for us about the relationship between students' literate proficiencies and use of technology. During science class, for example, we worked with students to identify keywords and then browse among Web sites for information on the geophysical characteristics of a planet or information about the life of a famous scientist. In the few minutes at the end of some classes, students were permitted to use the laptops to browse the Web or to go to popular sites they had already found online. Our observation was that although nearly all the students were proficient in the mechanics of conducting searches or typing in the URLs of Web sites, the general level of (print) literacy demanded by a particular Web site visited or searched for corresponded rather clearly with the general level of literate proficiency of the student who was visiting or searching. Students who read and wrote at or above "grade level," in other words, tended not merely to visit previously cached Web sites, but also seemed to conduct more original searches. Moreover, the sites that these students who were more proficient in print literacy visited during free time tended to have higher demands in terms of their literacy requirements. A favorite site of students who read and wrote well, for example, was the popular (at the time) game show, *Who Wants to Be a Millionaire?*, whereas students whose demonstrated proficiency was weaker tended to go to music Web sites, where they downloaded and listened to music videos, or clipped images to use as customized "wallpaper" for their laptops' screens.

Studies other than our own of technology's impact on the literacy practices of teachers and students in public schools also echo our findings. For example, O'Brien, Springs, and Stith (2001) presented the case of one struggling adolescent male whose lagging interest in literacy-based research was piqued when, as part of his placement in a high school "reading lab," he searched the World Wide Web for material on heavy-metal rock star Ozzy Osbourne and then used the graphics, photos, and information he'd collected to compose a Web page about Osbourne's life and music. O'Brien and his colleagues reported that the student, who had previously shown little interest in academic activity, became highly engaged in the process of researching during the project. But O'Brien et al. were more ambivalent in their appraisal of the overall effects of the project on the student's general interest in academics or of any general increase in his literate capacities.

Finally, more broadly based empirical investigations of computer-based technologies' capacity to transform the work of teachers and students also suggest that the outcomes produced by the introduction of computer-based technologies thus far have been more uneven and less encompassing in educational settings than in other spheres of activity. Cuban (2003), for instance, studied attempts to reform the curriculum of scores of public elementary and secondary schools in districts serving the Bay Area of northern California. Despite the ironic fact that these districts were located in or in close proximity to Silicon Valley, benefited from massive amounts of donated hard- and software from the computer industries located there, and were immersed in a culture of technological innovation, Cuban reported little or no real transformation of the ways in which teachers taught or students learned. In his analysis, he attributed the failure of technology to act as an engine for educational transformation to the fact that the underlying epistemological assumptions of the teachers and students with respect to what the curriculum should be or how it should be taught and learned were never challenged or effectively altered.

The Digitization of Social Reproduction

When we compare the theoretical discourses of New Literacies and their supporting case studies—conducted, it would seem, largely on the teenage children of university professors and other professionals (e.g., Bean, Bean, & Bean, 1999; Bruce, 2002; Leander, 2005)—to studies conducted in the more naturalistic conditions of actual schools or with a less advantaged group of students (Cuban, 2003; Dressman & Tettegah, in press; Dressman & Wilder, in press; O'Brien et al, 2001), then profound differences become apparent between the promises of New Literacies and the actual uses to which published studies show digital technology is typically put by educators and students in secondary schools. What would account for these differences and the disparities? It could be argued, perhaps, that a threshold of access or opportunity had not yet been crossed, so that the condition of pervasiveness on which many of the New Literacies' promises are so contingent was not realized. And yet, one of the most remarked upon aspects of the settings studied by both Cuban (2003) and us (Dressman & Wilder, in press) was the extraordinary wealth of hardware and software resources provided to the schools under study. In our setting, with a ratio of 30 wireless laptops to fewer than 50 students most of the time, high-speed wireless connectivity throughout all content classrooms, and almost limitless amounts of expertise, money, and good will, we frankly could not have imagined a more technology-saturated environment for curricular restructuring or the development of New Literacies.

The differences that we have noted in our review of the literature on digital technology bear notable resemblance to differences described by a large body of research and theory that characterizes schools and schooling processes as educating large numbers of students in ways that routinely sort students by their race, class, and gender into economic and cultural positions that align with those typically held by adults of the same race, class, and gender as theirs. Some of the mechanisms and practices within schools whereby this occurs are fairly obvious, such as through ability grouping and differential pull-out programs in elementary and middle schools and, in high schools, through overt tracking of some students into honors programs, other students into "comprehensive" tracks, and still others into remedial programs (Fine, 1991; Oakes, 1985: Rogers, 2002). Other, less formal mechanisms are more subtle but no less determining, such as teachers' and counselors' expectations for students within particular groups or tracks, differences in the materials and content covered within particular courses, and culturally and economically grounded instructional and curricular practices that differ from the cultural assumptions and practices of students whose cultural or gendered behavior is not considered "normative"—that is, White, middle- to upper-middle-class, heterosexual, and male-dominant (Anyon, 1981; Brantlinger, 2003; Finn, 1999; Lareau, 1989; McDermott, 1987; Rist, 1970).

This body of research and theory also holds that when children and adolescents from different social and cultural backgrounds encounter these mechanisms, they are not only treated differentially but respond in differentiating ways, according to the different practices and cultural logic of their home communities. For example, students whose home literacy practices encourage them to take a utilitarian or a literalist or a highly poetic, performative approach to reading and writing may be characterized by teachers as either backward or intellectually dull or undisciplined, and so in need of remediation or at least not prepared to handle the challenges of more complex literacy tasks (Christian-Smith, 1991; Dressman, 1997; Heath, 1983). By the time they reach high school, differently educated students may have had years of qualitatively very different types of interaction with the school curriculum and with teachers, and so as adolescents they may be thoroughly socialized to relate to the curriculum and to interact with teachers and administrators in qualitatively very different ways—for example, to curriculum as an engaging project, as work to be done, or as labor to be avoided, and to teachers as senior colleagues, as taskmasters to be (joylessly) served, or as easy marks for distraction and manipulation (Everhart, 1983; Finn, 1999; MacLeod, 1987; Weis, 1990; Wexler, 1992; Willis, 1981). Through such interactions, students not only teach their teachers to behave toward them and others like them in particular patterns, they also acquire for themselves a repertoire of practices to use in their future careers as professionals interacting with senior colleagues, as office workers dealing with an overbearing boss, or as manual laborers trying to disrupt or enliven a boring, repetitive task.

In this way, through a transactional process in which students of different genders and from different cultural and socioeconomic backgrounds are routinely sorted and routinely come to sort themselves, researchers and theorists narrate not only the ways in which schools reproduce cultural and social inequality along family lines from one generation to the next, but also the extent to which adolescents' academic and social practices in school result from an accumulation of differentiating processes that began early in their school careers and that, over a period of at least 8 or 9 years, have become not just habit, but, as Bourdieu (1984) would put it, *habitus*, that is, the "structuring structure" (p. 170) of their cognition and identity as social actors. Moreover, the rootedness of the processes described by these researchers and theorists in the history of educational practice, in the family histories of students, in the economics of particular school districts and the communities they serve, and in the very length and complexity of each student's educational career across 12 or more years also helps to account for the robustness—some would say, the ruthlessness—of these processes and their resistance, in the face of countless reform movements, to the interruption or alteration of their course.

We argue that it is social and cultural reproduction theory's historical multi-rootedness that makes it useful in explaining not only differences across case studies of adolescents' use of digital technologies but, more globally, digital technologies' general lack of impact on curriculum and instruction at the secondary level. Such a perspective makes clear why teachers and administrators habituated to thinking of students as falling into distinct tracks would also differentiate their expectations for students' uses of technology along similar lines, seeing "higher level" students as not only more capable of using but more in need of acquiring a relatively sophisticated understanding of how the Internet and search technologies worked, and seeing "lower level" students more as basic users or consumers of information available on the Internet who would need "short cuts" for finding and processing that information. It also explains why teachers who are already preoccupied with demands to "cover material" and pressures to raise achievement test scores might view digital technologies as "one more thing" to cover rather than as the opportunity to rethink their entire curriculum and mode of instruction.

Social and cultural reproduction theory's emphasis on economic and ideological exigencies also makes it clear how the additional expenses associated with digital computer technologies operate to differentiate students' out of school experiences with the Internet. Although theorists of New Literacies may point to falling prices in hardware and the relative cheapness of home access (AOL dial-up currently runs under $25; DSL service, in addition to basic cable service, runs around $40 per month), for working-class families in which one or both parents may work two jobs just to make ends meet, or even for middle-class families with salaried parents but declining benefits packages and high mortgage costs, even a basic level of home internet access may seem extravagant when such services are provided for free at their children's schools, at the public library, or at a relative's home. Moreover, reproduction theory explains how (at least in Champaign, IL), with local news broadcasts almost nightly of children being lured into the clutches of pedophiles on Internet chat rooms, the busting of Internet pornography rings, and the general xenophobia produced by 9/11, parents with very limited experiences with the Internet and computer technologies might understand such technologies as harboring more danger than opportunity for their children.

Stepping back from the futuristic vision of New Literacies to inventory exactly what type and level of literacy skills might be required to realize the educational potential of digital technologies demonstrates additional issues accounted for by reproduction theory but not by New Literacies. Despite the emphasis that New Literacies advocates place on multiple literacies, making use of e-mail, instant messaging, and the Internet still requires a high degree of proficiency in the conventions of print literacy, including the ability to spell and type with accuracy, the ability to identify keywords, the ability to make sense of and distinguish between abbreviated descriptions of sites, and the ability to skim, recognize, and extract information from extended passages of text. Moreover, as systems, computer technologies are highly literate in their organization. Their "user friendliness" is contingent on a user for whom basic literacy skills are automatic and transparent, and who already possesses a literate knowledge of the world—for example, who knows where countries are located relative to each other, who understands basic scientific concepts and terminology, who has a grasp of how different governments are organized, and who has a sense of when to be suspicious or when to trust information provided by a source. Students whose cultural logic and literate proficiencies are mirrored in the design and systematicity of computer technologies are more prepared to perceive computer technologies as transparent systems and are more likely to seize multiliterate opportunities than are students who struggle to spell correctly, whose reading of extended print texts is labored, and whose grasp of how the world outside their own communities works is relatively undeveloped.

In summary, social and cultural reproduction theory provides a compelling explanation of why, rather than revolutionize or at least interrupt educational practice, digital computer technologies instead seem to have been incorporated into the existing logic and design of educational programs. Yet that theory's greatest usefulness, we argue, is in explaining how, over time, the logic and practices of administrators, teachers, students, and their families combine in patterns of mutual reinforcement to produce outcomes in which some students graduate from high school as multiliterate, culturally capitalized, academically successful, and very confident citizens whereas others exit school with basic levels of literacy, knowing how to operate a computer but never fully mastering software applications or Internet search processes, and without a great deal of confidence or sense of empowerment as future learners or job seekers.

Six Students and the Internet

As a way of both illustrating and exploring the dynamics of social and cultural reproduction in the age of digitization, we present the cases of six ninth-grade students as they made use of computer technology during a cultural geography class to search the Internet for information about Caribbean islands and nations. Three of these students were members of a course section organized and taught for struggling adolescent readers, while the other three students were members of a section organized and taught as part of their high school's college preparatory program. One purpose in choosing to study and report on students who were grouped so differently was to dramatize the ways that both literacy and life experiences structure students' approaches to and success with digital computer technology.

An equally important purpose, however, was to develop a very thick and detailed understanding for ourselves and for readers of this chapter of the challenges that struggling readers face when they make use of at least one aspect of digital computer technology, with the ultimate goal of enhancing struggling readers' ability to use the Internet as an academic and personal source of information. For although we admit to the power of theories of social and cultural reproduction to explain past or present educational outcomes in general, we by no means subscribe to the inevitability of such patterns. Indeed, after the introduction of social and cultural reproduction theory in the 1970s and its development through much of the 1980s, a second generation of researchers and theorists in the 1990s, concerned by the totalizing implications of the theory, began to look for ways to retheorize educational practices as processes of social and cultural *production* rather than reproduction, in order to allow for possibilities of social change and to account for the many "exceptions" to patterns that had earlier been described with the force of law (e.g., Anyon, 1997; Bourdieu, 1989; Dressman, 1999; Dressman, Wilder, & Conner, in press; Fiske, 1989; Foley, 1990, 1991; Langer, 2001; Levinson, Foley, & Holland, 1996). We return to this later group of researchers and theorists and what their work may imply for the realization of the promises of New Literacies in our discussion at the end of the chapter.

ONE CURRICULUM, TWO CLASSROOM WORLDS

Introducing the Students

The six students whose cases we present were chosen from two classes of ninth graders studying the cultural geography of the Western hemisphere at Midland High, a comprehensive high school located in a midsized midwestern city. One class was taught by Helen Turner, a veteran teacher of social studies at Midland. The students in this class were considered "accelerated," and read above grade level. The second class was taught by co-author Phil Wilder, who was also Midland's reading coordinator. The students in his class were considered by school counselors and administrators to be "struggling;" all were at least one grade and most were several grades "below level" in reading. The curriculum content for both courses was ostensibly the same. Phil followed the same course outline as the other teachers of the course and routinely consulted with Helen during the semester about the content and sequence of course objectives. The two classes remained largely parallel throughout the semester and thus provided a reasonable context for making comparisons between the performance of students in both classes across the same course content, and, in one case, an identical research assignment.

All students in both classes who reported and could demonstrate basic proficiency with computers and the Internet were initially invited to volunteer to participate in the study. From those students who volunteered, we purposefully selected three students from Helen's class whose achievement tests indicated a reading level of 2 years or more above ninth grade and three students from Phil's class whose achievement tests placed them 2 or more years below ninth grade.

A brief summary of each student's background, academic history, and reported proficiency with computer-based technology is reported in Table 11.1. Placed into Helen's higher tracked geography class based on their academic history, Mary, Chris, and Hussein read at least two levels above grade level according to their performance on an eighth-grade national reading assessment. Mary was a biracial Asian American student who described herself in interviews as a "pretty good" student based on her academic success. Mary had her own personal computer, DSL Internet connection in her bedroom, and the opportunity to IM (Instant Message) with her friends for several hours every night. Kevin was a middle-class White male who also saw himself as a high-achieving student due to his ability to meet teachers' expectations. Although he preferred to learn from traditional texts, his mother's job as an elementary teacher had exposed him to the Internet at a very early age, and he reported being very comfortable using online applications of computers. Two years after immigrating to the United States from Lebanon, Hussein was a Palestinian enrolled in Midland's English as a Second Language program. Hussein characterized himself as a diligent, high-achieving student who had been academically successful in Lebanon and in the United States. Without a computer at home and with no experience with the Internet prior to his arrival in the United States, Hussein rarely used the Internet except as a resource for researching upcoming novels in his English class, or sometimes to e-mail family and friends in Lebanon.

Dan, Steve, and Keisha were placed in Phil's geography class on the basis of their achievement test scores. All three students read at least two levels below grade level according to their performance on the Stanford Achievement test. Dan was a male African American student who used an unreliable family computer at home for word processing and occasionally to post messages on a high school basketball Internet fan forum. His first memory of the Internet was in third grade when he used the Internet at the beginning of the school year to take a reading placement test. Steve was a European American male student who shared a home computer with his brother and used it primarily to play video games or to customize cars on automotive Web sites. Steve described himself as an "average student because I get Cs" and rarely used his home computer for homework because he preferred to read traditional (book) texts. Keisha was an African American student who described herself as an "okay" student and whose only access to computers or the Internet outside of school was at her aunt's house across town. Keisha's first use of the Internet occurred during seventh grade in Texas. When she did use the Internet in the school library during lunch or after school, it was primarily to look up music lyrics or to play on-line games.

As we learned from another study conducted at an alternative middle school in the same district (Dressman, Wilder, & Connor, 2005), the distribution of students with a history of struggle or success in school, particularly with regard to literacy, is far from even demographically. Although students in Helen's class were overwhelmingly of European descent, in Phil's class they were predominantly from African American or Mexican American backgrounds. Moreover, to judge from their dress and what they told us in interviews, the students in Helen's class were largely

TABLE 11.1

Students' Backgrounds, Reading Ability, and Self-Reported Computer-Based Practices

Student	Demographic background	Reading level[a]	Self-reported frequently visited web sites	Computer/Internet access	Self-reported computer-based activity	Self-described search practices
Helen Turner's Class						
Mary	Upper middle class Asian-American	Post-high school	www.goodquotes.com www.seventeen.com www.gap.com www.amazon.com www.pagesforallages.com	Has own PC with separate phone line in her bedroom. Three computers in home. Introduced to Internet in early childhood. Researched search engines in eighth-grade math class.	Uses Microsoft Word, Power Point, and AOL IM. Spends 6-8 hours IM chatting daily with friends. Uses Internet primarily for communication with friends and for homework. Seldom shops or purchases online.	Uses multiple search engines. Evaluates title, description, and address of Web sites in search results. Uses varied search terms and symbols to refine search. Cannot explain how Internet/search engines work.
Kevin	Middle-class White	Post-high school	www.nfl.com www.sportsillustrated.com www.google.com	Shares a home PC with brother. First used Internet in first grade. Taught how to search in second grade. Unlimited Internet access at mother's school as a child. Researched search engines in eighth grade math class.	Uses Microsoft Word Can use Power Point but doesn't like it Prefers learning from traditional texts. Infrequently uses the Internet for entertainment but sometimes follows his favorite NFL team and plays games with his younger brother online.	Uses multiple search engines. Evaluates title, description of Web sites in search results. Uses varied search terms. Cannot explain how Internet/search engines work.
Hussein	Palestinian immigrant; second year ESL student	Post-high school	www.sparknotes.com www.hotmail.com www.salmiya.net www.e-Bay.com	No computer at home. Used Internet for the first time after arriving in the U.S. in eighth grade. Uses computers in libraries for Internet access.	Uses Microsoft Word. Prefers learning from traditional texts. Rarely uses the Internet but does research upcoming novels for English class online, to email friends abroad or to research electronic gadgets. Says he has "no use for" Internet as entertainment.	Uses only Google. Reads description and sometimes the title of web sites in search results. Struggles to find effective search terms and unsure of how to refine search. Cannot explain how Internet/search engines work.

TABLE 11.1 (continued)

Student	Demographic background	Reading level[a]	Self-reported frequently visited web sites	Computer/Internet access	Self-reported computer-based activity	Self-described search practices
Phil Wilder's Class						
Dan	Middle-class African American	6.5	www.highschoolelite.com www.niketown.com www.nba.com	Describes home access to Internet and family computer as unreliable. First memory of the Internet was from third grade when he used the Internet to take a reading test.	Uses Microsoft Word. Uses the Internet to keep track of his favorite sports teams and to go to "biology" Web sites. Posts on a high school basketball message board "once a month." Has never used any IM technology and has never had an email account. Buys basketball shoes on the Internet.	Uses Google and Yahoo. Sometimes reads the description first few search results and usually visits the first "ones that show up" because they are "basically all the same thing." Cannot explain how to use varied search terms to refine a search. Cannot explain how Internet/search engines work.
Steve	Middle-class White	7.0	www.gamewinners.com www.gamecube.com www.ebay.com www.ebaymotors.com www.cartoonnetwork.com www.walmart.com www.bestbuy.com	Two computers in home. Shares a home PC with brother. May only use the Internet with parental permission. "I don't really get on the Internet unless I have a purpose … I don't use it much."	Uses Microsoft Word, Microsoft FrontPage and Adobe PhotoShop. Uses Internet to look up game codes, video games, cars and pictures of motorcycles. "Hardly ever" uses the computer for homework. Plays video games/computer games 2 hours per day. Has never used IM. Uses Internet to compare prices before buying item at store.	Uses multiple search engines. Skims description of web sites in search results. Does not refine searches. Can explain that servers store Web pages. Uses alternative web search features on Google. Can explain how to avoid school Internet filters. Can explain how to create a Web page and post it.
Keisha	Working class African American	5.5	www.bet.com www.azlyrics.com www.littlebowwow.com	Uses a computer once a month at her aunt's house. First Internet use at school. Never used a computer at public library. Never owned a computer. Seldom uses the internet at school.	Limited use of Microsoft Word. Uses Internet to look up rap lyrics, play games online. Has never used IM nor shopped or purchased items online.	Uses Google, Yahoo and AOL search engines. Usually skims title of Web sites in search results, sometimes skims the description of Web sites, and never looks at address. Uses a single search term and can not explain how to refine a search. Cannot explain how Internet/search engines work.

[a]Comprehensive score from Stanford Achievement Test administered in Grade 8.

from middle- to upper-middle class backgrounds, whereas the students in Phil's class were from working-class and working-poor homes. In the end, we would characterize our difficulties in balancing our participants along the lines of gender, social class, and race/ethnicity not as "design flaws," but rather as powerful indicators of the enduring societal and cultural divisions that separate students who succeed academically in U.S. high schools from those who struggle.

To gather information about the students' prior history of their use of computers and the Internet and to obtain baseline information about each class and the students' qualities as students, Phil conducted a series of interviews with each student and Mark interviewed both Phil and Helen about their backgrounds as teachers and their perceptions of their students and the course they were teaching. Mark, Phil, and Helen collaborated on the design of an assignment in which students were required to conduct multiple searches of the Internet to collect basic facts about the cultural geography of three Caribbean islands or nations. In addition, in the weeks preceding the assignment, Mark observed in Helen's and Phil's classrooms five times each.

Class Differences

From the outset of our investigations, distinctions between the proficiency and performance of the participating students in Helen's class and Phil's class were dramatically apparent. Our analytical task shifted from considering whether there would be a difference in the practices of students in the two classes to exploring how limitations or the lack of limitations in the students' preexisting literate practices affected their searches for information on the World Wide Web, and then connecting this analysis to information from the students' interviews about their prior experiences with computer-based technology and observations of the classroom curriculum.

Based on Mark's weekly observations of both classrooms and his conversations with both Phil and Helen, it seemed that with relatively slight variations, the curriculum of both classrooms and instructional approaches taken by both teachers were roughly equivalent, if not in many cases nearly identical. Both teachers were very adept classroom managers and had excellent rapport with their students, who in turn were typically very cooperative and engaged in the lesson throughout the 50-minute periods of instruction. One of the most striking similarities between the two classrooms was the engagement of both groups of students in the work of the class, particularly during issues-oriented classes. More than half the students in both classes enthusiastically offered responses to open-ended questions and at times offered information or details from their own knowledge bases, while the remaining students who did not directly contribute paid close attention to speakers and participated in other ways during the discussions, such as in note-taking exercises. In short, both demonstrated equivalent levels of active interest in course content and instruction.

Beyond these generalities, however, significant differences were observed in the ways that Helen and Phil organized and related information to the students and related to them personally, as well as in the ways that the students reciprocally related to and made sense of course content. For example, although both Helen and Phil made routine use of graphic organizers such as semantic webs and matrices to encourage note taking, the filling out and completion of these organizers was more individually and independently oriented in Helen's classroom than in Phil's, where such activities were more closely scaffolded via small group exercises or the use of more directive, step-by-step instruction—practices that took more time. One inadvertent result of this difference was that over the course of the semester, Helen's class moved farther and farther ahead of Phil's in its coverage of the course outline.

Even more significant differences were observed in the ways that students made connections to issues and information that were presented in class and in the ways that they seemed to go about "doing school" (Pope, 2001). For example, during a PowerPoint presentation about the Caribbean that Phil gave to his class, students' associations tended to be very personal and to drift away from the central topic. One student spoke about her "auntie" who had been to the Bahamas and had brought back a doll. As Phil showed photographs of the Florida Keys and Highway 1, a student remarked, "I couldn't drive on that road;" another remembered a segment of the TV show "Fear Factor" set in the Keys, in which there was a bungee jumping challenge, and described what it was like. For Cuba, students offered in free association "hand-rolled cigars," the movie *Blow*, the Cuban Missile Crisis, Fidel Castro, orphans, and Elian Gonzales, and concluded their discussion by asking Phil if he'd go to Cuba if he could. In contrast, when Phil presented the same slide show to the students in Helen's class using very similar language, students' free associations were more succinct and abstract. They used the term "poverty" in association with Cuba, for example, and asked more questions—and offered more answers—related to the categories of the semantic web they were filling out as they watched the slide show and listened to Phil. In part, this may have been due to Phil's status as a relative stranger and visitor in Helen's class; however, on other occasions when Helen was the instructor, most of the students' remarks were similarly detached, even when they discussed a topic as politically volatile as the issue of whether life in the United States or Canada was "better."

Overall, the differences observed in what counted as knowledge for students in the two classrooms were comparable to differences that Anyon (1981) and Keddie (1971) observed in the ways that knowledge was constituted in the middle-class and working-class classrooms that they studied, in which working-class students related to information provided by teachers by making personal connections with their own experience, whereas the impulse of students from professional managerial backgrounds was to look for how information might be placed within a preexisting scheme of other information—in other words, to look for ways to *manage* knowledge rather than engage it substantively.

Finally, in his observations Mark noted a significant, and ironic, difference in the ways that Helen and Phil related to the students. Because of Helen's sponsorship of the Key Club and involvement in other extracurricular organizations in which her students were also participants, she clearly knew more about her students' lives and used this information to personally connect with the students in the class, not only at the beginning or end but also at odd moments during each class. Thus, in her class, although course content was presented often in very abstract and detached ways, students ironically were never alienated by it, or at least not by the discourse of the classroom itself. In contrast, the students in Phil's class were largely not "joiners" of such extracurricular clubs, nor was Phil—the school's reading coordinator with multiple after-school inservice commitments, and a sponsor of many after-school activities—and so he could not and did not seem to relate to his students on the same personal level. Thus, in Phil's class, it was through Phil's allowance—indeed, encouragement—of students to relate personally to course content that they were able to avoid being alienated by the conventions and strictures of academic discourse (and to a lesser extent, to alleviate their marginalization within the high school as a whole).

One Assignment, Two Classroom Experiences

To compare differences between students in how they used the Internet for academic purposes, Phil, Helen, and Mark collaborated on the design of an assignment for both classes. This assignment was given in conjunction with a brief unit on the cultural geography of the Caribbean islands at the end of the Fall 2004 semester. It began with a PowerPoint™ presentation by Phil in both classes that provided an overview of four major regions of the Caribbean and the major islands within each, lasting approximately one class period. The day following the PowerPoint™, each student blindly selected three Caribbean islands and was provided a worksheet in matrix format for she or he was to find information on the World Wide Web about the three islands' populations, cultural/linguistic backgrounds, political histories, physical geographies, and locations. The students worked on this assignment individually in the computer center of Midland's library. The majority of students in Helen's class completed the matrix over a 2-day period, whereas for Phil's class, completing the assignment took 3 days. During their search process, the participating students in each class sat at adjacent computers and worked individually, while Mark and Phil took field notes, asked occasional questions, and, in the case of the students in Phil's class, offered enough help to keep the students productively engaged in the assignment. Following these sessions, the participating students' Internet caches were downloaded and recorded as part of the data base and photocopies were made of their written work for the assignment.

Despite wide variation in their quality of access, history of computer use, purposes, and quantity of experience, all six students could be characterized as "users of the internet"—that is, as individuals who could operate a computer and software systems with sufficient proficiency to locate specific Web sites or conduct a search for topics of interest and select at least one result from that search. For example, it became clear from the interviews that all six students had visited and memorized specific URLs, and that these sites were very closely related to their gender and cultural identities. Keisha, an African American female, reported that she had visited and knew the Web sites for Black Entertainment Television, as well as sites devoted to hip-hop and the artist Little Bow-wow; Kevin, a White male who played on Midland's high school football team, reported that he sometimes visited the National Football League's site, whereas Dan, an African American male whose sport was basketball, had visited the National Basketball Association site. A summary of each student's background, reading achievement as measured by standardized testing, and Internet activities and search practices as reported by the students during formal interviews, can be found in Table 11.1.

All six students also reported that they had used computers and the Internet for multiple purposes, even if the frequency of their use and the range of purposes varied. Except for Keisha, whose access to the Internet was the most limited of the six, all students reported having used the Internet not only to find information, but also more interactively, either through e-mail, instant messaging (IM), or online participation in games. Moreover, although the level of sophistication varied somewhat, all six students could describe and demonstrate the basic steps to conducting an Internet search. Only Hussein could not name multiple search engines, and all six understood the basic principles of keyword searches and could use keywords to search and retrieve Web sites (even though none could explain how the Internet or search engines worked, even in the most basic terms). If we discounted students' history of experience with the Internet and academic histories, focused exclusively on the students' own reports of their Internet activities, and allowed for some range in sophistication, speed, and accuracy, then it might also be expected that all six students would also be able to initiate and complete an Internet search of an academic topic relatively independently and at a basic level of competence.

But, as our findings from the assignment to search for information on Caribbean islands indicate, this was not the case. Instead, the data demonstrate a distinct division between the performance of the three focus students in Helen Turner's class and the performance of the three focus students in Phil's class, in terms of both the technical and academic aspects of the search process.

For the three focus students from Helen Turner's class, Hussein, Kevin, and Mary, the assignment to find specific information on three Caribbean islands was not easy or simple, but it was largely within their competence. Mary, whose typing was unorthodox ("I don't use—what do you call them, the regular [home] keys?" she told Mark) but as fast and accurate as any touch typist, went directly to the Encyclopedia.com site to look up Trinidad and Tobago, and within half an hour had completed the information for that island group. She then turned to a search engine to search for Curaçao, noting that "It's giving me sites in Spanish." The following morning, Mary resumed her search by going directly to the site Curaçao.com, and quickly skimmed through the text, extracting information from the text of the site to fill in each cell of the matrix for the island, and then quickly moving to another site for Aruba, noting as she did so that she would have to come back to "find (more) stuff about the government of Trinidad and Tobago." At the end of 2 days, Mary had easily completed her search for all requested information for the three islands.

Mary's classmate Kevin began his search by going to Google and saying, half to himself and half to Mark, "I'm not sure where to start this." Kevin chose to search for information on St. Vincent first, and after quickly locating from the menu of results a promising site, he skimmed the text to find information on the island's location and other categories of requested information. A half-hour later, Kevin had located a site that gave him information on the history of Bermuda. When he was unable to find the requested information on one site, Kevin moved to the slide-down menu on the search bar and retrieved the results page from Google to find another site. When he became frustrated with his search for information on Bermuda, Kevin again retrieved Google from the slide-down menu to conduct another search, this time for the island of Bonaire. During the second day of searching, however, Kevin was quickly confused during his search of Google for information on Saint-Martin/Sint Maarten, a single island whose northern half is part of the Netherlands Antilles and whose southern half is controlled by France. He tried several different searches using Google of multiple spellings and arrangements of Saint-Martin/Sint Maarten until Mark explained to him that the island was controlled by two European governments. In frustration, Kevin abandoned the topic and began to research Bonaire, using Google. Within a few minutes he had completed his data collection for Bonaire, and returned to another site, LonelyPlanet.com, which he had found during his browsing, that promised an "interactive map." Through LonelyPlanet.com,

Kevin eventually found information about French St. Martins and fully completed the assignment within the 2-day period.

Although Hussein told us in interviews that he seldom used Internet search engines, during the Caribbean assignment he was able to use multiple search terms in order to find relevant information about the geography, economy, and government of Aruba by paying attention to the titles of Web sites, the Web site address itself and the short description of the Web site in order to avoid tourist-centered Web sites. Unlike any of the other students we observed, rather than copy down facts from the outline format of the CIA Factbook's main page, Hussein found and used its internal links to read about the "Culture," "Geography," and "Economy" of Aruba. He meticulously jotted down a wealth of information about Aruba, and it became clear that he could extract main ideas from the text even though he often struggled to understand the details of what he was writing as notes. Most likely because he speaks English as a second language, he asked several times for an explanation of a term or idea (e.g., "offshore banking"). Hussein's ability to use numerous search terms, to skim and evaluate search results and Web pages, and his ability to recognize the main ideas of a text outweighed his occasional frustration with being an English-language learner.

In comparison, the search processes of the students in Phil's classroom were much more labored and unproductive. For example, Steve's search for information on Aruba began well from a technical perspective, but was stalled by the demands placed by the first site he visited on his ability to skim text efficiently and to understand common geographic concepts and vocabulary. Steve used the search engine, Ask Jeeves, to type in the key phrase "history on Aruba," which returned multiple promising Web sites. His first choice produced a significant amount of information on the history and culture of the island, in prose format. Steve began to read from the top of the page but soon stopped and began to scroll through the text very quickly. As Mark read along, he was able to locate all the information on the history and culture of Aruba that was requested on the worksheet. However, Steve did not record any of this information, and after scrolling back and forth several times, expressed frustration with the text format. He returned to Ask Jeeves and typed in the search window, "The geography of aruba" [sic], which provided the Web site for the CIA World Factbook—a site listing brief geographic facts for countries in an outline format—and began to scan the list of countries for Aruba, explaining that he'd found this site once before in a search. Steve was able to quickly scan the outline, and copied some facts down about Aruba on the worksheet. When Steve was unable to locate Aruba in one of the four regions that Phil had outlined in his presentation, he decided to search for information on Curaçao. But he had misspelled Curaçao on his worksheet and continued to misspell it when he searched. To offer some help, Mark wrote the correct spelling on a piece of paper for Steve, but when Steve mistook the "ç" in Mark's handwriting for a "g," that search also failed to produce results. Using the sliding search history menu, Steve relocated the CIA World Factbook; however, he was unable to find Curaçao listed there, either, because Curaçao, unlike Aruba, is not an autonomous state. He then returned to the search engine, and 10 minutes later, after trying multiple combinations of key words, he was able to locate a site with a significant amount of information about Curaçao—written in a lengthy prose format whose use of the terms *Dutch*, *The Netherlands*, and *Holland* led him to believe that the island had been the possession of three different nations in its history.

Dan's search process was equally frustrating, for both technical and literacy-related reasons. Using Google to search for information on Trinidad and Tobago, for example, Dan's strategy was to go to the first site on the list of results, quickly scan it for information, and then to use the back arrow on the browser tool bar to return to the list of results and choose the next site, scan it, then use the back arrow to return to the results for the first site. At promising sites, he frequently clicked on several menu items and then, within these linked pages, several other items, so that at times he was not one click but several clicks of the back arrow from the search engine list. Instead of using the slide-down menu to return directly to Google, at one point Dan clicked the back arrow on his browser so many times and so quickly that the screen locked, requiring him to restart the computer and begin his search all over again. In addition to these technical difficulties, literacy was also a problem for Dan. In his search for information on Curaçao, Mark observed Dan using the cursor much like some struggling readers use their fingers when they read, running the cursor over each word as he scanned a line of print in a Web site. When the information requested on the worksheet was in the text of a prose-rich Web site, like Steve, Dan often did not recognize it as information he could use. In the end, like Steve also (and in part, like Kevin and several other students in Helen's class, as well), Dan turned to the CIA World Factbook and its easily scanned outline for much of the information he needed.

Keisha's use of Google to search for information on Aruba was labored and produced limited new information on the geography, economy, or government. After typing in "arruba" and clicking on the Google-provided correct spelling, she struggled to distinguish among sites on the first page of more than twelve million results. She selected Web pages to visit based on the attractiveness of the title of a Web site, which repeatedly brought her to tourist sites with little information about the island's history, politics, or culture. In one instance, Keisha successfully selected a Web site with the desired information, but exited the site without clicking on an internal link titled, "Political System of Aruba." After 20 minutes of searching through multiple pages of results, Keisha returned to the first page and the CIA Factbook Web site on Aruba. Although the site was organized with clear topical headings that mirrored the requested information on the assignment sheet (e.g., "Culture;" "Geography;" "Economy"), she did not read through the extended text of the site for information. Terms used in the text, such as "parliamentary democracy," "dependency status," and "suffrage" seemed to restrict her comprehension. Despite a prolonged search process with many dead ends, Keisha persisted cheerfully and was able eventually to find and extract information from sites about Aruba's development based on the life expectancy, per capita GNP, and other development-indicating statistics found during the search.

Comparing Search Strategies Across Students

Table 11.2 provides a more systematic analysis of the strategies that each of the six students did or did not make use of in their search practices. The categories in this table were developed from an analysis of "moves" made by the students during one think-aloud protocol each, in which each student was asked to search for information on a Caribbean island they hadn't researched during the whole-class assignment. These findings also indicate a sharp division in the level of search skill between the students in Helen's and Phil's classes. For example, all three of the students in Helen's class routinely used varied search terms, and both Mary and Kevin

TABLE 11.2

Observed Internet Search Practices of Students

	Using search terms			Previewing Search Results			Finding relevant information		
	Used varied search terms	Used symbols to redefine search	Knew how to limit results	Skimmed Web site titles	Read Web site descriptions	Analyzed Web site addresses	Recognized organization of website	Skimmed text for relevant information	Related information to assigned task
Mary	Yes	Yes	Yes	Yes	Yes	Occ	Yes	Yes	Yes
Kevin	Yes	Occ	Occ	Occ	Yes	Occ	Yes	Yes	Yes
Hussein	Yes	No	No	Occ	Yes	No	Occ	Occ	Occ
Dan	Occ	No	No	Yes	No	No	No	Occ	Occ
Steve	Occ	No	No	No	Yes	No	Occ	Occ	No
Keisha	No	No	No	Yes	Occ	No	No	Occ	No

Note. Yes = Student was observed to use this strategy routinely. No = Student did not or very rarely was observed to use this strategy. Occ = Student was observed to occasion-ally use this strategy and demonstrated awareness of it as an option.

221

knew how to use symbols to redefine a search and to limit (narrow down) the number of resulting sites found, whereas only two of Phil's students, Dan and Steve, occasionally used varied terms in their searches, and were never observed to use symbols or to take steps to limit the number of results. Although students in both classes, with the exception of Steve, were observed skimming Web site titles for search results, students in Helen's class nearly always read the description of the site in each listing, whereas only Steve did so routinely in Phil's class; and none of the students in Phil's class were observed analyzing Web site addresses, while in Helen's class, Mary and Kevin did so occasionally.

The most significant differences between the practices of the students in the two classes, however, were not in the technical aspects of searching, but in those aspects requiring the highest degree of literate activity, that is, those aspects related to the finding of relevant information once a promising Web site had been located and opened. The analysis reported in Table 11.2 indicates that whereas Mary and Kevin were observed to recognize the organization of a Web site, to skim the text of the site for relevant information (that is, facts requested on the worksheet), and to recognize information as relevant within a text and/or be able inferentially to "translate" information found on a Web site *into* information relevant to the worksheet routinely (and Hussein was observed to do so occasionally), none of the students in Phil's class were observed to find relevant information routinely. Of the three students in Phil's class, Steve occasionally recognized the organization of a Web site, and Dan occasionally related information found on the Web site to the worksheet assignment, although all three students did occasionally skim the text of Web sites for relevant information.

New Literacies, Old Contingencies

When we return to the data from the students' online searches, from initial interviews about their histories as users of computer-based technology, and from their academic histories and achievement test scores, it seems apparent that the differences that we noted in the search processes of the two groups of students are attributable to two related but distinct factors: the quality more than the sheer quantity of the students' prior experiences with the World Wide Web in academic contexts, and their overall literate ability with respect to the reading and writing of print text. Differences in the literate behaviors of the two groups of students were very clear, and their effects on their search processes were quite direct. Although the processes of the three students in Phil's class were frequently stalled by typing errors or misspelled words, the three students we observed in Helen's class seldom misspelled words, and when a word or address was misspelled, it was quickly spotted and corrected. The students from Helen's class were also far more likely to play with key words and phrases or come up with alternatives than were the students from Phil's class. But the most significant difference in the two groups' literacies, we argue, was in the willingness and ability of students in Helen's class to read through paragraphs of print text online, to recognize relevant information that was embedded within these texts, and to then translate, or convert, information found into notes within the cells of the worksheet they had been given, with independence and speed. Largely as a result of differences in this last set of literate skills, nearly all the students in Helen's class were able to complete the assignment in two visits to the computer center, whereas students in Phil's class required at least 3 days, and many did not finish at all.

The two groups of students also demonstrated clear differences in their level of technical proficiency in using search engines to find information on academic topics, as indicated by the analysis reported in Table 11.2. Given the familiarity of all six students with specific sites on the World Wide Web and the wide range of personal uses of the Internet reported by students in both groups, we were initially surprised by the relative lack of sophistication that students in Phil's class demonstrated in their search practices. After all, one might reason, as in the theoretical literature on New Literacies it is access to technology that produces engaged learning, that whether students visited www.nfl.com or www.walmart.com or www.salmiya.net, or whether they used Instant Messaging or got their e-mail through hotmail.com, or used the Internet to post on message boards or comparison shop or download the latest raps and hip-hop lyrics, they were all participating in the new economic and political sphere of cyberspace and should all be developing, through one activity or another, equivalent cyber skills. Thus, assuming relatively equal access in their school careers to computer-based technologies at school, we would also expect that the students' technical abilities with the search process would show equivalent levels of sophistication.

How then can the dramatic differences in technical ability that we found be accounted for? Although we would not discount clear differences in the age at which students in the two groups began to use the Internet or other differences in the quality of students' home access, such as DSL in Mary's case or Kevin's early experiences with the Internet at the school where his mother taught versus the reported unreliability of the connection in Dan's home or parental restrictions on Steve's access, we would argue that the sort of personal uses of the internet described by the students in our study would not have significantly developed or inhibited the search skills that we observed and analyzed. Instead, we suspect the differences may in part be attributable to qualitative differences in the ways that search activities had been structured for students in their school careers. During their initial interviews, for example, all students described instances in which their elementary and middle school teachers had taken their class to the school's computer center to use the World Wide Web as a source of information about a particular topic. The three students in Phil's class described events in which they were either given a list of addresses for presearched sites or clicked links on their classroom's or library's Web page, went directly to specific sites, and copied information from them onto worksheets whose outline corresponded closely to the sites' organization. In contrast, two students from Helen's class, Mary and Kevin, described a research project in their advanced eighth grade math class in which they studied the characteristics of multiple search engines such as Google and Yahoo and then conducted a comparative analysis of them, as well as other instances in which they were required not just to "go to" a Web site, but to conduct actual searches and sift through text to find information. In short, although students from both groups described equivalent quantities of access to computer-based technology in their prior school experiences, the qualitative differences in their experiences—and the differential learning resulting from them—seemed vast.

CONCLUDING DISCUSSION

Although the findings and analysis that we have reported in this chapter are limited to a study of six students in two classrooms in a single U.S. school, we believe they also represent something of a challenge to any suggestion that the coming of computer-based technology may produce New Times for schooling in which previously undercapitalized students might evade the overdetermining forces of Old Practices. Instead, this study suggests that one's capacity to use New Literacies in academic contexts remains contingent on one's level of proficiency in Old (print text-based) Literacy, while the development of technical practices sophisticated enough to take full advantage of Web-based sources' academic knowledge depends on more than the assumed provision of access and opportunity at home.

We attribute the differences in search skill that we observed primarily to differences in the symbolic (and, correlatively, socioeconomic) capital in the two groups of students—capital that, in the form of higher (reading) test scores, in year after year of their school careers helped to place the students in Helen Turner's classroom in more advanced academic programs, such as those for the "gifted and talented." In such programs, the demands on students for "higher order" literacy activities are greater and students have more educational opportunities to develop sophisticated academic practices of all kinds, including learning how to conduct sophisticated searches of the World Wide Web for relatively sophisticated academic purposes, whereas next door or down the hall, students in "comprehensive" or even "remedial" classrooms might also be going to the computer center to use World Wide Web, but more likely to "take a reading test," as Dan recalled, or to copy information from presearched Web sites onto simple worksheets.

And so it also seems very arguable to us, based on our observations of six students whose ability to use print literacy, facility with computer technology, and ways of relating to school knowledge were clearly tied to their prior academic experiences and families' economic realities, that the same exigencies described in previous research and theories of social and cultural reproduction were also in operation at Midland High School, in the classrooms of Helen and Phil, and in the lives of Steve, Dan, Keisha, Mary, Kevin, and Hussein. The data of our investigations also suggest that rather than interrupt these reproductive processes, as an instructional and communicative tool, digital computer technology seems to have been assimilated into them.

Yet we do not accept the inevitability of these processes or of computer technology as the servant of them. The benefits of computer technology as a tool for learning and the need for every individual to become as proficient in the literate use of these technologies as previous generations were with using pencils, typewriters, and newspapers, are obvious. In our view, there is no question that computer technologies will become an increasingly central part of everyone's daily life, and that for economically and socially privileged individuals, the promises of the New Literacies are likely to be kept; but it is just as clear to us that these technologies in and of themselves provide no quick fix or easy way to interrupt historically and economically grounded inequalities, and that to pretend otherwise is to contribute to the maintenance and continuation of educational practices that reproduce those inequalities. How then might we theorize and develop educational practices that will keep the promises of the New Literacies for all students, rather than reproduce if not exacerbate the privilege of some students over others, when some students do not approach computers with the literate practices and knowledge that would make technologies seem transparent?

Theoretically, when we extend our review of the literature on social and cultural reproduction into the next generation of theory and research, we find significant ev-

idence that the processes described previously are not as monolithic as first presumed, and that within the scenarios described there are contradictions, gaps in
practice, and other spaces within which opportunistic students, educators, and
families can exercise some agency to disrupt them.

Previous studies have found that levels of low literacy and academic achievement presumed to characterize the student populations of schools that serve the
working poor and minorities are not nearly as uniformly low as earlier studies suggested. For example, in an earlier study conducted by Mark, Phil, and Julia Connor
(Dressman, Wilder, & Connor, 2005) in an alternative middle school in the same
school district as Midland High School, of eight struggling students from working
poor backgrounds, three read and wrote at or above grade level, as measured by
standardized achievement tests. In a follow-up study (Dressman & Wilder, in press)
conducted to assess the impact of wireless computer technology on the school's curriculum, one of these three students, an African American student with a severe
case of Attention Deficit Disorder, was documented as he developed advanced
proficiencies in using a wireless laptop computer to "multitask"—to work on
school-related tasks as he simultaneously downloaded hip-hop music, surfed the
Web, and negotiated back and forth among several Web sites at once. In another
study, Foley (1990, 1991) studied changes in academic achievement among gifted
Mexican American students in a South Texas high school in the years that followed
policy changes resulting from the Chicano Civil Rights Movement in the 1970s. In
Foley's analysis, in one community relatively slight changes in social policy were
enough to provide the children of working class families with a very modest
amount of academic and cultural capital with enough opportunity to "get
ahead"—to go to college and enter middle-class and professional
occupations—although many other students admittedly did not advance.

The documentation of these "naturally occurring" instances—that is, instances
unplanned by the researchers who documented them—provides evidence that processes of social and cultural reproduction are not inevitable, and that given some shift
in economic or political circumstances, they can be interrupted for some students.
Perhaps more promising, however, is the evidence of more deliberate instructional
practices, planned by educators with a reflexive grasp of reproductive theory, that
have been effective in countering historically situated educational practices. Langer
(2001) identified multiple middle and high schools located in impoverished school
districts in the United States where achievement levels in literacy exceeded the norm
for schools with low SES populations. From her analysis of instructional practices in
classrooms with high achievement rates, she identified patterns in which teachers
taught procedural "skills" explicitly and directly, but always within full, meaningful
contexts of literacy production—for example, writing authentic texts for real audiences; teaching full literary texts rather than discontinuous excerpts or unrelated
short texts—and through carefully scaffolded activities that provided guided practice and feedback. In another study, Anyon (1997) described a teacher education program in which preservice teachers are required to examine their own educational
backgrounds as well as study the experiences of students in urban and suburban
classrooms, and to develop instructional practices that negotiate between the tenets
of progressivist (project-based, constructivist) practices and the cultural expectations
of the working class for more directed instruction.

This brings us, in closing, to consider how the insights of theories of social and cultural postreproduction (that is, production) theory, in combination with recent stud-

ies of effective literacy instruction and preservice education and our own observations of the struggles of students when they used the internet as a research tool, might inform the development of instructional and curricular practices and teacher education programs capable of bringing every student in a school "up to speed" with digital computer technologies. Because the problems we noted of literate and technical proficiency seem in some ways to be separate, and because the technical problem alone might be characterized as a set of "little things" that could be easily remediated, a traditional program of intensive basic skills in reading, combined with some short-term explicit instruction in how to conduct a search, might seem appropriate. But we reject this possibility because it is not responsive to the arguments or findings of postreproduction theory or research. Moreover, on closer evaluation, the problems that the students in our study faced in terms of their literacy were not so "little" after all. They were mostly, we argue, with comprehension and were the consequence of a lack of prior knowledge about academic topics—with a lack of declarative academic knowledge of things and how they were related—problems that are typically only minimally addressed in skills-based programs of remediation (and may, in fact, be the consequence of an academic career spent in remedial programs weak in content knowledge). Moreover, a separation of instruction in literacy and search procedures would clearly not contribute to solving another problem that we noted, the ability to integrate literate and computer-based search activities.

A second possibility might be to short-cut the problems we identified in our investigation by providing students with a list of addresses to presearched Web sites on a particular topic along with explicit instruction to students at the same time in how to read through the site, gather information, and record it in some note-taking format, with a gradual release over time of more and more decision making to students. Such an approach might "guarantee" that all students in the class would receive instruction in how to read a Web site and conduct a search "properly," but we think it doubtful that many secondary students would pay attention in the ways that might be expected, that students would never become very independent in their practices through this process, and that, once completed, few students would be likely in the future to initiate searches of the Internet on their own. It would also be highly reproductive in its long-term consequences, as it would also short-change students who needed to develop Web-search skills that other students with high-speed connections in their homes and up-to-date hardware would likely pick up from older siblings, parents, or more knowledgeable friends.

Instead of these two approaches, and in place of assuming that students will "pick up" the literacy and other skills needed to efficiently and effectively search the Internet on their own, our reading of the literature suggests that an approach that builds on what students already know about an academic topic and their prior knowledge of the Internet, that encourages them to combine and share knowledge among themselves, that operates within an authentic instructional context and need to know, and that develops their metacognitive awareness of how the World Wide Web is organized as a source of academic knowledge, may prove more generative and motivational. For example, although Phil did ask students what they knew about the Caribbean and particular islands during the PowerPoint™ presentation that introduced the search assignment, he did so after the fact of designing the study. A more engaging and less frustrating approach might have been to design the assignment *after* determining what students knew and wanted to know about the Caribbean, and after a preliminary search of sites on the Web by the students suggested how and where information about the Caribbean was located on the Web, and what the literate challenges of finding information might be. Then Phil could have developed vocabulary and a richer organizational frame for the search project before the students began their full searches.

Second, after spending several days trying to help 20 students sit at individual computer terminals (designed for exclusively individual use) and struggle with 20 different problems, we wondered if it might not be more feasible and manageable if, in keeping with best practices in social constructivism, two or three students of varying abilities and competencies sat at a single computer and combined their knowledge about the topic and the search process. In keeping with the findings of Langer (2001), some timely direct instruction in specific procedures for conducting an efficient and effective search—how to identify keywords, how to distinguish promising Web sites from others in a list of search results, and how to use the features of a search engine to navigate efficiently—may also have been helpful at this point, especially if time could have been taken at the end of a class period to reflect on what had been learned, not only about the academic topic at hand, but about the process of searching itself. Through multiple research projects of this type—projects that were contextually authentic from the start but that increased in complexity from one to the next—over time we might have found the students in Phil's class becoming more willing to try to read through extended print text, to make more varied use of key words and phrases as well as other search symbols like "" and +, and to take notes that were incrementally more complete and accurate.

Beyond this project or the curriculum of any individual class, our reading of theory and research, and our consideration for the differences in quality and time online that students in Phil's and Helen's classes were allowed, we think it is crucial that schools open more times and spaces for students to use the Internet and other computer technologies in schools for their own individual purposes. Given the ideological conservatism of public education in these New Times, and the increasing pressure on schools to raise test scores and make every minute of the school day "count," we are aware of just how unlikely this is to happen, but we believe that, given the opportunities that such spaces have been shown to provide for the development of New Literacies and transferable skills, the suggestion needs to be voiced.

REFERENCES

Anyon, J. (1981). Social class and school knowledge. *Curriculum Inquiry, 11*, 3–42.

Anyon, J. (1997). *Ghetto schooling: A political economy of urban educational reform*. New York: Teachers College Press.

Bean, T. W., Bean, S. K., & Bean, K. F. (1999). Intergenerational conversations and two adolescents' multiple literacies: Implications for redefining content area literacy. *Journal of Adult and Adolescent Literacy, 42*, 438–448.

Bourdieu, P. (1984). *Distinction: A social critique of the judgment of taste*. Cambridge, MA: Harvard University Press.

Bourdieu, P. (1989). Social space and symbolic power. *Sociological Theory, 7*(1), 14–25.

Brantlinger, E. (2003). *Dividing classes: How the middle class negotiates and rationalizes school advantage*. New York: Routledge Falmer.

Bruce, B. C. (2002). Diversity and critical social engagement: How changing technologies enable new modes of literacy in changing circumstances. In D. E. Alvermann (Ed.), *Adolescents and literacies in a digital world* (pp. 1–18). New York: Peter Lang.

Christian-Smith, L. K. (1991). Readers, texts, and contexts: Adolescent romance fiction in schools. In M. W. Apple & L. K. Christian-Smith (Eds.), *The politics of the textbook* (pp. 191–212). New York: Routledge.

Cuban, L. (2003). *Oversold and underused: Computers in the classroom.* Cambridge, MA: Harvard University Press.

Dressman, M. (1997). *Literacy in the library: Negotiating the spaces between order and desire.* Westport, CT: Bergin and Garvey.

Dressman, M. (1999). Mrs. Wilson's university: A case study in the ironies of good practice. *Language Arts, 76,* 500–509.

Dressman, M., & Tettegah, S. (in press). Ordered by desire: School libraries in past and present times. In C. Kaptizke & B. Bruce (Eds.), *New libraries and knowledge spaces: Critical perspectives on information and education.* Mahwah, NJ: Lawrence Erlbaum Associates.

Dressman, M., & Wilder, P. (in press). Wireless technology and the prospect of alternative education reform. In J. Albright & A. Luke (Eds.), *Bourdieu and literacy education.* Mahwah, NJ: Lawrence Erlbaum Associates.

Dressman, M., Wilder, P., & Connor, J. J. (2005). Theories of failure and the failure of theories: A cognitive/sociocultural/macrostructural study of eight struggling students. *Research in the Teaching of English, 40,* 8–61.

Everhart, R. (1983). *Reading, writing, and resistance: Adolescence and labor in a junior high school.* London: Routledge and Kegan Paul.

Fine, M. (1991). *Framing dropouts: Notes on the politics of an urban public high school.* Albany, NY: SUNY Press.

Finn, P. (1999). *Literacy with an attitude: Educating working-class children in their own self-interest.* Albany, NY: SUNY Press.

Fiske, J. (1989). *Understanding popular culture.* Winchester, MA: Unwin Hyman.

Foley, D. (1990). *Learning capitalist culture: Deep in the heart of Tejas.* Philadelphia, PA: University of Pennsylvania Press.

Foley, D. (1991). Rethinking school ethnographies of colonial settings: A performance perspective on reproduction and resistance. *Comparative Education Review, 35,* 532–551.

Gee, J. P. (2000). Teenagers in new times: A new literacy studies perspective. *Journal of Adult and Adolescent Literacy, 43,* 412–420.

Gee, J. P. (2004). New times and new literacies: Themes for a changing world. In A. Ball and S. W. Freedman (Eds.), *Bakhtinian perspectives on language, literacy, and learning* (pp. 279–306). Cambridge: Cambridge University Press.

Haythornthwaite, C., & Wellman, B. (2002). The Internet in everyday life: An introduction. In B. Wellman & C. Haythornthwaite (Eds.), *The Internet in everyday life* (pp. 3–43). Oxford, UK: Blackwell.

Heath, S. B. (1983). *Ways with words: Language, life, and work in communities and classrooms.* Cambridge: Cambridge University Press.

Keddie, N. (1971). Classroom knowledge. In M. F. D. Young (Ed.), *Knowledge and control* (pp. 133–160). London: Collier-Macmillan.

Langer, J. (2001). Beating the odds: Teaching middle and high schools students to read and write well. *American Educational Research Journal, 38,* 837–880.

Lankshear, C., & Knobel, M. (2002). Do we have your attention? New literacies, digital technologies, and the education of adolescents. In D. E. Alvermann (Ed.), *Adolescents and literacies in a digital world* (pp. 19–39). New York: Peter Lang.

Lareau, A. (1989). *Home advantage: Social class and parental intervention in elementary education.* New York: Falmer.

Leander, K. (2005, February). *Imagining and practicing Internet space-times with/in school.* Paper presented at National Council of Teachers of English Midwinter Conference, Columbus, OH.

Levinson, B., Foley, D., & Holland, D. (1996). *The cultural production of the educated person: Critical ethnographies of schooling and local practice.* Albany, NY: SUNY Press.

Luke, A. (2000). New narratives of human capital: Recent redirections in Australian educational policy. In S. J. Ball (Ed.), *The sociology of education: Major themes.* New York: Routledge.

Lyotard, F. (1984). *The postmodern condition.* Minneapolis: University of Minnesota Press.

MacLeod, J. (1987). *Ain't no makin' it: Leveled aspirations in a low-income neighborhood.* Boulder, CO: Westview Press.

McDermott, R. (1987). Achieving school failure: An anthopological approach to illiteracy and stratification. In G. Spindler (Ed.), *Education and cultural process* (2nd ed.; pp. 173–209). Prospect Heights, IL: Waveland Press.

Oakes, J. (1985). *Keeping track: How schools structure inequality.* New Haven, CT: Yale University Press.

O'Brien, D., Springs, R., & Stith, D. (2001). Engaging at-risk high school students: Literacy learning in a high school literacy lab. In E. B. Moje & D. G. O'Brien (Eds.), *Constructions of literacy: Studies of teaching and learning in and out of secondary schools* (pp. 105–123). Mahwah, NJ: Lawrence Erlbaum Asspcoates.

Pope, D. C. (2001*). "Doing school": How we are creating a generation of stressed out, materialistic, and miseducated students.* New Haven, CT: Yale University Press.

Rist, R. (1970). Student social class and teacher expectation: The self-fulfilling prophecy in ghetto education. *Harvard Educational Review, 40,* 411–451.

Rogers, R. (2002). Between contexts: A critical discourse analysis of family literacy, discursive practices, and literate subjectivities. *Reading Research Quarterly, 37,* 248–277.

Weis, L. (1990). *Working class without work: High school students in a deindustrializing economy.* New York: Routledge.

Wexler, P. (1992). *Becoming somebody: Toward a social psychology of school.* London: Falmer.

Willis, P. (1981). *Learning to labor: How working class kids get working class jobs.* New York: Columbia University Press.

12

Literacies Through Youth's Eyes: Lessons in Representation and Hybridity

Kathleen A. Hinchman
Kelly Chandler-Olcott
Syracuse University

Adults can learn a lot from young people. Children are born with a clean slate, free from hatred, racism, sexism, homophobia and all their nasty cousins. Kids cooperate and share, skills requiring attitudes that many nations today seem to be lacking … From teens, adults can learn to renew their radical ideas and activist thoughts lost through life and their experiences. They can learn it is never too late to switch gears. They can learn that stubbornness and conviction are actually admirable qualities when compared with being passive and unquestioning.

—Zondlo, 1996, p. 14

Taken from a mid-1990s *Newsweek* editorial, these words were written by a young woman, now grown. Despite the passing of time, her argument continues to serve as a reminder of youthful communicative competence as well as the still viable complaint that youth are not given the respect they deserve in Western culture. As others have suggested, our negative connotation for the word *adolescent* provides strong hints of our culture's dominant stance toward this age group (Lesko, 2000). Our collective lack of respect is also indicated by the poor instruction and limited curriculum innovation that persist in much of youth's schooling (e.g., Cuban, 1993; Goodlad, 2004), despite promising alternative initiatives (e.g., Deschler, Schumaker, Lenz, Bulgren, Hock et al., 2001; Greenleaf, Schoenbach, & Cziko, 2001). Since the publication of this editorial, an increased emphasis on standards and high-stakes test performance in our educational climate sends new messages to our youth about the kinds of literacies that are valued. Some say that instructional initiatives in response to these concerns will help all youth toward greater literacy achievement, whereas others sug-

231

gest that such responses exacerbate existing challenges, especially for nonmainstream youth (Conley & Hinchman, 2004; Paul, 2004).

This chapter is an updated version of Hinchman's chapter in the earlier edition of this volume. Its purpose is to reconsider the ways researchers represent youth's perspectives in research and pedagogical recommendations, revisiting patterns of representation in five school-based qualitative studies of adolescent literacy and theorizing new pedagogical contexts that foreground adolescents' multiple literacies but also address today's heightened climate of accountability. In the following pages, we explain the evolution of this project and summarize the five texts. We explore the status of the youthful informants in each text and consider how these informants might participate in altered classroom literacy practices. Finally, we discuss the implications of our theorizing for others who are interested in enhancing adolescent literacy.

THE EVOLUTION OF THIS INQUIRY

Many literacy educators celebrate the initiations that are evident in young children's emergent oral and written language (e.g., Harste, Woodward, & Burke, 1984; Strickland & Morrow, 1989). Yet we sometimes roll our eyes in frustration as youth read only to answer teachers' questions (e.g., Alvermann & Phelps, 2004; Readence, Bean, & Baldwin, 2004; Vacca & Vacca, 2004). In response, literacy researchers have explored teachers' views of such limited reading, with focus on texts, tasks, and contextual pressures (for reviews in this area, see Alvermann & Moore, 1991; Moore, 1996; O'Brien, Stewart, & Moje, 1995). Other work has focused on capturing adolescents' views of reading and writing in classrooms (Alvermann et al., 1996; Bloome, 1987; Everhardt, 1984; Myers, 1992; Nicholson, 1984; Oldfather, 1995; Ratekin, Simpson, Alvermann, & Dishner, 1985; Santa Barbara Discourse Group, 1994; Smith & Feathers, 1983; Stewart, Paradis, Ross, & Lewis, 1996).

One line of work in this area, grounded in symbolic interactionism (Blumer, 1969; Denzin, 1992), queried teachers and students in classrooms about the meanings they made of texts and textual practices typical to those contexts. Taken together, these studies offered the insight that reading and writing in the manner envisioned by much recommended secondary school literacy literature has not been integral to secondary school's work, especially in content-heavy classes where teachers acted as brokers of required information (Dillon, 1989; Dillon, O'Brien, Moje, & Stewart, 1994; Hinchman, 1985, 1987; Hinchman & Zalewski, 1996; Moje, 1996; Stewart, 1989; Sturtevant, 1992, 1996). This work helped us to understand more about the very defensible and context-specific reasons for teachers' actions in secondary school classrooms. Moje (1996) explained this insight with irony: "It may be that inconsistencies lie not between what teachers believe and what they practice, but between what researchers believe and teachers practice" (p. 20).

Moje's suspicion that researchers' notions had clouded, and sometimes even prevented, appreciation of teachers' perspectives led Hinchman to wonder, in her earlier version of this chapter, if researchers' representations had analogously marginalized youth's views. Since the earlier version of this chapter, much research grounded in sociocultural perspectives has looked at youth's personal and academic literacies, in and out of school, in ways that both foregrounded and yielded powerful insights about youth's perspectives (e.g., Alvermann, 2002; Blackburn, 2003; Chandler-Olcott & Mahar, 2003; Hull & Schultz, 2002; Leander, 2002; Moje,

2000b; Sarroub, 2002; Schultz, 2002). This work has helped us to understand the increasingly important place of multimodal texts and digital technologies in youth's literacy development and identity construction, as well as highlighted differences in how young people view and employ literacies that are related to their membership in various discourse communities. It also hinted that youth might find heightened relevance when instruction acknowledges and enhances such literacies.

Yet our observations suggest that instructional implications of this work remain largely ignored. Instead, considerable evidence suggests that secondary school instruction remains substantially unchanged (Goodlad, 2004), continuing to marginalize many students, as Wilder and Dressman said in chapter 11. Moreover, when policy emphasizes high-stakes test performance, it is even less clear how we are to incorporate such research into our instructional planning, especially when the kinds of on-demand, formal expository writing privileged by high-stakes texts have little in common with the informal, interactive writing embraced by adolescents in online environments (Chandler-Olcott & Mahar, 2003; Lewis & Fabos, 1999).

This chapter revisits the way youth are represented in five studies. We conceptualized this work as an exercise in critical praxis (e.g., Harding, 1987; Lemke, 1995), that is, as systematic critique of one's own practice, in this case, our practice as researchers. For the purposes of this chapter, such critique meant examining our practice as researchers—directly in the case of Hinchman and Zalewski (1996), a study we review in the next section, and indirectly in the case of Chandler-Olcott and Mahar (2003), a study that we have included among those making recent, though limited, contributions to understanding of youth's perspectives on literacy. This orientation steered us toward critiquing, theorizing, and moving beyond assumptions made about representing others to imagine what could happen to these people in altered contexts.

The New London Group's (1996) notion of multimodal Design helped us to see literacy practices as a mix of old and new—a continual ReDesigning of experience, knowledge, and skills that learners bring to classrooms in light of new information and tools provided by joint activity in a community. Their proposal for multiliteracies pedagogy gave us a way to take what we know about youth's literacies into account in our instructional theorizing, with its framework of situated practice, overt instruction, critical framing, and transformed practice—a view that balances literacy learners' need for meaningful practice with their need for explicit guidance from more expert and experienced others. Moje's (2000a) proposal for hybrid pedagogy that incorporates cognitive, social, and critical views of subject-area literacies helped us to imagine classrooms that foreground youth's perspectives and simultaneously invite academic achievement of the kind envisioned by standards-based reformers.

We selected the same texts for review that were used in the original version of this text because of several common features: First, they represented a range of secondary-school disciplines (e.g., English, social studies, and science), yet they shared a common high school context. Second, they served a variety of foci (e.g., social organization, role of text and reading, contextualization of literacy processes, reading, and success), but used rich data, including extensive participant observation and in-depth interviewing to explore shared meanings in particular settings. Third, the texts were all composed to explore the relation between what is recommended and what is practiced to promote literacy in secondary schools (Alvermann & Moore,

1991; Sturtevant, personal communication, September 5, 1996). While we debated the wisdom of using somewhat dated texts, we realized that these classrooms look a good deal like many of the classrooms we visit today. We believed that, unlike more recent studies conducted outside of school, these classroom-based texts could provide good locations for considering alternative views of youth's literacies and pedagogy in response to these perspectives.

THE TEXTS IN REVIEW

In Sum

Following are brief summaries of each of the five pieces used for this inquiry, meant to introduce each study and to serve as a reference to the authors' premises for inquiry. Although no rewording of text can be entirely neutral, we tried to construct these summaries with close attention to authors' abstracts and summative statements as primary sources. We organized them according to features common across such research reports, including rationales, theoretical orientations, purposes methodologies, results, and implications for research and practice.

Dillon (1989).   The purpose of Dillon's (1989) piece was to "construct a description and interpretation of the social organization of one rural secondary, low-track English-reading classroom" (p. 227). Grounded in symbolic interactionist traditions, Dillon orchestrated this interpretive microethnography using field notes and interview data to generate a description of the classroom's social organization and a partial theory of the teacher's effectiveness. This teacher, Mr. Appleby, was reported to be effective because of his ability to create a classroom organization that accounted for the cultural backgrounds of his students. In addition, he was described as varying his teaching style during lessons to increase opportunities for student learning and improved student attitudes, establishing an environment where students felt good about themselves, structuring lessons that met the interests and needs of students, and implementing lessons so that all students could be successful within actions that were culturally congruent. Dillon ended her piece with a recommendation for more such studies to explain why participants in classrooms act in the ways that they do.

Stewart (1989).   The purpose of Stewart's text, representing his doctoral dissertation, was to examine the roles that textbooks and reading assumed within the social dynamics of Mr. Weller's secondary earth science classroom. Stewart's rationale for this inquiry was that little was known about the use of textbooks in science classrooms. Thus, he constructed a microethnography, anchored in symbolic interactionist and interactive sociolinguistic theory. His qualitative study primarily used participant observation and in-depth interviewing to provide data for a constant comparison analysis. Stewart found that, within a larger, control-oriented school context, the textbook was central to the teacher's choreography of instruction but not necessarily in ways that required extensive text-based information processing. As a result of this inquiry, Stewart suggested more work to explore how textbooks could be used differently, as a more dynamic and helpful source of information.

Sturtevant (1992).   Sturtevant's doctoral dissertation explored the types, amounts, and uses of reading and writing in two high school American history classes, as well as the contextual influences that affected such usage. Claiming a social constructivist framework, Sturtevant analyzed participant observation and in-depth interviews using constant comparison and domain analysis. Results suggested that reading and writing were primarily textbook directed and factual in emphasis. Apparently requiring more reading and writing than had been reported in previous studies, the two male teachers, Smith and Jones, also helped with study skills and essay and report writing. Conflicting demands of time pressures and content coverage, students' background and desire for good grades, teachers' beliefs about teaching, experiences with students, and collegial discussions influenced the conduct of classroom activities.

Hinchman and Zalewski (1996). The Hinchman and Zalewski (1996) piece represented Hinchman's year-long collaboration with Patricia Zalewski, a social studies teacher. Hinchman and Zalewski reported that their work was conducted to explore the role that reading played for students and their teacher, Zalewski, in a tenth-grade global studies class. Similar to Stewart, Hinchman and Zalewski found that although reading was instrumental in completing day-to-day classroom activities (e.g., lecture, question–answer sessions, small-group discussions, assessment), depth of understanding was not central to students' notions of success. As one student said, "I like it when I understand," but she found that there was not always time for understanding when grades overshadowed her more meaning-based concerns. The report recommended further situated study of teachers and students in classrooms and exploration of pedagogies within which ideas about success could be more easily discussed.

Moje (1996). Anchored in the traditions of symbolic interactionism and hermeneutic phenomenology (van Manen, 1990), Moje's (1996) ethnography focused on how and why a high school chemistry teacher and her students engaged in literacy activities. Based on data collected primarily through participant observation and in-depth interviewing, Moje argued that the relationship between Landy, the teacher, and her students shaped a particular construction of literacy activities. Landy's orchestration of literacy events came from her philosophy of science teaching, desire for organization, and interest in relationships. Students' purposes ranged from their interest in relationships to grades. As a result of this inquiry, Moje recommended more work to explore what teachers say and do, use of cases to teach connection between relationships and content, and exploration of trade-offs when students are helped to join Myers' (1992) achievement clubs because their teachers care about their success.

Considering Adolescents' Positions

For the next section, we consider the texts as constitutive discursive practices that reflect social constructions and particular systems of values, beliefs, and social practices (Fairclough, 1989; Gee, 1996; Hicks, 1995–1996). With Hodder's (1994) suggestion that thematic inquiry of written texts can, in essence, involve the same strategies as interpretations of oral texts gathered through participant observation and in-depth interviewing, we used the constant comparison method (Glaser & Strauss, 1967) to discern themes of social construction that seemed pertinent to the representation of youth's perspectives, recognizing that some of our insights have changed since the first version of this chapter. Using these texts as data meant ongoing attention to the fact that they were written for purposes that diverged from our concerns for their representations (Borland, 1991). Hodder (1994) explained:

> In both texts and artifacts the problem is one of situating material culture within varying contexts while at the same time entering into a dialectic relationship between those contexts and the contexts of the analyst. This hermeneutical exercise, in which the lived experience surrounding the material culture is translated into a different culture of interpretation, is common for both texts and other forms of material culture. (p. 394)

From rereading these text data, we developed a theory of the relative credibility afforded by the studies' participants as interpretive sources, copying key text segments, making notes about our thinking, developing a set of coding categories to represent themes related to this theory of apparent positioning, and refining our understanding of categories' parameters as we used them recursively across studies. We began with the Hinchman text so that we could work through the unsympathetic critical stance that can be used by those who critique other's texts. Within such constraints, we saw three themes as central to our questions about representing youth's perspectives: indications of participants' authority; unexplored ties to participants' gender, race, class, and identity; and unexamined acceptance of the larger context of schooling.

Indications of Relative Authority.   As is no surprise to critics of qualitative research as "colonizing discourse" (Fine, 1994, p. 70), each of the five reviewed texts represented a hierarchy of power, participation, and interpretation, framed by timely quirks in the research applications (e.g., focus on teacher effectiveness, teacher–researcher collaborations), yet varying in a larger sense only a little across pieces. Claimed as an artifact of twin demands for interpretative expertise and focused writing, the most dominant interpretations represented in the texts were the researchers'. Writing mostly in the third person, the authors were the usually invisible experts who conceived, designed, observed, interviewed, and authored representations of others in classrooms. The next most important interpretations belonged to teachers, the researchers' primary informants and the agents of their classroom access. Students' points of view were considered last and often in the aggregate, minimizing their more particularized potential for providing insights that could change the ways the rest of us see classrooms.

For instance, Hinchman's (Hinchman & Zalewski, 1996) outside-the-classroom words seemed the most apparent in the texts Hinchman composed with Zalewski, which is especially interesting given Hinchman and Zalewski's efforts to represent a collaborative front. Even as they reported Hinchman's effort to be a neutral observer to balance Zalewski's more active teaching role, they noted that data "collection became more focused until the categories that emerged were thought to be saturated" (Hinchman & Zalewski, 1996, p. 94), delivering procedural information in passive sentence constructions that belied her role as primary actor in this process. Dillon's, Stewart's, Sturtevant's, and Moje's texts all assumed similar roles for their authors, and their texts accounted for this position with varying explicitness. Current qualitative literacy researchers are far more likely to reflect on their involvement in and influence on research settings and informants (Kamberelis & Dimitriadis, 2005).

Additional evidence of the researchers' authority is found in the circumstance that all of the author-researchers claimed a phenomenological perspective, explaining their use of a variety of procedures to learn the defining processes of classrooms. Yet, all of them looked for reading and writing, acts that in the end seemed less than central to the classrooms they described. As Stewart (1989) explained, a phenomenological study in the idealized sense would not begin with such a preconceived search. Stewart thinly disguised the belief that we suspect all the authors shared to some extent, that one should see reading and writing instruction in all secondary school classrooms: "Thus describing science classrooms and how reading and textbooks are used for science instruction are especially important if content reading instruction is to become a ubiquitous component in science instruction" (Stewart, 1989, p. 8). The researchers' lenses also affected their ways of seeing others' classroom perspectives on literacy. For instance, Sturtevant (1992) explained that she omitted students' notes and other nonacademic print from her consideration because it was not suited to her more academic focus. From Finders' (1997) and Moje's (2000a) more recent work, we know that such practices are important sources of insight into youth's literacy and identity constructions.

The host teachers represented the next strongest voices in the respective texts. All were described with apparent great respect for their perspectives as primary orchestrators of classroom activities, whether they were characterized as struggling to cover content or as having developed a more student-centered pedagogy. For example, Dillon's (1989) Mr. Appleby, described by colleagues as an effective English teacher and by Dillon as the acknowledged focus of her inquiry, was a teacher who had reportedly developed many ways to help students feel successful in classroom interactions. His authority in the classroom and in Dillon's text seemed clear; Dillon noted that he referred affectionately to his students as "road dogs," meaning "students who keep trying despite their backgrounds and academic failures" (Dillon, 1989, p. 233). Appleby presumed some authority in the bestowing of such a nickname, and he was granted more by the text's respectful interpretation of its use.

Both Stewart's (1989) and Sturtevant's (1992) texts demonstrated analogous respect for their host teachers, Mr. Weller, Mr. Smith, and Mr. Jones, referred to as "Mr." throughout reports, whereas student informants were referred to by first names. Even as these teachers were described as primary sources of information in their respective classrooms, so too were they the locus of Stewart's and Sturtevant's interpretation that their shared struggle with covering content and addressing students' needs resulted in ambiguous text use and classroom reading activities. As second author of the Hinchman and Zalewski (1996) co-authored piece, Zalewski's teacher voice was clearly the second most authoritative. They consistently described her views of classroom activities before those of students, and their most basic statements of rationale privileged her concerns as teacher: "The class we selected was the one that caused Zalewski to ask the most questions about how to meet students' needs" (p. 93). Similarly, and beginning with the title's reference to teacher's beliefs, Moje's (1996) text also authorized Landy's voice over that of her students. We learned much more about Landy, her background, and her ideals, than about those same important identifying features in the students' lives, or about how these features differed among students or affected classroom interactions. The propensity to honor teachers over students was probably partly derived from the fact that teachers provided easier access when researchers construct a relationship with them that is anchored in respect. Yet left unexamined were the ways in which researchers' privileging of individuals' interpretations might obscure their ability to see the marginalization of some students (Alvermann, 2001).

Dillon's (1989) piece, the earliest in our chronology of studies, was also the first among the texts to suggest that students' perceptions of classrooms could be very different from their teachers'. As all of the researchers did to some degree or another, however, Dillon represented her students as a group, in her case as "a basic track class of juniors," citing particular students only in support of her study's assertions about Appleby. Stewart (1989) similarly described students as a group as having the power to "eat you alive" (p. 128) in the event of inappropriate activity choices by the teacher. Sturtevant (1992), in turn, confessed to the limitation that, "Scripting all [students'] discussion was not possible … when students met in small groups or worked independently" (p. 57), minimizing their priority as constructors of meaning in her observed classroom interactions even while demonstrating a significant limitation of participant observation research. The Hinchman and Zalewski (1996) text presented the researchers as determined to collect students' insights because "attention to students' views within the larger context of classroom interactions might change understanding about how reading works in these settings" (p. 93). Yet, these authors chose a few informants to represent the points of view of all students, and the text interpreted their words. Moje's (1996) text also represented some youth's perspectives, but the main point of their inclusion was to consider their response to Landy's classroom orchestrations. In contrast, much new work has looked at individual youth's perspectives more directly and individually, with regard to issues ranging from middle grade youth's technology use (Chandler-Olcott & Mahar, 2003) to older GLBT (e.g., Gay, Lesbian, Bisexual, Transsexual) youth's literacy enactments outside of school (Blackburn, 2003).

This business of who gets represented how in our research texts is a tricky one, limited by a host of conventions that are difficult to disrupt. We continue to find it contrary to consider producing discourse that more directly confronts our authority even as we revise this piece. Our field's tradition of neutral-sounding, third-person reporting of research adds a layer of discursive habits to be broken, and publication requires a focus that is likely to betray the variety of perspectives to be found in any social setting. We find it difficult to get around our claims to be able to write about others, but we understand that it is often equally problematic for teachers or teenagers to find time or inclination to author texts.

Mostly Unexplored Ties to Gender, Race, Class, and Identity.   As in most research traditions, all five of the texts alluded to researchers', teachers', and students' memberships in particular groups by gender, race, and class—sometimes directly, and sometimes indirectly. For instance, Hinchman and Zalewski (1996) reported that the high school location of the inquiry was considered middle class and suburban, and that Zalewski's class for college-bound students included 20 European American and 2 African American students. Although we acknowledged a search for balance in gender and achievement in the selection of student informants, particular ethnic identities and genders were claimed for neither the authors nor the five student informants—except as might be inferred from the names, Kathleen and Patricia, and the students' pseudonyms, Colin, Joe, Kiesha, Maria, and Tracy. Also, reported purposeful selection hinted of defining features that we thought significant bases for interactions in the social setting of the classroom. Yet, the remainder of the report never explored how perceptions of this import or the particulars of the mix were related to other aspects of classroom activities.

Stewart's (1989) text provided similar introduction to his study's informants. He, too, left unexplained the ties between the information in his introductions and participants' words and acts. He left unexamined his own observer's comment that "the staff and administration at Lincoln didn't really know how good they had it—that, in a lot of respects, the worst student at Lincoln wasn't all that bad" (Stewart, 1989, p. 103). Dillon (1989) noted that she selected her student informants according to her observations of class, achievement, and race, although individual students were not aligned with particular identities, and connections were not explored between these characteristics and the more idiosyncratic aspects of classroom actions or understandings. Dillon did, however, explore the connections between her background and her consideration of events in Appleby's classroom, Appleby's background and his ways of organizing class activities, and students' collective background and the community's resultant expectations for them—generally exploring the role of class but not race and gender. Similarly, in Sturtevant's (1992) text, Smith and Jones were also said to have backgrounds that directed them toward caring in particular ways about students:

> Mr. Smith is white; he believed the experience of living as a minority in a totally black population for two years [in the Peace Corps] made him 'more aware of race relations' and helped him to be able to 'relate more to black and minority students' (Sturtevant, 1992, p. 67)

Otherwise, Sturtevant also forged limited connections among race, class, gender, identity, and particular participation in classroom activities.

The ties of class to classroom action were dealt with a bit more explicitly in Moje's work, and in her suggestion that similar socioeconomic backgrounds of Landy and her students helped them to share notions of how to pursue success in school. The ties between particular participants' identity constructions, including gender, race, and class and their actual classroom actions, however, remained unexamined. That which could be explored as potentially meaningful is captured by a classroom discussion sequence included in Moje's (1996) text:

> Jay, seated in the last seat in the last row, interrupts the progress of students' observations to ask how far they were going to go around the room [with each student taking a turn at sharing an observation about the front-of-the-room experiment]. The rest of the class members laugh at Jay's question. Landy begins to have a sub conversation in which she trades statements with Jay as the rest of the students share observations… When it is Jay's turn, he offers this statement: "After Ms. Landy poured the unknown liquid into the two beakers, she put two smaller beakers over the top of the Erlenmeyer flasks." Landy also laughs and says, "I love this man; he's the only person to identify me!" (p. 182)

We were struck by Jay's panache in this example: Imagine the extent of his confidence, on stage in front of all his peers, making jokes along with effective observations while carrying on teacher–student quip trading as the class continued its discussion. In the manner suggested by Grumet (1988), we found ourselves wondering about Landy's position as female teacher in a discipline more typically viewed as dominated by men, and about whether her confessed attention to forming caring relationships minimized her authority as a content expert in the manner Hinchman and Young (2001) described elsewhere. They noted that, to become a successful social studies expert, a secondary teacher may be required to repeat dominant readings of the social studies (Noddings, 1992), rather than to engage such readings with concern for the multiple perspectives underlying the study of any culture (Flynn & Schweickert, 1986; Mills, 1994). Some aspects of Jay's performance may have evolved from his companions' valuing of his perspective over his teacher's, as well as other aspects of shared background and experiences.

We wonder similarly about social constructions underlying interactions among the participants in Appleby's, Weller's, Smith's, Jones', and Zalewski's classrooms. We realize that such undercurrents are difficult topics for explicit inquiry: Explanations of how gender, race, class, and identity work are not often well understood by those living the experiences. Lemke (1995) and others have suggested that our inability to interrogate that which cannot easily be seen may result in analyses that inadvertently misrepresent youth's identities, the social constructions that inform them, and the literacy practices that are tied to those identities. Ironically, studies that have been more successful at exploring such issues in connection with youth's literacy practices do not give us extensive ideas about how to structure classrooms that account for or invite such insights (see, for example, Blackburn, 2003).

Unexamined Acceptance of the Larger Context of Schooling.   Apple (1993) and Everhardt (1984) were among those who have pointed out that students and teachers can be viewed as anonymous workers for the status quo. Likewise, each of the reviewed studies explicitly represented schools as places within which teachers considered particular students' needs, but within a larger press for efficiently covered content. As was described in Hinchman and Zalewski (1996), success was defined as achieving passing grades through completion of activities, quizzes, and tests, rather than in terms of gaining disciplinary knowledge or insight. Some teachers, like Jones or Zalewski, were reported to be struggling to meet such obligations for as many students as they could, developing teaching methods to provide students with required information and using texts as a supporting but nonessential source. On the other hand, Appleby, Weller, Smith, and Landy were described as caring teachers who placed their relationships with students first, but who were nonetheless considered successful because they were productive with regard to students' proportionate demonstration of content acquisition.

Hinchman and Zalewski (1996), in particular, reported classroom activities through lenses that seemed thick with acceptance of an economic model, noting that, "Zalewski organized instructional activities to help the greatest number of students efficiently understand what she viewed as key concepts" (p. 96). Grades were given for completed activities, and "banked" for quarterly credit, forming a kind of bottom line. Passing grades were viewed as acceptable, and understanding was viewed by students as desirable but not essential. The text noted that students found small-group discussions more engaging than other forms of classroom activities, but it did not explore the possibility that they may have been coerced into this view by the grading system.

Similarly, students in Appleby's class were reported by Dillon (1989) as being primarily concerned with the question, "What do I need to do to make it from day to day, get by, pass my required classes, accumulate my needed credit hours, pass the BST, and eventually graduate from high school?" (p. 223). Appleby was said to have "interacted with students in ways that met their cognitive and affective needs" (p. 236), serving to reduce "resistance to learning" (p. 237). Appleby may have helped students to achieve what they saw as successful high school participation within a larger context that yielded them only a certain amount of access. For instance, he read much literature to his students, viewing knowledge of it as a status marker and fearing that they could not read it for themselves. Yet, in doing so, he may have helped to perpetuate the idea that real access to the literature of the dominant could never be theirs.

Hinchman and Zalewski's (1996) immersion in an economic model also was signified by reference to content-driven "units," perhaps as in units produced, as a central term in the explanations of classroom activities. Stewart used this term to mark a pattern in activities arranged by topic, including lectures, quizzes, and culminating unit tests. Stewart (1989) also described "down time" (p. 121) as those times when actions deviated from the topical. Sturtevant used instructional units representing content knowledge segments (e.g., Depression-era U.S. history) to mark time and artifact collection, despite evidence that participating teenagers may not have marked their attention to class participation in the same way. One student reported working on four required essays during the school year, whereas his teacher described such assignments in connection with specific units, although it should be noted that the student's words suited the question Sturtevant (1992) had posed.

Moje (1996) said, "In secondary content classrooms, the social context that shaped and is shaped by literacy learning and use is uniquely complex" (p. 175), suggesting literacy learning as a focus of what goes on in secondary schools by definition. Landy and her students viewed literacy differently, however. They looked at it as a text-based activity with an emphasis on successful ends, although notions of success were not explicit in this report. Sometimes, it seemed to mean achieving a passing grade, as it did in the Hinchman and Zalewski (1996) text, whereas at other times, it seemed to mean students perceiving themselves as understanding, as was connoted by Landy's talk about what being a good teacher meant to her. Moje (1996) stated, "Students also reported that they did not transfer such strategies to other classrooms," (p. 190) hinting that Landy's students would agree with those in Hinchman and Zalewski (1996) about the importance of content-specific productivity.

All these studies struggled, to varying degrees, with the tension between addressing students' needs and demands for content coverage. None of the researchers tackled directly the underlying premise of the importance of content coverage, however, or the idea that critical reading and writing were not the best skills for meeting such obligations (O'Brien et al., 1995). An academic literacy may have evolved that involved the students in learning appropriate communicative skills by virtue, in part, of ways their identities incorporated their varying gender, race, and class ties. These skills may have been used, in turn, to pass along teachers' acquired interpretations of the major content stories of the dominant culture, thus helping to perpetuate existing social hierarchies. Despite worthy intentions to the contrary, it can be argued that, because the current heightened emphasis on accountability has not been accompanied by multi-voiced debates about reaching toward more inclusive standards, we have further reified this stratification (Paul, 2004). It is especially difficult to attend to recommendations for embracing and building on youth's multiple literacies when standards are monolithic.

We fear that unwillingness to confront such issues in our representations, either by ignoring them in our school-based research or by exploring social constructions of subgroups without considering instructional ramifications, makes researchers

complicit in dominant larger social constructions, disempowering us from collaborating helpfully on developing new pedagogies that could yield an alternative
reality. It may even be that youth who are able to negotiate school participation successfully will have more power than anyone because this same savvy will help them
manipulate the world in which they find themselves as adults.

Through Particular Eyes

This next, nearly wholly fictionalized, section is meant to help us imagine the insights that might be added to our work by considering youth's interpretations of
classroom events and by imagining how these insights might be taken into account
as these youth assume the role of students in classrooms. We located a well-de-
scribed, adolescent key informant in each research report. Divergence by gender,
race, and class entered into this selection so that social ties to pedagogical participation could be explored and so we could theorize about relationships between
youth's and teachers' identity constructions and their literacy enactments in our
newly imagined, more hybrid classrooms. We collected all references to each individual and composed a paragraph describing what we could surmise about each.
We then reconsidered their classrooms as though we were seeing it through their
eyes, and then imagined alternative classrooms that would likely foreground their
concerns and still address the competing forces present in today's classrooms.

Our own stereotypes of youth's sense-making as well as our tendency to describe
issues of gender, race, class, and identity construction in simple, dichotomized fashion came into play and we read, reread, and revised our compositions to attempt to
control these tendencies. We also worked to guess at alternative explanations to represent several possible social worlds for each informant as a way to see our own views
through new lenses. Imagining these hypothetical texts helped provide us with important ways to reconsider our earlier interpretations of each text. We realize that,
were others to engage in a similar exercise, they would compose different stories.

Bernard.   Of the three informants that Dillon (1989) selected from Appleby's
low-track English-reading class, Bernard was the only male student. Dillon's
speech sample suggested that Bernard spoke in discourse resembling a rural African American dialect. Bernard may have been alluding to his class ties as well as his
insights about education when he reported that school was "a prison" and "boring," but "better than home" (Dillon, 1989, p. 243). If he was like most of his peers at
this disadvantaged school, he did not plan to go to college. Bernard noted that:

> Just by the way he'd talk, he were good to you … he don't be afraid to tell you how he
> feels—he don't talk mean to you, he just speak right to you … some teachers only likes
> the smart people—and Coach Appleby don't do that." (p. 241)

Bernard was not otherwise quoted in Dillon's (1989) text. She reported that he
seemed fairly reserved in all his classes, including Appleby's. We wondered about
Bernard's silence in this text, representing a classroom in a school where students
were blithely reported by administrators to be "uncaring" (p. 233). Did he suspect
that he had been tracked early for participation in a group for whom expectations
were limited? Could his silence be due to his status as male in a predominately female class? Or was he quieted by a fear that most of what went on in school did not

match his anticipated needs for communicative competence, thus allowing him to be perceived as one of the uncaring? Perhaps Bernard was silenced by a caring teacher serving as an unknowing conduit of a dominant group that wanted Bernard to "know his place" as an African American man. Yet Bernard's few but carefully chosen words hint of the kind of insight that would likely be wise to such subversion.

We think that Bernard would agree with the thesis of Dillon's (1989) report, that Mr. Appleby was an effective teacher who fostered meaningful learning by "showing them that I want them to learn and that I care about who they are" (p. 227), even as he likely would not realize that larger cultural constructions were precluding him from learning much that would help him toward connecting out-of-school and in-school literacies. But we can imagine Appleby's classroom using an alternative pedagogy involving more than essentially telling students about texts that have importance to the dominant culture. This alternative classroom may invite Bernard to study something of interest to him—perhaps critically framed inquiry into how our dialects position us in others' perceptions, with bits of overt instruction in code switching and its position in larger cultural studies (e.g., see Fecho et al., chap. 10, this volume). Students could participate in guided reading of varied texts to provide multiple views of this topic and develop reading strategies. They could use a variety of media to demonstrate new insights.

Teresa.   Stewart (1989) described Teresa, one of his student informants, as an endearing, hard-working sophomore, a B student who really enjoyed the content of her earth science course. She worked at a fast food restaurant to raise money for her hobby, horseback riding, with a non-college-bound ambition to become a jockey. Teresa seemed to like Weller's class and Weller, although she noted that she struggled with the technical vocabulary, confessing that the textbook was an important help to her: "Sometimes ... I have to go up in the back of the book to look up the definition" (Stewart, 1989, p. 140). She also noted that she "read the book entirely ... and I'll go back in the questions and problems and try to answer those" (p. 140). She described herself as studying more than most students because she found the vocabulary and reading difficult, although in Stewart's judgment, she was able to read the text and lacked "confidence" (p. 108).

As we considered the representation of her point of view, we wondered how many of Teresa's reactions could be attributed to her reportedly nonacademic ambitions, how these perceptions were threaded with discourses of gender (e.g., what girls can do) and class (e.g., not smart enough to go to college), that are common to working class youth (Hicks, 2002), and that may have informed her identity construction. We wondered if she was somewhat ambivalent about these ambitions by being attracted to this content. In addition, we wondered if there was an additional gendered undercurrent to Weller and Teresa's classroom transactions: Could their banter be interpreted as flirting, for control or other purposes? Did Weller use the logical outline of his presentation of science content to distance himself from students and, at the same time, send messages about their own possibly limited access to such understandings given their backgrounds? Did Weller's conspicuously middle-class upbringing cause communication difficulties with students from less academically oriented origins?

Teresa's struggles provided evidence that she perceived the focus of the class to be on learning the pertinent facts and generalizations for each unit, and that she accepted discourses that fed her construction of a lack of confidence in this subject area. But imagine Teresa in another type of science class, one like that recently described by Moje and her colleagues (2004). Within such a context, Teresa's interests in earth science could be deeply mined, perhaps leading her to different decisions about her ambitions, but most certainly helping her to transform her practices enough to gain confidence in additional academic literacies. Mr. Weller could use his interests and expertise to entice students, like Teresa, to explore various aspects of the discipline. Teresa and others could work in collaborative small groups to engage in Internet and library research, with Weller providing overt instruction in adapting and enhancing literacy strategies as they are needed. Students could be supported as they use the scientific method to test their own hypotheses, developed as they came to understand various theories. Critical framing could occur when they compare and contrast competing results of their research.

Don.   One of Sturtevant's (1992) informants, Don was described by Mr. Jones as an A student who had some difficulty writing. Don was a first-generation U.S. citizen, and as a result of living in a Vietnamese-speaking household, he received instruction for speakers of English as a second language until seventh grade. He reported that he had forgotten what he knew of the Vietnamese language. Mr. Jones suggested that he saw Don as part of a specialized group: "I have a number of Vietnamese students, Don is one of 'em; smart, good students, intelligent, make intelligent comments, they can get into the discussion. Trouble writing… he has a tendency to get pronouns in the wrong place … sentences that don't read too smoothly" (Sturtevant, 1992, p. 122). Don was reported to have a job outside of school at which he worked every day, and he was reluctant to waste any time in school, even working on schoolwork through his lunch hour.

As a "good student," Don believed it was important to do the reading and writing that was assigned in Jones' class: "Well, there's a lot of reading so every time he gives us an assignment … we have to read it, if we don't read we wouldn't know what he was talking about the next day in class discussion" (Sturtevant, 1992, p. 112). Don always wrote his assignment down and, thus, always had appropriate homework notes to refer to during the teacher's "pop" quizzes. To Jones' surprise, Don also noted that he could tell when a quiz was going to be "popped": "I can tell because some day only one or two people will speak out and the … rest just sit there quiet … they know they didn't read, so they just pretend they know it … so [Mr. Jones] gives us a pop quiz …" (p. 132). Don doubted that a person could get a good examination grade without reading and taking notes from the text: "They could pass with a D, [but] they wouldn't pass with a C because the test would involve a lot of reading" (p. 132).

By his own, his teacher's, and Sturtevant's measures, Don worked hard and long to do everything that was asked, apparently thinking the topic important enough for his attention, granting his teacher the authority to help him organize his attention, and accepting his class' product-driven ideology. Don gave notice that he was already developing a kind of assessment literacy from his participation in this classroom culture, learning to read the teacher's tacit notice that he was upset when students did not complete assigned reading. Imagine a classroom that made this study more explicit, one in which overt instruction invited youth to understand why people wanted them accountable for being able to demonstrate certain kinds of information. They could discuss, with the teacher, the pros and cons of these expectations and various measures of their performance. It is quite likely that students would be more motivated to engage in situated practice of such assessment literacy, eventually leading them to the kind of transformed practice that would allow them to choose whether and how to demonstrate expertise in such situations.

Maria.   One of five informants in Hinchman and Zalewski's (1996) report, Maria was a female youth in a tenth-grade, college-preparatory global studies class in a large suburban high school. Her text pseudonym hinted of possible Spanish, Portuguese, or Italian heritage in a class reportedly dominated by European Americans. In her quoted remarks she confessed that she did not "like social studies at all" (p. 101). Her work with others in small groups seemed collegial, anchored in the textbook as consummate information source (e.g., "That's what the book says" p. 100). She noted that "I learn more by listening than looking [reading] at the thing" (p. 96), yet, in apparent contradiction she referred to a particular lecture on period-specific architecture as "the most boring thing ever" (p. 97). Her words suggested an uncertainty and a throwing up of hands in the belief that those who "just like the subject" (p. 101) are the most successful.

Maria's words suggested that if she were positioned to do so, she might argue against Hinchman and Zalewski's (1996) thesis. She would say that, for her, the point was that not everyone was "born to" be interested in global studies, and therefore, not everyone could do well in its study. She did not allude to a sense for connections among classroom tasks and she found lectures boring but preferable to reading. We imagine that she would not see the fault for such disconnectedness as Zalewski's. In fact, Maria would admire this female teacher for her content mastery, a mastery Maria did not envision for herself. Instead, she would explain that the disconnectedness was a by-product of the content, as though it were something immutable.

Although Maria did not like social studies as a subject, she did not seem frustrated in a larger sense, perhaps because her various identity constructions were searching for connections between her existing literacies and any kind of schoolwork. But what if Zalewksi's global studies class had offered Maria an alternative invitation, orchestrating study of students' own cultural backgrounds and inquiry into how cultural values seemed to change in their families over time and emigration. Students could group themselves according to inquiry interests and interview family and community members to discern views over time about their countries of origin and American culture. Such students could read about ethnic and gender studies across cultures, with overt guidance from their teachers, researching and reporting on the ways in which enculturation in various parts of the world has developed over time. Within such a classroom, Maria's interest and enthusiasm for global studies could improve, and she would perhaps begin to forge better connections between her existing literacies and those needed for academic success.

Noreen.   One of Moje's (1996) student informants, Noreen was chosen as our student eyes in Landy's class because her voice was relatively quiet in this study compared with other informants. Quoted four times in Moje's text, little additional information was given about her background. Her admiration for her chemistry teacher was apparent in her enthusiastic talk—"She's spontaneous" (Moje, 1996, p. 184)—and in her assertion that "You can tell Ms. Landy is a good teacher because you can't look around the room and think that any one person is the stupidest person in the class," (p. 187). However, both the nature of her quoted arguments (e.g., " I know this is the best way [using SQ3R as a study strategy] for this material [because] I trust Ms. Landy;" p. 187) and some of her wording (e.g., "She like memorizes what she's going to say or something;" p. 184) hinted of a youth discourse that may not be comfortable in sterner academic settings. Thus, we chose to imagine Noreen as the "one student, a female, [who] appeared to be disengaged in class activities, but always responded appropriately when asked questions in class and consistently achieved high scores on homework and tests" (Moje, 1996, p. 179). As a caring teacher, Landy may have tried to involve such a reluctant speaker in class discussion by asking her to serve as recorder of the class observations, as Landy did with Noreen.

If she were the quiet student we imagine, perhaps partly tied to a lack of confidence in academic language, Noreen might have been a student not willing to take the risk needed for tasks considered to represent "critical analysis," described as our school children's deficit in the rationale for Moje's (1996) piece and a key demand of many of the tasks on our current high-stakes examinations. Noreen's representations of her own insights hinted of someone who may not see the critical as central to any of her multiple existences. Because it was not clear if she saw herself as having anything as intense as an "established relationship" with Landy, Noreen might also disagree just a bit with the study's main assertion that literacy was defined in Landy's classroom within a context where concern about relationships was foremost.

Landy taught strategies for independent study of text such as survey, question, read, recite, review (SQ3R), yet it was not clear if Noreen appreciated them for their help with understanding or because the resultant notes helped final averages. But what if Landy helped students to read about key chemistry concepts in a variety of texts—including those from the Internet, where scientific datasets are often available for student manipulation—and then asked them to report to one another on findings? They could then be invited to read and critique the textbook after gathering multiple perspectives, conducting experiments, and considering various ways to theorize around a certain topic.

Issues of Representation

This inquiry represents our response to calls for critical praxis, and our interest in issues of representation and classroom literacy pedagogy. We explored representations of adolescents' perspectives toward academic literacies in five classroom-based studies and found three central themes: indications of participants' varied authority; unexplored ties to participants' gender, race, class, and identity; and unexamined acceptance of the larger contexts of schooling. We theorized how we might design classroom literacy instruction to build on these young people's perspectives and multiple literacies within today's contexts of heightened accountability.

Because of the limitations of the original representations of the youthful informants, we know that our text-driven elaborations are not likely to match what really happened in these individuals' lives. We were also overwhelmed with the difficulties of discerning such perspectives for all students in a single classroom—yet that is what we believe the task of the teacher needs to be if she or he is going to construct pedagogy that invites youth to use and extend multiliteracies. Youth engage academic and nonacademic contexts as active constructors of identity (Hagood, 2002). Influenced deeply by growing insights into the social world, they try on, embrace, and discard ways of being that they borrow from peers, popular culture, and adults at variable speeds to construct identity "portfolios," as Gee describes elsewhere in this section. What youth tell us represents moments in time that are vastly different from other moments. Many are adept at manipulating, "playing" us adults, knowing how to produce effects that fit their varying motivations (Mahar, 2005).

Implications for Researchers.   It is clear that developing adequate representations of youth as the basis for pedagogy will be a central difficulty if we want to address multiliteracies well in today's schools. Incorporating all concerned constituencies presents an additional challenge, and yet, this is essential if we are to invite youth to be engaged and, at the same time, to address heightened curriculum standards. This caution also holds for those working on narrower interventions for the subset of youth who struggle with reading and writing but who likely desire access to the worlds in which they see their peers engaged—worlds that often reward quick and facile manipulation of multiple literacies (Lewis & Fabos, 1999).

This means we should continue to place youth, who are quite articulate about those things that are of interest and concern to them, in the center of research and subsequent discussion. We need to continue to find ways to represent their views, without violating those they would like to keep to themselves, and with a sense for their identity constructions and participations in many social worlds. On the way, we may have to interrogate much of what we think we know about developing cognitive and linguistic strategies, most of which was learned to promote content coverage. Work outside of classrooms that looks at youth's literacy and identity construction helps us to gain insights into individuals, but work inside classrooms may help us to understand better the kind of hybrid instructional models we will need if we are going to foreground youth while addressing others' concerns for what they learn. As Fine (1994) suggested:

> The project at hand is to unravel, critically, the blurred boundaries in our relation, and in our texts; to understand the political work of our narratives; to decipher how the traditions of social science serve to inscribe; and to imagine how our practice can be transformed to resist, self-consciously, acts of othering. (p. 75)

Implications for Teachers.   Since the last version of this chapter was written, much attention has come to be paid regarding our youth's reading and writing (e.g., Biancarosa & Snow, 2004; Jetton & Dole, 1994). However, only a limited number of the most publicized recommendations address youth's multiliteracies, much less explain how subject-area teachers might address them. It is important to remember that students will not necessarily feel empowered even if they are invited to share their perspectives in school (Ellsworth, 1989; Gore, 1993), and they have an equal right to know what their teachers think and understand about the world, without their teachers' views overshadowing their own.

This is not a call for idealized student-centered teaching; instead it is a call for construction that accommodates teacher and student views. We think the most effective study will involve enthusiastic teachers enticing students to work with them, recognizing each others' frailties and strengths in negotiated, responsive classrooms within which one's value does not rise and fall on a single utterance. We do not mean to be romantic because we know the kind of work that goes into the successful construction of such space. Yet if teachers look at their classrooms through their students' eyes, with their students' help, and maintain the essence of their subject-area study along with constituents' standards, they will have the tools they need.

Implications for Youth.   Orner (1992) suggested that calls for students to speak must themselves be examined: "For whose benefit do they/we speak?" (p. 77). She asked, "Where are the multiple, contradictory voices of teachers, writers, researchers, and administrators? The time has come to listen to those who have been asking others to speak" (p. 88). Shared authority only occurs when we have pedagogies that invite students to ask their teachers—and researchers and politicians—to share all their expertise as political agendas and not as immutable curricula. Teaching that invites students to speak should also allow them to be silent if they choose.

Teenagers, for their part, must similarly learn to look through the eyes of others, and to use these gazes to augment their own. They should be convinced that watering down curriculum is not in their best interests, but they should demand teachers who take the time, regularly, to find out what their interests and inclinations are, and to explore the fit between the content, skills, and ways of knowing associated with particular disciplines and students' own sensibilities. In a classroom of shared authority, students have the right to query authority when curriculum and assessment do not make sense to them, but they must learn to do so in collegial ways.

The question, what are adolescents to learn to be considered literate, has many different answers, depending on the contexts within which one asks the question. However, it leads to another, related question: What literacies do youth bring with them to their participation in secondary school classrooms that teachers can engage, learn from, and extend? This latter question is better answered for the short-term in particular classrooms on a day-to-day basis, and negotiated in terms of teachers' subject-area expertise and standards delineated by our larger society. We share the belief that if we begin with youth's existing literacies, and if they can see the point to others' interests and requirements, they will work with us to develop all kinds of strategies. In the long term, it will be even more important to be sure that we continue to answer both questions, and that we look through adolescents' eyes to help determine answers.

REFERENCES

Alvermann, D. E. (2001). Reading adolescents' reading identities: Looking back to see ahead. *Journal of Adolescent and Adult Literacy, 45*, 118–122.

Alvermann, D. E. (2002). *Adolescents and literacies in a digital world.* New York: Peter Lang Publishers.

Alvermann, D. E., & Moore, D. W. (1991). Secondary school reading. In R. Barr, M. L. Kamil, P. B. Mosenthal, & P. D. Pearson (Eds.), *Handbook of reading research* (Vol. 2, pp. 951–983). White Plains, NY: Longman.

Alvermann, D. E., & Phelps, S. F. (2004). *Content reading and literacy: Succeeding in today's diverse classrooms* (4th ed.). New York: Allyn & Bacon.

Alvermann, D. E., Young, J. P., Weaver, D., Hinchman, K. A., Moore, D. W., Phelps, S. F., Thrash, E. C., & Zalewski, P. (1996). Middle and high school students' perceptions of how they experience text-based discussion: A multicase study. *Reading Research Quarterly, 31*, 244–267.

Apple, M. (1993). *Official knowledge.* New York: Routledge.

Biancarosa, G., & Snow, C. (2004). *Reading next: Vision for action and research in middle and high school literacy: A report from Carnegie Corporation of New York.* Washington, DC: Alliance for Excellent Education. [Retrieved April 20, 2005 from all4ed.org]

Blackburn, M. (2003). Exploring literacy performances and power dynamics at The Loft: Queer youth reading the world and the word.*Research in the Teaching of English, 37,* 467–90.

Bloome, D. (1987). Reading as a social process in a middle school classroom. In D. Bloome (Ed.), *Literacy and school* (pp. 124–149). Norwood, NJ: Ablex.

Blumer, H. (1969). *Symbolic interactionism: Perspective and method.* Englewood Cliffs, NJ: Prentice-Hall.

Borland, K. (1991). "That's not what I said": Interpretive conflict in oral narrative research. In S. B. Gluck & D. Patai (Eds.), *Woman's words: The feminist practice of oral histor* (pp. 63–75). New York: Routledge.

Chandler-Olcott, K., & Mahar, D. (2003). "Tech-savviness" meets multiliteracies: Exploring adolescent girls' technology-mediated literacy practices.*Reading Research Quarterly, 38,* 356–385.

Conley, M., & Hinchman, K. A. (2004). No Child Left Behind: What it means for America's adolescents and what we can do about it. *Journal of Adolescent and Adult Literacy, 48,* 42–50.

Cuban, L. (1993). *How teachers taught: Constancy and change in American classrooms 1890 to 1990.* New York: Teachers College Press.

Denzin, N. K. (1992). *Symbolic interactionism and cultural studies.* Malden, MA: Blackwell Publishers.

Deshler, D., Schumaker, B., Lenz, K., Bulgren, J., Hock, M., Knight, J. et al. (2001). Ensuring content-area learning by secondary students with learning disabilities. *Learning Disabilities Research and Practice, 16,* 96–108.

Dillon, D. (1989). Showing them that I want them to learn and that I care about who they are: A microethnography of the social organization of a secondary low-track English classroom. *American Educational Research Journal, 26,* 227–259.

Dillon, D., O'Brien, D., Moje, E., & Stewart, R. (1994). Literacy learning in secondary school science classrooms: A cross-case analysis of three qualitative studies. *Journal of Research in Science Teaching, 31,* 345–362.

Ellsworth, E. (1989). Why doesn't this feel empowering? Working through the repressive myths of critical pedagogy. *Harvard Education Review, 59,* 297–324.

Everhardt, R. (1984). *Reading, writing, and resistance.* Boston: Kegan Paul.

Fairclough, N. (1989). *Language and power.* London: Longman.

Finders, M. (1997). *Just girls: Life and literacy in junior high.* New York: Teachers College Press.

Fine, M. (1994). Working the hyphen: Reinventing self and other in qualitative research. In N. K. Denzin & Y. S. Lincoln (Eds.), *The handbook of qualitative research* (pp.70–82). Thousand Oaks, CA: Sage.

Flynn, E., & Schweickert, P. (Eds.). (1986). *Gender and reading: Essays on readers, texts, and contexts.* Baltimore: Johns Hopkins University Press.

Gee, J. P. (1996). *Social linguistics and literacies: Ideology in discourses* (2nd ed.). Bristol, PA: Taylor & Francis.

Glaser, B., & Strauss, A. (1967). *The discovery of grounded theory.* New York: Aldine.

Goodlad, J. (2004). *A place called school: Twentieth anniversary edition.* New York: McGraw Hill.

Gore, J. (1993). *The struggle for pedagogies.* New York: Routledge.

Greenleaf, C., Schoenbach, R., & Cziko, C. (2001). Apprenticing adolescent readers to academic literacy. *Harvard Educational Review, 71,* 79–129.

Grumet, M. (1988). *Bitter milk: Women and teaching.* Amherst: University of Massachusetts Press.

Hagood, M. (2002). Critical literacy for whom? *Reading Research and Instruction, 41,* 247–265.

Harding, S. (1987). *Feminism and methodology.* Bloomington: Indiana University Press.

Harste, J., Woodward, C., & Burke, C. (1984). *Language stories and literacy lessons.* Portsmouth, NH: Heinemann.

Hicks, D. (1995–1996). Discourse, learning, and teaching. In M. Apple (Ed.), *Review of research in education* (Vol. 21, pp. 49–95). Washington, DC: American Educational Research Association.

Hicks, D. (2002). *Reading lives: Working-class children and literacy learning.* New York: Teachers College Press.

Hinchman, K. A. (1985). Reading and the plans of secondary teachers: A qualitative study. In J. Niles & R. Lalik (Eds.), *Issues in literacy: A research perspective* (34th Yearbook of the National Reading Conference, pp. 251–256). Rochester, NY: National Reading Conference.

Hinchman, K. A. (1987). The textbook and three content-area teachers. *Reading Research and Instruction, 24*(4), 247–263.

Hinchman, K. A., & Young, J. P. (2001). Speaking but not being heard: Two adolescents negotiate classroom talk about text. *Journal of Literacy Research, 33,* 243–268.

Hinchman, K. A., & Zalewski, P. (1996). Reading for success in a tenth-grade global studies class: A qualitative study. *Journal of Literacy Research, 26,* 91–106.

Hodder, I. (1994). The interpretation of documents and material culture. In N. K. Denzin & Y. S. Lincoln (Eds.), *The handbook of qualitative research* (pp. 393–412). Thousand Oaks, CA: Sage.

Hull, G. A., & Schultz, K. (2002). *School's out: Bridging out-of-school literacies and classroom practice.* New York: Teachers College Press.

Jetton, T., & Dole, J. (2004). *Adolescent literacy research and practice.* New York: Guilford.

Kamberelis, G., & Dimitriadis, G. (2005). *Qualitative inquiry: Approaches to language and literacy research.* New York: NCRLL/Teachers College Press.

Leander, K. (2002). Locating Latanya: The situated production of identity artifacts in classroom interaction. *Research in the Teaching of English, 37,* 198–250.

Lemke, J. (1995). *Textual politics: Discourse and social dynamics.* Bristol, PA: Taylor & Francis.

Lesko, N. (2000). *Act your age: A cultural construction of adolescence.* New York: Falmer Press.

Lewis, C., & Fabos, B. (1999, December). *Chatting on-line: Uses of instant message communication among adolescent girls.* Paper presented at the annual meeting of the National Reading Conference, Orlando, FL.

Mahar, D. N. (2005). *"I am not a number I am a free man": Suburban adolescents, multiliteracies, and tactics of resistance.* Unpublished doctoral dissertation, Syracuse University, Syracuse, NY.

Mills, S. (1994). *Gendering the reader.* New York: Harvester Wheatsheaf.

Moje, E. B. (1996). I teach students, not subjects: Understanding teacher–student relationships as contexts for literacy practices in a high school content classroom. *Reading Research Quarterly, 31,* 172–195.

Moje, E. B. (2000a). *"All the stories that we have": Adolescents' insights about literacy and learning in secondary schools.* Newark, DE: International Reading Association.

Moje, E. B. (2000b). "To be part of the story": Literacy practices of gangsta adolescents. *Teachers College Record, 102,* 651–690.

Moje, E., Ciechanowski, K., Kramer, K., Ellis, L., Carrillo, R., & Collazo, T. (2004). Working toward third space: An examination of everyday funds of knowledge and discourse. *Reading Research Quarterly, 39,* 36–70.

Moore, D. W. (1996). Contexts for literacy in secondary schools. In D. J. Leu, C. K. Kinzer, & K. A. Hinchman (Eds.), *Literacies for the twenty-first century: Research and practice* (45th Yearbook for the National Reading Conference, pp. 15–46). Chicago: National Reading Conference.

Myers, J. (1992). The social contexts of school and personal literacy. *Reading Research Quarterly, 27,* 296–333.

New London Group. (1996). A pedagogy of multiliteracies: Designing social futures. *Harvard Educational Review, 66,* 60–92.

Nicholson, T. (1984). Experts and novices: A study of reading in the high school classroom. *Reading Research Quarterly, 14,* 436–451.

Noddings, N. (1992). Social studies and feminism. *Theory and Research in Social Education, 20,* 230–241.

O'Brien, D., Stewart, R., & Moje, E. B. (1995). Why content literacy is difficult to infuse into the secondary curriculum: Strategies, goals, and classroom realities. *Reading Research Quarterly, 30,* 442–463.

Oldfather, P. (1995). "Songs come back to most of them": Students' experiences as researchers. *Theory into Practice, 34,* 131–137.

Orner, M. (1992). Interrupting the calls for student voice in "liberatory" education: A feminist poststructural perspective. In C. Luke & J. Gore (Eds.), *Feminisms and critical pedagogy* (pp. 74–89). New York: Routledge.

Paul, D. G. (2004). The train has left: The No Child Left Behind Act leaves black and Latino literacy learners waiting at the station. *Journal of Adolescent & Adult Literacy, 47,* 648–56.

Ratekin, N., Simpson, M., Alvermann, D. E., & Dishner, E. (1985). Why teachers resist content reading instruction. *Journal of Reading, 28,* 432–437.

Readence, J. E., Bean, T. W., & Baldwin, R. S. (2004). *Content area literacy: An integrated approach* (8th ed). Dubuque, IA: Kendall Hunt.

Santa Barbara Discourse Group. (1994). Constructing literacy in classrooms: Literate action as social accomplishment. In R. B. Ruddell, M. R. Ruddell, & H. Singer (Eds.), *Theoretical models and processes of reading* (4th ed., pp. 124–154). Newark, DE: International Reading Association.

Sarroub, L. K. (2002). In-betweenness: Religion and conflicting visions of literacy. *Reading Research Quarterly, 37,* 130–48.

Schultz, K. (2002). Looking across space and time: Reconceptualizing literacy learning in and out of school. *Research in the Teaching of English, 36,* 356–390.

Smith, F., & Feathers, K. (1983). The role of reading in content classrooms: Assumptions versus reality. *Journal of Reading, 27,* 262–267.

Stewart, R. A. (1989). A microethnography of a secondary earth science classroom: A focus upon textbooks and reading. *Dissertation Abstracts International, 50,* 3540A. (University Microfilms No. DA9003468)

Stewart, R. A., Paradis, E.E., Ross, B. D., & Lewis, M. J. (1996). Student voices: What works in literature-based developmental reading. *Journal of Adolescent and Adult Literacy, 39,* 468–478.

Strickland, D., & Morrow, L. L. (1989). *Emergent literacy: Young children learn to read and write.* Newark, DE: International Reading Association.

Sturtevant, E. G. (1992). *Content literacy in high school social studies: Two case studies in a multicultural setting.* Unpublished doctoral dissertation, Kent State University, Kent, OH.

Sturtevant, E. G. (1996). Lifetime influences on the literacy-related instructional beliefs of experienced high school history teachers: Two comparative case studies. *Journal of Literacy Research, 28,* 227–257.

Vacca, R. T., & Vacca, J. (2004). *Content area reading* (8th ed.) New York: Allyn & Bacon.

van Manen, M. (1990). *Researching lived expectations: Human science for an action sensitive pedagogy.* Albany, NY: State University of New York Press.

Zondlo, K. E. (1996, June 10). My turn: It's not just a phase. *Newsweek, 127,* 14.

IV

Changing Teachers, Teaching Changes

CHAPTER 13

The Literacies of Teaching Urban Adolescents in These Times   257
Susan L. Lytle

CHAPTER 14

Learning from Learners: Student Voices and Action Research   279
Jody Cohen, Cambria Allen, Heather Davis, Bruce Bowers, Elena Darling-Hammond,
and Li Huan Lai

CHAPTER 15

Reconceptualizing Adolescent Literacy Policy's Role: 297
Productive Ambiguity
Lisa Patel Stevens

Introduction to Part IV: Changing Teachers, Teaching Changes

Diane Waff
Strategic Literacy Initiative, WestEd

The chapters presented in this section describe an approach to adolescent literacy development that weaves strong connections among students, educators, policymakers and members of the academic community. Taken as a collective, these essays inspire the reader by illustrating how providing opportunities for diverse stakeholders to work together across traditional boundaries results in conceptual change about literacy teaching and learning. We are invited to rethink the logic of one-size-fits-all school reform efforts while benefiting from the wisdom of inclusive local inquiry communities to transform teacher practice, advance student learning, and bring about lasting school improvement.

Each chapter interrogates and makes problematic the concept of "literacy education" in order to reconceptualize who can participate in the conversation about making schools and schooling better places for adolescents' learning. In chapter 13, Susan Lytle writes about a collaborative practitioner inquiry community, of which I was a member, comprised of teacher leaders and college/university-based researchers. We explore, from our different vantage points, how teachers of adolescents define, enact, and assess teaching and learning in relationship to the growth and development of student literacy and school change. Through life histories, narratives, dialogues, transcripts of retreats, and fieldnotes, Lytle illuminates our diverse experiences around conceptions of race, gender, and class; student advocacy, social justice, collegial relationships, and what it means to learn from teachers' knowledge to effect change in local and national efforts to improve adolescent literacy.

Jody Cohen and her fellow authors in chapter 14 engage middle and high school students in collaborative action research projects that incorporate choice, personal relevance, high expectations, reflective dialogue, and writing. Through the words of the adolescents and the undergraduate students who coach them as researchers, this chapter gives particular attention to the caring relationships characterized as a form of "intimacy" that develops among the community of student researchers. The authors interrogate the notion of literacy as a "continuum of intimacy" that empowers learners to communicate successfully with peers and more formal audiences. The reader is invited to be systematically reflective about literacy instruction and to think deeply about the practices within schools and communities that have the potential to harness the collective energy of students and other stakeholders in meaningful intellectual work.

In the final chapter, Lisa Patel Stevens, despite the call for best practices and objective research to dictate teacher decision making and school reform efforts, proposes that policymakers develop a set of what she terms *enabling constraints* that require schools and school districts to look closely at their local context, draw on local knowledge and expertise, and use that data as its first referent point in the development of adolescent literacy policy. Stevens argues that teachers and students' voices have been either discounted or ignored when policymakers make decisions based on research that is frequently conducted on populations far removed from the local context. Ironically, it is the rich contextualized data from the voices of its own students and teachers that has the potential to provide local districts with some of the greatest insights for improving teaching and student outcomes.

13

The Literacies of Teaching Urban Adolescents *in These Times*

Susan L. Lytle
University of Pennsylvania

This chapter takes as a starting point the notion that reconceptualizing the literacies in adolescents' lives entails, in part, learning from teachers of adolescents what it means to teach them. Accessing teachers' knowledge most often involves creating a space for the telling and interrogating of stories of practice, a space that permits agency in the ways daily experiences are rendered, framed, and responded to, and a space that embraces the uncertainties and struggles endemic to this work. It also requires particular attention to the context: how teachers understand their work as deeply embedded within the cultures of local classrooms, schools, and school districts.

Secondary school teachers in the School District of Philadelphia have been working for the past several decades under conditions of continuing change and conflict. With racial segregation as a constant, there have been at least four successive and contrasting waves of reform, marked by centralizing, decentralizing, and/or recentralizing the district's role in determining curriculum, instruction, assessment, and school organization. Each wave has reflected the different visions of policymakers, superintendents, boards, and now CEOs. These consecutive waves of reform have been emblematic of and interactive with the political circumstances of the district that several years ago careened into the dissolution of the Board of Education and a state takeover of the school district. Now partially but progressively more privatized, and dealing with the far-reaching implications of federal and state policies, the district and its subcontractors are increasingly turning to publishers for scripted curricula and decontextualized programmed materials, to rigid tracking systems, and to a range of vendors for delivery of much of its teacher induction, professional development, and assessment. The increasing federal role in the way local districts function has thus had a very direct impact on the lives and work of Philadelphia teachers, a trend that is particularly relevant to this volume as No Child Left Behind (NCLB) begins to focus on high schools.

Amidst all of this turbulence swirls the rhetoric of attracting and maintaining a highly qualified teaching force, arguably that much more difficult to attain when urban districts are frantically scrambling just to cover classrooms, especially in the lowest performing and most underresourced middle and secondary schools. It is ironic and unsettling to urban educators (and prospective teachers) that the discourses of teacher deficits have never been more prevalent. Although teachers are widely regarded as the critical factor in improving student performance, critics of urban teachers nevertheless demean urban educators for what they don't know and can't do, for lacking in "content" knowledge, and for needing to be provided detailed and specific instructions for handling every aspect of what is less and less frequently regarded or treated as "professional practice." In many settings, improving teaching—both preservice teacher education and professional development for practicing teachers—has become equated with moving ideas and strategies top-down or outside-in, that is, the mandated implementation of "scientific research-based" practices certified as "best" by policymakers and academics and thus assumed to be universally effective. Regrettably, the debasing and deskilling of teachers and teaching is occurring at the same time district personnel mount a major push to attract capable people to the profession and retain them.

Even in this contradictory climate, and despite these widespread and expensive efforts to standardize sure-fire approaches to elevating student achievement as demonstrated by more and ever higher stakes tests, there has been as yet little compelling evidence for the logic or efficacy of orchestrating reforms that essentially by-pass the potential for teachers to become powerful contributors to positive change rather than ignored, regimented, or vilified as the source and essence of the problem. In my view, demanding high expectations for students while simultaneously holding low expectations for teachers has created serious impediments to districts accomplishing their goals for student outcomes.

RECONCEPTUALIZING TEACHING AS LITERACIES

This chapter draws on teachers' stories about their practice within and beyond their classrooms, stories of the complex social practices that constitute fundamental aspects of their daily work with urban adolescents. By *the literacies of teaching*, I refer here to a critical framework through which classrooms, schools, districts, and communities are viewed as texts with multiple possible interpretations and the potential to become generative sites of inquiry (Lytle, 1995; Lankshear & MacLaren, 1993). Rather than viewing the task of classroom teachers as simply putting distal theory into practice and/or implementing standards and curricula designed by others, the literacies of teaching framework fosters an image of teachers as creating and recreating their own practices and expanded theories of practice through systematic and sustained narrative inquiry that draws on multiple sources and experiences over the professional life span.

Over and against a singular and static image of teaching, no matter how enlightened, the literacies of teaching concept emphasizes the dynamic, complex, local, and deeply contextual nature of teaching, recognizing that teachers and their students are involved in a process of continuous engagement and interrogation of ideas and texts in the context of particular social, political, and cultural formations (Christensen, 1999). The framework thus becomes a heuristic for making visible teachers' active and ongoing investigations of their beliefs and assumptions about students, colleagues, schools, and systems as these inform their evolving practices and understandings of literacy teaching and learning. This conception explicitly counters the cookie-cutter image so commonplace in the current political discourse about education by forwarding a perspective on teaching as an active, intentional, and deliberative act in conditions of uncertainty. To be literate as a teacher means to engage in an ongoing, searching, and sometimes profoundly unsettling dialogue with students, families, administrators, policymakers, and other teachers, who may talk and read and write from very different locations and experiences. Classrooms and schools and communities and districts are like texts, subject to various and often competing interpretations even as they are rich and generative sites of inquiry (Street, 1984, 1995). The concept of the literacies of teaching thus speaks to the pressing need to create collegial contexts for learning that reflect local culture, exist over time, foster enduring relationships and networks, and intentionally interrupt the taken-for-granted alliances of power/knowledge implicit and often explicit in much of the current policy discourse related to teaching and student performance.

Teachers in communities of inquiry position themselves intentionally and self-consciously as learners learning from the daily exigencies of their work (Cochran-Smith & Lytle, 2002). In this process, they make their conceptual frameworks for teaching more explicit to themselves and more visible to others. Inquiry into practice is not primarily about taking on or trying out specific activities and behaviors, but rather about enriching teachers' own *theories* of teaching—by interrogating deeply held beliefs and assumptions and gathering "evidence" from their own and others' work for close and systematic analysis and interpretation (Cochran-Smith & Lytle, 1993). Teachers perceive making themselves vulnerable through story-telling and other forms of inquiry as a critical and powerful act, through which they diminish the potency of isolation, competition, and hegemonic systems that function as barriers both to teaching well and also to taking more meaningful and visible roles in shaping practice and policy in the field.

In this chapter, I present images of the work of teachers of urban adolescents constructed from my experiences in an urban writing project and from learning about teaching with graduate students enrolled in masters and doctoral programs in literacy. Having started The Philadelphia Writing Project (PhilWP) in the late 1980s, I have since taken part in and conducted research on/with many school–university teacher communities wherein participants conduct systematic and intentional inquiry into practice as urban K–12 or adult literacy educators (Cochran-Smith & Lytle, 1992, 1993, 2002; Lytle, 1996; Lytle et al. 1994). I regard my own intermingling of teaching, scholarly work, and professional practice as "working the dialectic"—a deliberative effort at mining the reciprocal, recursive, and symbiotic relationships of research and practice, analysis and action, inquiry and experience (Cochran-Smith & Lytle, 2004). To study and theorize the complex relationships of inquiry, knowledge, and practice has required intense immersion, over time, in contexts where practitioners (and others) share questions and stories of classrooms and schools, coconstruct knowledge about teaching, write and publish their inquiries, and investigate local and wider issues related to learning, language, culture, and literacy (for published accounts, see, for example, Banford et al., 1996; Fecho, 1995; Waff, 1994, 1995).

PROJECT SOULL AS A LEARNING COMMUNITY

One of these teacher inquiry communities that met for 4 years beginning in the late 1990s provides a particularly rich resource for insights about what it means to teach and learn from urban adolescents. Project SOULL, a *Study of Urban Learning* and *Leading*, was designed to investigate how teacher leaders in urban secondary schools define, enact, and assess leadership in relation to school change. Envisioned initially as a 3-year qualitative interview study, at the organizing meeting the project almost immediately morphed into a collaborative inquiry group of secondary school teacher leaders and university graduate students and faculty. Because of their prior experience in the writing project, teachers essentially insisted that SOULL be a space where they could meet regularly face-to-face to articulate and analyze their immediate and long-range concerns. Together we decided on a series of group retreats, to be held on a regular basis, as a setting for surfacing questions about their current issues in urban teaching and leading. Thus the project was transformed because of teachers' urgency about finding a context to struggle openly with day-to-day issues and support each others' efforts in a time of fundamentally destabilizing conditions. As the project evolved, our foci expanded to include not only discussions about how teachers lead, primarily from the classroom, but how they intervene at various levels of the system in the service of social justice and equity for urban students and communities. Group retreats became the primary site for storytelling where participants discussed and debated the meanings of their experiences, drawing on their common and varied interpretive frameworks for analysis, and considering promising actions. SOULL thus became a unique milieu for making public to each other the challenges and fundamental uncertainties of their daily practice.

Participants

The eight women teachers participating in SOULL had been teaching in the school district since the 1970s and, with the exception of one former Philadelphia high school teacher who during the time of the study became an assistant high school principal in a neighboring urban district, were all teaching high school English at various comprehensive and magnet high schools in the city. Composed of four White and four African American teachers, the group was intentionally diverse, parallel to the racial and ethnic makeup of PhilWP that from its inception addressed the teaching of writing and literacy in relation to issues of access and equity. SOULL teachers had been active in the reform initiatives of the 1980s and 1990s and also had track records as teachers and teacher researchers who demonstrated increasing success working with their students in small learning communities they helped craft with their colleagues (Cochran-Smith & Lytle, 1993; Fecho, 1994; Lytle et al., 1994; Waff, 1994). The SOULL group also included what we referred to as the research partners: an adjunct faculty member from a local university; a professor of English at an urban community college in Philadelphia; and me (all White women), as well as women graduate student research assistants, many of whom were formerly secondary teachers (including one Latina and one African American woman).

District Context

Because SOULL coincided with a particularly turbulent and dynamic period for the district, the local policy environment played a prominent role in what was taken up by the SOULL group. Throughout the life span of the SOULL project, the district moved steadily toward mandating specific texts and curricula, and the stakes for student performance on standardized tests continued to rise. During the final 2 years of the project, the organizing structure of small learning communities was threatened in many comprehensive high schools, and the district's cluster organization was dismantled. Other innovations SOULL teachers had worked hard to implement were being subtly or overtly trimmed or eliminated. In recounting their experiences with students, the teachers analyzed the ever-changing profiles of their school and the system, debating how (and whether) it was possible *in these times* for teachers to create and sustain rich learning environments in which urban adolescents would engage significantly with literacy learning and with school.

An Expanded Notion of Practice

From the outset of our work together, some common assumptions about inquiry and practice supported the group's efforts to grapple with and contest various interpretations of what it means to teach urban adolescents. Through PhilWP they had engaged in exploring what it means to have an *expanded notion of practice*, in other words, a deep belief in teachers as leaders in their own classrooms, as makers of knowledge about teaching and learning, and a parallel conviction that the walls of classrooms do not delimit their commitments and responsibilities as educators. Most of the group had also been part of a national discourse about urban teaching through the NWP Urban Sites Network (Banford et al., 1996). From these perspectives, there was a shared ideological stance that teaching is centrally about forming and re-forming frameworks for understanding practice: how students and their teachers construct the curriculum, comingling their experiences, their cultural and linguistic resources, and their interpretive frameworks; how teachers' actions are infused with complex and multilayered understandings of learners, culture, class, gender, literacies, social issues, institutions, herstories and histories, communities, materials, texts, and curricula; and, how teachers work together to develop and alter their questions and interpretive frameworks informed not only by thoughtful consideration of the immediate situation and the particular students they teach and have taught, but also by the multiple contexts within which they work (Cochran-Smith & Lytle, 2001).

Because of the makeup of the group, it was not necessary to spend a period of time figuring out how to talk with one another about critical issues of practice. SOULL teachers had extensive prior experience forming close collegial relationships, sustaining a teacher network within and across schools, and working collaboratively with school staff and administrators to try to improve the quality of teaching and learning in their schools (see Little, 1999; Lytle & Fecho, 1991). In addition, they had had a wide range of opportunities to facilitate formally organized professional development—as part of both writing project and district initiatives—within and beyond their own school and subdistrict sites. They were members of other teacher networks, and all had participated in national educational meetings and conference presentations.

While the participating teachers had these things in common, they also saw their collective work in SOULL—as teachers collaborating with university-based research partners—as a way to access salient differences in their knowledge and perspectives (Abowitz, 1999). Historically, teacher communities in PhilWP have been informed not only by current research in writing and literacy, but also by theories related to critical feminism, race, and ethnicity in which participants included themselves in their critiques of cultural practice and oppression (Cochran-Smith & Lytle, 1992; Delpit, 1995; Dillard, 2000; Lather, 1992; Luke & Gore, 1992; McIntosh, 1988; Nieto, 1995; St. Clair, 1998). Rather than a more narrowly defined or technical orientation, they regarded the social, cultural, and political dimensions of their practice as integral to engaging students and their families and communities in meaningful, agentive learning.

This expanded notion of practice had one further implication: the teachers saw mining their day-to-day work with adolescents with their SOULL colleagues as their primary way to understand what it meant to be truly responsive to the needs of urban students. From these close interactions and from being attuned to the effects of school and district culture on their own classroom work, they also believed they could determine how to make a wider impact in the school and district. This notion of "leading from the classroom"—albeit only recently recognized in the literature as necessary for distributed leadership and professional communities to take hold (Fullan, 1994; Hargreaves, 2003; York-Barr & Duke, 2004)—was a tacit assumption of the teachers in SOULL from the beginning.

For the remainder of the chapter, I re-present two of the interwoven themes about teaching urban adolescents that surfaced in the project: teaching and leading as advocacy for students and as the pursuit of "professional intimacy," both driven by teachers' perceptions of students' needs. I illustrate how teachers who grapple with the complex identities and representations of adolescents learning in and out of school make problematic their work as teachers, their representations of their students and relationships with colleagues, and the representations and attributions about their students made by others.

ADVOCACY FOR STUDENTS

It has almost become a commonplace in much of the professional literature (if not widely visible in practice) that literacy education needs to build intentionally and explicitly on the cultural and linguistic resources that learners at all levels of schooling bring to learning, resources that are explored in this volume from many different perspectives related to the lives of adolescents in school and out. Current accounts of K–12 *teachers'* prior knowledge and experience, however, mostly privilege content knowledge, even over and above the familiar triad of abilities, skills and dispositions. The debate around the meanings of "highly qualified" in NCLB policy has intensified this concern about what teachers know (and don't know) and the degree to which this can be ascertained through tests or course credits. Furthermore, the many arguments in support of standardized curriculum and assessment and its accompanying teacher training packages are often based on the implicit belief that both skills and knowledge need to be transmitted *to* teachers through a process of "embedding intelligence" in the curriculum itself (Lytle, Belzer, & Reuman, 1992). There is less, if any, emphasis on instructional processes that depend on mining the resources of diverse learners. Furthermore, because of the current emphasis on knowing content, the idea of dispositions—what may be construed as a reference to something related to character, temperament, or outlook—is perceived as too soft or obscure to test and are intentionally missing from the design of mandated or scripted instructional materials and curriculum.

At the same time, few would deny that teachers' own educational and life experiences, as learners as well as teachers, influence their formation of dispositions and expectations for teaching as a profession, as well as how they envision and enact their daily practice. As Britzman (1999) puts it, "Teachers' own educational experiences reverberate through each classroom they occupy, ultimately shaping the learning experiences of all of the children they teach" (p. 179).

The Salience of Herstory

In tracing their own educational herstories, all of the SOULL teachers described experiences that were formative of or precursors to taking an advocacy stance for urban students. African American teacher Vanessa Brown remembered being in a racially segregated elementary school with predominantly Black faculty whose personal style she has tried to emulate. She attributes her own success as a student to the high level of respect she was accorded, the many decisions she was allowed to make, and the way her fifth and sixth grade teacher confronted students with their decisions, asking them to explain their choices and their likely consequences. Her teachers were very involved in students' personal lives, listening to their stories and "trying to find opportunities for children to seek power out of their own lives." Her mother urged her to go to Gratz High School (a neighborhood school) over Girl's High School, a prestigious magnet school. There she encountered Marcus Foster, one of the first African American high school principals in Philadelphia and later superintendent in Oakland, California. His message provided a dramatic contrast to her junior high school principal, a White woman who said on her first day there:

> You're now part of the Gillespie student body. Schools all over the nation have a list of the schools and Gillespie Junior High is at the bottom of that list. And when you leave here people will know that you came from Gillespie Junior High.

Marcus Foster at Gratz made a radically different impression. As Vanessa explained it:

> At that time the school was well kept. So you didn't feel like you'd gone to a place that was less than another school. You didn't feel like you were in a place that was demeaning … It was clean, you know, and it was just a nice place to be at. And Marcus Foster … looked kind of distinguished, kind of like W.E.B Dubois. Real look of command. He spoke very intelligently with this booming kind of voice that you just had to listen to … He talked to us about how we could be anything we wanted to be, and high school would be a bridging place. I believe those were his words. And he just told us that from the moment we came into that building everything we ever dreamed of was open to us … And these kinds of words are the kinds of words I now use with students … giving that sense of hope and empowerment and possibility.

Interestingly, Vanessa also connects her experience as a student to those of her teachers, who were encouraged to get involved in teaching and learning beyond the classroom:

> Marcus Foster would do that with his teachers as well as with students, so not only did he try to get students to hold onto hope and looking forward to taking steps up, but he also did that for the staff. So you could see the staff also taking opportunities for leadership, which I hadn't noticed in Junior High School.

Vanessa recollects that what Marcus Foster was doing—empowering students to make choices—was not popular with the district and many believed that was the reason he was not offered the position of superintendent in Philadelphia:

Gratz was one of the schools where we walked out because we wanted Black Studies classes and … The day we marched out, he was on the loudspeaker speaking to students about thinking about what they were doing, and being sure that the choice they had made was a choice they had made in their hearts and not because it was popular. I can just remember his voice as kids were streaming out the door. Some kids streamed out because they believed in what they were doing. Some kids were just on the bandwagon—you know, "Everybody's leaving. I'm leaving." And he stayed in school, and he told teachers that they were not to do anything overt to stop us, but that we should think about what we were doing, and to make sure of that if there were consequences because of walking out … You could just hear his voice over the loudspeaker, and it was a powerful experience. And we walked from Gratz all the way down to the Parkway, in huge numbers, on the news … For the large number of us, we really believed that this was the way we were going to impact change. And that came out of what teachers had taught us in the classroom.

Vanessa also remembers being taken to concerts and the opera, and as a self-determined future history teacher, being encouraged to talk about her research with teachers in different parts of the city and to use university libraries at Penn, Temple, and Drexel and the Free Library, all of which she came to know well during her high school years. Debates outside of school around historical issues would come into the classrooms and "people would cut other classes to come to stand in the history classes to be part of the debates that would go on." Vanessa was explicit that these "heated philosophical debates" opened her up to possibilities for teachers taking risks to encourage that kind of discourse, encouraged by White teachers as well as African Americans:

> And a lot of times they were Caucasian teachers who were leading some of these discussions, and that's one of the things that helped me get a greater realization of how I could fit into the world. Because Caucasian teachers were so challenged to make changes in their own classrooms that they would have these difficult conversations and they wouldn't back down from it …

Vanessa's observations from her own herstory about the linkages between teaching and leading, racial identity and racially explicit content, teacher risk taking and student agency contributed to her growing images of what it meant to be a teacher, a first draft of the theory of practice she would eventually construct and reconstruct as a member of the profession.

Carol Merrill, also an African American teacher, had a much different experience—attending predominately White schools for all of her elementary and secondary education. In the following, she remembers the origin of her own intent to become a teacher:

> In elementary school I taught kids on my street how to draw. I taught Bible School at my church during the summers. There was an internal thrill about helping someone do what they could not do before, about seeing the look of accomplishment on a younger person's face. That desire to teach and the fun of learning new things myself fueled my academic adventures from second grade through high school. Whatever it took to get to college to become a teacher I was willing to do.

Like Vanessa, Carol's trajectory as a student included attention from role models and mentors at key moments in her life:

In ninth grade our pastor hired a youth minister who saw his ministry including Black history and college preparation. He was my first mentor, the first person I interacted with on a regular basis who knew about college and was willing to share. My school district was 95% Caucasian and 80% of the graduates went to college. Reverend Sims filled that academic void I lived in for six years through junior and senior high. He gave color and connection to the academic world I wanted to join. In this environment I learned to push myself, to take advantage of every opportunity even if teachers and counselors did not push me. Rev. Sims was there to provide the extra push. The church was there to provide leadership opportunities that were denied to Black students in school. It did not matter that my school just saw me as an ordinary Black student; my church family saw me and made me a leader...

Going on to college, Carol reports having Black teachers for the first time, learning about Black writers and musicians, and about "revolution in its many forms." With her Black classmates, she started a Black Student Union and organized a Black Arts magazine, for which she became editor. From these and other experiences, she discovered her mission: "to be a good teacher to Black students" in the city.

Marsha Pincus, a White woman, grew up in an area of the city where large high schools were predominantly White and working class. In contrast to Carol, whose racial identity was central to learning as an adolescent outside of school in her community, Marsha's herstory reveals a symbiosis with the intellectual expectations of school and an estrangement from some adults who were critical of her social affiliations:

So who was I as a girl, as a student, as one of nearly 1000 seniors in the class of 1970 at George Washington High School? Number 23 in my class, 93.25 average, but not a member of anything. Anonymous. I actually lied to make up activities under my name in the yearbook, ashamed of the way I went through high school. My friends were the druggies in the lower tracks. I was surly, disaffected, and angry. My family life was falling apart. But SCHOOL, READING, WRITING, they were my refuge. There I performed. There I achieved. There I succeeded. By 12th grade I was slovenly, with ripped jeans, frizzy hair, wore rimmed glasses, tie-dye t-shirts and an attitude—But I did my school work. For me, performing well in school was not just its own reward. It was the promise of escape—from a family which had fallen apart, from a peer group spinning out of control ... I don't know how I got through my senior year. I know I had no social life ... I took an SAT prep course, which my mother paid off at $10 a week and I earned straight A's. I got myself into college. No one there helped at all ... My French teacher told me I was too good for the people I was hanging out with and I hated her forever for that. She should not have bad-mouthed my friends. It was wrong and I vowed as a teacher that I would never do that to any student.

For Marsha, invisibility, alienation, and anonymity were juxtaposed with rich experiences reading and writing, leaving her highly attuned to the extent that adults in school contexts can be counted on or are perceived as "helpers," or not.

Diane Waff, an African American teacher, also had deep roots in the Philadelphia system. Yet her memories of her education as an adolescent highlight the historical gap between students' racial, cultural, and ethnic identities and the underlying assumptions of their secondary education:

I was an only child. I grew up in Philadelphia, attended Philadelphia public schools, and earned my undergraduate degree at the University of Pennsylvania. Although there were many positives in my early school experiences, there were many painful omissions in the curricula and discipline-based texts used in the schools during my formative years. The kind of knowledge seen as important did not include the writing of minorities, women, or members of society who were not politically well positioned. The perspectives that were taught reflected the cultural hegemony of the dominant group. The traditional canon did not allow for the integration of my voice as an African American female or the voices of my male counterparts into the classroom discourse. We were taught by culturally different instructors who privileged their knowledge by ignoring ours. While we were taught to read and write in the dominant discourse to gain the skills necessary to compete in American society, we were never encouraged to question what we read, to critically analyze the status quo, or to struggle with questions relating to the inequities we experienced in our everyday lives. Education was presented as the "Great Escape," not as the way to transform limiting real life conditions.

Other participants had similarly compelling and consequential herstories: One teacher spoke of the Socialist roots in her family and her own struggles in school with testing and learning to read. Another recounted early experiences with anti-war activism, trade unionism, and the painful school experiences of her biracial child. Yet another teacher started a drama club for students at her daughter's school when she held a position as a secretary there, prior to becoming a teacher. Taken as a set, these herstories suggest the inevitable variation in educational backgrounds and cultural and linguistic resources teachers bring to teaching. Articulating these stories, through talk and writing, became ways to trace some of the deep influences on why teachers teach as they do and what they have to teach each other.

Becoming a Student of Students

SOULL teachers talked often and at length about particular students, issues they were facing or had faced working with them, and the many deep lessons they had learned that shaped their concepts of teaching. As Marsha put it:

> I remember my students by the stories they tell. Long after their names and faces have faded, their stories shimmer in my memory with a life of their own ... I have felt most like a teacher in those quiet and private moments of receptivity. The people who know me as a teacher leader know me by the stories I tell about the lessons I have learned from my students' stories.

A key dimension of student advocacy came from teachers' deliberate efforts to become students of their own students. For Carol, this pervasive curiosity began early in her career because what she encountered in schools did not coincide with her lived experience as a Black woman. This required that she take an ongoing stance of inquiry about what it would mean to get students to relate what is being talked about in school to their own lives:

> When I came to Cooke [Middle School in the early 1970s] gang conflict was building up, so my first five years there I kept going to kids' funerals. The gang fights [were] outside the school on the corners. That was the backdrop. That was counter to what I learned and built my own philosophy in terms of what Black people need to be doing ... what makes these kids want to, why do they hate themselves? Why do they want to act the negative things out on each other? They can't do it maybe to the real source and so how do you use the classroom, how do you use literature, how do you use writing to

try and get them to learn more about themselves and to think more highly of themselves? And to get them to ….appreciate what they can do?

In every piece of her herstory, Carol referenced her own uncertainties and questions about how to best relate to and meet students' needs. In the 1980s she was repeatedly transferred among three racially different middle and high schools, one where she remembered students didn't like her because she was "Black and female." Recognizing that the school was mostly White and that none of the students were going to have that many Black teachers (the school at the time had not filled its minority quota of teachers), she made Black literature integral to the curriculum and tried to build relationships with the Black students. In the mid-1980s her middle school was one of the first to get involved in a cross-district writing across the curriculum initiative. There she had unusual opportunities for professional development and meeting other teachers participating in what she termed "ground floor reform in schools." Transferring back to West Philadelphia High School in the early 1990s (where she continues to teach), she became part of an African-centered small learning community where she countered again what she regarded as students' "level of dislike for their culture and themselves" by teaching from an African perspective, inviting Black women, artists, and anthropologists to interact with her students.

Participating in a PhilWP institute on teacher research, Carol interviewed a young student with sickle cell anemia who was frequently out of school and had family problems. Documenting systematically her interactions with this particular student, Carol brought her data to the teacher community and thus "was able to make a big difference in one kid's life." This rhythm of taking courses, documenting what she was learning from her students, and sharing her work with various teacher communities became a pattern in her professional life. Documentation, she suggested, forces you to scrutinize what you are doing, to see "what was really happening" and to make sense by trying to convey these observations and analyses to others. Other teachers learned about students' lives by creating clubs (e.g., for Latino or LGBTQ students), by sponsoring multicultural day performances, and by making the necessary contacts and arrangements so that students could work in their communities. Many of these efforts to advocate for students by knowing more about them were also explicitly designed to help students become leaders themselves.

Coming to know students differently was also integral to the way students were positioned in the taught curriculum. There were numerous discussions in the SOULL group about how essential it is to follow students (as opposed to the script) when discussing literature, to use noncanonical texts, to make spaces for their many different stories and interpretations. In Marsha's Gratz High School classroom, for example, in the face of increasing standardization, she began working with local playwrights who were part of the Philadelphia Young Playwrights Festival (PYPF). Through collaborating with writers, Marsha said she was "invited into her [African American] students' lives through playwriting" and through these experiences, she reimagined her responsibilities to her students. When she moved to a magnet school, however, this desire to be a student of her students took an unexpected turn:

I mean, Masterman is different … And I will say … that magnet schools have done far more to damage community schools than these charter schools ever will. I understand the complications and complexities of all that. I know why there's magnet schools … to keep white kids in the city, white families from fleeing. And, well, that's another whole story. This girl said to me at Masterman on Friday, she asked me if this was true ... She asked me if I could tell her, that she had heard something and she really wanted to know if it was true. White girl who lives in the northeast, gone to Masterman since fifth grade. She told me that she heard that the inner city schools like West Philadelphia, University City and Gratz are getting all the supplies and that the supplies are just sitting there and they don't know what to do with them. And the reason that Masterman and Conwell and these other schools in the Northeast aren't getting their supplies is because they have to give it to the inner city schools to make it look good and because the parents at Masterman and these other places will go out and have fundraisers and get money for materials ... She meant it. So in some ways, when I was able to say to her, "No, Sarah, this isn't true, this is some crazy story, this is like urban folklore. Let's deconstruct it and figure out where it's coming from." ...

The telling of this story made an opening for Marsha to try to teach the student, over time and in various contexts, where stories like these come from and what they represent. Trusting relationships with students obviously make it more possible for a teacher to advocate for a student, in this case, by intervening in a White student's uninterrogated perception of herself as inherently superior to others.

Diane discussed her way of advocating for students by inviting them to the table as discussants with teachers. She began by creating discussion groups for students to talk about their experiences in her courses and their desires for change. This evolved into a Girl Talk group (Waff, 1994) and other initiatives where student voices and experiences were sought after not only as learning support but also to enable students to play a wider role in influencing practices and policies in schools. A recurrent pattern in Diane's practice involved identifying innovative ways to bring students into conversations typically reserved for adults and to insert their voices into teachers' professional development by drawing on students' written work.

Intervening on Behalf of Students

Teachers' interventions on behalf of students took a variety of forms. Diane describes her disposition to question herself and her aspirations for students as a kind of stance, a set of deep questions that guide her practice:

> I'm thinking about what it is that really drives the work that we do. In my role, I see myself as an African American teacher leader, and African American really has double lines under it for me. In my cluster there are not many Black leaders. There's one Black principal and I am the African American Teaching and Learning Coordinator. And what I find is that who I am as a person of color has made me very sensitive to the experiences of the African American and Asian American students and teachers who go to school and work in that community. And it's always in my mind, what kind of experience do they have in these schools? And my own experience: What kind of experience am I having? How do I resist or change a lot of what I perceive as very discriminatory practices that go on, even to book selection, to the kind of curriculum that's taught? How do I work with teachers on an ongoing basis to talk about these issues and to think about what they're teaching, how they're working with colleagues, how they're viewing what's going on in the school system, what it is that they object to and why they object to it? How do we work together to change things?

Carol, too, speaks to a set of fundamental beliefs that inform her day-to-day decisions about how to think about what she is doing:

I'm like a surrogate parent. I'm fighting for kids, for basic things. This one student got a scholarship from the school and it's September and the kid hasn't gotten the money. So he's borrowing books. When other kids finish studying he'll call them up and see if he can borrow their books … and so [during my sabbatical] I'm coming and I'm bugging people to the point that now a check is to be going out to him on Tuesday. So I'm a pain in the ass at school this year. So that's what I am trying to explain to people when they say, "You're on sabbatical; why are you here?" I have a right to come into the school. Just because I'm on sabbatical doesn't mean that my teaching stops and my relationships with students stop.

As already mentioned, many of the teachers in SOULL sponsored marginalized groups of students in activities. They also regularly sought to redress specific injustices they perceived had been visited upon students by the system. For example, White teacher Mickey Harris' stories of advocating for students at Central High School through a range of interventions speak strongly to the centrality of this role for SOULL teachers. Over the life span of the project, Mickey spoke about supporting and intervening for a student who was raped; confronting the administration of her school on the inequitable treatment of late students based on race; intervening on behalf of a student and his father to keep the child from being expelled; interceding with the principal about changing a student's roster necessitated by barriers to communication based on language, race, and class; creating a Latino student association; supporting diverse body images among members of the cheerleading squad; protesting the expulsion of a National Merit Scholar who was being kicked out for looking like a "thug;" protesting the administration's prerogative to discriminate against Latino students purportedly around issues of lateness and drugs; advocating for a student to be able to go to the prom; going to the administration about a teacher who consistently failed Latino students; walking out of a retirement dinner in response to sexist, insulting jokes and trying to model resistance responsibly for students; speaking out against colleagues' derogatory comments about pregnant students and students with low grades; calling parents of summer school students to give them good news of their children's progress; finding a placement for a homeless young woman; and having students write about suicides at her school and other problematic topics. On one particularly memorable day, Mickey intervened on behalf of an Asian student:

I had this wonderful young woman in my class who didn't tell me why she had been out for three weeks and the discipline office told me, "I think her brothers are part of an Asian gang in South Philly so she'll probably be dropping out." And they wrote this stuff down and they said, "Don't be easy on her. She's on daily report." You see, when our school sees Asian students they assume they must be members of gangs, particularly if they live in South or Southwest Philly. But I said to her, "Kim, why were you out?" And she got all clouded up and she said, "You're the first person who asked me. My sister killed herself two weeks ago." Here is a child whose nurturing is, whose background is, you don't tell people your business, particularly your family business, so assumptions were made. I was ready to say, "Well, here's your daily report. It has to be signed by me and everybody else." And then I just thought it didn't feel right. And believe me, I apologized to her and ran around to the discipline office to give them shit. The system, the institution, the school, was saying to her, "You've been out for three weeks. Your family doesn't speak English. You're on daily report. You better watch your tail."

When asked by one of the graduate students, "So, you apologized for the institution?" Mickey replied, "But I'm part of the institution so I'm very much a part of that apology."

Another whole category of interventions related to teachers' willingness to participate in district-sponsored test construction or curriculum writing or book selection or any of the myriad tasks that were designated to teachers at that period of the district's history. Teachers saw volunteering to participate in these activities as related to their concern for what would be foisted on students as a consequence of teachers not speaking up on their behalf. Dina Portnoy, a White teacher at University City High School, tried to counter what she felt was a pervasive attitude about urban students and their commitment to their education:

> In spite of what you see as resistance to learning, the fact is that most (and I mean most) of the kids really resent the fact that they haven't been "educated." And they know it …. It's not necessarily considered hip to be complaining about it, but they do, and you have to assume that they really do want some education. Otherwise, why go in every day? If you enter the classroom believing they are "unteachable" you will surely communicate that to them, and they'll be insulted. Trust me on that.

In describing how and why they entered teaching, many teacher leaders explicitly named their involvement with movements for social justice as a prime motivating factor. This naming of activism within struggles for civil rights, women's liberation, and workers' rights frames their practice as teachers and teacher leaders as a form of political activism, a construct in which student advocacy is one manifestation.

PROFESSIONAL INTIMACY

Carol introduced the term *professional intimacy* during the first whole group retreat (September 1999). She was naming the kinds of issues and ideas she would like to explore in SOULL and noted that the idea of "professional intimacy" came to her mind when thinking about her experience in PhilWP and especially about her relationship to Mardys Leeper, a White teacher also a member of PhilWP and a colleague at her high school. In this section I trace some of the teachers' definitions and enactments of professional intimacy as another way of understanding how student advocacy was accomplished and represented in SOULL. Connectedness to colleagues enabled teachers to deepen and extend their practice, not only by collaborative work but by the inevitably productive and sometimes painful conflicts that occur when teachers together interrogate their fundamental beliefs and practices in and beyond the classroom.

Connecting On Behalf of Students' Life Chances

For Carol (and others), professional intimacy described collegial relationships that fostered a space for experimentation, a context for naming perceived weaknesses in one's practice, posing questions about students and school culture, and collaborating in analyses of events and issues. Formed through the recognition of shared philosophies that could support joint work on special projects, curriculum development, and the creation of new opportunities for students, this kind of relationship also functioned as a catalyst for doing work beyond the conventional curriculum but critical to the intellectual life of students. For example, in her first dialogue, Carol described coteaching at her high school with Eleanor Novek, a Penn doctoral student/journalist, and beginning a community newspaper. She depicted her partnership with this woman as two professionals from different arenas working together to create an educational experience for students. The community focus of the paper "forced [her] out of the classroom," out of her "comfort zone," and into a space where she could "read" her students in new ways. The newspaper provided a context for taking a closer look, talking about students' strengths, and inventing ways to group them effectively for various aspects of the research and production processes. She and this graduate student coplanned, cotaught, and engaged in daily journaling and dialogue. Doing ever more explicit analysis and interpretation of the work—because of the close collaboration—became critical to Carol's practice.

Carol often cited Mardys as the reason why she did certain things. In their small learning community (SLC), she and Mardys voluntarily took on roles as the "workers," "doers:" the "solid rocks," who were always planning and writing up notes. For a project on the underground railroad, Carol, Mardys, and another PhilWP teacher, recognizing the potential value of truly cross-disciplinary inquiry to their students, tried to pull in the math and science teachers. Concerned about West High School students not going on to college and wanting to provide more assistance to students in the application process, Carol and her colleagues brought these concerns and ideas to the SLC and ended up inventing what they called "the Achievers Club," a student-centered project she documented systematically and shared through participation in another PhilWP inquiry community made up of teachers, parents, and students investigating the implementation of the standardized curriculum from their diverse locations (Gold, Rhodes, Brown, Lytle, & Waff, 2001). This was not a simple coming together around shared purpose; Carol reports that there were times when she "dragged" Mardys into things and visa versa. Mardys took the lead in starting a media arts project, for example, which required not just grant writing but creating a media lab and writing curriculum for themselves and other teachers, as well as doing professional development for others participating. All this was accomplished in what Carol described as conditions at West "in an environment of chaos and disorder."

There are many other permutations of the concept of "professional intimacy" that marked the work of these urban teachers as student advocates. As the concept became part of the group's discourse, many of the instances discussed had a very positive valence. Marsha collaborated with an Alaskan teacher she met through a national teacher research group modeled after PhilWP's cross-visitation program. She and the Alaskan teacher had their students sending their plays back and forth between Ketchikan, Alaska and north Philadelphia, thereby encountering firsthand each other's social and cultural worlds and making a space for a kind of multicultural education beyond even what published literature could afford. Dina worked closely with colleagues in her SLC when they wanted to expel a student whom Dina believed, with an appropriate contract, would have a real chance of making it in school. Later she used her network with teachers outside the SLC to advocate for the same student, who was going to be expelled for fighting, a situation Dina knew was not of the student's making. In both cases, it was the long-term professional connections that made it possible for Dina to work on the student's behalf, a reflection of the kinds of networks and relationships that are often needed to enable urban students to stay in school and learn. Vanessa, an English teacher, kept a dialogue journal over many years with a math teacher, as a way to counter what they perceived to be an antichild, antieducation atmosphere in the school; together, they used the journal to try to better understand their students and make their classrooms compelling environments for learning.

Collegial Relationships as Sites of Struggle

Like other teacher leaders, Vanessa and African American teacher Annette Sample emphasized the centrality of collaboration with colleagues to their teaching, learning, and leading. However, both also raised issues of tension and failure around collaboration, noting, for example, how pursuing collaborative relationships can actually further a sense of isolation. Annette, for example, elected to bypass her colleagues when they were unresponsive and develop a series of student-centered, student-led activities beyond the regular curriculum. In Vanessa's case, working with colleagues collaboratively (or trying to) created a context in which pedagogical and philosophical values came into contention, where she, like Annette, risked distancing or even hostility in order to foster change.

Going against the grain of institutional racism, sexism, and classism by holding alternative views of students and pedagogical practices can be a treacherous process with uncertain outcomes. Vanessa, for example, began to conceptualize writing a grant that would bring together special education teachers, a group that rarely has the chance to work together. This experience was the most sustained collaborative effort ever attempted in her SLC. She invited other special ed teachers to develop interdisciplinary curricula, a process that involved pulling three classes together and a move that went against the tradition of special education teachers working alone. Vanessa tried to be a catalyst for the change but soon realized she was always the one responsible for coming up with ideas, organizing meetings, and so on. Their interactions around the proposal surfaced conflicting notions of collegial relationships, pedagogical practice, and perspectives on students, resulting in tension and isolation that impacted not only the grant work but had ramifications across the SLC: a severe "breech" in one relationship, fracturing of others.

Later in the year, in response to strict mandates around testing, Vanessa met with two trusted colleagues to discuss their concerns and responses. She eventually decided to resist the mandates, recounting this story as an example for others to reflect on how taking a stance like this—even when done by just one teacher in one room—can serve as a form of teacher leadership, what she calls *unprofessional professional development*. In her view, acting alone was productive, resulting in a positive change in her practice and more meaningful and substantive encounters with her colleagues.

Another set of stories related to risk in professional relationships surfaced when Diane spoke about her relationship with Ellen, a White woman and new member of PhilWP, at almost every retreat. Although then the Teaching and Learning Coordinator of a subdistrict of the school district, Diane chose to spend part of her time coconstructing and coteaching an English class with Ellen. The course, "Literature of Social Vision and Social Change," was designed to engage students in examining the social construction of systems of race, class, and gender oppression in human society and to prepare students to meet the district's standards for eleventh-grade English.

Tensions related to race, class, and sexuality emerged in the coteaching relationship and were worked through in front of the students. In these situations, Diane saw it as her professional responsibility to confront assumptions so that alternative perspectives could be forwarded. These situations were often personally challenging and painful for both Diane and Ellen:

> Well, it's not even easy with Ellen and I because the first day I was in there, it's just interesting the images the people have of different schools and she made a statement about, you know, if she were at Ben Franklin [HS] or King [HS], I don't even know if she said Olney [HS], that kids bump into each other in the hall and then they just either curse each other out or fight each other or something. She didn't say it that explicitly, but she was making a statement about Northeast having like 3,400 kids and it's really crowded in the hall and how different it would be if we were at Gratz or …

At that moment in the dialogue, I asked for clarification about whether this was being said privately or in front of students, and Diane affirmed the latter:

> I said, "Because that wasn't my experience at Olney. I didn't experience that. I didn't see people bumping into each other and getting into large altercations around things like that. I mean, it wasn't that volatile." And then another student said, "Yeah, that's just a stereotype." And then she said, "Well, I had a student from King who told me that." And I said, "Well, maybe it's important for us to think about that statement and what it means and what images people take away when you make statements like that." And, you know, the kids got involved in the conversation and I felt proud of them. I felt distressed that she would say something like that. I'm thinking, "Why would she say something like that?" It just made me see, you know, the work is never done, that you constantly have to have these conversations, you have to engage your kids in conversations … I need to be here, I need to be that other point of view, to provide just another way of seeing the world. And we need to feel comfortable challenging each other.

Diane remembers being very upset that day, and trying to work it through with Ellen:

> "You know, aren't you aware of the images that you're putting out there? And that's what people are saying about the Black kids who are coming to Northeast, that we're bringing with us this hoodlum way of interacting to this school, that we're destroying the environment up here … It really put me in a difficult place and I had to contain myself not to lash out at you, but I was disappointed that you would say something like that." So we wrestle with those kinds of things together and recently we've been calling [SOULL teacher] Mickey … we have conference calls around how to present these issues in the classroom, how do you intelligently get these differing perspectives and what kinds of writing experiences and interactive experiences do you provide in the classroom? And she's shared with us a lot of what she's done …

Sometimes the clash occurred within the SOULL group itself when complexities surfaced around advocating and the extent and nature of teachers' responsibilities to students who fail and to the system itself. Dina and Diane frequently found themselves seemingly on different sides of these issues, for example, on the occasion when a debate broke out about whether teachers should be responsible for writing descriptions of their students who failed so that summer school faculties could use them in planning instruction. Dina takes the first shot at this:

This is some of the tension that Diane and I have a tendency to talk about … around this advocacy for kids … And a very little example is … a week before school closed we were given these forms that we had to fill out for each 9th grader who failed. And, the purpose of them, although I suspect they're not going to be used this way, because I think they'll get lost in the paper shuffle, but the purpose was when these kids go to summer school the teachers would have information about the kids—which is not a bad purpose. But we got them a week before school ended. I had a pile of final exams to read. I had grades to do. I had a classroom to clean up. I had preparation to do. Fundamentally, my response when the vice principal gave them to me, she said, "And they're due Friday" and I said, "Well, I'm not going to do them by Friday." And she said, "Well, you're taking a risk." I said, "Tell you what, write me up" was my response to that. And I wasn't the only one … Within and against the system is very complicated because the way in which the school district did that, although they could say it was in the best interest of the kids, the way they did that belied that notion.

Diane announced that she wanted to respond with a counterstory of her own:

I think those forms are pretty damn important in terms of teachers having some knowledge of who the kids are who are sitting in front of them because if you're going to fail masses of students, you need to take the time to fill out the form. And I make sure that I go to every school, that those forms are filled out, and I had the teachers who are working in our summer program, we paid them for four hours to go through all of the forms … That's the purpose for summer school—to help students who weren't able to master the work during the school year, they're supposed to get intensive support …. I went back to the teachers and said, "If you flunked this child, I want to know more information. What kinds of things did you do? Where does he need help?" I think that that's part of the obligation of being a teacher, to care about the kids … And when we sat there with those forms, [we] were reading them through and saying, you know, "How could somebody write something like that?" and that is the culture that I try to cultivate. We even had some teachers in our room who wrote these forms that had no information on it and I remember pulling one up and I said, "Barbara G.?" and she was sitting right there. She was one of the subs for our program and I called her up and I said, "What are we supposed to do with this? We don't know anything about this kid. What kind of help does he need? What should we do with him in this summer?" She didn't write anything.

Margo Ackerman, a White teacher at University City High School, laughed and said:

Well, I'm with Barbara [laughs] because although I understood what you said, … I've had lots of experience with IEPs and I know the language of special ed. But this form, Diane, and the amount of time they gave us to do it. They ask you to describe a child in between lines that I can't even see the spaces between. So they're not, to me, they're not really interested. There's no way that I can explain why a child failed in two little lines that says, "Well, how should they be assessed? What is their learning style?" … if they cared about the kids that were failing in my class, they would have allowed time to sit down and discuss with me or they would have given me time to write anecdotals that would really have shared what this kid was like. This was purely a cover your ass form.

To Margo and the group, Diane replied with a question: "What do you see is the obligation of teachers towards those students that they failed?" and a deep discussion ensued about teachers' responsibilities in influencing the ways policies are enacted.

WHO NEEDS TO HEAR THE STORIES OF TEACHERS OF URBAN ADOLESCENTS?

Teachers like those in Project SOULL do not oppose standards, the need for highly qualified teachers, the assessment of outcomes, or policies that seek to rectify long-standing inequities in the system. What they resist is the gross oversimplification of the complexity of the task at hand, the proliferation of policies and high-stakes tests that fail to take into account that teaching is not fundamentally technical work, but rather what many have argued is a highly complex, deliberative, and adaptive process (see, for example, Meier, 1992; Zumwalt, 1982). They know from the inside out that repetitive presentation and testing of material is not the primary way to improve student performance and is least likely to engage urban adolescents who often have more reasoned and studied resistance to business as usual in schools.

Drawing from the case of Project SOULL, what is at stake here is nothing less than urban student survival (a preeminent goal of student advocacy) and urban teacher survival (a probable consequence of significant student-focused professional collaboration). Arguments for democratic education make a clear case for the relationship between teachers' active participation in the cultures of teaching and schooling and the lessons that are learned by students who observe their teachers being and becoming agents of change (Fuhrman & Lazerson, 2005; Johnson, 2005). Highly significant instruction occurs everyday beyond delivery of the mandated curriculum. And whereas it would be difficult to claim that Project SOULL represents a "typical" case of work accomplished in teacher groups, one can argue that these teachers' insights and struggles, their interpretations and enactments of leadership from within and beyond the classroom, provide a telling case of the literacies of teaching urban adolescents that might inform the work of teacher educators and those responsible for creating learning opportunities for experienced urban teachers *in these times*.

As Johnson (2005) points out, recent studies of new teachers suggest that most will not make the kind of lifetime commitment to urban education that is evidenced in the careers of the teachers in Project SOULL; the next generation is much more likely to have what are termed *serial careers*. Yet evidence is also accumulating that those who elect to teach will come expecting to have opportunities to grow in the profession, to exercise influence beyond the classroom. It is not surprising, then, that schools that promote interdependence and space for teachers to take a meaningful role in curriculum development and to participate actively in the shaping of school culture are more likely to retain those new to the profession.

These stories of urban teachers reflect their fundamental need to understand their students' aspirations, strengths, resilience, and struggle; as literacy educators, they recognize the seriousness of what is at stake in their everyday teaching, within and beyond the classroom. Their choices as leaders are often motivated by a heightened awareness of their own identities and the identities of their students, and of the power of teaching so that adolescents learn to advocate for themselves. Because many current policies related to the literacies of urban adolescents factor out or do not acknowledge or address the complexities of teaching as a deeply social, cultural, and political practice, there is much to be learned from the stories of teachers who understand this profoundly and are willing to make public the challenges and uncertainties essential to this work.

ACKNOWLEDGMENTS

I would like to acknowledge the Spencer and MacArthur Foundations and the Graduate School of Education at the University of Pennsylvania for support of Project SOULL. I would also like to thank Elizabeth Cantafio and Torch Lytle for superb feedback on drafts of this chapter and Kelly Wissman for valuable assistance in data collection and analysis for Project SOULL.

REFERENCES

Abowitz, K. K. (1999). Reclaiming community. *Educational Theory. 49*(2), 143–159.

Banford, H., Berkman, M., Chin, C., Cziko, C., Fecho, B., Jumpp, D. et al. (1996). *Cityscapes: Eight views from the urban classroom.* Berkeley, CA: National Writing Project.

Britzman, D. P. (1999). Cultural myths in the making of a teacher: Biography and social structure in teacher education. In E. Mintz & J. T. Yun (Eds.), *The complex world of teaching: Perspectives from theory and practice* (pp. 179–192). *Harvard Educational Review, 56*(4), 442–456.

Christensen, L. M. (1999). Critical literacy: Teaching reading, writing, and outrage. In C. Edelsky (Ed.), *Making justice our project: Teachers working towards critical whole language practice* (pp. 53–67). Urbana, IL: National Council of Teachers of English

Cochran-Smith, M., & Lytle, S. L. (1992). Interrogating cultural diversity: Inquiry and action. *Journal of Teacher Education, 43*(2), 104–115.

Cochran-Smith, M., & Lytle, S. L. (1993). *Inside/outside: Teacher research and knowledge.* New York: Teachers College Press.

Cochran-Smith, M., & Lytle, S. L. (2001). Beyond certainty: Taking an inquiry stance on practice. In A. Lieberman & L. Miller (Eds.), *Teachers caught in the action: Professional development that matters* (pp. 45–60). New York: Teachers College Press.

Cochran-Smith, M., & Lytle, S. L. (2002). Teacher learning communities. In J. Guthrie (Ed.), *Encyclopedia of education* (2nd ed., pp. xx). New York: Macmillan.

Cochran-Smith, M., & Lytle, S. L. (2004). Practitioner inquiry, knowledge, and university culture. In J. Loughran, M. L. Hamilton, V. K. LaBoskey, & T. Russell (Eds.), *International handbook of research in self-study of teaching and teacher education practices* (pp. 601–650). Dordrecht/Boston/London: Kluwer.

Delpit, L. (1995). *Other people's children: Cultural conflict in the classroom.* New York: New Press.

Dillard, C. B. (2000). The substance of things hoped for, the evidence of things not seen: Examining an endarkened feminist epistemology in educational research and leadership. *Qualitative Studies in Education, 13*(6), 661–681.

Fecho, B. (1995). Language inquiry and critical pedagogy: Co-investigating power in the classroom. In M. Fine (Ed.), *Chartering urban school reform: Reflections on public high schools in the midst of change* (pp. 180–191). New York: Teachers College Press.

Fuhrman, S., & Lazerson, M. (Eds.). (2005). *The public schools.* New York: Oxford University Press.

Fullan, M. (1994). Teacher leadership: A failure to conceptualize. In D. Wallin (Ed.), *Teachers as leaders: Perspectives on the professional development of teachers* (pp. 241–253). Bloomington, IN: PDK Educational Foundation.

Gold, E., Rhodes, A., Brown, S., Lytle, S. & Waff, D. (2001). *Clients, consumers, or collaborators? Parents and their roles in school reform during children achieving. 1995–2000.* Philadelphia: Consortium for Policy Research in Education.

Hargreaves, A. (2003). *Teaching in the knowledge society: Education in the age of insecurity.* New York: Teacher's College Press.

Johnson, S. M. (2005). Working in schools. In S. Fuhrman & M. Lazerson (Eds.), *The public schools.* New York: Oxford University Press.

Lankshear, C., & McLaren, P.L. (1993). *Critical literacy: Politics, praxis and the postmodern.* Albany: State University of New York Press.

Lather, P. (1992). Post-critical pedagogies: A feminist reading. In C. Luke & J. Gore (Eds.), *Feminisms and critical pedagogy* (pp. 120–137). New York: Routledge.

Little, J. W. (1999). Organizing schools for teacher learning. In L. Darling-Hammond & G. Sykes (Eds.), *Teaching as the learning profession: Handbook of policy and practice* (pp. 233–262). San Francisco: Jossey-Bass.

Luke, C., & Gore, J. (Eds.). (1992). *Feminisms and critical pedagogy.* New York: Routledge.

Lytle, S. L. (1995, May). The literacies of teaching. *Graduate School of Education News,* 4–13. Philadelphia: University of Pennsylvania.

Lytle, S. L. (1996). "A wonderfully terrible place to be:" Learning in practitioner inquiry communities. In P. Sissel (Ed.), *The future of community-based literacy* (pp. 85–96). San Francisco: Jossey Bass.

Lytle, S., Belzer, A., & Reumann, R. (1992). *Invitations to inquiry: Rethinking staff development in adult literacy education.* Technical Report TR92-2. Philadelphia: National Center on Adult Literacy.

Lytle, S. L., Christman, J., Countryman, J., Fecho, R., Portnoy, D., & Sion, F. (1994). Learning in the afternoon: When teacher inquiry meets school reform. In M. Fine (Ed.), *Chartering urban school reform: Reflections on public high schools in the midst of change* (pp. 157–179). New York: Teachers College Press.

Lytle, S. L., & Fecho, R. (1991). Meeting strangers in familiar places: Teacher collaboration by cross-visitation. *English Education, 23*(1), 5–28.

McIntosh, P. (1988). *White privilege: Unpacking the invisible knapsack.* Excerpt from: *White privilege and male privilege: A personal account of coming to see correspondences through work in women's studies.* (Working paper No. 189). Wellesley, MA: Wellesley College Center for Research on Women.

Meier, D. (1992). Reinventing teaching. *Teachers College Record, 93*(4), 594–609.

Nieto, S. (1995). *Affirming diversity; The sociopolitical context of multicultural education* (2nd ed.). New York: Longman.

St. Clair, R. (1998). On the commonplace: Reclaiming community in adult education. *Adult Education Quarterly, 49*(1), 5–14.

Street, B. (1984). *Literacy in theory and practice.* New York: Cambridge University Press.

Street, B. (1995). *Social literacies: Critical approaches to literacy in development, ethnography and education.* New York: Longman.

Waff, D. (1994). Girl talk: Creating community through social exchange. In M. Fine (Ed), *Chartering urban school reform: Reflections on public high schools in the midst of change* (pp. 192–203). New York: Teachers College Press.

Waff, D. (1995). Romance in the classroom: Inviting discourse on gender and power. *The Quarterly of the National Writing Project and the Center for the Study of Writing and Literacy, 17*(2), 15–18.

York-Barr, J., & Duke, K. (2004). What do we know about teacher leadership? Findings from two decades of scholarship. *Review of Educational Research, 74*(3), 255–316.

Zumwalt, K. (1982). Research on teaching: Policy implications for teacher education. In A. Lieberman & M. McLaughlin (Eds.), *Policy making in education: 81st Yearbook of the National Society for the Study of Education* (pp. 215–248). Chicago: University of Chicago Press.

14

Learning From Learners: Student Voices and Action Research

Jody Cohen
Bryn Mawr/Haverford College

Cambria Allen
Heather Davis
Li Huan Lai
Bryn Mawr College

Bruce Bowers
Mastery Charter School

Elena Darling-Hammond
Haverford College

This chapter examines an action research project in which college students worked with urban secondary school students in two sites to coresearch and take action on an education-related issue. At the high school, students investigated the dress code and presented their research and recommendations to the administration. At the middle school, students investigated the implications of the No Child Left Behind Act (NCLB) for urban schools, and wrote letters to the president and the Kerry campaign. In both instances, the processes of locating the issues, developing the research, and communicating findings required that the secondary students discover and express their perspectives in new ways and that the college students listen and respond in new ways. While both projects led to products or "actions," the processes also offer insights and questions about youths' identities in relation to making knowledge, coming to voice, and instigating change. Furthermore, through reflecting on this project, we have reached fresh understandings of literacy that we believe have implications for teachers, learners, and researchers.

We argue here for action research with adolescents as both a powerful venue for teaching and learning literacy and a compelling way to learn *about* teaching and learning literacy. First, when action research focuses on students' (rather than researchers' or teachers') concerns, it is likely to elicit and make audible a broad register and range of student voices as students engage in meaning making for themselves and others (Rudduck, 2002; Shultz & Cook-Sather, 2001; Weis & Fine, 2000). Second, in this project, all of us from our positions as teachers, researchers, and students struggled within and against standard expectations about literacy. Our goals as action researchers made us confront the ongoing tension between honoring a critical perspective on language and schooling on the one hand and recognizing the primacy of the mainstream "language of power" (Delpit, 1998) on the other. Third, action research entails its own set of literacy skills, evident in the tools required to draft, implement, and document an interview. This "action research literacy" throws into relief skills embedded in more conventional forms of literacy teaching and learning. Finally, action research is a radical form of research, utilizing and challenging the conventions much as critical literacy utilizes and challenges conventional literacy. As such, action research can help to illuminate an expanded definition of literacy that includes a multiplicity of literacies and shifts the locus of authority to bring students into a position of more power *vis a vis* their own learning.

Although we worked with two school sites, we developed our thinking about literacy teaching and learning and action research together, using cross-site comparisons to help us come to fuller understandings. We begin with a description of the sites. Then we organize the chapter according to a linked series of insights/hypotheses about literacy teaching and learning through employing action research. Within each section, we offer an insight arising from our work, along with vignettes intended to clarify, instantiate, and raise questions arising from this work. Finally, we argue for a reconsideration of literacy as a venue for not only increasing students' repertoire of competencies but also for expanding the discourses and meanings to which we all have access.

THE COLLEGE AND SECONDARY SITES

This project sits at the intersection of several college and K–12 programs: The project is based in a course within the Education Program at Bryn Mawr and Haverford Colleges. The field component is arranged through Bryn Mawr's Praxis Program, and in this case Jody, the course teacher, had a grant to develop a community-based research component. Her purpose was three-fold: to highlight for students the relationship of theory to practice; to engage with urban schools in ways that meet real needs and desires; and to use action research to develop students' skills and to impact their situation.

The college has been developing partner relationships over several years with both secondary school sites, a charter high school called City Charter High School (CCHS) and a middle school with its college access program, called Urban Middle School (UMS) and College Prep. This chapter represents our work in these sites during the spring semester of 2004. The co-authors include four undergraduates, referred to as teacher-researchers (Heather and Li Huan at CCHS, Cambria and Elena at UMS), the high school teacher (Bruce), and the college teacher (Jody). We write from our distinct roles as well as collectively. Our intent is to share what we learned about teaching and learning literacy, with the hope of enriching others' understandings of literacy and of how action research can enhance, deepen, and complicate "coming to voice."

CCHS is located in the bustling center of the city. The entrance is reminiscent of an office building, and the theme of professionalizing education permeates the school. A sign on the wall declares the mission of the school in huge letters: ALL STUDENTS LEARN THE SKILLS THEY NEED TO REALIZE THEIR DREAMS. The school is divided into a Lower House and an Upper House, and all students are required to dress professionally. The head of the school is the "CEO" and has a corporate background, and several large corporations sponsor the school.

At the time of our research, the school was in its third year, with approximately 300 students. It boasts relatively small classes, a technology-infused curriculum, courses organized around projects, and a "mastery" system according to which students must attain competence in a subject area in order to go on to the next level. While six college students worked in three classrooms at CCHS, here Heather and Li Huan share their experiences working with Bruce's mainly first-year Humanities class of 26 students. As Heather noted in her field log, "When we asked them (on the first day) what they wanted to research, what came up overwhelmingly was the dress code." The college students met with the class every Friday to conduct research on the dress code. Li Huan facilitated a group that constructed, distributed, and analyzed surveys, while Heather worked with students to write and conduct interviews. The team analyzed the data and presented their work to the school administration.

UMS is located in the west end of the city in an area populated mainly by working-class African Americans living in tightly packed row houses on the edge of the river. Although the building is far from new, its architecture suggests that it was once a masterpiece. Atop a series of granite steps, all but one of the windowless metal doors is padlocked. In the foyer, a huge banner proclaims that the school met minimum standards set forth by NCLB: WE MADE AYP [Adequate Yearly Progress] IN 2003. Above this is an American flag; below is the visitor check-in, requiring valid photo identification. The library has been closed since the librarian took early retirement and the gym doubles as a cafeteria. Of the more than 1,100 students enrolled here, 99% are African American, with 70% considered to be low income. Like CCHS, UMS has a dress code.

College Prep is a federally funded program geared toward readying students in Grades 6 to 12 for higher education. Students need only express interest and obtain a parent's signature to enroll. The program offers assistance with the college preparatory process, including college and career workshops, visits to college campuses, and summer academic institutes. The college students planned and conducted a weekly college prep class, beginning with a loose curriculum that they adapted to address student concerns.

LITERACY: DEFINITIONS AND CONSIDERATIONS

In this chapter we use the action research projects we conducted with urban students to explore literacy as a communicative tool, embedded in a specific context and involving a personal journey or struggle. We acknowledge and deem as important the fact that the students with whom we worked tended to make and communicate meaning in a range of ways including the use of African American English Vernacular. Thus our task involved both respecting and supporting their evolving identities as intertwined with their meaning making and helping them to stretch their communicative skills to meet expectations held by their readers or listeners, the intended recipients of their communications. Furthermore, because the project involved action research, our goal required that our students communicate with recipients clearly and compellingly, such that students would be effective in voicing their understandings and effecting change.

We begin with the premise that being literate in an area involves more than just knowledge in terms of information, but also entails being able to understand meaning and communicate within that area. Gee (2003) distinguishes between the passive accumulation of content and active engagement with the text in order to make and apply meaning. To be literate is not only to know, but also to be able to use that knowledge, make meaning with it, draw on it to understand the world differently, use it to make change. We would not consider someone literate who was merely able to form the correct sounds from printed symbols, even if they were able to reiterate dictionary definitions, if they were unable to make and communicate meaning. Meaning must be realized and brought to fruition in a communicative context.

The communicative function of literacy is strangely absent from conventional definitions. When someone "reads" or makes meaning from symbols, they interpret what another person chooses to communicate. Even if the communicator is presenting "facts," they are doing so from a necessarily biased perspective, emphasizing some and leaving others out. Not only is the presentation of the facts a contextualized communication but also "facts" themselves are embedded in context. Gee (2003) acknowledges the social and historical context of linguistic theory as an example: If different people had contributed to the body of knowledge, "it might be equally good now but somewhat different" (p. 29).

Understanding that knowledge is contextually based acknowledges the primacy of literacy's communicative role. Furthermore, only through immersing oneself within a given context can one contribute to and alter the nature of "facts" within that area. This limitation of access to those already immersed in the dominant perspective applies to less recognized contexts as well. People whose communicative mode does not include what society values have a hard time impacting social values from the outside.

This demonstrates Gee's (1998) claim that one always speaks within a certain "discourse," or "a socially accepted association among ways of using language, of thinking, and of acting that can be used to identify oneself as a member of a socially meaningful group or 'social network'" (p. 51). To effectively communicate within a certain context, then, requires one to take on a certain persona. The process of becoming literate is much more than acquiring knowledge. It is a personal struggle, not separate from identity formation. As Neilsen (chap. 1, this volume) puts it, becoming literate is a process of "developing critical awareness and agency in one's own life" (p. 8). The opportunity to explore possible identities and ways of communicating impacts identity formation. Freire (1983) acknowledges this extension of the use of literacy, not only explaining that "language and reality are dynamically intertwined" but also acknowledging the personal engagement involved in that connection: "The texts, the words, the letters of that (home) context were incarnated in a series of things, objects, signs. In perceiving these, I experienced myself, and the more I experienced myself, the more my perceptual capacity increased" (p. 1).

Thus, we might define literacy in this way: the ability to effectively use a communicative tool (which necessitates the ability to understand meaning from "text") embedded in a specific context, and necessarily involving a personal journey/struggle. By defining the process of becoming literate in terms of the identities people play with and question while speaking and listening, reading and writing, we see the potential for conflicting discourses, or conflicting allegiance to "ways ... of thinking and of acting" (Gee, 1998, p. 51), complicating the notion of literacy as learning a skill set.

By recognizing that expanding our definition of literacy expands the population that we can define as literate, we acknowledge the current limited access to literacy as traditionally defined and correlated to a lack of access to power. Traditionally conceptualized literacy, or the ability to read and write text in "standard English," privileges a certain way of communicating. This becomes problematic when we acknowledge the extent to which becoming literate is a personal process of identity formation. When value is limited to a certain way of understanding and communicating meaning, not only are some people disadvantaged who do not easily adopt the expected set of values, but also options for identity exploration and for making and communicating meaning are thereby limited for everyone.

LITERACY TEACHING AND LEARNING AT OUR SITES

As we began to talk across our two school sites, we found ourselves describing instances of students' talk in terms that reminded us of Gee's (1998) primary and secondary discourses. In developing a framework that elucidates students' different challenges as literacy learners, Gee argues that we all have primary and secondary discourses: Primary discourses are those that we acquire in our close communities; as we enter more distant situations such as school, we learn the secondary discourses necessary to negotiate these new settings. Those whose primary discourses are significantly different from the dominant secondary discourse have to "learn" deliberately rather than "acquire" unconsciously this secondary discourse. Although "learning" promotes meta-cognitive understanding, according to Gee it does not allow for the "mastery" that characterizes our grasp of "acquired" primary discourse.

Early on, the students at our sites called on a style of conversation that seemed to us primary discourse: When they became excited about explaining their experiences, they used a language mode involving freewheeling talk, interruptions, laughter and body language, and spontaneous connections that built on each other's meanings; this discourse met the immediate need to make sense of their experiences and explain these to the teacher-researchers, whose task was to listen for their students' experiences in order to develop an action research project. As the project progressed, however, students would have to struggle with the requisite skills for reading/writing/speaking/listening in other ways that met project goals; for these purposes, secondary discourse became necessary. In this sense, Gee's framework "fit" our experience with our students.

We also found Gee's framework to be an awkward fit: First, along with Delpit (1998), we worried that the distinction between "acquisition" and "learning" might work to undermine teachers' expectations of some students, or, in Ladson-Billings' (2002) phrase, to legitimate "permission to fail." Furthermore, we became wary about participating in what McDermott and Varenne (1995) call "culture *as* disability," that is, the way culture captures some people for less powerful social positions, thereby bolstering others into advantageous positions. From this perspective, for example, although we acknowledge the value of African American English Vernacular as a language, we are also concerned not to foreclose the possibility of mastery of "standard English" to any group. Finally, because we believe that literacy learning involves a process of identity formation, we hypothesize that language might function as a continuum along which we/students move. Understanding literacy as a continuum of intimacy to distance helps us use Gee's framework in a way that illuminates what we're learning about literacy teaching and learning. Next, we conceptualize literacy learning in terms of such a continuum, offering four propositions to flesh out this framework and sharing site stories to clarify and complicate our understanding of teaching and learning literacy through action research.

LITERACY LEARNING BEGINS INTIMATE AND BECOMES INCREASINGLY DISTANT

By "intimate," we mean the expression of experiences, knowledge and understandings that are part of one's struggle/journey and in a context with others who share those experiences and understandings. By "distant," we refer to the existence of a wide range of (others') experiences, contexts, and language/communication expectations. Literacy learning involves communicating with those within and outside of the "intimate" group that shares one's experiences. Thus in the move from intimate to distant, literacy learning requires that learners not only make known to themselves what they know but also reconsider, revise, and enhance their knowledge to communicate successfully—with clarity and impact—in a new context and with a more removed audience.

This way of looking at literacy teaching/learning seems to us almost the converse of our usual assumptions. Teaching "to the test" offers a useful counterexample: First, as the people writing the tests are not in the classroom, teachers may feel that they're being given curriculum distant to them no less than to their students; their task is to bring their students to the (static) material. Even in daily teaching, we recognize the assumption that the teacher has the material—the alphabet, the book, the assignment—and that her or his challenge is to bring students to that material and prepare them to make the "learning connection," for example, read that sentence, understand that story. The teacher's challenge, then, is to begin with intrinsically distant material and move the students to this material.

Because we were involved in an action research project in which our task was to work with students to identify and pursue issues *of concern to them*, our job began with the need to ascertain the knowledge and concerns intimate to the students; this necessarily preceded bringing students to our conception of what they should know, and for us this entailed an unlearning process. Heather notes, "In the beginning I was worried more about getting students to my own predetermined understanding, thinking about their ideas as a production or at least a reflection of my work." Teachers also may need to unlearn what they know to open up the possibility of moving from students' intimate meaning making into the more distanced mode of communicating with others in a perhaps unfamiliar context. Although the move from intimate to distant isn't counterintuitive in the deepest sense of that word, we experienced it as counterintuitive given the ways that we've been socialized to understand teaching and learning.

The High School

Heather writes, based on her field notes:

> I struggled in the beginning with the students' insistence on researching the dress code. To me, and most of my team, it seemed superficial and not worth our time (and, we were sure, not worth the students' time either). I was sure nothing would come of it but complaints; and what more could you say but, 'this sucks' …. 'yep, I agree.' However, through the nature of our project, I was forced to start where the students wanted, with their desires and their conceptions. At the time it seemed nearly impossible; now I realize it was vital. Starting with the students, and having no set agenda, made the project personal, meaningful, and fruitful for both the students and us. Beginning intimately, the students' work meant something to them. The project was theirs. They did not need to be motivated to do "work" on this project. Expressing themselves, being taken seriously, and sharing intimate knowledge were exciting and inherently worthwhile. Most of them volunteered to do work outside of class, and none of them were getting official credit for their work.

Bruce recalls:

> When the students decided that they wanted to research the dress code, they were opting to examine an important part of their world. The fact that this decision did not coincide with my own thoughts about what was "important" was insignificant. It was incumbent that my thinking had to change. How could the adults assist the students in their research project? Was it possible to mentor and assist in this process without subverting the students' intentions?

Although having an intimate starting point was essential to the students' experience of meaningful work, equally important was their goal of distant communication or action, a place to go with their intimate knowledge. This is where the teacher's role as guide was crucial. Heather recaps a critical point from her field notes:

> One girl, who had previously seemed the most excited/engaged was just like, "There's no point. I already knew the answers" [referring to the interview]. When I told her we could present this to (the CEO), she was still discouraged/self-defeating, saying that they wouldn't listen or change the dress code no matter what. I tried encouraging them, telling them that the dress code could very well change, but also told them that it would be cool to be able to present their opinion in a project they initiated, even if it didn't change anything, and that they could learn something in the process … For some reason, this was the first time I was satisfied by my interaction with the students. I had to transform my image of an effective teacher role from that of a far off lighthouse director illuminating a destined path, to the role of a guide, always by the students' side. It meant I did not know where we were going, and, consequently, I was learning and growing with them.

Bruce wondered, "How could we help the students become aware of the underlying issues of power and control of dress code regulations or would they discover this on their own?" Heather writes based on her field notes:

(The dress code) has potential for bringing in much bigger issues. We talked about the issue of imposing a standard: was it telling them what they were wearing wasn't good enough? not giving them enough credit? getting them ready for the business world? This relates to the imposition of "standard English"—does this perpetuate their marginalization/segregation/not feeling adequate? Also, the question arose of whether there are unwritten dress codes everywhere, in society, and in schools with or without a written dress code.

The Middle School

The teacher-researchers were frustrated that the students appeared to be going through the motions of beginning an "educational autobiography" but did not seem involved. During the third session, the tone suddenly shifted as the students began talking about what was going on in their school—their frustrations with testing, the physical condition of the building, the service-learning project. Their experiences began to coalesce into collective knowledge making as they confirmed, complicated, and illustrated one another's points. The session shifts from distanced to excited and frustrated in Cambria and Elena's summary of their field notes:

The students had already written "educational autobiographies" in previous years. They had difficulty finding positive experiences and felt stifled, not empowered, by this assignment. In an attempt to reframe the curriculum around our students' needs in a context appropriate to the mission of College Prep, we opened the third class by asking students why they were in College Prep and what they wanted to get out of it. At first, students listed ideas such as inviting older students to visit and share the strategies they had developed to succeed. Then some students requested help on standardized test taking; this request came in light of the new district exam that the students had to pass to advance to ninth grade. At this point the tone of the discussion changed, as our students had a forum where they could openly express some of their criticisms of school without being dismissed because of their status as adolescents. A student who had been withdrawn blossomed into one of the most vocal students that day. We allowed the discussion to completely veer from our original plan to provide a space for their voices:

- Students were generally in favor of some type of tracking. They felt that the quality of their education was undermined in large classes with too many disruptive students.
- The students wanted tutors; NCLB had eliminated volunteer tutors from the classroom.
- Students were concerned about the level of preparation by some of their teachers, especially one long-term substitute. They challenged the idea that a teacher could force them to accept incorrect "facts" because that individual is an adult and they are children.
- Students questioned how prepared they were for standardized tests and for life. They were concerned that they could be made to stay back if they failed one of these exams, regardless of how outstanding their academic performance might be.
- The students felt they had to take too many standardized tests, and that time spent in the classroom preparing could be better spent teaching them material.

Through this discussion, we began to see that the students could not visualize themselves taking an active role in their education because they felt suffocated by the system; they focused on the negative without feeling empowered to effect change.

In both sites, the teacher-researchers opened themselves up to their students' experiences. This was both uncomfortable and exhilarating because it reversed the usual order of teacher bringing the students to the material and inaugurated instead the order of students bringing the material to the teacher. We hypothesize that this reversal can set the stage for student investment in a literacy process and product.

LITERACY LEARNING DOES NOT OPERATE UNIDIRECTIONALLY FROM INTIMATE TO DISTANT, BUT RATHER INVOLVES CREATING BRIDGES FROM THE INTIMATE TO THE DISTANT AND ALSO FROM THE DISTANT BACK TO THE INTIMATE

The initial sessions at our sites fit Freire's (1983) description of "reading the world," as students are making sense by speaking and listening to each other on whatever topics they've identified as important. The sessions were characterized by high energy—a response to the invitation to talk about what's really going on. These modes of expression are informal rather than prescribed, exploratory rather than focused, and based on an assumption rather than an explanation of shared intent. Common experiences and/or a real willingness to "get it" are assumed and part of the pace and energy of this discourse, associated with how people speak in communities where they feel relatively understood. Teacher-researchers listened, encouraged expression, and cared, even if at times they struggled with how seriously to treat students' concerns.

A danger in literacy teaching is to assume that once students have engaged in intimate expression through talk or writing, they are then ready to move to the more distant task of creating a product for an audience, usually the teacher. However, we learned that this process works more like weaving in that it is necessary to keep returning to the intimate even as understanding and expression increasingly account for the expectations of a more distant audience. The movement is not linear from brainstorming to communicating with an audience but rather a recursive process in which periodic returns to primary discourse help to determine and deepen both meaning and communication. To forget this is to risk students' disengagement with the material.

Furthermore, looping back to the intimate creates a system of checks whereby, as students revise and enhance their meaning making, they are able to use their personal identities and their shared struggle as a template against which to assess their evolving understanding. Thus, returning to contexts where students legitimately turn to primary discourse can sustain and deepen their insight and ultimately enrich their communication. Conversely, when they are not invited to move back and forth between the intimate and the distant, students may experience meaning as fixed and frozen or flat and without savor; their motivation to express what they know to more distant audiences may lose vitality, becoming rote rather than infused with the discovery of meaning.

The intent of literacy teaching and action research is to help students move toward communication that is real and efficacious—aimed at an audience and fueled by a desire for impact. As the audience becomes more distant, there is a need to scaffold students in terms of both motivation and the means to conduct effective communication. Why *should* students continue to put energy into such an endeavor? The teacher-researchers worked to maintain students' engagement, including confidence in their knowledge and investment in expressing it, and at the same time encouraged students to expand their knowledge and expression beyond the parameters of the early sessions. Bruce notes, "A lot of times students don't see the purpose in writing a paper, and when you tell them to 'write more about this' they don't see why." Working with students to weave the intimate and the distant can help to address that "why." In our stories, we note instances in which we worked with students to bridge the intimate and the distant as well as cases in which we failed to do so; both teach us about the importance of this process.

The High School

Heather writes, based on her notes:

> The students don't just "get it" all of a sudden, but their learning is constant, and the connection between intimate understanding and distant communication needs to be enforced and reinforced. When the students talked too much about their experiences with the dress code, they started to feel discouraged. They needed to feel purpose in their work to be motivated to further their research and communicate their understandings. This was a struggle because they were not used to doing this type of literacy work: with their own direction and for their own purpose. While they needed to keep a hope for powerful distant communication in mind in order to do the somewhat tedious work of completing interviews and surveys, they also needed to keep their intimate knowledge of and investment in the dress code in mind and go back to it, in order to stretch their understanding.

> At some points, I think we pushed them to think about communication before they'd had enough time to deepen their own understanding. Soon after we asked questions of them, they had to come up with questions to ask other students. We only knew the kinds of questions to ask them because we had an idea of what "distant" looked like; we'd already taken this kind of journey. For instance, we'd needed to come to a deeper understanding of issues surrounding the dress code in order to know what questions to ask. Now we had to help the students formulate questions that other students could answer, questions that would elicit the kinds of answers that would contribute to a final presentation intended to change the opinion of the administration. This, I now see, was an extremely distant place to start. So I wish they'd had more time to understand what they wanted to convey, so that they would be better prepared to take a step back and brainstorm effective ways to communicate it.

> While sometimes I felt like we were not connecting enough of their new learning back to the intimate, in some instances this connection *was* made palpable: The "Standup" activity was a key moment in the process because it gave students strategies for reflection. They sat in a circle and I read quotes, e.g. "I feel informed about the policies of this school," and "I feel like I know how to get information I need." Sitting in near silence and standing when a statement applied to them gave them the chance to stretch their personal understanding of the dress code, by reflecting and making connections scaffolded by the activity. But instead of focusing on grasping the fullness of their understandings, we had to move on to having them learn about others' opinions.

> We had another point of great connection when the students went as a group to interview students in another classroom. They'd been having a hard time comprehending the interview process: instead of asking their interviewee questions and taking notes, they'd been handing their list of questions to people to fill out. I tried again to explain

the interview process, keeping in mind our goals for the final presentation. Watching our students walk into the other classroom with a sense of pride and ownership and then engage the other students in an exploration of their own opinions was incredibly powerful and exhilarating. Our students had the experience of inviting other students to access and express their intimate knowledge, which was realized because our students were able to connect their goal of distant communication with the power of their ideas. Their intimate understanding was pertinent to their success in encouraging the other students' exploration. The previously distant tool of interviewing was suddenly given life as they made the connection between their goal of communicating with a presentation and their work of deepening intimate understanding.

Bruce reflects:

Students learned how to construct and use research tools such as interviews and surveys. On a deeper level they have also learned that research often results in changing your initial research question/focus as you gather information. This idea translated to the classroom as they were able to apply that knowledge to work they were doing. Their understanding that your questions and ideas changed as your knowledge and experience increased was invaluable.

The Middle School

Cambria and Elena narrate from their notes:

We faced our own difficulties in establishing the bridge between intimate and distant centers of knowledge. After that initial breakthrough where the students gave us insight into their intimate experiences as learners, we struggled to construct a framework that built on what they'd offered. Mindful of the somewhat fatalistic way in which the students considered these problems, we worked to plan an action research project in which the students' voices would be heard. We felt that writing letters to President Bush and the Kerry campaign would serve as a form of social action. We began by introducing the students to the letter-writing project through an examination of the lyrics written by a popular hip-hop artist.

The class read and discussed a rap song by Nas called "Can I Talk to You?" The song is about Nas talking to various government officials about the problems in his neighborhood that go unaddressed. We thought that by introducing students to the project through rap we would be able to connect the idea of expressing societal concerns with their own experiences. The students connected to the material. By introducing the letter-writing project with a nod to a popular form of artistic expression, we were able to demonstrate how written language is a viable method of protest to enact change. We used the Nas piece to create a bridge between something as intimate as music and the now less-distant goal of enacting change in public schools.

After reading the song, we asked the students what they thought of what they had read. They all agreed that Nas raised important issues; they also pointed out that many of the public officials making decisions would not want their children living in the neighborhoods in which the students resided. The students began to ask which public officials were responsible for certain policies and conditions, about the civil rights movement and the history of school desegregation litigation, which interested them because their school is so obviously isolated on the basis of race. We then handed out copies of *Letters to the Next President* (Glickman, 2004)—an especially appropriate text considering that this was the spring before the 2004 presidential election. The book included letters from students, teachers, politicians, and laymen, all focused on the issue of public education. We used the book to introduce the letter-writing project, which would illuminate the issues the students had identified in that first dynamic session. After a vote, the students chose to craft letters in two groups: one about NCLB, and the other about "poor schools" in the area, a category that students defined as involving schools with poorer students and less resources than their own.

By allowing the students to choose their topics, we created a bridge between the intimate and the distant that we hoped would allow the students to lend their voices to a national debate and participate in the political process. Our intent was to empower the students to believe they could enact change. Later, we saw ways that we'd injected our own aims, and we considered how we might have helped the students build recursively toward communicating with a distant audience. Our goal was to write Kerry and get a response from him; we were jazzed about it! The students seemed considerably less enthusiastic. They felt more connected to a local politician—they knew exactly who he was. Directing our letters to someone more tangible might have made more sense.

When the students internalized what they were learning, they approached it from a different angle than what we expected. I had an idea of how they'd write their letters—not a five-paragraph essay. But it ended up as that because we didn't have enough time. They would have had to unlearn the five-paragraph essay and relearn a way to write outside that structure. They couldn't get to the more intimate response since they had this learned idea of literacy as a distanced thing. So it's not so simple to just start with the intimate because kids begin with the already ingrained idea that literacy is distant.

Additionally, the students were not very familiar with NCLB, even though this legislation affected those areas of education with which the students seemed most concerned. We did not have enough time or resources (for example, the school library was closed) to fully realize our instructional goals. Looking back, we might have approached the topic using the students' existing knowledge: There was an AYP (Adequate Yearly Progress) banner up in the front hall of the school and we could have used that as a basis for starting to work with the students on NCLB, in relation to the passionate interest they had expressed about standardized and high-stakes testing.

The idea of beginning with the banner is reminiscent of Freire's (1970) approach to teaching literacy: the teacher works with learners to identify a "codification," a symbol that signifies the group's central issue; this then becomes a touchstone to generate meaning-laden reading and writing—literacy as reading and writing the world and the word. The AYP banner signified students' shared intimate knowledge, and might have helped students deepen their research and their communication.

Action research as a literacy venue highlights the importance of time because students are committed to an action with intent to impact. First, students may need to unlearn literacy as communication with a remote audience in order to allow for the unpredictability of working recursively between the intimate and the distant. Furthermore, there is tension between the time pressure on tasks and the need to explore the implications of intimate knowledge. The experience of the students who worked additional hours with Heather and Li Huan suggests the correlation between time spent weaving back and forth between students' old and new knowledge and students' increased expression and sense of efficacy. As Li Huan notes, "When the focus group students were respected and heard, they expected more and wanted to change things."

THE DYNAMIC BRIDGING OF INTIMATE AND DISTANT KNOWLEDGE CAN SET THE STAGE FOR STUDENTS TO EXPERIENCE A SUDDEN NEED AND CAPACITY FOR A LEAP IN LITERACY LEARNING—THAT IS, SUDDEN AND SIGNIFICANT GROWTH—IN THE FORM OF A LEAP FROM CLOSE OR PERSONAL UNDERSTANDINGS TO COMMUNICATION WITH A MORE REMOTE AUDIENCE

Heather describes such a moment at CCHS:

> The day of the presentation came for me with lots of conflicting feelings. We had worked really hard, and yet not hard enough. It was a great collaboration, and yet I was afraid we pushed and led too much towards the end. Because there was too little time we ended up doing a lot of in between steps, both the tedious process work that they could have learned a lot from, and the theoretical questioning that we were one step ahead, pulling at every step. We planned on meeting ten minutes before the presentation so that they could prepare, but it seemed like they didn't see this as important. Most of them were late. Li Huan and I frantically went over the plan for the presentation with them, and they didn't seem excited or scared. They asked few if any clarifying questions. (I don't know if they were actually feeling nonchalant, or just felt like they had to act that way with peers.) The first boy to show up said, "So this is actually going to happen, huh?" In an effort to make the short prep time they had valuable, we had planned ahead by jotting notes underneath the topic they were supposed to address in the presentation. We meant the notes only to spark ideas.

> We picked the two students we knew had thought deeply about their topics and could communicate well to explain the hardest points. We had jotted down notes underneath the boy's topic, and before the presentation he seemed the most confident. We had not been able to come up with precise notes to jog ideas on the topic the girl was going to present, and figured we'd talk with her about it beforehand. While we were waiting in the hall and other students were chatting about unrelated things, she was the only one that was preparing, jotting down what she was planning to say in a notebook leaned up against the wall. Before the presentation, I had every reason to believe they would perform similarly. But the boy recited almost verbatim the points we intended as starting ideas, whereas the girl used her own words, and successfully conveyed the point.

LITERACY TEACHING AND LEARNING INVOLVE SOME KIND OF PRODUCTION IN WHICH STUDENTS MEDIATE THE STRETCH BETWEEN THE INTIMATE AND DISTANT IN ORDER TO COMMUNICATE. ULTIMATELY, STUDENTS' PERSPECTIVES AND KNOWLEDGE INFUSE THE WIDER AUDIENCE, CHANGING WHAT "WE KNOW" ABOUT A GIVEN SUBJECT

In conventional terms, this talk of "production" would point to the individual student's ability to demonstrate the move from intimate to distant by conveying their meaning–perspective to the teacher. The action research project helped us to understand the value of having the students' production reflect the dynamic relationship between the intimate and the distant. For the student, this would entail negotiating along the continuum of primary to secondary discourse, whereas for the audience this would involve the added value of a fresh, authentic perspective on an issue of mutual concern. Furthermore, we noted the value of the collective production in a situation perhaps more similar to many workplaces than to the testing setting that often characterizes "product" in school.

For the individual, our project suggests that students' literacy learning is profoundly shaped by the meaningfulness of the production in connecting intimate experiences with a broader context and an intention to effect change. Bruce notes that the students often have a hard time understanding the concept of revision or the idea of working toward a final product. They lack a framework within which revision is meaningful because their literacy learning appears to be self-referential; the teacher gives the assignment and as the students didn't initiate the task, they may have little investment in its completion. The dress code project helped students see that their work could culminate in something beyond fulfilling an assignment.

To scaffold this process, the teacher has to help students bring their intimate knowledge to meet distant audiences and communicative expectations. The teacher must understand the intimate experiences of the students in order to help them mediate and frame their knowledge into a product that creates a point of convergence with an outside audience. Although certainly the goal of literacy teaching and learning involves the growth of students in terms of their identities as well as their critical and communicative skills, we believe that literacy learning is also and importantly tied to outcomes that stretch the boundaries of what's known or understood about a given subject and thus impact the "real world" of the school, the community, and/or the wider social and political context. These two aspects of literacy teaching and learning—students who are skilled meaning makers and communicators and real world impact—seem to us deeply intertwined.

The High School

Jody draws on her field notes:

> Students presented their research process and findings to the dean and the CEO. The students speak with clarity, focus and seriousness of purpose. Afterwards the dean and CEO respond: The dean tells the students they "did a great job" and "this is the best way to go about making your voices heard." She notes that there are two issues—the dress code and the colors—and asks students whether they're saying that they don't want the dress code but if they have to have it, here are their preferences. The students nod.

> The CEO also tells the students they did a great job and that "decisions should be based on real data—this is good for you to learn as you become adults." He gives a brief history of school's decision to have a "professional look" and says that if they were in a democracy with regard to issues like the dress code, they'd have decision-making power. He explains that there are things students have "authority over" and that "students are consulted about the dress code." For next year, decisions have been made and the process "has included the voices of students, teachers and parents, all of whom were at the table … I know day to day what you wear is important to you. To me the most important issue and what I want your participation in is academics, and how to help us have no fights, and student involvement in school culture and clubs." Students raise a number of points, about the dress code and about other issues, such as the schedule and language offerings. The dean responds to student frustration by noting that students asked for black as dress code color and they are getting this. When a young man returns to the idea that they should just be able to wear what they want, the dean notes that

there are more discipline referrals on dress down days. "You act different if you wear what you want to wear."

The students felt as if they had not made the hoped-for impact. Even though some of what they were asking for was coincidentally met, they hadn't "won" in the sense of precipitating an immediate change in policy. At the same time, the students expressed a sense of completion and efficacy; they'd seen the project all the way through and communicated with those with authority in the school community.

Bruce reflects on outcomes:

Students have been exposed to concepts that inform their "institutional" knowledge. Some of them expressed surprise that not all teachers thought in the same way about the dress code, i.e. there was not a monolithic belief in the dress code. Some of the students extended this knowledge to the curriculum by asking questions or making statements such as: "So this is why Ms. C. does things differently!", "Do all teachers agree about the discipline policy?", "Do you (a teacher) get in trouble when you disagree with (the CEO)?", "How do teachers work together?" This new information helped the students to reexamine relationships among the school staff. Students initially took their seeming inability to affect policy as a disappointment. It may have shattered some of their initial, more elementary considerations that "a person should be listened to," yet this also became an object lesson in the realities of the politics that often accompany policy construction.

Although the CEO indicated his preference that students share their perspectives on issues he considered important, the students' work on the issue of the dress code has the capacity to expand the community's understanding of what counts.

The Middle School

Cambria and Elena describe the final sessions:

Students wrote paragraphs and we put them together and added transitions. (One student) had even written two drafts of her section and incorporated some of our suggestions before typing it onto a laptop we brought. (Another), usually talkative and sometimes unfocused, worked hard on his contribution from an outline he had created the week before. This process was incredibly powerful; the students were beginning to feel knowledgeable about their given topic and to hope that someone would read their letters.

The NCLB group's letter included this passage:

NCLB has set a high standard that most students here don't appear to accomplish according to test scores. These tests are not telling our abilities proven by our grades. Students are not adapting to these tests because the tests don't test what we're learning in our classes. Plus, these tests are mostly consuming our time from the classroom and making it so that our teachers teach too much of only stuff that we're going to need for the test but not the stuff that we need as a foundation for our whole education. We think these tests count for too much!

The poor schools group's letter included this passage:

Some schools have lap top computers for each student while other schools don't have enough books. We realize that poor schools do not even have basic functioning equipment or resources while other schools look like palaces; they have things such as auto-matic (sensor-started) bathroom utensils and central air. Many poor schools have broken windows, no toilet tissue, nonworking toilets and sinks in even worse condi-tions. Students do not want to attend schools with such poor conditions and these schools do not provide an environment that encourages learning and excellence.

The teacher-researchers struggled to keep their students engaged in a project that required the middle schoolers to mediate the stretch between their close-up experi-ence of schooling and communication with an audience both distant and powerful. Although the students did not receive immediate feedback, their words carry insid-ers' knowledge that can enrich our understanding of how testing and funding impact student learning.

CONCLUSION

In the course of this project, we recognized the importance of learning from stu-dents, not only in terms of allowing students to improve our teaching but also be-cause students know things we don't know. We understand our task as teaching literacy in such a way as to facilitate our students' teaching as well as learning. Compton-Lilly (2003) puts this in terms of mainstream and alternative discourse:

> (A)lternative discourses that children bring to school reflect useful, powerful and pro-ductive ways of being and making sense of the world. Although acquisition of main-stream discourses may benefit my students in some, perhaps many, contexts, alternative discourses challenge mainstream interpretations and understandings; these contradictions present the possibility of change ..." (p. 28)

Our experience at CCHS provides a powerful example of these "contradictions," where the teacher-researchers had to acknowledge their own temptation to disre-gard dress code as an inadequate subject for investigation, much as the CEO did at the final presentation. About midway through the project, Li Huan sought to make sense of the dress code as the focus to which students consistently returned:

> The dress code emphasizes "professional" attire to prepare students for the real world. The representation that students must acquire to be part of the "professional world" overlooks an alternative discourse where students' desires reside. For students, the real world is to dress "hip" and be an individual, a discourse seen as less valuable to the society because dressing "hip" is not the road to success. This parallels the issue of power and language: Students need to learn standard English to be accepted and heard in mainstream society, whereas alternatives such as Ebonics are seen as equipped with "wrong" grammar and therefore when students speak in this way, their validity and power are stripped.

In this chapter we suggest the importance of opening to that place of "students' desires," where we can tap into students' intimate knowledge as a primary source for making and communicating meaning. As Rudduck (2002) argues, advertisers are way ahead of educators in terms of the image they offer young people of them-selves as active, empowered agents rather than as passive recipients of others' deci-sions. Action research as a strategy for literacy teaching and learning can offer not only a location for teaching students to understand, revise, and communicate but also a venue for addressing students as people with valuable perspectives and efficacy, and for challenging and expanding mainstream knowledge. In this case, literacy assumes an importance that extends beyond the classroom walls, and what occurs within those walls takes on a corresponding significance.

REFERENCES

Compton-Lilly, C. (2003). *Reading families: The literate lives of urban children.* New York: Teachers College Press.

Delpit, L. (1998). The politics of teaching literate discourse. In V. Zamel & R. Spack (Eds.), *Negotiating academic literacies: Teaching and learning across languages and cultures* (pp. 207–218). Mahwah, NJ: Lawrence Erlbaum Associates..

Freire, P. (1970). *Pedagogy of the oppressed.* New York: Continuum.

Freire, P. (1983). The importance of the act of reading. *Journal of Education, 165*(1), 5–11.

Gee, J. P. (1998). What is literacy? In V. Zamel & R. Spack (Eds.), *Negotiating academic literacies: Teaching and learning across languages and cultures* (pp.51–60). Mahwah, NJ: Lawrence Erlbaum Associates.

Gee, J. P. (2003). *What video games have to teach us about learning and literacy.* New York: Macmillan.

Glickman, C. (Ed.). (2004). *Letters to the next president: What we can do about the real crisis in public education.* New York: Teachers College Press.

Ladson-Billings, G. (2002). "I ain't writin' nuttin": Permission to fail and demands to succeed in urban classrooms. In L. Delpit & J. Dowdy (Eds.), *The skin that we speak: Thoughts on language and culture in the classroom* (pp.109–120). New York: The New Press.

McDermott, R., & Varenne, V. (1995). Culture as disability. *Anthropology and Education Quarterly, 26,* 324–348.

Rudduck, J. (2002). The sera lecture 2002: The transformative potential of consulting young people about teaching, learning and schooling. *Scottish Educational Review, 34,* 123–137.

Shulz, J., & Cook-Sather, A. (Eds.). (2001). *In our own words: Students' perspectives on school.* Lanham, MD: Rowman & Littlefield.

Weis, L., & Fine, M. (2000). *Speed bumps: A student-friendly guide to qualitative research.* New York: Teachers College Press.

15

Reconceptualizing Adolescent Literacy Policy's Role: Productive Ambiguity

Lisa Patel Stevens
Boston College

Desiree is an African American girl attending eighth grade in an urban city in the western United States. Desiree spends her time outside of school writing in her personal journal, penning short stories and poems about her experiences as a young woman and an outsider to her mostly White middle school and working on her fan-based Website dedicated to the R&B group, Destiny's Child. In particular, Desiree spends a great deal of time instant messaging other fans of Destiny's Child and communicating online with other Website masters learning about their practices in constructing various Website features. Formerly a straight A student, Desiree grades have flagged lately, due to a lack of motivation and her inability to see relevance in the curriculum to her questions about race and gender.

Sharon is a European American in her mid-40s and is Desiree's physical science teacher. Sharon has been teaching physical science for 15 years and maintains a healthy skepticism for educational fads and policies. According to Sharon, she is concerned about her kids and how to help them, and she mostly regards educational reforms that filter down from the "powers that be" as little more than nuisances. Her school administrator and school district have recognized her as an excellent teacher, and she has gained expertise in guiding students through physical science content by relying on heavy use of the class textbook, in-class lectures and notes, and homework out of the class textbook. Although Sharon considers herself to be somewhat technologically proficient, she feels it best to stick to the traditional print basis of her classroom. Recently, she has become concerned about Desiree's less-than-adequate performance in science and has referred Desiree to the special education coordinator for assessment of potential reading difficulties.

Sharon and Desiree draw our attention to a quintessential quandary facing current educational research, practice, and policy: How can education best create productive space for individuals' literacy practices? Desiree is clearly proficient in some literacies and opting out of others. Sharon has experienced success teaching traditional, print-based literacies, but is challenged in recognizing not only Desiree's current literacy practices but also what skills Desiree might need beyond the context of schooling. This chapter is centered on exploring the potential role that adolescent literacy policy could play in productively shaping the interactions between teachers like Sharon and young people like Desiree.

Adolescent literacy policy has been, for most of the past several decades, a rather nonexistent entity. In fact, in a field where different discourses often divide parties from the fields of research and practice, adolescent literacy teachers and researchers have long held common ground in sharing the frustration of being underresourced, forgotten, and often overlooked. However, at the time of the writing of this volume, the United States is engaged in an unprecedented level of policy discussion about adolescent literacy. While the exact nature, role, and scope of these nascent policies remains to be seen, this is an important time to advise caution for what one wishes. In the case of adolescent literacy, the lack of previously existing policies and the beginning groundswell provides researchers, educators, and policymakers with a unique opportunity to pause and consider carefully what role adolescent literacy policy should play in their lives, and more importantly, in the lives of young people. This chapter focuses on a few key questions: (a) what counts as policy, (b) how have past adolescent literacy policies conceptualized roles for teachers and young people, (c) what sources of information should inform policies, (d) what should be the role of adolescent policy, and (e) how can complexity theory be used to transform policies on adolescent literacy instruction ?

To first explore these questions, we must consider what counts as policy and what spaces it has previously occupied in the field of adolescent literacy.

WHAT IS POLICY?

Why should educators and researchers who work at local levels, often far removed from the daily workings of official policymakers, be concerned with policy? Whereas we often speak of research and practice and how to bridge the two, a third and equally significant component of educational professional pursuits is policy, deliberately conveying to educators what to do, how to do it, and for what purposes. Policy is defined as the captured essence of values (Ball, 1990). In this way, policy serves no less an important function than communicating what kind of literate subject of the state is to be nurtured through schooling. For example, when educators receive a curriculum outline, with standards of achievement for each grade level, this document, or policy, is setting forth what it means to be literate in contemporary society. If the standards reach for factual comprehension as literacy, this will likely produce pedagogy that supports that kind of reading practice. If the standards promote proficiencies with digitally mediated literacies, including the ability to design and create Web pages, critical literacy, and the active questioning and positioning of texts, different pedagogies would need to provide scaffolding for teaching that kind of literate student.

At all times, policymakers should be concerned with what types of literate citizens are needed for society (Luke, 2002). One of the key functions of schools is to prepare students for current and future possible worlds and life pathways. Some schools approach this mission from a stance of social justice, others from more utilitarian and technicist perspectives of literacy. Educators should be interested in what values and whose voices are conveyed to them through educational policy and its relationship to daily practices. What policies are informing Sharon's literacy decisions as a secondary science teacher? Although this seems like a rather simple question, pinpointing what counts as policy can be a nebulous exercise.

The crystallization of values in policy is both explicit and implicit. Clearly, documents such as state and national curriculum guidelines contain explicit statements about what counts as literacy, in the form of objectives, goals, standards, and levels of achievement. However, policies can also be conveyed, sometimes quite explicitly and forcefully, through speeches and images, as values and shared understandings of those values. These types of texts are complex aspects of policy, mediated by words, images, and actions (Lingard, Henry, Rizvi, & Taylor, 1997). Adding to this complexity is the frequent contradiction that can occur when messages conveyed through formal, institutionally sanctioned policies differ from those found within more informal texts, such as supervisory conversations between a principal and a teacher. In essence, all of these instances of policymaking provide opportunities to articulate, influence, and enact shared sets of values. Sharon might well have culled her sense of purpose and charge from curriculum documents, state standards, or conversations with her administrators, to name just a few sources that count as formal and informal policies in adolescent literacy. To explore what literacy policies might include, then, we must consider policy as much an activity or a process as a textually captured object. All of these sources communicate messages about what is possible, what is not possible, by whom, and on whose behalf.

Policies, broadly construed and narrowly enacted, act as a key technique of the state, communicating what is meant to be done by educators on behalf of the government. In this way, administrators, teachers, and students draw on explicit policies to see what type of literate subject the state is creating. Social theorist Foucault (1972) discussed contemporary developments that have created states of governmentality. Governmentality works as individuals read and understand what is expected of them by the state and then gradually begin to monitor and surveil themselves in meeting those expectations. If Sharon's school district mandated that teachers should coordinate and reference their lesson plans according to a set of narrowly defined learning outcomes, Sharon, along with many other teachers, would most likely begin coding lesson plans accordingly. Although the district officials might not be dropping in to check for this practice, Sharon might engage in this regular referencing in anticipation of a check from the district officials. As a result, Sharon's definitions of important literacy practices may become narrow and rigid. Desiree, already having opted out of literacy practices that she sees as overly didactic and disconnected from her life, may feel further marginalized from this classroom and its sanctioned practices. This mediation between the policy, its interpretation by recipients like Sharon, and the stakeholders like Desiree works to construct both what is possible and what is not possible. The stakes, then, are high indeed when we consider Desiree's ability to engage in the social construction of her sense of self in schooling spaces.

This social, political, and historical context for policy as a key instrument of governmentality increases the need for all stakeholders to engage regularly in various forms of policy analysis, examining the purpose, fruition, and other aspects of policy (Stone, 1997). These analyses are necessary, as policies can simultaneously limit the options for educators and young people and open up possibilities for pedagogy and curriculum. In keeping with that perspective, how have past efforts at setting adolescent literacy policy informed Sharon's work as a secondary science teacher and the literacy practices that she sanctions in her classroom?

ADOLESCENT LITERACY AND POLICY: PAST EFFORTS AND MISTAKES

Since the 1990s, the field of secondary literacy research has undergone epistemological, methodological, and impactful shifts in its fundamental questions. The focal points for secondary literacy research prior to the 1990s were content-area literacy strategies and older struggling readers. The field of content-area literacy was, for the bulk of the 20th century, comprised of experimentally and quasiexperimentally trialed reading strategies (Alvermann & Moore, 1991). The focus here was on the textbook and assisting young people to be successful in school-sanctioned literacy practices. Somewhat similarly, the focus on struggling readers addressed remedial instruction in the basics that had not been learned in elementary school. In fact, we can see both of these strains through Sharon's decision making. Her reliance on the textbook marks what counts for her in terms of literacy practices: proficiency in literal comprehension of the nonfiction science text. When Desiree resists the performance of this proficiency, Sharon has one other domain of adolescent literacy to invoke: the struggling reader. In these ways, Sharon's "reading" of Desiree and her literacy needs, abilities, and prior experiences mirrors areas of needs in past adolescent literacy policy. Working from past adolescent literacy policy instantiations, Sharon, in essence, has a very small set of resources to draw on, and those resources do not reach widely enough to conceptualize the literate lives of young people and what their future needs might be.

The history of adolescent literacy policy reveals a few trends and mistakes. The first trend is its own mistake: an overwhelming absence of explicitly articulated policies on adolescent literacy. For many schools, states, and districts, formal statements about expectations for literacy development and pedagogy with older readers and students have been largely absent. Instead, the focus of literacy policy has been on the young reader, with the implicit understanding and assumption being that meaning making is a process and set of skills acquired, mastered, and finalized during the early years of schooling. Luke and Luke (2001) have argued that, in fact, this absence of explicit attention on older readers is tightly implicated in a larger sense of distrust and disregard for young people. Although the factors associated with this absence of explicit policies would surely vary from context to context, the effects of the absence have had an impact on young people and the adults who work with them.

Without an explicit interrogation of who young people are and what forms the basis for their needs and ontological and epistemological stances in the world, a dominant discourse about the age/developmental stage called "adolescence" has been the default point of reference. Many scholars have critiqued the historically situated creation of the Western stage of adolescence and questioned its application in a postindustrial information age (e.g., Finders, 1998/1999; Lesko, 2001; Stevens, 2005a; Wyn, 2005); however, the age/stage discourse enjoys an almost unrivaled elevation as truth.

However, not all of adolescent literacy policy has been defined through absence. Various initiatives have been put forward to address young peoples' literacy development, either in the form of efforts to boost students' content-area literacy or, more commonly, to provide remedial reading instruction for older struggling readers. In each case, the focus has been on the context of the school and how to support older students so that they can become successful readers of school-sanctioned literacies. Both of these highly limited referent points are at work when Sharon equates Desiree's lack of articulated literal comprehension of the textbook with a need for special education assessment and resources. With few resources and policies developed for adolescent literacy, Sharon proceeds with the assumption that elementary reading processes were not mastered. Overall, Sharon is equating literacy proficiency with school-sanctioned literacy practices, a logical deduction from past conceptualizations of adolescent literacy policy. A potential countering force to these past traditions in adolescent literacy policy is the more recent research conducted into young peoples' literate lives outside of school contexts. Complementing and, arguably, distinguishing itself from the earlier themes of content-area reading strategies and remediation, this more recent movement in the field of literacy research has reconfigured itself under the moniker "adolescent literacy."

First gaining momentum in the late 1990s (e.g., Alvermann, Hinchman, Moore, Phelps, & Waff, 1998), the term adolescent literacy was reconceptualized in research studies, policy statements, and edited volumes addressing literacy pedagogy beyond the elementary years. Although much debate has taken place over the precise meaning of the term, this shift in name is largely meant both to be symbolic and to have material consequences, with a primary repositioning of the young person as the focus of theoretical and empirical work in literacy research with older students (Moore, Bean, Birdyshaw, & Rycik, 1999). And, not surprisingly, given the concurrent explosion of digitally mediated texts and textual practices, researchers interested in adolescent literacy have begun to recognize young peoples' out-of-school and self-sanctioned literacies (e.g., Hagood, 2003; Moje et al., 2004; Stevens, 2005a).

Of particular note in many of these studies is the rupture between young peoples' perceived competencies in educational settings and those competencies that they exhibit in self-selected literacy practices (e.g., Knobel, 2001; Stevens, 2005b), a scenario that also marks the interactions between Desiree and Sharon. Also of note is the expanded definition of literacy and its related competencies that are privileged in these studies. Studies into young peoples' literacies support definitions of literacy that work across the modes of auditory, image-based, and logographic, and multimediated texts. For example, in Bean's co-authored article with his two daughters (Bean, Bean & Bean, 1999), he documented how their print-based and digitally mediated literacy practices permeated, informed, and shaped their daily ideas and practices. For this research to productively influence adolescent literacy policy, though, substantial shifts will need to take place in how policy is conceptualized, what informs it, and what role it plays in young people's and educators' lives.

INFORMATION SOURCES THAT NEED TO INFORM POLICY

If policy is to truly act as the crystallization of values, the most logical questions to arise should be those that ask whose values and from what stances do we formulate these values and policies? A specific way to take up these questions is to consider what sources of information and evidence inform adolescent literacy policy.

As mentioned earlier, at the time of this writing an unprecedented amount of policy attention is being paid to adolescent literacy. In many cases, these discussions are couched within larger discussions of moving the accountability and measurement tactics of the federal policy, No Child Left Behind, to the arena of secondary education. For example, consider *Every Child a Graduate: A Framework for an Excellent Education for All Middle and High School Students* (2002), published by the Alliance for Excellent Education. In the report, the organization cites an increasing and alarming crisis in secondary literacy rates. The document, published by the self-described "national policy, advocacy, and research organization created to help middle and high school students receive an excellent education," defines neither literacy nor young people explicitly but maintains a strong theme of failing secondary literacy rates. According to the document, six million secondary students are failing to achieve in literacy. Purportedly, this figure is based on national standardized assessments, but these specific source details are not provided in the report. The policy document links itself to other existing federal policy initiatives, as indicated in the following statement: "We are promised that no child will be left behind, but these promises do not include adolescents who continue to struggle to meet high standards, or, worse, simply give up and leave school without a high school diploma" (p. 1).

In *Every Child a Graduate* and in other documents like it (e.g., Snow & Biancarosa, 2003), the central topic of the young person is not theorized explicitly. Rather, the explicit focus and references are fixed on reading success in the secondary school setting. Furthermore, many references are made to being able to read content-area texts and perform in those classroom settings. A few references to students being computer literate are made, but the overwhelming majority of specific details, descriptions of need, and calls for action are directed toward basic print reading fluency and content-area literacy competencies. Ironically, this unitary focus on secondary school achievement as the basis for forming adolescent literacy policy may well succeed in garnering significant monies to help students succeed in secondary schools but still create legions of young people ill-prepared for the dynamic demands of succeeding in an information age (Hargreaves, 2003) where the attention economy (Lankshear & Knobel, 2002) is alive and well. School-sanctioned literacies and their assessments have been widely criticized on two major grounds: lack of resonance with self-sanctioned literacies engaged by many young people (e.g., Chandler-Olcott & Mahar, 2003; Knobel, 1999; Moje et al., 2004) and lack of resonance with the dynamic, multimediated literacies required in an information age and globalized economy (e.g., Hargreaves, 2003; New London Group, 1996; Stevens & Bean, in press). Therefore, policies that are drawing on traditionally school-sanctioned literacies and their accompanying measures may in fact be preparing students better for the 1950s (days of blackboards and chalk talk) than for the life pathways they are likely to encounter in a digitally mediated world (Gee, 2002). For Desiree and other students like her, more money and policies articulating the need to succeed with content-area textbooks are unlikely to help her use literacies to mediate her sense of self and the world.

What, then, would make a more appropriate referent point for adolescent literacy policy? Part of the answer is found within the field of research into adolescent literacy that has begun to document the varying literate practices of young people. From the emerging studies that inform the field about young peoples' uses of IMing and zines (e.g., Chandler-Olcott & Mahar, 2003; Leu, Kinzer, Coiro, & Cammack, 2004) to the market research (Rushkoff, 2001) that shows the current generation of young people to be more comfortable mediating the multiple literacies of a first-person shooter video gamer than the comparatively linear flow of print in a book, we are being forced to redefine how we understand youth. The important referent point here is not a glossier, urban, savvy, and hip portraiture of young people. While, for example, Desiree spends much of her out-of-school time choosing Internet-based literacy practices, she has a varied and far-reaching repertoire of literacy practices, and she is one member of a large and incredibly varied segment of the population: young people. In fact, the research field would be wise to be leery of reifying an equally inappropriate and sweeping image of all young people as multitasking, plugged-in technophiles.

Rather, the instructive point here is that adolescent literacy policy must have localized knowledge as its first referent point. This is in keeping with the long-standing tradition of others who have appropriately named the importance of situated knowledge in effective pedagogy. From Moll's conceptualization of funds of knowledge (Moll, Amanti, Neff, & Gonzalez, 1992) to Au's (1998) culturally responsive work with native Hawaiian children, an anthropological view of young people would first inform adolescent literacy policies from arguably the most important stakeholders' perspective: the young person. Pedagogically, it is futile to plan without a specific learner's needs, abilities, and interests in mind. Policies that require local knowledge of participants work from the same premise. A productive adolescent literacy policy that might affect Desiree, then, would be one that had specific, grounded, and current information about her and others like her in her peer community. Such policies would be informed not only by accurate statistics and demographic information, but also by the articulated needs, interests, and desires of young people themselves. By altering the reference point from a sweeping and assumed stereotype of the adolescent, adolescent literacy policy could be informed by actual voices, both young and older (see Harper & Bean, chap. 8, this volume).

The second referent point for adolescent literacy policy is concerned with the literacy proficiencies we are seeking to enable in our students. Currently, the referent point for those proficiencies is the secondary school curriculum, and to a lesser extent, the didactic traditions of tertiary institutions. This referent must change; it needs to move from the local to the global. Educators need to develop an awareness of the trends in economics, politics, and social science that are shaping the world. Knowing what literacy demands are in place on the SAT is still important, but educators also need to acknowledge the literacy demands required to understand, code-switch, and mediate a world with blogs, Web mail, video on demand, and text messages. Rather than asking solely what literacy practices Desiree needs to be successful in school, we should also be asking, and incorporating into policy, what she is likely to need for multiple and future life pathways.

Consider, for example, a recent study conducted by Beck and Wade (2004), studying the various characteristics demonstrated by young managers and corporate workers who grew up playing video games. In a study comprising 2,500 participants, Beck and Wade found that in those participants who considered themselves to be gamers, characteristics such as calculated risk taking, perseverance, competitiveness, leadership, and commitment to the organization were statistically more significant. The researchers posit that this gaming generation has experienced a differing construction of neural pathways and cultural practices during their teenage years, largely spent gaming, and that those shifting mindsets are resulting in a youth-led transformation of the business world.

Although Beck and Wade's claims are provocative, the merits of their study are not within the scope and sequence of this chapter. Their work seeks to investigate two large areas: how the multibillion dollar industry of videogames has changed the experiences of millions of young people and what effect it is having on their interactions in the business world. Although the research processes and data-gathering techniques employed by Beck and Wade may or may not be useful to educators, these are the types of questions that explore larger societal conditions and factors and that should be taken up and considered in teaching and learning contexts. Educators and policymakers should be continually engaged in these types of questions—those that inquire about the lives of young people, the worlds they are living in and likely to find themselves living in, and how to mediate the connections between those two. However, adolescent literacy policy must learn to see these inquiries differently than others have: it should engage in these questions as a habit of organization and mind. The answers to these questions will never be statistically known and rigid. If that occurs, the policy, both as a text and a process, will have become defunct, outdated, and inevitably replaced by the next policy subject to only the same fate. One key way out of this cyclical refabrication of panaceas is to engage in policymaking as a necessarily ambiguous and recursive process, continually examining the referent points of young people and their possible future lives. This iterative stance will provide one necessary component to engaging and defining policy as a process; however, adolescent literacy policy must, like other policies, also reconceptualize the context of the classroom and its participants. Engaging in questions about relevancy and priorities in the current and future life pathways is an essential practice for educators and policymakers to enact effective policy and practices.

THE ROLE OF ADOLESCENT LITERACY POLICY

Inevitably, policies are written in one context and then enacted in other contexts. Policies are subsequently taken up, modified, rejected, altered, ignored, overlooked, put on pedestals, and vilified. Inevitably subject to a limited shelf life, these policies then give way to the next wave of policies that will only witness the same types of reactions. These variations occur, in large part, because policies are trying to predict actions and sequences for systems that are largely unpredictable. Consider how policies might have very different roles if schools were conceptualized not as sites for the implementation of prescribed sets of practices but rather as complex learning settings. Seen through the lens of complexity theory, schools, districts, and other educational contexts can be significantly reconceptualized.

In short, complexity theory posits two key characteristics to complex systems: one, the systems are composed of necessarily different parts, and two, these systems occur in nested and mutually dependent fashions. The constituent parts are diverse, self-organizing, self-regulating, and constantly shifting in unpredictable ways to result in synergistic fruitions, pointedly different to the disparate possibilities of the individual parts (e.g., Bowers, 1995; Capra, 1982). As an example of this nestedness in complex systems, people are composed of interconnected sets of complex systems such as cells, tissues, and organs. Each of these systems individually attend to stimuli, or contexts, but do so at once individually and in relation to each other, to form and transform embodied responses and experiences. Similarly, we can apply these concepts to educational systems. Within a school, for example, the necessarily complex system of a single student sits alongside other and diversely constituted students and teachers. These "systems" are nested within the larger system of the classroom, which is nested within the school system itself. This analogy can be applied to the district, state, and even national government as well. Although these systems are not strictly biological in nature and caution should be exercised to avoid equating biological phenomena with synthetic and political structures, using the lens of complexity theory offers a compelling metaphor for reconceptualizing learning systems.

In particular, one key feature of complexity theory that may be of use in reconceptualizing learning systems is the unpredictability of the complex systems. Healthy systems made up of disparate parts that work together to accomplish a common goal, such as tissue production or larger organ functions, act in unpredictable, self-organizing ways that, while meeting the needs of the system, do not follow prescribed pathways. It is precisely this characteristic of unpredictability that offers a seminal turn from prevailing models of educational policy and planning procedures. To date, educators have worked from premises that use techniques such as lesson plans to map out the predicted, expected, and planned behaviors and interactions in the classroom. If educators were to operate from an assumption about the learning setting as necessarily complex, they could potentially engage with a productive release from this type of predicting. Instead of working to forecast a linear sequence of behaviors, complexity theory assumes that the practices within the learning setting will be spontaneous, interrelational, and even fickle. Because complex systems defy preconceived hypotheses mapping these responses, they remain purposefully and productively ambiguous. That is, a context cannot be predetermined or statically relegated to a particular purpose outlined by an external agent because only the self-organizing practices of the participants can craft, erase, recraft, and modify such purposes.

Thus, whereas Sharon may well view her classroom's purpose as a site of the acquisition of a set of skills, including literal comprehension of the content-area textbook, Desiree assigns a different purpose, one that causes her to disconnect from the learning space that Sharon has organized. Participants in complex settings have an interactive relationship with the setting, changing its functions and purposes to meet shifting needs. A reconceptualization of classrooms and learners as complex systems provides opportunities for re/mediating the theories that underpin policies; at the same time it presents challenges to shifting the role of policy. In taking up the ideas of complexity theory and viewing education through these scientific lenses, neither absent nor prescriptive policies would best nurture healthy and complex learning settings. How then could this subjective, shared, and complex space of the classroom be reconceptualized under adolescent literacy policy?

USE OF COMPLEXITY THEORY TO TRANSFORM POLICIES ON ADOLESCENT LITERACY INSTRUCTION

In their work that examines the epistemologies of learning typically found in schools, Davis, Sumara, and Luce-Kapler (2000) use complexity theory to examine how educators might structure teaching and learning in the context of productively unpredictable complexity. The authors propose that complexity theory alters the traditional role of lesson planning and policymaking. Instead of predicting what the participants will do and in what order, a view of classrooms as complex settings asks what sets of conditions are best for a variety of practices and results.

Typically, policymakers write policies that seek to provide administrators and teachers with the answers to the perennial question of "What works?" with discrete, sequential, and often constraining procedures and rules. By contrast, Davis et al. (2000) envision pedagogy that focuses less on control of predictable behavior and outcomes and more on facilitating generative structures. These generative structures are ones that provide support for learners to work toward goals that they have informed, work with each other, and improvise multiple pathways to achieving these goals. However, this type of synergistic improvisation occurs more easily within a few constraints rather than a longer list of expected behaviors and outcomes. For example, rather than provide young people with a prescribed reading list and a format for book reports, a teacher could, through a view of learning as complex, outline possible topics to be explored and provide a few key constraints. Students could be required to include multimedia texts, standard referencing of a minimum number of sources, and the acknowledgment of community-based issues that relate to the topic at hand. These few constraints provide sufficient focus yet allow for multiple pathways in complex learning.

From this stance, adolescent literacy policy can be reconceptualized to ask not what should be going on discretely in classrooms across the United States, but instead, what enabling constraints would allow for a productively diverse set of interactions, learnings, and synergistic results. Adolescent literacy policy could productively constrain districts and schools by requiring that school-wide literacy plans be researched and written based on the local needs of the young people in those communities. To ascribe from on high what the literacy plan should be works from an assumption that the needs of young people can be known and delineated from a generalized, removed distance. In contrast, I propose that adolescent literacy policy could and should require a shift in referent point for practice from making assumptions about adolescents to considering inquiry-based evidence about young people and their worlds. Such a policy would necessarily communicate that literacy lesson plans differ from site to site to site, thus setting the ground for the expectation of diversity in complex learning settings. In fact, policymakers who understand systems to be complex regard diversity as a prerequisite, not as a burden to be dealt with. Reconceptualizing adolescent literacy policy from this perspective would then have far-reaching implications for young people and the teachers who work with them.

Under such a vision of adolescent literacy policy, the classroom interactions between Desiree and Sharon would differ significantly. Sharon, along with other school-based personnel, would be charged with knowing and basing their pedagogical decisions on two anchoring sources of inquiry: the local and contextualized literate lives of the young people with whom they work, and the likely future life pathways of those young people. Strongly privileged in this approach to literacy policy are the voices and perspectives of young people, primarily because prevailing assumptions that distant policymakers have adequate knowledge about what adolescents need would no longer suffice. Desiree and other young people would have opportunities to share their views of literacy, how they use textual practices to mediate their senses of self and the world, and what they need educationally.

Complementing these locally informed knowledges would be a second source of inquiries: exploration of the global demands, trends, and practices that should inform pedagogical goals. As teachers and learners interact with broader sets of questions of what young people should be learning and how they might engage with this learning, literacy practices would widen, perhaps preventing the marginalization that has to date marked Desiree's schooling. Seen from the lens of complexity theory, the possible roles afforded to adolescent literacy policy, the young person, the teacher, and pedagogy would be radically transformed.

SUMMARY AND CONCLUSION

Policy is often regarded as formally construed from afar, something that is developed by elected officials in closed rooms. As can be seen through the various responses to literacy policy initiatives like No Child Left Behind, teachers are rarely afforded opportunities to actively engage, interpret, and transform educational policies. In typical hierarchical and teleological fashion, policies are devised, encoded, and transmitted from persons removed from local teacher/student contexts. If the only people who can inform and transform policies are those who work outside of classrooms, this has the potential to devalue educators who work with young people.

To be locally anchored and responsive, policies need the professional input and refraction provided by various stakeholders, including young people themselves, community members, teachers, parents, and so forth. And as much as policymakers need to be better informed by the perspectives of these interested parties, the stakeholders themselves need to be aware that they can be more than the assumed recipients of values crystallized by others. If Desiree were given a view of the academic standards that have, to date, governed her expected achievement in school, what revisions might she offer? One could guess many.

The elegantly simple concept of enabling constraints to productively support complex systems offers a compelling alternative to the overly didactic and regulatory tone of No Child Left Behind and many other contemporary education policies. Instead of policies that seek to rein in the synergistic possibilities of human beings in complex settings, an alternative might be to delineate a few constraints, restrictions, or goals and then allow for divergent, creative, and necessarily unpredictable pathways to those goals. Such a fundamental but significant shift could transform interpretation of a policy from an exercise in obedience and/or resistance to one that is more participatory and holds potential for generating more relevant and inventive teaching. As federal government policies forge their strongest roles in U.S. education to date, the need for accountability that cuts both ways has never been higher. In that sense, educators and other key stakeholders should interrogate current policies for the appropriateness of their underlying theories, design, and resultant effects. Along with this kind of questioning should come reconstructive efforts to envision language and literacy policies differently. This will require a broader base of input into policymaking, including young people and teachers (see Harper & Bean, chap. 8, this volume).

With the rising discussion and attention being paid to adolescent literacy policy and the general lack of preexisting explicit traditions in national adolescent literacy policy, the opportunities to inform, participate in, and affect policymaking are considerable. One such opportunity would be to look upon schools as complex systems, necessarily charged with diversity and unfolding in unpredictable and self-negotiating ways. We would change the role of policy. It is time for the magnifying lens of accountability to be applied refractively to policy; policies should not be allowed to function and plan for predictable outcomes that might only occur in simple, homogenous settings with few variables such as language, context, and culture. For Desiree and Sharon, current policies that support content-area literacy proficiency and assume reading to have been acquired in the elementary years are contributing to a profound loss of opportunity. Because the shared sense of values in the adolescent literacy policies affecting them speak neither to Desiree's needs nor to her possible future pathways, Desiree has become disengaged and Sharon is left with insufficient approaches and strategies. Recast within complexity theory, the policies affecting these two people might afford both of them more efficacy and involvement in investigating and appropriating the skills, strategies, and processes that they determine to be most relevant. Effective policies for complex systems should seek to establish the best conditions for individuals' mediation of learning settings—diversity, enabling constraints, flexibility, and perhaps little else beyond that.

REFERENCES

Alliance for Excellent Education (2002). *Every Child a Graduate: A framework for an excellent education for all middle and high school students.* Washington D.C.: Alliance for Excellent Education.

Alvermann, D. E., Hinchman, K., Moore, D. W., Phelps, S. W., & Waff, D. (Eds). (1998). *Reconceptualizing the literacies in adolescents' lives.* Mahwah, NJ: Lawrence Erlbaum Associates.

Alvermann, D. E., & Moore, D. W. (1991). Adolescent literacy. In R. Barr, M. L. Kamil, P. Mosenthal, & P. D. Pearson (Eds.), *Handbook of reading research* (Vol. II, pp. 951–983). New York: Longman.

Au, K. (1998). Constructivist approaches, phonics and the literacy learning of students of diverse backgrounds. In T. Shanahan & F. V. Rodriguez-Brown (Eds.), *National Reading Conference Yearbook, 47,* 1–21. Chicago, IL: National Reading Conference.

Ball, S. (1990). *Politics and policymaking in education.* New York: Routledge.

Bean, T. W., Bean, S., & Bean, K. (1999). Intergenerational conversations and two adolescents' multiple literacies: Implications for redefining content area literacy. *Journal of Adolescent & Adult Literacy, 42,* 438–448.

Beck, J. C., & and Wade, M. (2004). *Got game: How the gamer generation is reshaping business forever.* Boston, MA: Harvard Business Press.

Biancarosa, G., & Snow, C. (2004). *Reading next: A vision for action and research in middle and high school literacy: A report from the Carnegie Corporation of New York.* Washington, DC: Alliance for Excellent Education.

Bowers, C. A. (1995). *Educating for an ecologically sustainable culture: Rethinking moral education, creativity, intelligence, and other modern orthodoxies.* Albany, NY: State University of New York Press.

Capra, F. (1982). *The turning point: Science, society and the rising culture.* New York: Bantam.

Chandler-Olcott, K., & Mahar, D. (2003). "Tech-savviness" meets multiliteracies: Exploring adolescent girls' technology-related literacy practices. *Reading Research Quarterly, 38,* 356–385.

Davis, B., Sumara, D., & Luce-Kapler, R. (2000). *Engaging minds: Learning and teaching in a complex world.* Mahwah, NJ: Lawrence Erlbaum Associates.

Finders, M. (1998/1999). Raging hormones. *Journal of Adolescent & Adult Literacy, 42,* 252–263.

Foucault, M. (1972). The discourse on language. *The archeology of knowledge* (A. M. Sheridan, Trans.). New York: Harper Colophon.

Gee, J. P. (2002). Millennials and bobos, *Blues Clues* and *Sesame Street:* A story for our times. In D. E. Alvermann (Ed.), *Adolescents and literacies in a digital world* (pp.51–67). New York: Peter Lang.

Hagood, M. C. (2003). New media and online literacies: No age left behind. *Reading Research Quarterly, 38,* 387–395.

Hargreaves, A. (2003). *Teaching in the knowledge society: Education in the age of insecurity.* New York: Teachers College Press.

Knobel, M. (1999). *Everyday literacies: Students, discourse & social practices.* New York: Peter Lang.

Knobel, M. (2001). I'm not a pencil man: How one student challenges our notions of literacy "failure" in school. *Journal of Adolescent & Adult Literacy, 44,* 404–420.

Lankshear, C., & Knobel, M. (2002). Do we have your attention: Attention economies and multiliteracies. In D. E. Alvermann (Ed.), *Adolescents and literacies in a digital world* (pp. 19–39). New York: Peter Lang.

Lesko, N. (2001). *Act your age!: A cultural construction of adolescence.* New York: Routledge.

Leu, D. J., Kinzer, C. K., Coiro, J. L., & Cammack, D. (2004). Toward a theory of new literacies emerging from the Internet and other information and communication technologies. In R. B. Ruddell & N. J. Unrau (Eds.), *Theoretical models and processes of reading* (5th ed., pp. 1570–1613). Newark, DE: International Reading Association.

Lingard, B., Henry, M., Rizvi, F., & Taylor, S. (1997). *Educational policy and the politics of change.* London: Routledge.

Luke, A. (2002). What happens to literacies old and new when they're turned into policy. In D. E. Alvermann (Ed.), *Adolescents and literacies in a digital world* (pp. 186–204). New York: Peter Lang.

Luke, A., & Luke, C. (2001). Adolescence lost / childhood regained: On early intervention and the emergence of the techno-subject. *Journal of Early Childhood Literacy, 1,* 91–120.

Moje, E. B., Ciechanowski, K. M., Kramer, K., Ellis, L., Carrillo, R., & Collazo, T. (2004). Working toward third space in content area literacy: An examination of everyday funds of knowledge and discourse. *Reading Research Quarterly, 39,* 38–70.

Moll. L. C., Amanti, C., Neff, D., & Gonzalez, N. (1992). Funds of knowledge for teaching: Using a qualitative approach to connect homes and classrooms. *Theory into Practice, 31,* 132–142.

Moore, D. W., Bean, T. W., Birdyshaw, D., & Rycik, J. (1999). Adolescent literacy: A position statement. *Journal of Adolescent & Adult Literacy, 43,* 97–110.

New London Group (1996). A pedagogy of multiliteracies: Designing social futures. *Harvard Educational Review, 66,* 60–92.

Rushkoff, D. (2001). *Playing the future: What we can learn from digital kids.* New York: Riverbend Books.

Snow, C., & Biancarosa, G. (2003). *Adolescent literacy and the achievement gap: What do we know and where do we go from here? A report for the Carnegie Corporation of New York.* New York: Carnegie Corporation.

Stevens, L. P. (2005a). Renaming "adolescence": Subjectivities in complex settings. In J. A. Vadeboncouer & L. P. Stevens (Eds.), *Re/Constructing the 'adolescent': Sign, symbol, and body* (pp. 271–282). New York: Peter Lang.

Stevens, L. P. (2005b). Youth, adults, and literacies: Texting subjectivities within and outside schooling. In J. A. Vadeboncouer & L. P. Stevens (Eds.), *Re/Constructing the 'adolescent': Sign, symbol, and body* (pp. 49–68). New York: Peter Lang.

Stevens, L. P., & Bean, T. W. (in press). *Critical literacy in the United States: Research and policy at the nexus of practice.* New York: Peter Lang.

Stone, D. (1997). *Policy paradox: The art of political decision making.* New York: W.W. Norton.

Wyn, J. (2005). What is happening to "adolescence"? Growing up in changing times. In J. A. Vadeboncouer & L. P. Stevens (Eds.)., *Re/Constructing the adolescent: Sign, symbol and body* (pp. 25–48). New York: Peter Lang.

Author Index

Note: f indicates figure.

A

Abowitz, K. K., 261, *276*
Achebe, C., 74, *79*
Alderman, M. K., 30, *44*
Alexander, P. A., 35, *44*
Allen, A., -R., 166, 170, *184*
Allington, R. L., 35, *44*, 68, *79*
Alpert, B., 141, *144*
Althusser, L., 134, *144*
Alvermann, D. E., xxii, *xxxii*, 30, *44*, 62, *63*, 68, *79*, 148, 152, 154, 155, *159*, *160*, 232, 233, 238, *248*, *250*, 300, 301, *308*
Amanti, C., 303, *309*
Anderman, E. M., 30, 35, 38, *44*
Angelou, M., 192, *203*
Anyon, J., 208, 211, 216, 225, *227*
Anzaldua, G., 114, *126*
Apple, M., 150, *159*, 240, *249*
Archer, M. S., 135, *144*
Au, K., 303, *308*
Avi, 50, *63*

B

Bahktin, M. M., xxi, *xxxii*, 136, *144*, 190, 194, 202, 203, *203*
Baldwin, R. S., 152, *160*, 232, *250*
Bales, S., 148, *160*
Ball, A., 198, *203*
Ball, S., *308*
Bandura, A., 144, *144*
Banford, H., 259, 261, *276*
Barthes, R., 134, *144*
Barton, D., 34, *44*
Baudrillard, J., 134, *144*
Bauer, E., 43, *45*

Bauman, Z., 165, *184*
Beach, R., 31, *45*
Bean, K. F., 206, 208, 227, 301, *308*
Bean, S. K., 206, 298, 227, 301, *308*
Bean, T. W., 148, 152, 155, 156, *159*, *160*, 206, 208, 227, 232, *250*, 301, 302, *308*, *309*
Beck, J. C., 303, *308*
Beck, U., 165, *184*
Behrman, E. H., 155, *159*
Belzer, A., 262, *277*
Berkman, M., 259, 261, *276*
Bernstein, B., 180, *184*
Biancarosa, G., 247, *249*, 302, *308*, *309*
Birdyshaw, D., 301, *309*
Blackburn, M., 142, *144*, 232, 238, 240, *249*
Bloom, A., 151, *159*
Bloome, D., 42, *44*, 232, *249*
Blumenfeld, P., 30, 35, 38, *44*, 90, *106*
Blumer, H., 232, *249*
Borkowski, J. G., 144, *144*
Borland, K., 236, *249*
Bourdieu, P., 109, 110, 126, *126*, *127*, 181, *184*, 209, 211, *227*
Bowers, C. A., 304, *308*
Bowles, S., 132, *144*
Boyd, F. B., 155, *160*
Bransford, J. D., 143, *144*
Brantlinger, E., 208, *227*
Britzman, D. P., 263, *276*
Brown, A. L., 143, *144*
Brown, C., 192, *203*
Brown, S., 271, *276*
Brozo, W. G., 155, *160*
Bruce, B. C., 206, 208, *227*
Bryk, A. S., 132, *145*
Buber, M., 137, *144*
Buckingham, D., 8, *26*

Bulgren, J., 231, *249*
Burbules, N. C., 143, *144*
Burke, C., 232, *249*

C

Cain, C., xxi, xxiii, xxiv, xxv, xxvi, *xxxii*, 129, 139, *145*
Cammack, D. W., 43, *45*, 302, *309*
Capra, F., 304, *308*
Carlson, D., 151, 152, 153, *159*
Carr, M., 144, *144*
Carrillo, R., 90, *106*, 152, 154, 155, *160*, 244, *250*, 301, 302, *309*
Carter, P. L., 109, *127*
Cazden, C., 194, 196, *203*
Chandler-Olcott, K., 232, 233, 238, *249*, 302, *308*
Chhabra, V., 35, *45*
Cherland, M. R., 9, *26*, 158, *159*
Chin, C., 259, 261, *276*
Chomsky, N., 134, *145*
Christensen, L. M., 258, *276*
Christian-Smith, L. K., 208, *227*
Christman, J., 259, 260, *277*
Christmas-Best, V., 148, *160*
Ciechanowski, K. M., 90, *106*, 152, 154, 155, *160*, 244, *250*, 301, 302, *309*
Cisneros, S., 47, 50, *63*
Clark, A., 37, *44*
Clark, R., 194, *203*
Clinton, K., 168, 170, *184*
Cochran-Smith, M., 259, 260, 261, 262, *276*
Cocking, R. R., 143, *144*
Coiro, J. L., 43, *45*, 302, *309*
Colapietro, V. M., 135, *145*
Collazo, T., 90, *106*, 152, 154, 155, *160*, 244, *250*, 301, 302, *309*
Commeyras, M., 62, *63*
Compton-Lilly, C., 294, *295*
Conley, M. W., 129, *145*, 232, *249*
Connor, J. J., 211, 212, 225, *228*
Cook-Sather, A., 280, *295*
Corno, L., 144, *145*
Countryman, J., 259, 260, *277*
Crawford, V., 168, 170, *184*
Cuban, L., 207, 208, *228*, 231, *249*
Culler, J. D., 134, *145*
Cunningham, F., 148, 149, *159*
Cunningham, J. W., 129, *145*
Cunningham, P. M., 68, *79*, 129, *145*
Cziko, C., 69*f*, *79*, 231, *249*, 259, 261, *276*

D

Davidson, A. L., 66, *79*
Davies, B., 83, *84*, 135*n*2, 136, *145*
Davis, B., 305, 306, *308*

Delanty, G., 148, *159*
Delpit, L., 189, 193, 194, 198, 203, *203*, 262, *276*, 280, 283, *295*
Denzin, N. K., 232, *249*
Derrida, J., 134, *145*
Deshler, D., 231, *249*
Dewey, J., 149, 150, 151, *159*
Dillard, C. B., 262, *276*
Dillon, D., 232, 233, 234, 237, 238, 239, 240, 242, 243, *249*
Dillon, D. R., 85, 88*f*, 91, 92, 93, 97, 99, 101, *105*
DiMaggio, P., 109, 110, *127*
Dimitriadis, G., 151, 153, *159*, 236, *250*
Dishner, E., 232, *250*
Diversi, M., 148, *160*
Dole, J., 247, *250*
Doneman, M., 29, 36, *44*
Dressman, M., 206, 208, 211, 212, 225, *228*
Du Bois, W. E. B., 65, *79*
Duke, K., 262, *277*

E

Eccles, J. S., 30, 35, 38, *44*
Edelsky, C., 48, *63*, 149, *159*
Egan-Robertson, A., 42, *44*
Elenes, C. A., 151, 154, *160*
Elkins, J., 155, *159*
Ellis, D., 156, *159*
Ellis, L. M., 90, *106*, 152, 154, 155, *160*, 244, *250*, 301, 302, *309*
Ellsworth, E., 48, 62, *63*, 247, *249*
Emerson, C., 136, *146*
Everhart, R., 209, *228*, 232, *249*

F

Fabos, B., 233, 247, *250*
Fairclough, N., 235, *249*
Farrell, E., 132, *145*
Feathers, K., 232, *251*
Fecho, B., 200, *204*, 259, 260, 261, *276*
Fecho, R., 259, 260, 261, *277*
Finders, M. J., 9, *26*, 69, *79*, 140, 141, *145*, 237, *249*, 300, *308*
Fine, M., 208, *228*, 236, 247, *249*, 280, *295*
Finn, P., 208, 209, *228*
Fiske, J., 211, *228*
Flake, S., 156, *159*
Fletcher, J. M., 35, *45*
Flynn, E., 240, *249*
Foley, D., 211, *228*
Foucault, M., 134, *145*, 299, *308*
Foehr, U. G., 36, 37, *45*
Foley, D., 211, 225, *228*
Ford, M.. E., 144, *145*
Frankl, V. E., 135, 142, *145*

Freccero, J., 182, *184*
Freebody, P., 65, *79*
Freire, P., 114, *127*, 151, 152, *159*, 190, 193, 199, *204*,
    282, 287, 290, *295*
Fuhrman, S., 275, *276*
Fullan, M., 262, *276*

G

Garcia, E., 71, *79*
Gay, G., 67, 68, *79*
Gee, J. P., xxiii, *xxxii*, 34, 39, 43, 44, 48, 49, 50, 51, *63*,
    70, *79*, 88, 89, 90, 102, *105*, 108, *127*, 139,
    145, 163, *164*, 166, 168, 170, 174, 180, 183,
    184, 190, 202, *204*, 206, *228*, 235, *249*, 282,
    283, *295*, 302, *308*
Gibson, W., 191, *204*
Giddens, A., 135, *145*, 165, 166, *184*
Gilyard, K., 188, *204*
Gintis, H. I., 132, *144*
Giovanni, N., 187, *204*
Giroux, H., 148, 150, 152, 155, *159*
Glaser, B., 235, *249*
Glickman, C., 289, *295*
Gold, E., 271, *276*
Goldman, S. R., 90, *105*
Gonzalez, N., 303, *309*
Goodlad, J., 231, 233, *249*
Gordon, L., 190, *204*
Gore, J., 247, *249*, 262, *277*
Graziano, M., 36, *45*
Greenblatt, S., 166, *184*
Greene, M., 149, *159*
Greenleaf, C., 69f, *79*, 231, *249*
Gregory, D., 73, *79*
Greider, W., 166, *184*
Grumet, M., 239, *249*
Guerra, J. C., 89, *105*
Guthrie, J. T., 30, 38, *44*, *46*

H

Hagood, M. C., 30, *44*, 139, 141, 141n2, *145*, 153, 154,
    159, 247, *249*, 301, *308*
Hamilton, L., xxii, *xxxii*
Hamilton, M., 34, *44*
Hamilton, V., 76, *79*
Harding, S., 233, *249*
Hargreaves, A., 262, *276*, 302, *308*
Harker, R. K., 109, *127*
Harklau, L., 140, *145*
Harper, H. J., 156, 158, *159*
Harré, R., 83, *84*, 135n2, 136, *145*
Harste, J., 232, *249*
Hawisher, G. E., 42, *45*
Haythornthwaite, C., 206, *228*
Heath, S. B., 208, *228*

Hellman, L., 5, 6, 27
Henríquez, A., xxiii, *xxxii*
Henry, M., 299, *309*
Hicks, D., 89, *106*, 235, 243, *249*
Hinchman, K. A., 68, *79*, 129, 137, *145*, 148, 152, 155,
    159, *160*, 232, 233, 235, 236, 237, 238, 239,
    240, 241, 245, *248*, *249*, *250*, 301, *308*
Hinson, D., 62, *63*
Hirsch, E. B., 151, *159*
Hock, M., 231, *249*
Hodder, I., 235, 236, *250*
Hodges, C. R., 139, *146*
Hoffman, E., 6, 27
Holden, J., 143, *145*
Holland, D., xxi, xxiii, xxiv, xxv, xxvi, *xxxii*, 129,
    139, *145*, 211, *228*
hooks, b., 114, *127*
Hubbard, L., 139, *146*
Hudicourt-Barnes, J., 90, *106*
Hull, G. A., 69, *79*, 166, *184*, 232, *250*
Hurwitz, C., 69f, *79*
Hynds, S., 139, *145*

I

Ivanic, R., 34, *44*, 194, *203*

J

Jackson, D. B., 139, *145*
Jakobson, R., 134, *145*
Janks, H., 48, *63*
Jenkins, H., 9, 27
Jetton, T. L., 35, *44*, 247, *250*
Johnson, A., 76, *79*
Johnson, S. M., 275, *276*
Juel, C., 35, *44*
Jumpp, D., 259, 261, *276*

K

Kahne, J., 149, 155, 156, *160*
Kamberelis, G., 236, *250*
Kanter, R. M., 166, *184*
Kass, P. M., 156, *159*
Keddie, N., 216, *228*
Kellner, D., 30, *44*
Kendall, S., 34, *44*
Kenway, J., 154, *159*
Kinkaid, J., 191, *204*
Kinzer, C. K., 43, *45*, 302, *309*
Knight, J., *249*
Knobel, M., 29, 34, 35, 36, 37, 38, 43, *45*, 154, 155,
    159, 206, *228*, 301, 302, *308*
Kochman, T., 182, *184*
Kohl, H., *127*
Krajcik, J., 90, *106*

Kramer, K., 152, 154, 155, *160*, 244, *250*, 301, 302, *309*
Kramer, K. E., 90, *106*
Kress, G., 40, *44*, *45*
Kuhn, T. S., 134, *145*

L

Labov, W., 180, *184*
Lacan, J., 134, *145*
Lachicotte, W. Jr., xxi, xxiii, xxiv, xxv, xxvi, *xxxii*, 129, 139, *145*
Ladson-Billings, G., 68, *79*, 198, *204*, 283, *295*
Lam, W. S. E., 167, *184*
Langer, J., 211, 225, 227, *228*
Langhorne, R., 154, *159*
Langmead, D., 154, *159*
Lankshear, C., 29, 34, 35, 36, 37, 38, 43, *45*, 154, 155, *159*, 166, *184*, 206, *228*, 258, *276*, 302, *308*
Lareau, A., 208, *228*
Lather, P., 262, *276*
Lave, J., 89, 103, *106*
Lazerson, M., 275, *276*
Leander, K. M., 40, *45*, 206, 208, *228*, 232, *250*
Lee, C. D., 85, 90, *106*
Lee, P. W., xxii, *xxxii*
Lee, V. E., 132, *145*
Lefebvre, H., 40, *45*
Lemke, J. L., 89, 90, 93, *106*, 233, 240, *250*
Lenhart, A., 36, *45*
Lenz, K., 231, *249*
Leonardo, Z., 134, *145*
Lesko, N., 150, 152, 153, 155, *159*, 231, *250*, 300, *309*
Leu, D. J., 43, *45*, 302, *309*
Levinson, B., 211, *228*
Lévi-Strauss, C., 134, *145*
Lewis, C., 233, 247, *250*
Lewis, M. J., 232, *251*
Lindfors, J. W., 188, *204*
Lingard, B., 299, *309*
Lipman, P., 68, *79*
Little, J. W., 261, *276*
Little, T. D., 144, *146*
Long, R., 34, *45*
Lorde, A., 114, *127*
Luce-Kapler, R., 305, 306, *308*
Luke, A., 48, 50, *63*, 155, *159*, 206, *228*, 298, 300, *309*
Luke, C., 262, *277*, 300, *309*
Lyon, G. R., 35, *45*
Lyotard, F., 205, *228*
Lytle, S. L., 258, 259, 260, 261, 262, 271, *276*, *277*

M

Macedo, D., 151, *159*
MacLeod, J., 209, *228*
Mahar, D., 232, 233, 238, 247, *249*, *250*, 302, *308*
Maher, F., 151, *159*

Mahiri, J., 69, *79*
Malone, M. J., 169, *184*
Martin, M., 8, *27*
Martin, N., 194, *204*
Martino, W., 48, *63*
Marx, R. W., 90, *106*
McCallister, C., 139, *145*
McCarthy, S. J., 139, *145*
McDermott, R., 208, *228*, 283, *295*
McIntosh, P., 62, *63*, 262, *277*
McKay, S. L., 141, *145*
McLaren, P. L., 118, *127*, 152, *159*, 258, *276*
McLaughlin, M., 148, *160*
McMillan, S., 144, *146*
Meacham, S. J., 126, *127*
Mead, G. H., 136, *146*
Mehan, H., 139, *146*
Meier, D., 275, *277*
Michaels, S., 89, *106*
Mills, S., 240, *250*
Mishler, E. G., 180, *184*
Moats, L., 35, *45*
Moje, E. B., 69f, *79*, 85, 88f, 88, 90, 91, 92, 93, 97, 99, 101, *105*, *106*, 139, *145*, 152, 154, 155, *160*, 232, 233, 235, 237, 238, 239, 241, 244, 245, 246, *249*, *250*, 301, 302, *309*
Moll, L. C., 303, *309*
Moon, J. S., 30, *44*
Moore, D. W., 68, 69f, *79*, 129, 140, *145*, *146*, 148, 152, 155, *159*, *160*, 232, 233, *248*, *250*, 300, 301, *308*, *309*
Moore, S. A., 129, *145*
Morgan, W., 48, *63*
Morrow, L. L., 232, *251*
Morson, G. S., 136, 143, *146*
Mouffe, C., 151, 154, *160*
Myers, J., 232, 235, *250*
Myers, W. D., 74, *79*, 147, 156, 158, *160*

N

Nadesan, M., 151, 154, *160*
Naidoo, B., 156, *160*
Neff, D., 303, *309*
Neilsen, L., 5, 8, 25, 26, *27*
Nespor, J., 130, 131, 132, 134, 137, *146*
Nicholson, T., 232, *250*
Nieto, S., 262, *277*
Noddings, N., 240, *250*
Norton, B., 139, *146*

O

Oakes, J., 208, *228*
Obidah, J. E., 107, *127*
O'Brien, D. G., 29, 30, 31, 35, 43, *45*, 92, 93, *105*, 207, 208, *228*, 232, 241, *249*, *250*
O'Connor, M. C., 89, *106*

Ogbu, J., 69, *79*, 141, *146*
Oldfather, P., 232, *250*
Orner, M., 248, *250*
Osborne, K., 150, *160*

P

Pailliotet, A. W., 30, *45*
Paradis, E. E., 232, *251*
Pari, C., 152, 155, *160*
Parker, W. C., 148, 149, 155, 157, *160*
Paul, D. G., 232, 241, *250*
Peek-Brown, D., 90, *106*
Perry, T., 110, 111, 126, *127*
Phelps, S. F., 68, *79*, 148, 152, *159*, 232, 248
Phelps, S. W., 301, *308*
Pintrich, P. R., 30, 35, *45*
Pope, D. C., 216, *229*
Porter, M., 8, *27*
Portnoy, D., 259, 260, *277*
Powell, R., 152, *160*
Pratt, M. L., 89, *106*
Pressley, M., 34, *45*, 68, *79*, 144, *144*

Q

Quinn, N., 49, *63*

R

Randall, S., 62, *63*
Ratekin, N., 232, *250*
Readence, J. E., 69f, *79*, 148, 152, *159*, *160*, 232, *250*
Reeves, A. R., xxii, *xxxii*
Reich, R. B., 166, *185*
Rellinger, E., 144, *144*
Restak, , R., 37, *45*
Reumann, R., 262, *277*
Rhodes, A., 271, *276*
Rickelman, R. J., 152, *160*
Ricks, B., 48, 50, *63*
Rideout, V. J., 36, 37, *45*
Rifkin, J., 165, *185*
Riley, P., 150, *160*
Rist, R., 208, *229*
Rizvi, F., 299, *309*
Roberts, D. F., 36, 37, *45*
Roeser, R., 30, 35, 38, *44*
Rogers, A. G., 9, *27*
Rogers, R., 89, *106*, 208, *229*
Rosenblatt, L., 10, *27*, 149, 150, *160*, 190, *204*
Ross, B. D., 232, *251*
Rouse, K. A. G., 144, *146*
Rudduck, J., 280, 294, *295*
Rushkoff, D., 37, *45*, 302, *309*
Rycik, J., 301, *309*
Rymes, B., 69, 78, *79*

S

Salinger, J. D., 10, *27*
Sarroub, L. K., 233, *250*
Scharber, C., 31, *45*
Schilling, C., 135, *146*
Schmit, J. S., 143, *145*
Schoenbach, R., 69f, *79*, 231, *249*
Schultz, K., 69, *79*, 232, 233, *250*, *251*
Schumaker, B., 231, *249*
Schunk, D. H., 30, 35, *45*
Schweickert, P., 240, *249*
Scott, K., 143, *146*
Sefton-Green, J., 8, *26*, 30, *45*
Selfe, C. L., 42, *45*
Seligman, M., 30, *45*
Semali, L., 30, *45*
Shannon, P., 150, *160*
Shaywitz, S. E., 35, *45*
Sheehy, M., 40, *45*
Shor, I., 152, 155, *160*
Shulz, J., 280, *295*
Shumaker, B., *249*
Silbereisen, R., 148, *160*
Simon, M., 36, *45*
Simpson, M., 232, *250*
Sion, F., 259, 260, *277*
Skinner, D., xxi, xxiii, xxiv, xxv, xxvi, *xxxii*, 129, 139, *145*
Smith, F., 232, *251*
Smith, J. B., 132, *145*
Smitherman, G., 198, *204*
Snow, C., 247, *249*, 302, *308*, *309*
Snyder, I., 42, *45*
Soja, E. W., 40, *45*
Springs, R., 29, 35, *45*, 207, 208, *228*
St. Clair, R., 262, *277*
Stevens, L. P., 155, *160*, 300, 301, 302, *309*
Stewart, R. A., 92, 93, *105*, 232, 234, 237, 238, 239, 241, 243, *249*, *250*, *251*
Stith, D., 29, 35, *45*, 207, 208, *228*
Stolle, E. P., 48, 50, *63*
Stone, D., *309*
Strauss, A., 235, *249*
Strauss, C., 49, *63*
Street, B. V., xxiii, *xxxii*, 34, 35, *46*, 88, *106*, 259, *277*
Strickland, D., 232, *251*
Sturtevant, E. G., 155, *160*, 232, 234, 237, 239, 241, 244, *251*
Sumara, D., 305, 306, *308*
Sutherland, L. M., 90, *106*
Swartz, D., 109, *127*
Sztompka, P., 135, *146*

T

Tannen, D., 34, *44*, *46*

Tarantino, Q., 8, 13, 27
Tatum, A. W., 66, 67, 69, 70, 77, 79
Taylor, C., 165, 185
Taylor, S., 299, 309
Tettegah, S., 208, 228
Thrash, E. C., 232, 248
Toohey, K., 139, 146
Torgesen, J. K., 35, 45
Trousdale, A. M., 144, 146
Tsolidis, G., 157, 160

U

Upchurch, C., 65, 66, 79

V

Vacca, J., 232, 251
Vacca, R. T., 232, 251
Van Leeuwen, T., 40, 45
van Manen, M., 235, 251
Varenne, V., 283, 295
Villanueva, I., 139, 146
Volkmann, M., 92, 105
Vygotsky, L. S., xxi, xxiv, xxxii, 136, 146

W

Wade, M., 303, 308
Waff, D., 68, 79, 148, 152, 159, 259, 260, 268, 271, 276, 277, 301, 308
Wallis, C., 153, 160
Walls, T. A., 144, 146
Walmsley, S. R., 35, 44
Weaver, D., 232, 248
Weil, S., 18, 27

Weiner, E. J., 155, 160
Weis, L., 209, 229, 280, 295
Welch, O. M., 139, 146
Welchman, J., 150, 160
Wellman, B., 206, 228
Westheimer, J., 149, 155, 156, 160
Wexler, P., 209, 229
Wigfield, A., 30, 35, 38, 44, 46
Wilder, P., 206, 208, 211, 212, 225, 228
Wiley, N., 135, 136, 146
Williamson, K., xxiii, xxxii
Willis, P., 89, 106, 141, 146, 209, 229
Wilson, A., 191, 204
Wong, S.-L. C., 141, 145
Woodson, J., 76, 79, 156, 160
Woodward, C., 232, 249
Wright, R., 192, 204
Wyn, J., 300, 309

Y

Yancey, K., 41, 46
Yoon, K. S., 30, 35, 38, 44
York-Barr, J., 262, 277
Young, J. P., 48, 50, 51, 53, 62, 63, 69f, 79, 232, 239, 248, 250
Youniss, J., 148, 160

Z

Zalewski, P., 232, 233, 235, 236, 237, 238, 240, 241, 245, 248, 250
Zondlo, K. E., 231, 251
Zumwalt, K., 275, 277

Subject Index

Note: *f* indicates figure, *t* indicates table.

A

Abandoned Generation, The, 148
Academic-track students, 86
Achievement
  low, 30
  motivation, 30
  student, 76–78
Action research, 88, 255, 280–284, 287, 290–291, 294
Adulthood, 18–26
Advancement Via Individual Determination (AVID), 139
Advisory Council on Advancing Adolescent Literacy, xxiii
Advocacy for students, 262–270
African American
  adolescents, 67
  dialect, 242
  culture, 187
  English vernacular, 281–283
  soldiers, 147
  students, 86, 113–114, 116, 126, 187–188, 194–196
  teachers, 263–265
  youth, xxiv
African Americans, 65–66, 110–111
  teachers of, 68
Agency, xxv, 139
  affirming, 132–133
  in cultural worlds, xxvi
  denying, 133–135
  a perspective on, 135–137
Alliance for Excellent Education, xxiii
Angelou, Maya, 114
Apple computers, 205
Appropriation, 197
Art school, 24–25

"As if" learning communities, 108*f*, 109–111, 116–119, 121, 126
Authority, 138, 144, 236–238, 244, 246, 280, 292–293
  questioning, 19–20
  shared, 248
Autobiography
  Black, 190
  educational, 286
  inquiry into, 192

B

"Beautiful Black Men, " 187
Bilingualism, 155, 167
Black
  dialect, 187
  English, 192–193
  literature, 190
  teachers, 263–265
Blaxploitation, 8
Brain plasticity, 37
Bread Loaf School of English, 188, 194

C

Caroline in the City, 14
Catcher in the Rye, The, 7–12, 17, 20
Caulfield, Holden, 7, 10–12, 20
Causal determinism, 133
Chicano/Latino students, 113–114
Children's Aid Society in New York, The, xxvi
Choices for the 21ˢᵗ Century, 157
Chomsky, Noam, 24
Chrystos, 114
Citizenship, 148–149, 155–158
Classroom

identities, 85
  mulitcultural, 194
  relationships, 85, 94–96, 99–100
Classtalk, 187, 194–195
Codes, 188–191, 202–203
Code switching, 164, 188–189, 192–193, 196–197,
    203, 243
Cognitive scientists, 37
Community forces, 69
Comprehension
  improving, 30
  literal, 300–301, 305
Computer-based
  practices, 213–214t
  search strategies of students, 220–222
  technology, 205–207, 212, 215, 222–223, 226
Content-area
  classrooms, 83, 85–90
  identities, 90–101
  literacy, 85, 87
  planning and teaching, 103–104
Context(s), 197, 211, 236
  academic, 222
  altered, 233
  district, 260–261
  instructional, 226
  of literacy production, 225
  local, 256
  pedagogical, 232
  of schooling, 240–241, 246
Core linguistic deficits, 34
Crisis of courage, 9
Critical
  consciousness, 118–126
  literacy, 3, 9, 47–51, 56–57, 61–62, 151, 156, 164,
      280, 298
Critical language awareness (CLA), 194
Cultural
  capital, vii, x, 8, 108f, 109–111, 113, 117, 126,
      225
  competence, 72
  diversity, 180
  divisions, 215
  ecology, 42
  heritage, 123–124
  identities, 68
  models, 49, 52–53, 57–62
  reproduction, 164, 209–210, 224
Culturally engaged instruction (CEI), 198
Culture, xxv
  as disability, 283–284
  of power, 194
Curriculum
  interventions, 90
  orientations, 74–76
Cyber
  skills, 223
  technology, 206
Cyberspace, 154, 223

Cyborg theory, 36–37

D

Decentering the subject, 134
Decision making, 87
Decoding, 34–35
Deerhunter, 39, 41
Deliberative forums, 157
Democracy, 147–158
  and literacy education, 149–152
  pluralistic, xxv
  radical, 152–155
Design, 41
Desire, 25
Dialects, 112, 180, 191, 194, 197, 200, 242–243
Dialogic relationships, 137
Digital
  generation, 37
  media, 29–31
  technology, 206, 233
Disciplinary identities, 85
Discourse community, 34, 85, 89–90
Discourse, 49, 57–62, 94–96, 282
  academic, 217
  in the African American community, 198
  of the classroom space, 99
  colonizing, 236
  of gender, 243
  of struggle, 118–126
Disengagement, 30, 38
Distribution, 41
"Doing school," 216
Dostoevsky, 136
Dragonwings, 141
Dress code, 157, 279, 281, 285–286, 288, 292–294
Duddy Kravitz, 20
Dunlevy Milbank Center of the Children's Aid So-
      ciety, xxvi

E

Economic, 150, 219–220
  capital, 109
  class, 150, 165, 208
  consequences, 35
  factors, 133
  globalized, 302
Economy
  new, 165
Emotional
  resonance, xxi
Enabling constraints, 256
English
  as a second language, 212, 219, 244
Equal-status interactions, 196
Ethics, 26

Every Child a Graduate, 302

F

Fahrenheit 911, 114
Fallen Angels, 147, 158
Family background, xxii
Fences, 191
Figured worlds, xxiv
Framing, 41
Freedom, 23
Friends, 14
Front Page, 206

G

Game Cube, 33
Garcia, Jerry, 38, 41
GEAR UP Program, 113, 121
Gender
    constructions, 47, 50–51, 62
        in advertising, 23
    discourses of, 243
    in feminism, 134
    identities, 9, 18, 23, 48, 50–57, 62, 114, 217
    oppresssion, 272
    stereotypes, 3–4, 51, 55
Gender-based power structures, 141
Generation M, 37
Generation X, 14
Gilligan, Shannon, 39
Girl, 191
Goals
    conflicted, 189
    pedagogical, 306
    personally relevant, 30, 42, 43
    setting, 38
    tangible, 31
Google, 39
Grammars, 41
Grateful Dead, 38, 41–42
Guardian, Weekly, The, 20

H

Habitus, 209
Harbaugh, Jim, 32–33
Hardware resources, 208
Harry Potter, 33
Heteroglossia, 190
Hidden messages of texts, xxii
Hill, Lauren, 114
Hispanic students, 86
History-in-person constructs, xxi
Home/community literacy, 107, 108f, 125
House on Mango Street, The, 47, 50, 57, 60

I

"I Walk in the History of My People," 114
Identities (*see also* Adolescent identities *and* Cultural identities *and* Gender identies *and* Racial identities), xxi, 166
    academic, 139–141
    classroom, 85, 88–89
    demanded, 102
    disciplinary, 85
    exploring, 6
    using language to fashion, 168
    multiple, 66–67
    as recognized, 102
    socially situated, 48–49
Identity, 25
    across discourse communities, 89–90
    complacent, 91–92, 97–99, 101
    construction, 66–67
    in cultural worlds, xxvi
    defined, 66
    re/construction, xxiv
Imagined possibilities, xxii
Indianapolis Monthly, 32
Inquiry (*see* Language inquiry)
Instant messaging (IM), xxx–xxxi, 36, 212, 217
Institution of Old Learning (IOL), 43
Internet, 36, 154, 167–168, 205–206, 209–215, 217, 223, 226–227, 244, 246
    access, 15
    generation, 37
Internet-based messaging, 152
Internet-based literacy practices, 303
I-Statements, 169–180

J

Jackson, Samuel, 8
Jonas, Sarah, xxvi–xxxii
Justice, 7, 60, 66
    lack of, 167
    social, 26, 143, 148, 155–156, 255, 260, 270, 298

K

Kids in the Hall, 22
Knowledge, 9, 14, 16, 18, 25, 51, 67–68, 77, 92, 94, 96, 108, 166, 170, 194, 198, 210, 224, 233, 240–241, 259, 282, 290–294
    content, 104, 226, 241, 258
    identity, 97

L

Labels, 35
Language, xxv
    communication based on, 269

deconstructing, 48
inquiry, 201–202
of power, 280
as subject of critical inquiry, 189–200
universal, 195–196
validating, 119
Language learning
approaches to, 188–189
reconceptualizing, 191–201
Learned helplessness, 30
Letters to the Next President, 289
Literacies (*see also* Multiple literacies *and* School
        literacies)
of teaching, 258–259
of technology, 42–43
Literacy (*see also* Content-area *and* Radical literacy
        and TechnoLiteracy *and* Textured liter-
        acy), 26
achievement, xxi
    gap, xxiii
    improving, xxiii–xxvi
definitions and considerations, 281–283
development, 65–66
factual comprehension as, 298
framework, 68
overload, 69–70
learning, 86–87, 129, 144, 241, 261
    distant, 284–294
    intimate, 284–294
policy, 304–305
practices, 97–99
    in academic areas, xxiv
as semiotic, 8
shifts, 76–78
Literate currency, 84, 107–109, 111–119, 122–124
Little House on the Prairie, 23

M

MASPAS Program, xxvii
Mastery, 245
learning, 92
of standard English, 284
system, 281
Media
new, 36
project, 33
Media-centric, 29, 31
view of competence, 36–37
Mediasphere, 37
Mediating practices, xxv
Microethnography, 234
Millenials, 37
Miracle Worker, The, 191
Moore, Michael, 24, 114
Motivation(*see* Achievement motivation)
Multiliteracies, xxv, 37, 158, 164, 233, 247
Multimediating, 29, 36–37
competence in, 38–40
as a form of compostion, 41–42
mapping the space of, 40

in schools, 43–44
Multimodality, 40–41, 233
Multiple
literacies, 148
texts, 148
Multitasking, 36

N

Narrative(s), 169, 174, 180–182, 247, 255, 258
pop culture, 8
text, 33, 41
Nas, 114, 289
National Adolescent Literacy Coalition, xxiii
New Brain, 37
New Literacies, xxiii, 29, 34, 36, 38, 40–43, 84, 154,
        164, 206–208, 210–211, 222–224
Newsweek, 231
No Child Left Behind Act (NCLB), xxii, xxvi, 113,
        257, 262, 279, 281, 286, 290, 293, 302, 307
impact on youth advocacy groups, xxii–xxiii
Noncomformist, 6

O

One-size-fits-all school reform, xxv
Osbourne, Ozzy, 207
Other People's Children, 194
Other Side of Truth, The, 156

P

PEACE Program, 113–114, 119, 126
Pedagogy, 43, 66, 68, 72, 78, 88, 105, 110, 118,
        150–158, 164, 189–190, 198, 200, 232,
        247–248, 272, 298–303, 306–307
liberal-humanist, 149
Peer literacy, 107, 108*f*
Pentimento, 5
Personal learning plans (PLPs), 199
Persuasive writing, 83, 130–132, 134, 137–139
Philadelphia Writing Project, The (PhilWP),
        259–261, 267, 270–272
Picture of Dorian Gray, A, 20
Playstation, 39
Pluralistic
democracy, xxv, 151, 153, 157–158
society, 148, 154
Policy, 102, 104–105, 143–144, 157, 189, 262,
        297–300
and adolescent literacy, 300–301
    implications for, 104–105
    informing, 301–304
    the role of, 304–305
changes, 225, 293
transforming, 305–306
Policymakers, 3, 34, 200–201, 245, 255–259, 298,
        304, 306–307
Political

activists, 26
  issues inherent in language, 189
  nature of language study, 200
Pop culture, 9, 43, 148
Popular culture literacy, 107, 108f
Positioning
  youth as readers and writers, xxiv–xxv
Power, 9, 18, 48, 66, 236, 238, 285–286
  in alliance with knowledge, 259
  codes, 188–193, 200–203
  culture of, 194
  dialect of, 72f
  of language, 152, 187, 294
  of poetry, 119
  political, 149
  in relationships, 88–89
  seeking, 263
  structures (gender-based), 141
  of teaching, 275
  of theories of social and cultural reproduction, 211
PowerPoint, 39, 217
Print-centric, 29, 31
  view of competence, 34–36
Print media, 31
Production, 41
Professional
  development
    support, 68–69, 71–74, 78
    unprofessional, 272–273
  intimacy, 270–274
Project SOULL, 259–262, 267, 269
Pulp Fiction, 8–9, 13–15, 19–20

R

Race, xxv, 47–51, 57–62, 118, 132, 187–188, 191, 196, 202–203, 206, 208, 215, 238–242, 255, 272–273, 297
  Black, 65
Race-based experiences, 70
Racial identities, 47, 50–52, 57–62, 114, 264
  slur, 191
Racism, 7, 47, 57–61, 123
  in Pulp Fiction, 8
Radical democracy, 148–149, 151–155
  educators, 149, 151
  literacy education, 151, 153
  pluralism, 84, 158
Reading against the grain, 48
Ready for the World: Americans Speak on High School Reform, xxiii
Re/construction, 47–48, 50–62
Redressive texts, 47–50, 56–57, 61–62
Register shifting, 196
Remedies for racial inequality, 157
Resistance, 37, 50–51, 59, 62, 89, 91–92, 110, 141, 156, 209, 240, 270
Richler, Mordecai, 20
Role Playing Game (RPG), 33–34

Rolling Stone, 38, 141

S

Salinger, J. D., 7, 20
Saturday Night Live, 22
Saved By the Bell, 23
School literacies, xxxi, 38, 68–70, 74, 86, 101, 107, 108f, 126, 129, 148, 150, 232
Schools, rethinking, 21–22
Scripting, 6
Seinfeld, 14
Self-fashioning, xxv, 165–167, 182–183
Self-understandings, xxi
Semiotic modes, 40–41
Serial careers, 275
Sexism, 7
Shakur, Tupac (2 Pac), 114
Shape-Shifting Portfolio People, 166, 182
Shortcuts, xxx–xxxi
Single Guy, 14
Slang, 192
Small learning community (SLC), 271–272
Social
  constructs, 18, 60, 227, 235, 240–242, 272, 299
  interactions, 107, 176–177, 180, 235
  languages, 163
  life, 23
  network, 282
  practices, 48
  reproduction(digitization of), 207–210
  weighing of understanding, xxi
Socioeconomic levels, 86, 114
Software, 31, 38, 183
  programs, 205–206, 217
  resources, 208
Sports Illustrated, 32
Standardized tests, 33
Steele, Ariel, xxvi–xxxii
Stereotypes, 9, 48, 50, 55
Striving readers, 34
Structuralism, 134
Struggling readers, 34–35
Subjectivities, 85–86, 88f, 88, 90–93, 114, 141n3
Subtexts, xxii
SuperCard, 32
Survey, Question, Read, Recite, Review (SQ3R) strategy, 98
Symbolic interaction, 232, 234
Symbols, 38, 41, 213t, 221t, 222, 227, 282
Symphonia, 33

T

Tarantino, Quentin, 8, 13–14, 16, 19
Teaching Democracy: Unity and Diversity in Public Life, 157
Technoliteracy, 42–43

Technology (*see also* Computer-based technology), xxv, xxxi
    cyber, 206
    infused curriculum, 281
Technology-based texts, 152, 205
Text as discourse, 6
    male-centered, 18
    media as, 22–24
    messaging, xxx–xxxi
    re-envisioning, 20–21
    as symbolic resources, 17
Textured literacy, 41–42
Three-three structure, 131
Touchstone texts, xxiv, 5–6, 9
Travolta, John, 8, 13–14
True Confessions of Charlotte Doyle, The, 50, 52

U

Upchurch, Carl, 65–66

V

Victimization by words, 192
Video games, 31, 43
Violence Project, 31
Voice(s), 23, 48, 61, 65, 77, 88, 92, 101, 112–124, 155, 200, 203, 266, 278–279, 289–292, 299, 303, 306
    authoritative, 138, 143, 237
    "coming to, " 280
    contradictory, 248
    of disaffected youth, 7
    internally persuasive, 136–137, 143
    providing a space for, 286
Voices of the Self, 188

W

Waiting for God, 18
Wal-Mart, 23–24
WarioWorld, 34
Washington, Eric, xxvi–xxxii
Webbrowsing, 31
    sites, 32–33, 39, 168, 183, 206–207, 212, 217–220, 222–227
White
    students, 86
    superiority, 111
Who Killed Elspeth Haskard: The Magic Death, 39, 41, 43
Who Wants to be a Millionaire?, 207
Windows software, 206
World Wide Web, 205–207, 222, 224
Word recognition, 34–35

X

Xenophobia, 210